Readings in Microeconomics

Readings in Microeconomics

Tim Jenkinson

OXFORD UNIVERSITY PRESS
1996

Oxford University Press, Walton Street, Oxford OX2 6DP

Oxford New York
Athens Auckland Bangkok Bombay
Calcutta Cape Town Dar es Salaam Delhi
Florence Hong Kong Istanbul Karachi
Kuala Lumpur Madras Madrid Melbourne
Mexico City Nairobi Paris Singapore
Taipei Tokyo Toronto
and associated companies in
Berlin Ibadan

Oxford is a trade mark of Oxford University Press

Published in the United States
by Oxford University Press Inc., New York

British Library Cataloguing in Publication Data
Data available

Library of Congress Cataloging in Publication Data
Jenkinson, Tim, 1961–
Readings in microeconomics / Tim Jenkinson.
Includes bibliographical references and index.
1. Microeconomics. I. Title.
HB172.J46 1996 338.5—dc20 95–51468
ISBN 0–19–877493–1
ISBN 0–19–877492–3 (Pbk.)

Typeset by Graphicraft Typesetters Ltd, Hong Kong
Printed in Great Britain
on acid-free paper by
Bookcraft, Bath Ltd., Midsomer Norton, Avon

Preface

Demand often results in supply. The idea of producing a book collecting together many of the important and widely cited papers published in the *Oxford Review of Economic Policy* initially came from my students. They complained to me about the difficulty of finding copies of the *Review* in libraries when everyone taking a course was after the same issue. They told me how good it would be to have a selection of the most useful papers readily available. They even told me they might buy such a collection. And so the idea to produce this reader on microeconomics, along with the companion volume on macroeconomics, was born.

The first volume of the *Oxford Review of Economic Policy* was published in 1985. Two features have continued to distinguish the *Review* from other economics journals: the thematic approach, whereby each issue is focused on a particular subject, with leading authorities commissioned to contribute, and an insistence that articles should be written in a non-technical style. From the start the editors have stressed that articles should be accessible to students, policy-makers, journalists—in fact, anyone with an interest in economic issues. There has also been an insistence that policy implications should be discussed fully, rather than relegated to an occasional footnote. As much of economics has become more technical, specialized, and mathematically sophisticated, the role played by the *Review* in cutting through the algebra and stating ideas in words has become increasingly valuable. As a result, the *Review* has established a strong and growing readership amongst students, academics, journalists, teachers, and economists in the private and public sectors, as well as an impressive list of contributing authors.

These volumes of collected papers draw together some of the most important and widely cited articles published in the first ten volumes of the *Oxford Review of Economic Policy*. I hope that the books will fulfil a number of aims. First, they will ensure that the original articles remain easily accessible. Second, they will provide a resource to those teaching core micro- and macroeconomics courses, and may be used as a ready-made 'reading pack' by lecturers (hence avoiding the trouble and cost of obtaining copyright clearance on individual articles). Third, they will enable students and others interested in economic policy to acquire a selection of the most useful papers at a low cost and reduce the need to spend hours slaving over the photocopier.

The production of these volumes also presented a useful opportunity to update or revise the original articles in the light of developments since they were first published. Many of the authors have taken advantage of this opportunity and updated and revised their papers to take into account recent advances in the literature, policy developments, and more recent data. This periodic spring-cleaning should ensure that even the papers published in early volumes of the *Review* stay relevant and useful. Some papers, especially those published relatively recently, have not been changed.

By far the most difficult task in putting together these volumes was to decide which papers to include. Over the last ten years a large number of high quality and widely cited papers have been published in the *Review*—many more than could be included in two books of a reasonable length. In making the selection I was concerned to cover all the main areas of macro- and microeconomics, which inevitably meant that some of the less 'mainstream' areas were neglected altogether. This is not to deny the significance and importance of these areas. Indeed, it is hard to think of an economic policy area more important than, say, the economics of transition to market economies, to which the *Review* devoted two issues in 1991–2, even though this specific topic is excluded from these more general volumes. A slightly different problem was that some issues contained many important articles, but only one or two could be included. There are thus many interesting and important papers not included in this selection.

An important criterion used in selecting papers was that the volume should contain a balance between those papers that surveyed a particular theoretical literature and those that were more focused on applied policy issues. It was also decided to go for depth of coverage rather than breadth. Consequently, the volume contains two or three articles on each of the six selected areas:

- Industrial Organization
- R&D
- Competition and Industrial Policy
- Externalities and the Environment
- International Trade
- Education and Training

While this has resulted in the exclusion of several other areas—such as the microeconomics of the labour market and corporate finance—all the selected subject areas have been the focus of extensive academic research and policy debate in recent years, and would be covered by intermediate or advanced courses on microeconomics.

Finally, I should like to thank a number of people who helped turn the idea to produce these volumes into reality in little more than six months. An important role was played by Andrew Balls who, rather than spend the weeks immediately after his final examinations relaxing on the beach, instead read large numbers of articles and advised me on the content of the volumes, the required revisions to papers, and also on student preferences. Most of the editorial work on the volumes took place while I was on leave at Dartmouth College, USA. Dartmouth provided me with a haven from normal administrative chores, and an excellent e-mail link that kept me in touch with those who actually produced the books. Among these, Tracy Mawson and Jenni Scott at OUP supervised the production process with great efficiency and speed, and Alison Gomm shouldered much of the responsibility for dealing with revisions, liaising with authors, and much more with her characteristic effectiveness. Over the years that I have been managing editor of the *Oxford Review of Economic Policy* I have accumulated a tremendous debt of gratitude to Alison, whose contribution has been far greater than that of a conventional production editor.

Last and certainly not least, the success of the *Oxford Review of Economic Policy* owes much to the efforts and vision of its editors—Chris Allsopp, Andrea Boltho, Dieter Helm, Gerry Holtham, Colin Mayer, Ken Mayhew, and Derek Morris—greatly assisted by an active and supportive editorial board. Their editorial input was critical in the commissioning and production of the original papers.

Tim Jenkinson
January 1996

Contents

List of Figures

List of Tables

PART I

INDUSTRIAL ORGANIZATION

Strategic competition among the few—some recent developments in the economics of industry

JOHN VICKERS

All Souls College, Oxford

I. Introduction

The title of this article is intended as a signal of two things. First, we are concerned with industries where several—but not many—firms are actually or potentially in competition with each other. Thus our topic is competition among the few,[1] or oligopoly, rather than the polar extremes of textbook perfect competition and pure monopoly. Secondly, we are interested in the *strategic* nature of competition between firms, where the meaning of 'strategic' can be explained as follows:

> If the essence of a game of strategy is the dependence of each person's proper choice of action on what he expects the other to do, it may be useful to define a 'strategic move' as follows: A strategic move is one that influences the other person's choice, in a manner favourable to one's self, by affecting the other person's expectations of how one's self will behave. Schelling (1960, p. 150)

The definition is taken from Thomas Schelling's classic book *The Strategy of Conflict*, which has inspired much recent work on strategic moves such as threats, promises and commitments in the economics of industry. This work is sometimes described as 'The New Industrial Economics', but we shall steer clear of the controversial business of applying that label.

The recent work on strategic competition among the few can be compared with the older traditions in industrial economics associated with Harvard and Chicago. The structure–conduct–performance paradigm pioneered by Edward Mason at Harvard in the 1930s was developed by Joe Bain and others in the 1950s and 1960s. This approach regards market *structure* (the number and sizes of firms in the industry, entry barriers, etc.) as determining the *conduct* of firms (their policies regarding price, advertising, capacity, innovation, etc.), which in turn determines the *performance* of the industry (its allocative efficiency and technological progress, for example). Of course proponents of this view would not claim that causality flows in one direction only—from structure to conduct to performance—but they do emphasise relationships involving that causal flow (see Scherer (1980) pp. 4–5). The recent work on strategic competition has explored many of the aspects of industry structure and conduct that were recognised as being important by economists in the Harvard tradition. A prime example is the theory of entry barriers and entry deterrence, which will be described below. But there are important differences between the approaches that should be noted. The apparently general applicability of the structure–conduct–performance paradigm caused attention to be focused on features shared by different industries, rather than upon the idiosyncrasies of particular industries. More recently, however, there has been some tendency to study industries on a case by case basis (see Schmalensee (1982) and Spence (1981)). A second difference is that much recent work has been concerned with the determinants *of* market structure, rather than with the dependence of conduct and performance *upon* structure. One concern has been to

First published in *Oxford Review of Economic Policy*, vol. 1, no. 3 (1985).

[1] This phrase is borrowed (i.e. stolen) from the title of Fellner's (1949) book on oligopoly. For an excellent recent survey of the economics of industry, see Waterson (1984).

show how the fundamentals of consumer preferences and technological relationships, together with the behaviour of firms, determine market structure endogenously.

The 'Chicago tradition' has been to view industrial economics 'through the lens of price theory'.[2] This approach places much greater faith in the operation of market forces than does the Harvard approach, and is correspondingly less convinced of the need or desirability of government intervention to do something about apparent 'market power'. To the contrary, government policy is seen as being one of the main causes of restrictions upon free competition—for example legal barriers to entry into certain markets. These views are closely linked with the emphasis of the 'Austrian School' upon dynamic competition by innovation and the threat of new entry. Such topics as these have also been addressed in the recent work that is reported below, but the conclusions reached—especially regarding government policy—have often differed markedly from those of the Chicago school.

The lens of *game theory* has been used to study the economics of strategic competition. Game theory provides a framework for analysing situations in which there is interdependence between agents in the sense that the decisions of one agent affect the other agents. It is not necessary to use game theory to study pure monopoly (where there is only one decision-maker) or perfect competition (where each individual is too small to have any appreciable effect upon others), but game theory is most appropriate to the study of competition among the few. The next section contains a very brief outline of some basic notions in game theory, and introduces some illustrative examples that are developed in the subsequent discussion.

Section III discusses strategic competition between existing firms, and section IV is concerned with strategic competition between existing firms and potential rivals. These two issues are closely related, but it is helpful as a first step to address them separately. Section III has three main themes: the dynamic nature of strategic competition between firms, the dependence of market structure on the fundamental conditions of consumer preferences and technology, and the role of strategic commitment. The first theme is illustrated in part 1 of the section, which is about collusion between firms. Using the perspective of repeated games, it is shown how firms may be able effectively to collude noncooperatively, i.e. in the absence of explicit cartel arrangements. This demonstrates that it would be fal-

lacious to argue that such collusion would inevitably be undermined by each firm's incentive to undercut its rivals. The theme of the endogeneity of market structure is developed in parts 2 and 3, which are concerned with R & D competition and product differentiation, respectively. The final part discusses strategic commitment of R & D as an illustration of how the decisions of a firm are made partly with a view to influencing the behaviour of its rivals in the industry. Each firm attempts to gain a position of strategic advantage over its rivals, and to avoid being put at a disadvantage by its rivals' efforts. It is hoped that these examples convey some of the flavour of main theories of strategic competition between existing firms. They do not constitute an exhaustive survey.

Section IV is concerned with the effect of potential competition upon firms already in a market. The seminal work of Bain (1956) on barriers to new competition has recently been subject to intensive reappraisal. Baumol (1982) and others have proposed a controversial theory of 'contestable markets', in which there are no barriers to new competition. Other authors, more in the spirit of Bain, have shown in a rigorous fashion how an existing firm in a market might be able to deter entry into the market by strategic investment in capacity, R & D advertising, brand proliferation, or predatory pricing, for example. These developments are reviewed below.

Section V draws some broad implications for policy. The other articles in this volume provide more detailed discussions of antitrust and industrial policy. The first broad implication is that market structure and conduct are determined jointly by the fundamental conditions of consumer preferences and technological relationships. This contrasts with the view that market structure is somehow given, and that it determines conduct in the industry. Rather, industry structure may be as much a symptom of underlying factors as a root cause of undesirable conduct and performance. A related implication is the importance of potential competition. The threat of new entry can be a potent influence upon the behaviour of existing firms; on the other hand that threat may be thwarted by strategic moves by existing firms. A third broad implication is that competition among the few does not necessarily produce socially desirable results—a point well illustrated by R & D competition. It follows that there is an important role for public policy to influence the outcome of strategic competition among the few. As a final point, recent work in industrial economics should not be seen as delivering generally applicable policy prescriptions. On the contrary, it has served to highlight the heterogeneous nature of industries while providing useful tools

[2] This phrase is due to Aaron Director—see Williamson (1979, p. 919).

and valuable perspectives for the study of particular cases.

II. Interdependent decision-making

When there are only a few firms in an industry, they are *interdependent* in the following sense. The behaviour of any one firm has an appreciable effect upon the other firms, and the best plan of action for one firm to adopt depends upon the plans of action chosen by the other firms. Each firm is trying to second-guess the others—the behaviour of one firm depends upon what it expects the other firms to do, and they in turn are making their decisions on the basis of their expectations of what their rivals (including the first firm) will do. The situation is rather like that found in games like poker, bridge, or the children's game involving scissors, paper and rocks. Indeed, the framework for studying situations of interdependent decision is called the *theory of games*. This theory was developed by von Neumann and Morgenstern and has been refined and employed in numerous applications.

This section has two purposes. The first is informally to describe some basic notions of game theory, which will be useful for the economic analysis to follow. The second is to introduce two illustrations of games—concerning cooperation between firms and predatory pricing—which will be developed in the subsequent sections.

1. Some elements of game theory

A situation of interdependent decision-making, as described in the paragraphs above, is called a *game*. The participants in the game are the *players*. In our case the firms in the industry are the players. Each player pursues some objective: each player is intent upon maximising his *payoff*. The payoff that a player receives measures how well he achieves his objective. We shall suppose for the most part that the payoff of a firm is its profit (or, in dynamic contexts, the discounted value of its profit stream). Thus we are assuming that firms are intent upon maximising their profits. The payoffs of the players depend upon the decisions that they make. In general, the payoff of player 1 depends not only on his decision, but also upon the decisions made by the other players. This is precisely the element of interdependence that game theory attempts to study.

Each player chooses a *strategy*. A strategy is a plan of action, or a complete contingency plan, which specifies what the player will do in any of the circumstances in which he might find himself. A strategy is therefore quite different from a *move*. A move is the action that a player makes on a particular occasion, whereas his strategy specifies for the whole range of possible circumstances what move he would make in each particular circumstance. The distinction is rather like the difference in chess between Karpov's game plan (his strategy) and his move pawn-to-king-four.

To summarise so far: the description of a game includes:

(i) the set of *players*;
(ii) the set of *strategies* available to each player from which each player chooses one; and
(iii) each player's *payoff*, which depends on the strategies chosen by the various players.

It is sometimes necessary to describe a game in more detail. A fuller description would include:

(iv) the *move order* in the game—i.e. who moves when; and
(v) the *information* conditions in the game.

By (v) is meant the knowledge that each player has at every stage concerning (a) the prior moves made by the various players, and (b) the motivations of, and strategies available to, the other players in the game.

One way to categorise games is according to the degree of harmony or disharmony between the interests of the players. At one extreme is the pure *coordination* game, in which all players have the same objective. At the other extreme is the game of pure *conflict*, in which there are two players with completely opposed interests—what is good for one is bad for the other. Usually, however, there is a mixture of conflict and coordination of interests. Such *mixed motive* games will be our main concern.

It was stated above that in most games the best strategy for one player to choose depends upon what the other players choose. Hence the importance of expectations about the others' choices. But sometimes a player has a strategy that is best irrespective of what the others do. This is called a *dominant* strategy, and the other, inferior strategies are called *dominated* strategies. The first example in the next subsection is one in which each player has a dominant strategy.

It is easy to deduce what will happen in games with dominant strategies—each player simply chooses his dominant strategy. But in general it is hard to work out what will happen, because the best strategy for each player depends upon what the others do. A situation in which each player is choosing the best strategy available to him, given the strategies chosen by the other players, is called a *Nash equilibrium*. Nash equilibrium corresponds to the idea of self-fulfilled expectations. If each player expected the others to play their part in the equilibrium, then it would be rational for him to do likewise. If the same is true for all players, then all have their expectations fulfilled at equilibrium. Similarly, Nash equilibrium corresponds to the idea of a tacit, self-supporting agreement. If the players were somehow to agree to a plan of Nash equilibrium behaviour, then none would have an incentive to depart from the agreement. No external mechanism would be required to enforce the agreement. However, any agreement that is not a Nash equilibrium would require a means of enforcement.

The concept is named after John Nash, an economist who made some fundamental advances in game theory in the 1950s. The concept is in fact a development of that introduced in the 1830s by Cournot, a French mathematician, who examined the output decisions of the two firms in a duopoly. He defined equilibrium as a position in which each firm is producing his optimal output level, given the output level chosen by the other firm.

2. Two illustrations

Following the rather general outline of game theory above, we now consider two illustrative examples. They are concerned with

(i) the problems of collusion; and
(ii) predatory pricing.

Both examples will be developed in later sections of this paper.

(i) The problem of collusion

Figure 1.1 represents a very simple game[3] in which the players are two firms, A and B. Each firm has a choice between two alternatives—a high output strategy or a low output strategy. The numbers in the boxes give the payoffs of the players, which can be thought of as the firms' profits. The convention is that firm A's payoff is written in the bottom left-hand corner of a box, and B's payoff appears in the top right-hand corner.

In the example, the best thing that can happen for a firm is for it to produce high output while its rival produces low output. The low output level of its rival means that price is not driven down too much, and so a good profit margin is earned. The worst thing that

Figure 1.1. The Prisoners' Dilemma

can happen is to produce low output while the rival produces high output. Then price is fairly low—due to the rival's high output—and revenues are barely sufficient to cover total costs. If both firms produce high output, then price is low but profits are positive. It is better for both to restrain output, and thereby to raise price. We shall refer to this as the collusive outcome.

What will happen in this game? In fact it is a dominant strategy for each firm to choose a high output level. This is the best strategy for firm A whether firm B produces a high level of output or a low one. Similarly for firm B. Thus the 'noncooperative' outcome is for each firm to get a payoff of 1. However, if the firms had somehow been able to attain the collusive outcome (i.e. both produce low levels of output), then both would have received a superior payoff of 2. The problem of collusion is for the firms to achieve this superior outcome notwithstanding the seemingly compelling argument that high output levels will be chosen. In section 3 it will be seen how this problem can be resolved when a game such as that depicted in figure 1.1 is repeated. After all, in reality firms are in competition on a long-term basis; they are not engaged in a 'one-shot' game like the one just considered. When account is taken of this fact, collusion can be sustained by threats of retaliation against non-cooperative behaviour.

(ii) Predatory pricing

Figure 1.2 represents a simple game[4] in which predatory pricing is possible. Note that the method of representation differs from that in figure 1.1. Here we have made the order of moves explicit. The players are two firms—a potential entrant is contemplating entry into a market currently dominated by an incumbent firm. The potential entrant chooses between going IN to the market, or remaining OUT of it.

---

[3] The game is a version of the well-known Prisoners' Dilemma Game.

[4] Dixit's excellent (1982) survey contains an account of this game.

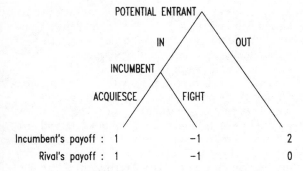

Figure 1.2. An entry game

The two examples above were intended to illustrate how game theory is used to analyse strategic competition among the few, and to prepare some of the ground for the discussion to follow.

III. Strategic competition between existing firms

The aim of this section is to describe some recent developments in the analysis of strategic competition between existing firms. The next section considers competition between existing firms and potential rivals. Neither section is intended to be anything like a survey. Rather, the intention is to try to convey the flavour of some recent developments, by way of illustrative examples.

The present section has four parts. The first continues the discussion of collusion from the previous section. It is shown that, using the perspective of repeated games, it may be possible for firms effectively to collude in the absence of explicit agreement to do so, even though each is exclusively concerned to maximise its own profits. The second and third parts of this section both develop the theme of the 'endogeneity' of market structure by showing the importance of the fundamentals of consumer preferences and technological relationships. The model of R & D competition by Dasgupta and Stiglitz (1980) is the main subject of part 2, and part 3 discusses recent work on product differentiation, notably that of Shaked and Sutton (1983). Strategic commitment is the topic in the final part of this section, which contains an account of Brander and Spencer's (1983) model in which firms choose their levels of R & D activity partly with a view to influencing their rivals' behaviour.

If entry occurs, the incumbent can either FIGHT entry, which is costly to both firms, or he can ACQUIESCE so as to arrive at some peaceful coexistence, which is more profitable. The best thing for the incumbent is for entry not to take place. In that event, the potential entrant does better than if its entry were fought, but not as well as if its entry were met with acquiescence.

What will happen in the game? In fact there are two Nash equilibria:

(a) Potential entrant chooses IN, and incumbent chooses to ACQUIESCE in the event of entry, and

(b) Potential entrant chooses OUT, and incumbent chooses to FIGHT in the event of entry.

In each case, each player gets his maximum payoff given the strategy chosen by the other player. But equilibrium (b) is implausible, because it is clear that, faced with the fact of entry, the incumbent would find it profitable to ACQUIESCE, rather than to FIGHT entry. Relying on this fact, the potential entrant would choose IN, and we would get equilibrium (a). In other words, the incumbent's threat to FIGHT is not *credible*—it is an empty threat that would not be believed. The concept of Nash equilibrium has been refined to rule out these peculiar equilibria involving incredible threats. The concept of *perfect equilibrium*, developed by Selten (1965; 1975), requires that the strategies chosen by the players be a Nash equilibrium, not only in the game as a whole, but also in every subgame of the game. In figure 1.2 there is a subgame beginning at the node alongside the word 'incumbent'. Perfect equilibrium rules out the undesirable equilibrium (b), leaving only the intuitively reasonable equilibrium (a): entry occurs and is met with acquiescence.

The game in figure 1.2 is sufficiently simple for it to be possible to work out what will happen without bothering with the jargon above. But in more sophisticated—and realistic—examples this is not so.

1. Non-cooperative collusion

The paradoxical title of this subsection indicates that we are asking whether collusive outcomes can be sustained by non-cooperative behaviour, i.e. in the absence of explicit, enforceable agreements between firms. In the simple illustration of figure 1.1 above this was not possible, but that illustration had evident shortcomings. In particular, it represented a 'one-shot' game, whereas in reality firms are commonly in competition with their rivals on a longer term basis. That is to say, they are in a *repeated* game. Is non-cooperative collusion possible in a repeated game?

The answer to this question depends upon at least four things:

  (i) whether the game is repeated indefinitely, or only a finite number of times;

 (ii) whether the players in the game are fully informed as to the objectives of, and opportunities available to, their rivals;

(iii) whether the players know the prior moves made by their rivals—so that 'cheating' can be detected; and

(iv) how much weight the players attach to the future in their calculations.

The particular circumstances of an industry determine what it is appropriate to assume in relation to (i)–(iv). Rather than look at particular industries, our approach here will be to explore the consequences of the various assumptions that could be made.

Initially, we shall do this by developing the illustrative example shown in figure 1.1.

Suppose for the moment that the game is repeated a finite number of times, and that there is complete and perfect information. Firms are assumed to maximise the (possibly discounted) sum of their profits in the game as a whole. Unfortunately (for the firms) the collusive low output outcome cannot be sustained. Suppose that the game is repeated 137 times. At the last round, it is clear from previous argument that it is a dominant strategy for both firms to produce high output. This fact implies that neither firm has any incentive to cooperate by producing low output at the 136th repetition, since it is clear to all what will happen at the last round. And the same is true at the 135th repetition. The argument proceeds, by backwards induction, to the conclusion that there is never any collusion—both firms produce high output at every stage of the game. Since there is nothing special about the number 137, the same conclusion holds for any finite number of repetitions of the game.

As well as being unhappy (for the firms), this result is rather unsatisfactory. First, our intuition suggests that some collusion would occur, at least early on in the game, despite the fact that the number of repetitions is finite. Secondly, the experimental evidence (see Axelrod (1984)) accords with this intuition. How can this intuition, supported by experimental evidence, be squared with apparently compelling game theoretical logic?

Before answering this question, let us consider the *infinitely* repeated version of the game depicted in figure 1.1. Suppose that firms discount the future at rate w, where w is a number between zero and one. That is,

firms attach weight w to what happens next period, weight w^2 to what happens the period after that, and so on. The closer w is to zero, the less weight they attach to the future relative to the present, i.e. the more short-sighted they are.

Provided that w is not too small, it is now possible for non-cooperative collusion to occur. Suppose that firm B plays the *trigger strategy*, which is to choose low output in period 1 and in any subsequent period provided that firm A has never produced high output, but to produce high output forever more once firm A ever produces high output.[5] The idea is that firm B cooperates with A unless and until A 'defects', in which case B is triggered into perpetual non-cooperation. What is A's best response to this trigger strategy by B? If A were also to adopt the trigger strategy, then there would always be collusion—each firm would always choose low output and receive 2 in each period. The discounted value of this profit flow is

$$2 + 2w + 2w^2 + \ldots = 2/(1-w).$$

In fact A gets this payoff with any strategy in which he is not the first to defect. If, however, A chooses a strategy in which he defects at any stage, then he gets a payoff of 3 in the first period of defection (because B chooses low output), and a payoff of no more than 1 in every subsequent period (because B has been triggered into perpetual non-cooperation). So his payoff is at most

$$3 + w + w^2 + w^3 + \ldots = 3 + w/(1-w).$$

Comparing the two payoffs, we see that it is better not to defect so long as

$$w \geq 1/2$$

This precise answer depends of course upon the particular numbers chosen for the illustration. But the general point is clear. Provided that the firms give enough weight to the future, then non-cooperative collusion can be sustained, for example by trigger strategies. The collusion is non-cooperative in the sense that the firms are not acting in concert; each is independently doing the best it can given the strategy adopted by the other firm. In other words, the trigger strategies constitute a Nash equilibrium, or a self-enforcing agreement. Trigger strategies are not the only way to sustain the collusive outcome non-cooperatively. Another leading strategy is tit-for-tat, according to which a player chooses in the current period what the other player chose in the previous period.

---

[5] See Friedman (1971).

Now let us return to the question of how collusion might occur non-cooperatively, even in the finitely repeated game. Recall that we found a tension between intuition and experimental evidence on one hand, and game theoretic logic on the other. Intuition said that collusion could happen—at least in the earlier rounds—but game theory apparently said that it could not. An important and elegant resolution of this paradox has been provided by Kreps *et al.* (1982). They relax the assumption of complete information, and suppose instead that one player has a small amount of doubt in his mind as to the motivation of the other player. Suppose, for example, that A is not absolutely certain that B's payoffs are as described above (i.e. the discounted sum of the payoffs in figure 1.1). Suppose that A attaches some tiny probability p to B preferring —or being committed—to playing the trigger strategy.[6] It turns out that even if p is very small indeed, the players will effectively collude until some point towards the end of the game. This occurs because it is not worth A defecting in view of the risk that the non-collusive outcome will obtain for the rest of the game, and because B wishes to maintain his *reputation* for possibly preferring, or being committed to, the trigger strategy. Thus the analysis also yields a satisfying account of how reputation can operate to maintain effective collusion, at least for a substantial part of the time. What is remarkable about the result is that a small degree of doubt about the motivation of one of the players can yield much effective collusion. Once the strict assumption of complete information is slightly relaxed, the outcome of the game changes radically.[7]

So far in the discussion of collusion we have focused on the simple example in figure 1.1, in which two firms have a choice between a high or a low output level. But there may be several firms in an industry, and in fact firms have a much broader choice. If output is their decision variable, they can choose from a wide range of possible output levels. Or it may be that their decision variable is price, not to mention other aspects of company behaviour such as investment, advertising and R & D. Be that as it may, more or less the same analysis can be applied straightforwardly in the more complex settings. In those settings new possibilities arise. For example, Abreu (1984) has investigated the most effective credible strategies for 'punishing' deviations from collusive behaviour. The more effective the punishment, the greater is the deterrent effect, and the

greater is the degree of collusion than can be sustained. In an infinitely repeated game where firms choose output levels, the most effective credible punishment strategy consists of a stick and a carrot—the carrot is the attraction of collusion, and the stick is a swift episode of high output levels and a correspondingly low price level. If any firm deviates from collusive behaviour, there would immediately occur one unpleasant period of punishment (the stick), followed by a return to collusion (the carrot). This punishment strategy is credible because it would be entirely rational for the other firms to punish the defector in the way described. In the model no firm actually chooses to defect, because the credible threat of punishment acts as a sufficient deterrent.

We have not yet faced up to the problem of detecting defection from a collusive arrangement. Implicity we have been supposing that firms can observe one another's behaviour, but this assumption of perfect information may be unjustified. It is perhaps more reasonable to suppose that the firms in a collusive arrangement can observe the price prevailing in their market, but not the output levels chosen by the individual firms that are party to the arrangement. If the demand curve facing the industry is not known for certain, then one firm cannot infer exactly what the others have done. Suppose that a low price is observed in some period. That might be because demand for the product of the industry is low; or it might be because some firm has defected from the collusive arrangement by producing a high level of output. There is the problem of inferring which is the true cause.

This question has been examined by Green and Porter (1984). They consider equilibrium strategies in which firms collude so long as price remains above some critical level P, but they revert to an episode of more aggressive, non-cooperative behaviour if price ever falls below P, before restoring collusive behaviour T periods after the initial price drop.[8] The (credible) threat of the episode of non-cooperative behaviour is sufficient to deter defection from the collusive outcome, but occasionally there is an episode of non-cooperation when demand is especially low. This theory offers an interesting interpretation of the pattern of prices in an industry characterised by occasional, temporary falls in price. One view is to regard the falls in price as *collapses* in cartel discipline, but the account given by Green and Porter suggests the alternative view that they *help ensure* cartel discipline.

---

[6] In fact Kreps *et al.* (1982) suppose that the small probability is attached to B playing the tit-for-tat strategy, which had emerged as a successful strategy in experiments—see Axelrod (1984).

[7] The same point emerges in the work on predatory pricing by Kreps *et al.* (1982).

[8] Abreu *et al.* (1984) have shown that in Green and Porter's (1984) model, the most effective way to police the cartel is to have a severe reversionary episode lasting one period. The parallel with Abreu (1984) is clear.

There are numerous other devices that might be used by firms to facilitate non-cooperative collusion by ologopolists. Salop (1985) has explored *facilitating practices* such as most-favoured-nation (MFN) clauses and meeting-competition-clauses (MCCs) that are commonly observed in sales contracts. An MFN clause is one that promises the buyer that the seller will not supply another buyer at a lower price. (If the commodity in question is an input for the buyer's business, then the buyer would not face the risk that another buyer would gain a competitive advantage over him by obtaining the input more cheaply). Several common pricing conventions—for example posting list prices—have effects similar to an MFN clause. An MCC says that the seller will match the price of any seller supplying at a lower price. The effect of practices of this sort is to alter the incentives of the firms in the oligopoly in such a way that price reductions are less attractive. In addition, they tend to make it easier for one firm to monitor the behaviour of others. Thus they facilitate oligopolistic collusion. In similar vein Klemperer (1984) has shown how switching costs can promote collusive behaviour.[9] Switching costs are present when it is costly for a consumer to switch from his current supplier to a different supplier (even though ex ante suppliers are on a par). Examples are accountants, and airlines that offer frequent flyer discounts. Sometimes switching costs occur naturally (as with accountants), but sometimes they occur because of the deliberate actions of firms (as with airline discounts), although the motivation for those actions is not necessarily to facilitate collusion.

We conclude this discussion of non-cooperative collusion by mentioning some problems for public policy that will be developed in section V. We have seen that effective collusion does not necessarily require explicit agreements between firms. Antitrust policy generally declares explicit agreements to be unlawful, but it is not clear how it can or should be directed against tacit, non-cooperative collusion. One difficulty is to identify the actions of firms that are unlawful. After all, if each firm is independently pursuing its legitimate business interests. Nevertheless we saw that in some contexts the process of collusion might be facilitated by certain practices—for example price clauses in sales contracts. The question arises of whether these facilitating practices are a suitable target for antitrust policy.

2. Market structure and cost reducing innovation

One of the themes emphasised in the introduction was the endogeneity of market structure. Rather than take market structure as given, we wish to understand how the basic conditions of consumer preferences, technology, and so on determine market structure and the conduct of firms. To make the point very crudely, we wish to see how the basic conditions jointly determine structure, conduct and performance, whereas the traditional S–C–P paradigm is more concerned with the causal flow from structure to conduct to performance.

Below we set out the model of market structure and cost-reducing innovation due to Dasgupta and Stiglitz (1980).[10] It is very much a 'bare bones', stylised model, and deliberately so. It shows with great clarity that relationships and correlations—such as those between market structure and R & D efforts—do not necessarily imply causality, and that other explanations are available. This affects how we interpret empirical correlations between market structure and innovation.

The model brings out another, quite separate point. The message of much economic theory concerning the production decisions of firms is that the free market generates results that are broadly desirable from the social point of view, especially if the market is competitive. It is well-known, however, that this happy conclusion breaks down in a wide range of circumstances. Technological competition is a leading case in point. After presenting the Dasgupta-Stiglitz model, we shall discuss why this is so.

The model

The unit costs of a firm are assumed to depend on its R & D efforts. Let $c(x)$ be the unit production costs of a firm that spends x on R & D. As x increases, c falls. There are n identical firms in the industry producing the same product. We will see shortly how n is determined. If total industry output is Q, price is $P(Q)$, where P falls as Q rises. The profits of a firm with output q and R & D expenditure x can be written

$$\pi = [P(Q) - c(x)]q - x$$

The term in square brackets is the profit margin. When multiplied by q this gives gross profit, from which R & D expenditure x is deducted. If all firms produce the same level of output q then total industry output Q is equal to nq.

[9]   By contrast, von Weizsäcker (1984) has constructed a model in which higher switching costs cause there to be more competition. See Klemperer (1984) for a discussion.

[10]   See also Dasgupta (1985) for a review of the theory of technological competition.

Each firm chooses its output q and its R & D expenditure x to maximise its profits π. Each firm assumes that its own decisions about x and q do not affect the decisions of other firms about their output and R & D. In other words, we are interested in the Nash equilibrium of the game.

As to the determination of n, the number of firms, there are two leading possibilities. One is that n is given exogenously—there happen to be n firms and that's that. But this assumption seems to be rather arbitrary. At least it calls for some justification. Another possibility is that n is determined endogenously, by *free entry* into the industry. If there is free entry, then firms will continue to come into the industry until it would be unprofitable for the next firm to do so. As an approximation, we may say that entry occurs up to the point where profits are zero. The free entry condition is not the only way that n could be determined endogenously. Alternatively one could suppose that barriers to entry do exist, and these could be modelled explicitly. However, we shall assume free entry in this illustration, because it suffices to make the points at hand.

Let us remind ourselves of the variables of interest. Our index of market *structure* is n, the number of firms. As n falls, the industry becomes more concentrated. The *conduct* of firms includes their decisions on output q and R & D expenditure x. The *performance* of the industry is measured by such things as profits π, the price-cost margin $(P - c)/P$, and innovative advance (i.e. the rate of cost reduction).

It remains to say more about consumer *preferences* and *technological* relationships. Consumer preferences determine demand conditions for the output of the industry, i.e. the relationship between P and Q. To be specific, let the (inverse) demand curve have the form

$$P(Q) = \sigma Q^{-\varepsilon} \quad ; \quad \sigma, \varepsilon > 0.$$

This specification turns out to be particularly convenient. The size of the market is measured by σ and the sensitivity of price to output is measured by ε. The price elasticity of demand is $1/\varepsilon$. As to technological conditions, the relationship between unit costs and R & D expenditure is given the form

$$c(x) = \beta x^{-\alpha} \quad ; \quad \alpha, \beta > 0.$$

Here β measures the level of costs, and α measures the sensitivity of unit costs to R & D expenditure. When α is large, unit costs fall more rapidly with R & D efforts. Thus, 'innovative opportunities' are greater.

The four parameters, α, β, ε and σ are the basic conditions of demand and technology. Together they determine the structure, conduct and performance

variables in the model. It turns out that α and ε (the elasticities of cost reduction and of demand) are especially important. A number of interesting results hold at the (free entry) equilibrium in the model.

The number of firms is given by

$$n = \varepsilon (1 + \alpha)/\alpha.$$

Thus an industry is more concentrated (n is smaller) when innovation opportunities (α) are greater. Industries with less elastic demand (that is, lower $1/\varepsilon$, or higher ε) are less concentrated. The size of the market (σ) does not affect n. If the market is larger, the level of R & D per firm is greater, and unit costs are correspondingly lower.

The price-cost margin at equilibrium is

$$\frac{P - c}{P} = \frac{\varepsilon}{n}$$

Thus the price-cost margin is negatively related to the elasticity of demand $(1/\varepsilon)$ and positively related to the level of concentration $(1/n)$. However, care is necessary in interpreting this familiar relationship, because n is determined endogenously, within the model, rather than being fixed. Indeed, by combining the last two equations we obtain

$$\frac{P - c}{P} = \frac{\alpha}{1 + \alpha}$$

The price-cost margin is seen to depend on the basic parameter α. This margin is greater in industries where innovative opportunities are greater. This is because firms' R & D expenditures—which have to be covered by the price-cost margin—are higher in these industries. In fact research intensity, as measured by the ratio of R & D expenditure to sales revenue is

$$\frac{nx}{PQ} = \frac{\alpha}{1 + \alpha}$$

which is the same price-cost margin. Recall that industries with greater innovative opportunities also tend to be more concentrated. *Thus there tends to be a positive relationship between concentration, the price-cost margin, and research intensity, but there is no causal relationship between these variables*: they are all determined by the underlying parameters of technology and demand.

The equilibrium outcome described above can be compared with the socially optimal research and production plan. In the Dasgupta-Stiglitz (1980) model, costs are not reduced as much as is socially optimal, and price is too high. At the same time, total R & D expenditure is likely to be too great, because there is excessive duplication between the research efforts of different firms.

Spence (1984) examines cost reducing innovation in a richer model. He focuses on the classic appropriability problem in R & D. The problem has two parts: (i) the incentive of a firm to do R & D depends on the degree to which it appropriates the benefits of its R & D; if there are 'spillovers', so that one firm benefits from the R & D of another, then incentives are reduced; (ii) on the other hand, knowledge is optimally diffused among firms if it is priced at the marginal cost of its dissemination (which is often close to zero). The problem, then, is that incentives for innovation require inefficient diffusion of knowledge. Spence shows that the market may perform poorly irrespective of concentration and the extent of spillovers, but potential performance improves when spillovers are high. R & D *subsidies* improve market performance substantially. They drive a wedge between the price received by a supplier of R & D output and the price paid by its buyers. A possible solution to the problem of excessive duplication of R & D efforts is to encourage cooperative R & D. However, there is the danger that this facilitates anticompetitive behaviour, such as collusion in product markets or entry deterrence. For a discussion of policy towards R & D intensive sectors, see Ordover and Willig (1985).

This subsection has described only a tiny fraction of the work that has been done on the relationships between market structure and innovation. It has concentrated on cost-reducing innovation, where the costs of a firm depend smoothly upon its (and possibly its rivals') R & D efforts. Product innovation has not been discussed, and nor have R & D contests such as patent races. On these important matters see the extensive surveys by Kamien and Schwartz (1982), and Stoneman (1983).

3. Product differentiation and market structure

The study of product differentiation has been central to industrial economics ever since its inception. The 'spatial' representation of product differentiation, first used in Hotelling's 1929 *Economic Journal* article, has been the basic framework for much work on the topic. In Hotelling's representation, sellers are positioned at points along a line, along which consumers are distributed. One can think of the line as, for example, a stretch of beach (with the sellers being ice-cream vendors) or as a representation of the sweetness/dryness of cider (with very sweet cider at one end and very dry cider at the other). Consumers prefer to patronise sellers positioned close to them (because they save on 'travel costs'), and are therefore prepared to pay some price premium to obtain their favoured variety. The framework can be extended in many directions—to several dimensions, circles rather than lines, and so on. Several interesting questions can be posed within this framework. For example, will there be a tendency for sellers to differentiate their products as much as possible, or will they tend to agglomerate at a point? How does the nature of price competition between firms depend on their locations? Can an incumbent monopolist deter entry into his market by introducing a proliferation of brands at different locations? And so on.

Rather than discuss any of these questions in the Hotelling tradition, I shall focus instead upon recent work on *vertical* product differentiation, and its bearing on the issue of the determination of market structure. Products are said to be 'vertically differentiated' when they differ in respect of *quality*. If two vertically differentiated products were offered to consumers at the same price, one of the two products would be preferred by all—i.e. the one with higher quality. (This is of course *not* the case in Hotelling's framework, where there is 'horizontal' product differentiation. In that case, if two goods were offered at the same price, some consumers would prefer one of them, and other consumers would prefer the other—a consumer would prefer the product closer to him in product space). Since quality differences are manifest features of many markets, it is clearly important to study vertical product differentiation.

Shaked and Sutton (1983) have examined the determination of market structure in markets with vertically differentiated products (see also Shaked and Sutton (1982)). Their major result concerning market structure is that there may be an upper limit to the number of firms than can coexist at equilibrium irrespective of the size of the market. In that case, a certain degree of market concentration is inevitable. (By 'equilibrium' is meant Nash equilibrium in prices given quality levels).

A market in which this property holds is called a *natural oligopoly*. This result contrasts with the property of horizontally differentiated markets that there is no limit to the number of firms that can coexist at equilibrium if the market is large enough.

Whether or not a market is a natural oligopoly depends in a subtle way upon the interaction between consumer preferences and the technology of product improvement. Let c(u) be the unit variable cost of supplying a product with quality level u. We would expect c to increase with u, but what matters is how rapidly c increases with u. If unit variable costs rise 'sufficiently slowly' as quality increases, then the market is a natural oligopoly—there is a limit to the number of firms that can coexist at equilibrium, no matter how big the market is. More generally, this result holds if it is the case that all consumers would have the same ranking of products if all products were offered at their respective unit variable costs. If this property does not hold, it is possible for a new firm to attract custom by entering with a quality level intermediate between two existing quality levels and selling at a price close to unit variable cost. It follows that there is no limit to the number of firms that can exist as the market grows. However, when the property does hold, a firm adopting such a policy would not necessarily gain any custom, because consumers would be prepared to pay the extra for the higher quality product already on the market, for example.

The details of Shaked and Sutton's analysis are complex and subtle; the account above does not do justice to them. The central point to emerge is that market structure depends critically upon the technology of product improvement and upon consumers' preferences—in particular their willingness to pay for quality improvements.

Shaked and Sutton observe that the condition that the cost of quality improvement does not rise rapidly in relation to consumers' willingness to pay for it, is most likely to be met in industries where product quality depends more on fixed costs (e.g. R & D) than on unit variable costs. Expenditure on quality improvement and the number and sizes of firms in the market therefore jointly depend upon consumer preferences and upon technological relationships. Thus we have seen in this section—as in the last—that market structure is not the exogenously given determinant of firms' conduct. Rather, conduct and structure are jointly determined by the fundamentals of preferences and technology.

4. Strategic commitment with R & D

Strategic moves are an important feature of competition between existing firms. Recall that a strategic move is one designed to induce another player to make a choice more favourable to the strategic mover than would otherwise have happened. The purpose of this subsection is to examine strategic commitment in the particular contexts of R & D competition, following Brander and Spencer (1983).

Consider an industry containing two firms, each of which is to decide on its level of cost-reducing R & D expenditure. Whereas in subsection (2) it was assumed that firms chose their R & D and output levels simultaneously, we shall now suppose that R & D decisions are made *before* output decisions are made. This is realistic inasmuch as R & D expenditures are irreversible and long-term in nature, whereas output decisions are more readily changed. Since the firms' output decisions now depend partly upon their R & D decisions, a *strategic motive* is added to the efficiency motive for research expenditures. In particular, firm 1 would like to curb the output of firm 2, because market price is then higher. By reducing its own costs through research expenditure, firm 1 credibly threatens to produce greater output. This has the desired effect of discouraging firm 2 from producing such high output. High R & D expenditure is thus a strategic move that works by influencing the output decision of the other firm. Owing to the attractiveness of this move, firms tend to overinvest in R & D, in the sense that the output that they eventually supply is produced inefficiently: too much R & D, and too little of the other factors of production, are employed. This strategic source of inefficiency is quite separate from those mentioned earlier in this section.

In more precise terms, the problem is analysed as a two-stage game. Levels of R & D are chosen at stage one, and output levels are chosen at stage two. Being interested only in threats that are credible, we characterise the perfect equilibrium of the game. The easiest way to do this is first to calculate the equilibrium outputs at stage two as a function of the R & D levels chosen at stage one. Having found the dependency of outputs upon R & D, it is then possible to find equilibrium in the choice of R & D levels at stage one. In fact the analysis does not depend on the strategic variable being R & D. Exactly the same applies to any fixed factor of production that reduces costs—such as capital. However, the analysis is sensitive to the assumptions that are made about stage two of the game. We assumed that the firms achieved equilibrium in output levels, in which case there is excessive R & D. But if equilibrium is in prices, the opposite result can hold: each firm underinvests in R & D to induce the other to charge a higher price. The intuitive explanation is that by investing less in R & D, a firm causes its equilibrium price to be slightly higher. This in turn causes the rival's equilibrium price to be slightly higher, which is beneficial to the first firm. This sort of sensitivity of results to assumptions that appear equally plausible bedevils theorists of market structure.

Strategic commitment with R & D is but one illustration of the strategic nature of competition between existing firms. Other instruments of commitment include advertising, the introduction of new brands, and patenting. These themes are taken up again when strategic commitment to deter new entry is examined.

IV. Potential competition and strategic entry deterrence

The threat to existing firms posed by potential competitors has long been recognised as an important influence upon market structure and conduct. The force of this threat depends on the extent to which there are *barriers to entry* into the market. In his classic analysis, Bain (1956, p. 3) defines barriers to entry as

the advantages of established sellers in an industry over potential entrant sellers, those advantages being reflected in the extent to which established sellers can persistently raise their prices above a competitive level without attracting new firms to enter the industry.

He identified three sources of barriers to new competition:

(i) Product Differentiation: customer loyalty to existing products puts new entrants at a disadvantage.

(ii) Absolute Cost Advantages: incumbent firms might enjoy absolute cost advantages, due perhaps to exclusive access to superior technologies, or to accumulated experience.

(iii) Economies of Scale: if the minimum efficient scale of production for a firm is large in relation to total demand in the market, then a new entrant faces a dilemma—entry at small scale involves high production costs, but entry at efficient scale would expand industry supply so that price would fall.

Bain's analysis has been subject to recent critical scrutiny (see for example von Weizsäcker (1980)) and at the same time attempts have been made to develop his insights in a rigorous, detailed fashion. As to the causes of barriers to entry, an important distinction, due to Salop (1979), is between *innocent* and *strategic* barriers to entry. An innocent barrier to entry is the incidental result of the short-run profit-maximising behaviour of existing firms. A strategic barrier to entry is constructed by design, with the intent of deterring new entrants into the market. The erection of a strategic barrier to entry involves the sacrifice of short-run profits with a view to the longer-run gains of deterring entry. Strategic entry deterrence is the subject of section IV.2. The next section, however, is about the controversial theory of contestable markets, in which there are no barriers to

new competition and the threat of entry is at its most potent.

1. The theory of contestable markets

The idea that potential competition affects the conduct of existing firms is by no means novel, but it has recently been examined in its purest form in the theory of contestable markets, developed by Baumol, Panzar and Willig (1982) and their colleagues. Much of their work concerns the economics of multi-product industries, but here we shall concentrate on their analysis of *new entry* into markets. (Although there are important relationships between the topics of entry and multiproduct firms, most of the main ideas concerning the former can be discussed with reference to singleproduct industries). Important claims have been made on behalf of contestability theory. Baumol (1982, p. 1) in his Presidential address to the American Economic Association claims that the theory

enables us to look at industry structure and behaviour in a way that is novel in some respects, that it provides a unifying analytical structure to the subject area, and that it offers useful insights for empirical work and for the formulation of policy.

A contestable market is one into which there is ultrafree entry (to use Shepherd's (1984) phrase). All firms —actual and potential—have access to the same technology and hence they enjoy the same cost function. Furthermore, and most importantly, exit from a contestable market is absolutely costless, in the sense that an entrant incurs no *sunk costs* (i.e. irrecoverable expenditures). Thus a contestable market is vulnerable to *hit-and-run entry*:

Even a very transient profit opportunity need not be neglected by a potential entrant, for he can go in, and, before prices change, collect his gains and then depart without cost, should the climate grow hostile. (Baumol (1982, p. 4)).

Contestability is not inconsistent with the existence of economies of scale. Even if there are fixed costs of production, a market can be contestable provided that there are no sunk costs.

The following conditions hold at equilibrium in a contestable market.

(i) Profits are zero. If they were positive, then new firms would be attracted to enter. If they were negative, then some existing firms would exit from the market.

(ii) Production is efficient. Otherwise a new firm would enter the market, attracted by the prospect of producing efficiently, undercutting the existing inefficient firms, and making a profit.

(iii) Price P is at least as great as marginal cost MC. Otherwise a new firm would be able to make more profits than some existing firm by entering on a slightly smaller scale.

(iv) When there are two or more firms in the market, P cannot exceed MC. Together with (iii), this implies that P = MC. This condition is desirable from the point of view of welfare (ignoring 'second best problems'), because it implies that production occurs up to the point where the marginal cost of output equals its marginal benefit as measured by price. (When just one firm is in the market, this condition might not hold: see Baumol (1982, p. 5)).

(v) There is no cross-subsidisation between products. Otherwise there would again be a profit opportunity for a new firm. This follows from (iii).

(vi) The number and configuration of firms is always such as to produce the industry's output at minimum total cost.

Properties (i) to (vi) are highly desirable, according to the canons of traditional welfare economics.[11] The final property is of particular interest. It is another instance of the idea that market structure is endogenously determined by the basic conditions of demand and technology, rather than being given exogenously.

The theory has been subject to critical review—see, for example, Shepherd (1984). It is most implausible that real-world markets (or at any rate a significant number of them) fit the assumptions of the theory of contestable markets, even approximately. In particular, the theory depends on the twin assumptions:

(a) that there are no sunk costs; and

(b) that an entrant can come into a market, and set up on full scale, before the existing firm(s) respond by changing price.

Both these assumptions are dubious in respect of real-world markets. Assumption (b) is the *opposite* of the natural assumption to make, since price can be generally altered more rapidly than a new firm can establish itself in a market.

Against these criticisms, it might be said that, although real-world markets do not exactly fit the assumptions of the theory, a significant number of them approximately do so, or could be made to do so by appropriate policy measures. It is unclear how this response could meet the objection to assumption (b), and in any event there is a further difficulty. It is that if the assumptions of contestability theory are changed slightly (for example by supposing that sunk costs are positive but small), the predictions of the theory can alter radically. For instance, even tiny sunk costs can substantially reduce—or even eliminate—the force of the threat of entry upon existing firms. This *lack of robustness* is a major reason to doubt the applicability of the theory to practical problems.

That being said, the theory of contestable markets is a timely reminder that the threat of new entry can be a potent force that shapes market structure and the conduct of existing firms. It underlines the importance of measures to liberalise markets by reducing barriers to entry and exit, where it is possible to do so.[12] However, the theory is not built on sufficiently strong foundations to justify the confidence that is sometimes placed in the 'invisible hand' results derived from it. For example, it would be a grave error to suppose that there is no need to regulate private natural monopolists, on the grounds that the threat of entry compels them to behave benignly.

2. Strategic entry deterrence

In a contestable market, the only way to deter the entry of new firms is to meet the needs of consumers with maximum efficiency. This is far from being true in other, perhaps more plausible, contexts. The purpose of this subsection is to describe some of the devices that existing firms might use to deter entry in a strategic fashion. That is to say, we are interested in strategic moves designed to benefit existing firms by inducing potential rivals to choose not to enter their markets. Salop (1979) gives an account of early work on this topic. See also Salop (1981).

For the sake of simplicity, we shall focus on the case where one incumbent firm is seeking to deter the entry of one potential rival.[13] The entry decision of the rival depends upon his beliefs as to the likely profitability of being in the market. Entry will occur if and only if the expected profits exceed the expected costs of entry. How can the incumbent influence those beliefs in such a way as to deter entry?

---

[11] Another property is that in multiproduct natural monopoly industries, 'Ramsey prices' obtain at equilibrium for the product set of the industry in question: see Baumol *et al.* (1982). Ramsey prices maximise social welfare subject to the constraint that the firms earn a given profit level.

[12] Most economists would agree with the proposition that on the whole it is desirable for entry to be as free as possible. This statement is qualified because in some circumstances it is possible that free entry would damage welfare: see e.g. von Weizsäcker (1980).

[13] The case where several incumbents seek non-cooperatively to deter entry has been studied by Gilbert & Vives (1985).

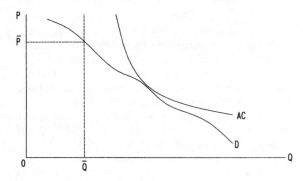

Figure 1.3. Limit pricing

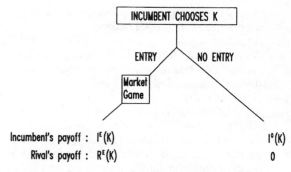

Figure 1.4. Commitment and entry deterrence

We shall address this question in two steps. First, we shall suppose that each firm is fully informed about the behaviour, opportunities and motivation of the other. In that case, the game between firms is one of complete and perfect information. Secondly, we shall relax these assumptions about the information available to the firms, and examine the roles of signalling and reputation in entry deterrence.

An instructive place to start is with the Bain-Sylos model of entry deterrence.[14] According to the Bain-Sylos postulate, the rival assumes that the output of the incumbent after entry would be the same as his output before entry. Given this postulate, it follows that the incumbent can influence the rival's assessment of post-entry profitability by varying his own pre-entry output. Figure 1.3 shows the 'limit output', and corresponding 'limit price' sufficient to deter entry. The demand curve for the industry is D, which is drawn relative to the vertical axis at 0. The AC curve is the average cost curve of the rival. It is drawn relative to the vertical axis given by the dashed line at output level $\overline{Q}$ because the D curve relative to that axis is the residual demand faced by the rival.

The limit output and limit price are $\overline{Q}$ and $\overline{P}$, respectively. If output is less than $\overline{Q}$, the AC curve is shifted left, and a portion of it would lie below the demand curve, in which case the rival could enter profitably. An output level greater than or equal to $\overline{Q}$ suffices to deter entry. The incumbent may choose to deter or to accommodate entry, depending on the profitability to him of each course of action.

The above analysis is instructive, but not altogether convincing. The difficulty lies with the postulate that the rival expects the incumbent not to change his output level in the event of entry. Dixit (1980, p. 97) questions the postulate on two counts:

First, faced with an irrevocable fact of entry, the established firm will usually find it best to make an accommodating output reduction. On the other hand, it would like to threaten to respond to entry with a predatory increase in output. The problem is to make the latter threat credible given the prospective entrant's knowledge of the former fact.

Similarly, Friedman (1979) has observed that in a game of complete and perfect information, and with no intertemporal interdependences of cost or demand conditions, the incumbent's output level before the entry decision ought to make no difference to the rival's assessment of the profitability of entry. Once entry occurs, a new game begins, and the parameters of that game are independent of previous behaviour.

This suggests that flexible instruments such as price or quantity are less likely to be the means of entry deterrence than instruments that have a more lasting effect upon cost or demand conditions. The key is for the incumbent to *commit* himself to a course of conduct that would be detrimental to an entrant. A large literature, from which but a few items will be mentioned,[15] has explored this theme. Figure 1.4 above sketches a simple schema.

First, the incumbent chooses the level of some strategic variable K. Numerous interpretations can be given to K, but for the moment regard it as the incumbent's capacity level. If the rival chooses not to enter, he gets zero, and the incumbent gets $I^O(K)$, as shown at the foot of the right-hand branch. Note that the incumbent's payoff depends on K even if entry does not occur. If entry does take place, a duopoly exists. Without examining the details of the duopolists' interactions, let us assume that the upshot of the 'market game' between them is that the incumbent gets $I^E(K)$ and the rival gets $R^E(K)$ in the event of entry. The schema is broad enough to allow for the rival also to choose some

---

[14] See Bain (1956) and Sylos-Labini (1964).

[15] A fuller survey, and an extensive bibliography, are provided by Geroski and Jacquemin (1984).

strategic variable, after the incumbent's choice of K. This would be included in the black box of the market game.

The incumbent's choice of K deters entry if $R^E(K) < 0$. It may be that entry is deterred even by the level of K that would have been chosen by a pure monopolist facing no threat of entry. Then entry is said to be block-aded. Or it may be that the incumbent does better to permit entry than to deter it. But here our concern is with the remaining case, in which strategic entry deterrence is optimal for the incumbent.

What are the likely instruments of entry deterrence? It is useful to distinguish between those that affect costs (the incumbent's and/or the rival's) and those that affect demand. As to the former, Dixit (1980) showed how the incumbent's choice of *capacity* could deter entry, but in Dixit's model, excess (in the sense of idle) capacity is not observed.[16] More generally, K can be interpreted as the incumbent's level of *capital input*. Strategic entry deterrence commonly implies over-capitalisation, in the sense that the output eventually produced by the incumbent could have been produced more efficiently with a lower level of capital, and a correspondingly higher level of variable factors of production (see Spence 1977). The same holds when K is interpreted as the incumbent's cost-reducing R & D expenditure. (Note the parallel with section III.4 above). In all these examples, the incumbent's commitment of high K promises that he will supply a high output level, or charge a low price, in the market game. The choice of K is therefore unattractive to the rival, not because of its direct effects, but because of its indirect influence upon the outcome of the market game.

In criticism of the Bain-Sylos analysis, it was stated above that the incumbent's pre-entry output would not affect the rival's entry decision if there were no intertemporal interdependences of cost or demand. But such interdependences do hold if the *experience curve* effect operates—i.e. if a firm's cost level is a declining function of its cummulative output. In that case it is possible for the incumbent's choice of output to deter entry strategically: see Spence (1981) and Fudenberg and Tirole (1983).

As well as the incumbent lowering his own costs, there may be ways for him to *raise the rival's cost*: see Salop and Scheffman (1983). For example, by setting high wage rates in the industry, the incumbent increases his own costs and those of an entrant. The direct effect of this upon the incumbent is unfavourable, but if the indirect effect is to deter the rival's

entry, then the ploy may well be beneficial to him in overall terms.

Another way in which entry might be deterred is for the incumbent to deny the rival access to technology that would allow him to compete. Gilbert and Newbery (1982) examine *pre-emptive patenting*—the acquisition of a patent by an incumbent firm with the purpose of denying the patent, and hence an entry opportunity, to a potential rival. An important factor here is that the incumbent's incentive to win the patent is likely to exceed the rival's incentive, even if the patent is for a technology inferior to that already enjoyed by the incumbent. This is because the incumbent's monopoly persists if he denies entry to the rival, whereas competition, which is less profitable than monopoly, occurs in the event of entry. This result has an important bearing on the question of the persistence of monopoly, for the advantage of the incumbent arises from his *strategic position*; intrinsically the incumbent may be no different from the rival. The result also offers an explanation of the phenomenon of sleeping (i.e. unused) patents, because the pre-emption result does not depend upon the patent being for a technology that is superior to the incumbent's existing technology.

Turning from the cost side to the demand side, there are further ways in which an incumbent firm can make the prospect of entry unattractive for a rival firm. In some circumstances, strategic *advertising* deters entry, although in Schmalensee's (1983) exploration of advertising and entry deterrence, it emerged that low advertising was the way to deter entry. The reason was that high advertising would cause the incumbent to have a higher price in the market game. For the rival, the favourable latter effect outweighed the disadvantage of high advertising, and made entry more attractive. *Brand proliferation*—the introduction of numerous new products—can also serve to deter entry (see Schmalensee (1978)). To use the locational analogy common in the analysis of product differentiation, brand proliferation fills up product space in such a way that there are no remaining slots or niches for profitable entry.

Product differentiation was one of Bain's three sources of barriers to entry. Although advertising is often regarded as a measure of product differentiation, Bain did not see it as the heart of the problem. Schmalensee (1982) shows how buyers' uncertainty about the quality of new brands can give established (or pioneering) brands an advantage in a differentiated market. The new brand would have to be priced substantially below the existing brand to induce consumers to experiment with it; part of the cost of the experiment is the loss of surplus currently being

---

[16] Bulow *et al.* (1985a) show that idle capacity is possible when Dixit's assumptions on demand are relaxed.

enjoyed on the existing brand. This is again an example where the incumbent has strategic advantage solely because of already being in the market.

To summarise so far, there are numerous ways in which an incumbent firm can influence cost and/or demand conditions by strategic investments in such a way as to discourage entry into his market. Bulow *et al.* (1985b) and Fudenberg and Tirole (1984) have examined in general terms various types of entry deterrence. Returning to the schema of figure 1.4 above, we can ask whether over-or-under-investment in the strategic variable K deters entry. The answer depends of course upon the specificiation of the market game. In some instances (such as excess capacity deterring entry), the incumbent deters entry by being 'large'. Fudenberg and Tirole call this the Top Dog Effect. In other instances, the incumbent deters entry by being 'small', and thereby promises an aggressive response in the event of entry. This is the Lean and Hungry Look. It may be better for the incumbent to accommodate, rather than deter entry. Then he will act strategically to influence the nature of entry, either by being 'large' (a Top Dog) or 'small' (the Puppy Dog Ploy). The aim of all these strategic moves is to cause the rival to choose to act more favourably for the incumbent than he would otherwise do.

So far we have supposed that firms are fully informed about each other's opportunities and motivation, but we now turn to the second step in the analysis of strategic entry deterrence by relaxing this assumption. Milgrom and Roberts (1982b) have shown how limit pricing may be used to deter entry when the potential entrant is uncertain as to the cost level of the incumbent firm. The rival's expectations concerning that cost level—and hence his entry decision—are influenced by the price charged by the incumbent before the entry decision is made. Therefore the pre-entry price can act as a *signal* of the incumbent's efficiency. An incumbent with low costs would like to signal that fact, because the potential rival would then be more reluctant to enter his market. By the same token, an inefficient incumbent would like to masquerade as a low-cost firm in order to make entry less likely. This incentive to signal in an uncertain environment means that the incumbent's pricing may be used as an instrument of entry deterrence. Note that consumers benefit from this kind of limit pricing insofar as it lowers price. Other interesting issues arise when there is uncertainty about demand as well as the incumbent's cost level. Then a low pre-entry price might signal either low demand or low costs: see Matthews and Mirman (1983).

Milgrom and Roberts (1982a) and Kreps and Wilson (1982) have explored another context in which uncertainty about the incumbent plays a role in entry deterrence, namely in connection with *predatory pricing*. They examine a game due to Selten (1978) in which an incumbent firm—a chain store—is threatened by entry in each of a number of towns. More precisely, they look at a game in which the predatory pricing game in figure 1.2 is repeated a finite number of times. Intuitively, one would expect that the incumbent would fight entry if challenged in town early in the sequence, in order to deter later entrants. However, this is not so if the entrants have complete information about the opportunities and motivation of the incumbent, because in that case he would never fight entry. This is because it is common knowledge that he would not fight in the last town; and so he would not fight in the last but one; and so on. But if the assumption of complete information is very slightly relaxed—so that there is a possibility that the incumbent is somehow committed to fighting—then even an uncommitted incumbent would (rationally) fight entry in early towns to keep up the *reputation* of possibly being a committed fighter. This reputation effect is very powerful, in the sense that a very small amount of imperfect information can make it rational to fight in a large number of towns. There is an exact parallel between this and the work of Kreps *et al.* (1982) on the repeated Prisoners' Dilemma described in section III.1.

3. Potential competition: concluding remarks

To summarise, potential competition affects the behaviour of existing firms insofar as it impels them to behave in such a way that entry is an unattractive prospect. In a contestable market, where entry is ultrafree, entry is unattractive only when existing firms, singly and in combination, meet consumers' demands with maximum efficiency. In other, perhaps more realistic circumstances, this need not be so. Incumbent firms may choose to act strategically to deter entry. Since the key to strategic commitment is some degree of irreversibility, price is perhaps less likely to be the instrument of strategic entry deterrence than non-price instruments such as capacity, R & D or brand proliferation (although price was regarded as the instrument in conventional theory of entry deterrence). However, when firms are uncertain about each other and their environment, richer possibilities exist, and firms' behaviour may be chosen partly with a view to the signals conveyed to rivals. The theory of industrial organisation has made important advances in understanding these matters.

V. Conclusions and policy implications

The purpose of this paper has been to explain some recent developments in industrial economics so as to give a background for the consideration of policy. In this concluding section, some of the main themes of the foregoing discussion are highlighted, and it is suggested how they bear on policy questions.

A major theme is the *endogeneity of market structure* (see e.g. sections III.2 and III.3 above). Recent theory has examined the dependence of market structure and conduct upon the basic parameters of technology and demand, whereas previously much emphasis was placed upon the causal flow from structure to conduct and performance. If structure is regarded as a symptom of underlying forces, rather than as the root cause of (say) undesirable forms of conduct, then the perspective on policy alters.

A related theme is the role of *potential competition*. If conditions of entry into an industry are free and easy, then, even though there may be only a few firms actually in the industry, they may be compelled to perform well, in terms of productive, dynamic and allocative efficiency, due to the threat of entry. It is for this reason that policies designed to liberalise entry are on the whole desirable. The results of the liberalisation of the US airline markets, and of the market for terminal equipment in telecommunications, are examples in point. As a theoretical proposition it is not always the case that liberalisation is desirable, but there must be a strong—though rebuttable—presumption in favour of that claim.

There are numerous ways in which incumbent firms can seek to thwart the threat of entry—for example by predatory practices. Unless these practices are somehow checked, the danger is that other measures of liberalisation will not be effective. If threats of predatory behaviour deter entry, then liberalisation has not properly taken place.[17] In any event, it would be a serious mistake to suppose that measures of liberalisation are always sufficient to ensure good industry performance. In a contestable market (see section IV.1 above) that is indeed the case, but the assumptions of the theory of contestable markets are both strict and sensitive to small variations. The implications of that theory for policy are therefore doubtful, save insofar as the theory underlines the point that entry conditions are important. In some industries (including natural monopolies) no amount of liberalisation will ensure good

industry performance. There is then a case for regulation—either in the form of control of public enterprise, or as regulation of private enterprise.[18]

Another broad theme is that strategic competition among the few can produce results that are not socially desirable. For example, it was shown in section III.1 that effective collusion between firms can occur even when there is no opportunity for them to make enforceable agreements. In section III.4 it was shown how a firm might over-invest in R & D or capital equipment (and therefore produce its output inefficiently) in an attempt to gain strategic advantage relative to its competitors. Section IV.2 on strategic entry deterrence contained numerous examples of entry deterring devices that are costly to society both directly and because they thwart competition.

The classic example of market failure is perhaps that of R & D competition (see section III.2), which has been a major topic in recent industrial economics. The free market allocates resources inefficiently to R & D for several reasons, including appropriability problems (the innovator requires reward, but static efficiency requires free access to his results) and duplication of research. These considerations are the justification for government policies such as patent protection, subsidies for R & D, and measures to promote collaborative R & D (e.g. joint ventures). By its industrial policies, government can influence conditions in the game between firms—their payoffs, strategies, and so on—and thereby influence its outcome. Moreover, one government may be engaged in a game with others, in which each is choosing industrial and commercial policies to further its objectives. Many of the tools and concepts recently employed in industrial economics—such as commitments, threats and collusion—are being applied to the study of government policy using this game perspective.

Recent developments in the theory of industrial organisation have added considerably to our understanding of the workings of competition between the few. Although the perspective gained should and will influence the making and the implementation of competition policy and industrial policy, the new theory has not delivered generally applicable policy guidelines, and it is unlikely that it will do so in future. It would be wrong to blame theory for this shortcoming, for the reason is that industries are intrinsically different from one another, and the prospect of generally applicable guidelines is therefore unlikely. However, recent

---

[17] For a brief account of the economics of predatory practices, see Vickers (1985) and the references therein.

[18] The natural monopoly problem in general, and electricity and telecommunications in particular, are discussed in Vickers and Yarrow (1985).

developments in industrial economics are providing most illuminating perspectives on the nature of industrial conflict.

Appreciation of the strategic nature of competition among the few underlines this point. The successful strategist (say a threatener or a promiser) is he who arranges things in such a way that the other parties think it sufficiently likely that the threat or promise will be carried out. Whether and how this can be done depends on the particular circumstances at hand, and is largely a matter of tactics and opportunism. The economists recently studying strategic competition among the few have been investigating phenomena well-known to others: an eminent businessman, who had just been told of recent developments in the economics of industry exclaimed: 'I feel like the character in Molière who learns that all the while he has been speaking prose'.

References

Abreu, D. (1984), 'Infinitely repeated games with discounting: a general theory', unpublished paper, Princeton University.

Abreu, D., D. Pearce and E. Stacchetti (1984), 'Optimal cartel equilibrium with imperfect monitoring', Harvard Institute of Economic Research Discussion Paper 1090.

Axelrod, R. (1984), *The Evolution of Cooperation*, (Basic Books, New York).

Bain, J. (1956), *Barriers to new competition* (Harvard University Press, Cambridge, MA).

Baumol, W., J. Panzar and R. Willig (1982), *Contestable markets and the theory of industry structure*, (Harcourt Brace Jovanovich, San Diego, CA).

Baumol, W. (1982), 'Contestable Markets: an uprising in the theory of industry structure', *American Economic Review*, **72**, 1–15.

Brander, J., and B. Spencer (1983), 'Strategic commitment with R & D: the symmetric case', *Bell Journal of Economics*, **14**, 225–35.

Bulow, J., J. Geanakopolos and P. Klemperer (1985a), 'Holding idle capacity to deter entry', *Economic Journal*, **95**, 178–82.

Bulow, J., J. Geanakopolos and P. Klemperer (1985b), 'Multimarket oligopoly', *Journal of Political Economy*, **93**, 488–511.

Dasgupta, P. (1985), 'The theory of technological competition' in F. Mathewson and J. Stiglitz (eds.) *New developments in the analysis of market structure*, (MIT Press, Boston, MA).

Dasgupta, P., and J. Stiglitz (1980), 'Industrial structure and the nature of innovative activity', *Economic Journal*, **90**, 266–293.

Dixit, A. (1980), 'The role of investment in entry deterrence', *Economic Journal*, **90**, 95–106.

Dixit, A. (1982), 'Recent developments in oligopoly theory', *American Economic Review Papers and Proceedings*, **72**, 12–17.

Fellner, W. (1949), *Competition among the few*, (Knopf, New York).

Friedman, J. (1971), 'A non-cooperative equilibrium for supergames', *Review of Economic Studies*, **28**, 1–12.

Friedman, J. (1977), *Oligopoly and the theory of games*, (North-Holland, Amsterdam).

Friedman, J. (1979), 'On entry preventing behaviour and limit price models of entry', in Brams *et al.* (eds.) *Applied Game Theory* (Physica-Verlag, Vienna).

Fudenberg, D., and J. Tirole (1983), 'Learning by doing and market performance', *Bell Journal of Economics*, **14**, 522–30.

Fudenberg, D., and J. Tirole (1984), 'The fat-cat effect, the puppy-dog ploy, and the lean and hungry look', *American Economic Review Papers and Proceedings*, **74**, 361–6.

Geroski, P. and A. Jacquemin (1984), 'Dominant firms and their alleged decline', *International Journal of Industrial Organisation*, **2**, 1–27.

Gilbert, R., and D. Newbery (1982), 'Pre-emptive patenting and the persistence of monopoly', *American Economic Review*, **72**, 514–526.

Gilbert, R., and X. Vives (1985), 'Non-cooperative Entry deterrence and the free rider problem', mimeo, University of Pennsylvania.

Green, E., and R. Porter (1984), 'Non-cooperative collusion under imperfect price information', *Econometrica*, **52**, 87–100.

Kamien, M., and N. Schwartz (1982), *Market structure and innovation* (Cambridge University Press, Cambridge).

Klemperer, P. (1984), 'Collusion via switching costs', Stanford University Graduate School of Business Discussion Paper no. 786.

Kreps, D., P. Milgrom, J. Roberts and R. Wilson (1982), 'Rational cooperation in a finitely repeated prisoners' dilemma game', *Journal of Economic Theory*, **27**, 245–252.

Kreps, D., and R. Wilson (1982), 'Reputation and imperfect information', *Journal of Economic Theory*, **27**, 253–279.

Matthews, S., and L. Mirman (1983), 'Equilibrium limit pricing: the effects of private information and stochastic demand', *Econometrica*, **51**, 981–996.

Milgrom, P., and J. Roberts (1982a), 'Predation, reputation and entry deterrence', *Journal of Economic Theory*, **27**, 280–312.

Milgrom, P., and J. Roberts (1982b), 'Limit pricing and entry under incomplete information: An equilibrium analysis', *Econometrica*, **50**, 443–459.

Ordover, J., and R. Willig (1985), 'Antitrust for high-technology industries: assessing research joint ventures and mergers', Woodrow Wilson School Discussion Paper no. 87.

Salop, S. (1979), 'Strategic entry deterrence', *American Economic Review Papers and Proceedings*, **69**, 335–338.

Salop, S. (ed.) (1981), *Strategy, predation and antitrust analysis*, (F. T. C., Washington, DC).

Salop, S. (1985), 'Practices that facilitate Oligopoly Coordination', in F. Mathewson and J. Stiglitz (eds.), *New developments in the analysis of market structure* (MIT Press, Boston, MA).

Salop, S., and D. Scheffman (1983), 'Raising rivals' costs', *American Economic Review Papers and Proceedings*, **73**, 267–271.

Schelling, T. (1960), *The strategy of conflict*, (Harvard University Press, Cambridge, MA).

Scherer, F. (1980), *Industrial Market Structure and Economic Performance*, (2nd ed., Rand-McNally, Chicago).

Schmalensee, R. (1978), 'Entry deterrence in the ready to eat breakfast cereal industry', *Bell Journal of Economics*, **9**, 305–327.

Schmalensee, R. (1982), 'Product Differentiation Advantages of Pioneering Brands', *American Economic Review*, **82**, 349–365.

Schmalensee, R. (1983), 'Advertising and Entry Deterrence: an Exploratory Model', *Journal of Political Economy*, **90**, 636–653.

Selten, R. (1965), 'Spieltheoretische Behandlung eines Oligopolmodells mit Nachfrageträgheit', *Zeitschrift für die gesamte Staatswissenschaft*, **121**, 301–324 and 667–689.

Selten, R. (1975), 'Re-examination of the Perfectness Concept for Equilibrium Points in Extensive Games', *International Journal of Game Theory*, **4**, 25–55.

Selten, R. (1978), 'The Chain Store Paradox', *Theory and Decision*, **9**, 127–159.

Shaked, A., and J. Sutton (1982), 'Relaxing Price Competition through Product Differentiation', *Review of Economic Studies*, **49**, 3–14.

Shaked, A., and J. Sutton (1983), 'Natural Oligopolies', *Econometrica*, **51**, 1469–1484.

Shepherd, W. (1984), '"Contestability" vs. Competition', *American Economic Review*, **74**, 572–587.

Spence, M. (1977), 'Entry, capacity, investment and oligopolistic pricing', *Bell Journal of Economics*, **8**, 534–544.

Spence, M. (1981), 'The learning curve and competition', *Bell Journal of Economics*, **12**, 49–70.

Spence, M. (1984), 'Cost Reduction, Competition, and Industry Performance', *Econometrica*, **52**, 101–121.

Stoneman, P. (1983), *The Economic Analysis of Technological Change* (Oxford University Press, Oxford).

Sylos-Labini, P. (1962), *Oligopoly and Technical Progress*, Cambridge, Mass.: Harvard University Press.

Vickers, J. (1985), 'The Economics of Predatory Practices', *Fiscal Studies*, **6**(3), 24–36.

Vickers, J., and G. Yarrow (1985), *Privatization and the Natural Monopolies*, London: Public Policy Centre.

von Weizsäcker, C. (1980), 'A Welfare Analysis of Barriers to Entry', *Bell Journal of Economics*, **11**, 399–420.

von Weizsäcker, C. (1984), 'The costs of substitution', *Econometrica*, **52**, 1085–1116.

Waterson, M. (1984), *Economic Theory of the Industry*, Cambridge: Cambridge University Press.

Williamson, O. (1979), 'Symposium on Antitrust Law and Economics: Symposium Introduction', *University of Pennsylvania Law Review*, **127**, 918–924.

2

Tacit collusion

RAY REES

University of Munich[1]

I. Introduction

The word collusion describes a type of conduct or form of behaviour whereby decision-takers agree to co-ordinate their actions. This in general would seem to involve two elements: a process of communication, discussion, and exchange of information with the aim of reaching an agreement; and, where there are gains to reneging on the agreement given that the others comply, some kind of mechanism for punishing such violations and so enforcing the agreement. In the economics of oligopolistic markets the distinction between 'explicit' and 'tacit' collusion turns on the first of these elements. It is possible that firms could agree to co-ordinate their actions in some way without explicit communication and discussion. For example, it may become tacitly accepted practice in a market exactly to match the price changes of the largest firm. All firms are aware of this 'tacit agreement' or 'conscious parallelism', and no process for reaching agreement is strictly necessary. However, the second element must always be present: typically there are at least short-run gains from reneging on an agreement and so tacit collusion requires the perception that to do so would in the end turn out to be unprofitable because of punitive reactions by the other firms.

Indeed, at the extreme, it could be argued that whether or not there is explicit communication is irrelevant: what matters is whether a collusive agreement, however arrived at, can be sustained by the self-interest of the parties involved. If this is not the case,

then explicit communication is simply 'cheap talk'. This is most easily seen in the context of a market which takes place only once. For example, suppose that a government wishes to sell off, once and for all, the mineral rights on a tract of land and invites sealed bids which will specify required acreage and a price per acre. There are just two firms which will bid, though the minerals extracted will subsequently be sold on a competitive world market. Each firm knows that the value of the land is £100 per acre, and knows the other knows this and that the government does not. The government places a reservation value of £10 an acre on the land. If the firms bid competitively, they will each bid £100 an acre for the entire acreage. It would clearly be in their interests for them to agree to bid £10 an acre for one-half the acreage each. Such an agreement would not, of course, be legally enforceable. Moreover, it is not sustainable by the self-interest of the firms. If one firm believed that the other would bid according to the agreement, it is in its interest to bid slightly more than £10 an acre for the entire acreage. But then it would realize that the other firm would have also worked that out, and it should raise its bid. But the other firm will also have worked this out . . . and so on. Whatever the firms may have discussed and agreed, this is merely cheap talk if the agreement cannot be enforced: under the conditions of this example, the firms will end up making competitive bids.

The enforceability of collusive agreements by some means can, therefore, be taken as a necessary condition for their existence. We shall consider at some length below circumstances under which this condition is met even when enforcement through the courts is not available. If the distinction between tacit and explicit collusion is to mean anything, it must also be shown that the ability to communicate in some way affects the likely existence and stability of collusion. Is collusion indeed *ever really* 'tacit', or is it the case that

First published in *Oxford Review of Economic Policy*, vol. 9, no. 2 (1993). This version has been updated and revised to incorporate recent developments.

[1] I am grateful to Asha Sadanand and to participants at the conference run by *Oxford Review of Economic Policy* and the Centre for Business Strategy at the London Business School in January 1993, in particular to Donald Hay, for helpful comments on an earlier draft of this paper.

what may appear to be tacit collusion is actually explicit collusion in which the process of agreement is simply concealed? The statement by Adam Smith that businessmen's meetings, even for 'merriment and diversion', usually end up in connivance to restrict competition, is often quoted, but the sentence which follows it is equally perceptive: 'It is impossible indeed to prevent such meetings, by any law which either could be executed, or would be consistent with liberty and justice.' Moreover, short of methods of surveillance which are also not 'consistent with liberty and justice' it may be impossible to obtain evidence on what transpired at such meetings.

Turning now to antitrust policy, a major difference among advanced industrial countries in respect of their policy towards collusion lies in whether collusion is in most instances *per se* illegal, as in the US, or whether attention is directed at appraising the results of collusive behaviour, as for example in the UK. In the former case there is understandably much more emphasis on deciding whether or not collusion has in fact taken place. The problem here is that, quite apart from the possibility that collusion might be concealed, the observation that firms communicated and appeared to reach agreement need not imply that the collusive outcome was actually achieved (as in the above bidding example), while if collusion is tacit there will be no evidence of communication and negotiation. The observation of communication is neither necessary nor sufficient for existence of collusion.

II. Equilibrium concepts

Until relatively recently, oligopoly theory was typically presented as a collection of models each based on a particular *ad hoc* set of assumptions about firms' perceptions of their rivals' reactions to their own choices of prices or outputs. The leading models in the literature are:

The Cournot model: in the traditional story firms independently choose outputs on the assumption that their rivals make no response to their choices—even though this assumption may be continually falsified—and market equilibrium is achieved through a sequence of alternating output choices which converges over time.

The Stackelberg model: a leader makes a choice of output, the other firms act as followers and make their profit-maximizing response to this output. The leader takes account of these responses in choosing its output and is able to do better than it would under Cournot

reactions—there is a 'first mover' or precommitment advantage.

The 'kinked demand curve' model: each firm believes that an increase in its output (reduction in its price) will be matched by its rivals, while a reduction in output (increase in price) will not be followed. This creates a kink in the firm's perceived demand curve at its current price–output pair (the levels of which are, however, unexplained) which then tends to remain the same despite changes in marginal cost, because of a discontinuity in the firm's marginal revenue at the kink.

The Bertrand model: again in the traditional story firms independently choose prices, on the assumption that their rivals make no response to their choices. Where firms produce identical outputs and have identical constant marginal costs equilibrium price ends up equal to this common cost. If the constant marginal costs differ, then only the firm with the lowest marginal cost is left in the market and it sets a price just below the marginal cost of the next-to-lowest cost firm. If marginal costs are non-constant then no equilibrium price exists unless outputs are non-homogeneous, i.e. there is product differentiation.

The Edgeworth model: firms choose prices as in the Bertrand model, with identical constant marginal costs, but with fixed output capacities. There is a range of possible types of outcome, including those of the Cournot and Bertrand models, but the novel possibility is that of 'price cycles'. There is a range of prices the upper and lower limits of which are determined by demand, cost, and capacity parameters. As firms set prices alternately over consecutive periods, price falls by small steps from the upper limit of the interval until it reaches the lower limit and then jumps back to the upper limit and the cycle begins again.

Recent developments in game theory have had an important impact on the way we interpret these models. Game theory forces us to be precise about three sets of assumptions on which a model rests:

(i)   the possibility of binding commitments. If it is possible for firms to make binding commitments, for example legally enforceable contracts, to carry out certain agreed actions, then this raises a fundamentally different set of issues than if no such commitments are possible. In the former case the firms are involved in a *co-operative game*, the problem is to reach agreement on division of the gains from co-operation. In the latter case, whether or not explicit communication takes place, each firm has to decide on the choice of action which is in its own best interest in the light of the fact that the others are behaving in the same way: we have a *non-co-operative game*. All the oligopoly models just discussed are examples of non-co-operative games, and in the light of the antitrust laws in most advanced industrial countries this would seem to be appropriate.

(ii)   The frequency of market interaction. This is something that is often somewhat ambiguously specified in the traditional economic models. The models are usually formulated as 'one-shot games': firms are making their choices relative to market and cost conditions at a given point in time as if there were no past and no future. Nevertheless, time enters through the back door in the discussion of reaction patterns. The very concept of 'action' and 'reaction' must presuppose at least two points in time, but the discussions underlying the Cournot and Bertrand models implicitly require much more, possibly an infinity of time periods as the processes of convergence to an equilibrium work themselves out. Likewise the price cycles in the Edgeworth model take place through real time. If market interaction takes place repeatedly, however, why is it that firms are assumed to ignore this and treat each decision as if it were a move in a 'one-shot' game? Surely if the market is held repeatedly firms would realize this and formulate strategies that determine their actions over time. But then, as we shall see, it may become possible to rationalize the kind of collusive behaviour which is simply not contemplated in the standard models.

(iii)   The way in which firms form their expectations of their rivals' choices. A rational player in a game cannot be thought of as simply taking his rivals' actions as given by some *ad hoc* assumption. The analysis of a game is concerned precisely with the question of the expectations of the behaviour of his rivals it is rational for any one player to form. The general answer game theory gives to this question is contained in the concept of Nash Equilibrium (NE). The choices made by players in a game must be mutually consistent in the sense that each player's choice is the best for him given the choices made by the others. The NE choices have the property that if each player knows the others will make their NE choices, he has no reason to deviate from making his own NE choice. The argument to suggest that a non-NE set of choices cannot be an equilibrium outcome of the game proceeds as follows. Suppose player 1 assumes that player 2 will choose action A, and that 1's best (most profitable) response to this is action B. Suppose, further, that 2's best response to B is *not* A. Should 1 continue to assume that 2 will choose A? If 2 *had* been going to choose A, she would work out that 1 would plan to choose B, in which case she would change her planned action to whatever is the best response to B, so falsifying the initial assumption that she would choose A. Thus 1 cannot persist in believing

2 will choose A if he knows that she is as rational and well-informed as he is. Only the NE choices are immune to this kind of contradiction.

The classic oligopoly models can then be thought of as one-shot, non-co-operative games to which the NE concept can be applied to find a solution. They differ not in respect of reaction patterns but in the economic characteristics of the market concerned, and it is a matter of fact, not logic, to decide which model is appropriate for any particular market under study. An interesting point is that in the three leading models, those of Cournot, Bertrand, and Stackelberg, the NE outcomes are identical to those traditionally derived; only the reasoning underlying the derivation of those equilibria changes. Since the games are played just once, with the firms making output or price choices simultaneously, the equilibria cannot be rationalized by appeal to a process of action and reaction through time. The explanation of the equilibrium outcomes is that they *are* the NE outcomes in these games.

It is useful to consider the antitrust implications of the outcomes in these three market games. First, firms are behaving non-co-operatively and, it seems safe to say, non-collusively. Communication between firms is unnecessary to achieve the market equilibrium, since this is done by the firms independently thinking through the logic of the situation.[2] In the absence of the ability to make binding agreements any such communication would in any case be cheap talk—the only outcomes that are sustainable by the self-interest of the firms are the NE outcomes, and any agreement to choose non-NE outcomes would be reneged upon, as in our earlier example (which can be thought of as a model of Bertrand competition). Thus a charge of collusion could not be made to stick.[3] At the same time, in two of the three models the equilibrium outcomes could be quite bad from the welfare point of view. In the Bertrand case with constant identical marginal costs we have, in fact, the perfectly competitive market outcome, with price equal to marginal cost and no excess profit, but in the Cournot and Stackelberg cases prices exceed marginal costs and the firms make excess profit. Moreover, in these models, if the firms have different and non-constant marginal costs, a further source of inefficiency is that total market output will be produced at more than minimum total cost—the marginal costs of firms are not equalized at the equilibrium. It is

---

[2] Note, however, that the firms are assumed to have full knowledge of each other's profit functions, which, at the least, requires knowledge of each other's cost functions. There is clearly a role for exchange of information to achieve this, as we discuss more fully below.

[3] This is, in fact, recognized in US antitrust law, as we discuss more fully in section III.

certainly true that the Cournot and Stackelberg equilibria in general involve smaller welfare losses, and lower levels of excess profit, than would be the case if the firms acted as a joint profit-maximizing monopoly or cartel but, none the less, contingent on market parameters, allocative inefficiency could still be quite large.

It seems clear then that an antitrust policy based on the behaviour of firms, in particular on whether or not this is collusive, could come to different conclusions to one which was based upon appraisal of the inefficiency and extent of excess profits associated with the market outcome. Except in the special Bertrand case, even if the self-interest of the firms does not lead them to collude, it would not lead them to behave as perfectly competitive firms either.

The assumption that the market takes place just once is, of course, patently unrealistic: repeated market interaction among firms would appear to be the rule. Some care has to be taken, however, in specifying the time horizon in a model of a multi-period market. To simplify the dynamics of the model, it is usual to assume that the market situation in each period is the same: the same population of firms faces the same market demand with the same cost conditions in each period. The key distinction is that between the case in which there is a known, finite number of periods in which firms will choose prices or outputs, and those in which either the number of periods, though finite, is not known with certainty, or the time horizon can be regarded as infinite. When there is a known, finite number of periods, an argument based on backward induction can be constructed, to the effect that the equilibrium strategies for the multi-period game consist simply of repetitions of the single-period NE, for example the one-period Cournot equilibrium outputs in a market in which firms make output choices.[4] Nothing of substance, therefore, is added by analysing the market in a multi-period setting. On the other hand, if there is no known, certain last period from which this

backward induction argument can begin, it makes sense to discuss the conditions under which *collusive* behaviour can be sustained as a *non-co-operative* equilibrium of the repeated game.

The intuitive argument is straightforward. If firms agree to set outputs or prices which give them higher profits than those they would earn in a one-shot NE, and one of them reneges on this agreement, then in the following period(s) punitive actions can be undertaken, for example a price war, to wipe out the gains from the deviation. The threat of this *ex ante* can then be used to ensure adherence to the agreement. The existence of a future in which to apply punishment allows current collusion to be sustained by the self-interest of the firms.

There are two respects in which this intuition must be taken more rigorously. First, it must be established that sufficiently large future losses can be threatened so that, when discounted to a present value, they offset the gain from reneging in the current period. Second, the threat to inflict these losses must be credible. We consider each of these points in turn.

The fact that future losses from punishment have to be set against current gains to defection implies that the rate at which a firm discounts the future will be important. This rate will in general reflect a firm's (marginal) cost of capital. In an imperfect capital market it need not be the same for all firms, and in an economy subject to cyclical fluctuations in economic activity it need not be the same over time. In general, the more heavily firms discount the future (i.e. the higher their cost of capital) the smaller will be the present value of future losses of profit caused by punishment, relative to the immediate gains from cheating on an agreement. In a particular market, given its underlying cost and demand parameters, it will usually be possible to define a range of discount rates over which agreement on some collusive set of outputs or prices can be sustained by some threatened punishment strategy. In general this range will vary with the set of outputs or prices to be sustained, the punishment strategy and the characteristics of the individual firm. We shall explore how these factors interact more fully below. It suffices to note here that the more heavily firms discount the future the less likely is it that collusion among them can be sustained.

The gain to a firm from reneging on the collusive agreement will depend partly on cost, demand, and capacity parameters and partly on the length of time for which a higher profit than that realized under the agreement can be earned before retaliation by the other firms takes place. For example, if technology is such that production is subject to a fixed maximum rate of

---

[4] Even in finite horizon games, there are cases in which collusive behaviour may constitute a non-co-operative equilibrium. If there are multiple Nash equilibria of the constituent game, over which players have strict preferences, then collusion can be sustained by threats to play less-preferred Nash equilibrium strategies. If the end-period of the finite horizon game is not known with certainty, then at each period there is a probability there will be a next period in which punishment can take place, and by factoring this probability into the discount rate the model becomes similar to the infinite horizon case. Finally, if each player believes that there is a non-zero probability that the other will play co-operatively, because she is 'crazy' or not individually rational, than as Kreps *et al.* (1982) show, even in a finite horizon game, if the horizon is long enough, firms may play co-operatively. In the interests of simplicity, and since similar issues arise, we subsume all these cases under the 'infinite horizon' case.

capacity output, and for each firm its output under the collusive agreement is just about at capacity, then there would be virtually no short-run gain to reneging on the agreement. On the other hand, if there is significant excess capacity at the agreed output, and the agreed price is well above marginal cost, then a significant output expansion would be both feasible and profitable and so reneging on the agreement could appear attractive. The longer the other firms take to detect a deviation and implement a punitive response, the greater will be the duration of the flow of profit from reneging and the further into the future the losses from punishment will be delayed, thus reducing their present value.

The extent of losses from punishment of course depends on the form of punishment adopted (we consider the question of the *credibility* of this punishment below, here we examine only its extent). In the literature[5] three main types of punishment strategy have been analysed.

(i) *Nash reversion.*   It is generally expected that the profits firms receive as a result of collusion exceed those they would earn in the one-shot NE, otherwise they might as well not collude. In that case, one way of inflicting a loss of profit in retaliation for reneging on the agreement would be to revert to the NE of the one-shot game, either permanently or for a number of periods sufficient to wipe out the gains from reneging, if that is possible. One limitation of this as a punishment is that it may not be very severe—it may imply a moderate loss of profit relative to the collusive agreement—and so may support collusion only for a small set of discount rates. A second limitation, at least if the joint profit-maximizing (cartel) allocation is thought to be a likely objective of the collusion, is that this allocation may not be sustainable by threats of reversion to a Cournot–Nash equilibrium. It is not difficult to construct cases in which firms have unequal marginal costs and some firms earn higher profits at the Nash equilibrium than at the joint profit-maximizing allocation.

(ii) *Minimax punishment.*   For each firm in the market, it is possible to define its profit maximizing action (an output or price) or *best response* given the actions of all other firms. We can then find the values of the latter which make the firm's best-response profit as small as possible. This is the firm's minimax profit, and it is also often referred to as its 'security level', since the firm cannot be forced to take a lower profit than that. Clearly the most drastic punishment for a firm

that has reneged on the collusive agreement would be for the other firms to force it to its security level, either forever or for some specified number of time periods. It is straightforward to show that the threat of minimax punishment forever is always capable of enforcing a collusive agreement which gives a firm a higher profit than its security level for *some* set of interest rates. Thus denote the firm's security level profit by π^s, the profit level under the agreement by $\pi^* > \pi^s$, and the maximum profit the firm can earn when it reneges on the agreement in a single period by $\pi^R > \pi^*$. Then in contemplating reneging the firm must weigh up the one-off gain $\pi^R - \pi^*$, against the present value of the infinite future stream of profit it loses as a result of punishment, $(\pi^* - \pi^s)/r$, where r is the per-period interest rate. The firm will not renege if

$$\pi^R - \pi^* \le (\pi^* - \pi^s)/r$$

or

$$r \le (\pi^* - \pi^s)/(\pi^R - \pi^*)$$

and since the right-hand side is always positive there must be some set of interest rates for which this will hold. This proposition goes under the name of the Folk Theorem in the theory of repeated games. In a given market, the set of profits which can be sustained by minimax punishments could be very large indeed.

(iii) *Simple Penal Codes*:   Abreu's theory of simple penal codes involves a 'stick and carrot' form of punishment. For each firm that is party to the agreement, a 'punishment path' is formulated, which specifies outputs (or prices) for each firm to be adopted if the firm in question deviates from the agreement. This punishment path involves two phases: a phase of expanded outputs (lower prices) which inflicts loss of profit on the deviant; then the remainder of the path consists of a return to the original collusive outputs. Thus the path could be thought of as a period of price warfare followed by reversion to collusion. The loss of profit in the punishment phase must be enough to wipe out the gain from reneging. If the deviant reneges again in the punishment phase, this is met with a reimposition of the punishment phase *from its beginning*, thus postponing the date of reversion to the more profitable collusive phase. This reversion to collusion is the carrot to induce the deviant to accept whatever is meted out to it in the punishment phase. If one of the non-deviant firms fails to carry out its role in punishing the cheat by producing its punishment output, it in turn is treated as having reneged and the firms adopt the punishment path for this firm. It can be shown that again a large set of collusive allocations can be

[5]   For expository surveys, at varying levels of difficulty, see Friedman (1986), Gravelle and Rees (1992), Martin (1992), Tirole (1988), Fudenberg and Tirole (1989), and Shapiro (1989).

supported by threats of punishment of this kind provided firms do not discount the future 'too heavily'.

These three types of punishment strategy will sustain different sets of collusive allocations, but the main point of interest in comparing them is that of the credibility of the strategies. Clearly, if a threat of punishment is to be effective in sustaining collusion the firms must believe that the punishment would actually be carried out if the need arose. This not only requires the firm reneging on the agreement to 'accept its punishment'. Since in general inflicting punishment may be costly to the non-reneging firms, it must be credible that they would in fact do so. In the case of the first two of the above punishment strategies, Nash reversion and minimax, the acceptance of punishment by the deviant is not an issue. In each case the punishment profit corresponds to its best response to the actions of the other firms. In the case of a simple penal code, acceptance of its punishment is the best action by the deviant given that the alternative is reimposition of the punishment path: punishment outputs are so chosen that it is better not to postpone the date of reversion to collusion than to make a short-term gain from deviating from the punishment path. We shall, therefore, focus on the question of the credibility of the threat that the non-deviating firms will actually carry out the punishment.

Study of the general question of credibility of threats in dynamic games has led to the formulation of the 'refinement' of the Nash equilibrium concept termed 'subgame perfect equilibrium'. We can illustrate with the case of minimax punishment and, for simplicity, assume that there are just two firms. If each firm believes the other's threat to minimax forever following a defection, its best response is not to defect. Now, consider what would be the situation at the beginning of the period immediately following a defection. In the game beginning at that time, which is a proper subgame of the original game, it is not in the best interest of the non-deviating firm actually to minimax the other. For suppose this firm believes that the deviant believes that it will be minimaxed, and so will produce the corresponding output. Then the punishing firm's best response to this is *not* to carry out the punishment but to produce its corresponding profit maximizing output. There is nothing to make it in the firm's best interests actually to follow through with the punishment in the *period following* a deviation, given the game that then presents itself. This will then be perceived in the previous period, and so the threat of minimax punishment will not be credible. To be credible, it must be in a firm's best interest to carry out the threat at the time it is called

upon to do so. This criterion of credibility is more formally embodied in Selten's equilibrium concept of *subgame perfection*. According to this, a subgame perfect equilibrium strategy for a game is one which gives a Nash equilibrium strategy for *every subgame* of the game. The above example of a minimax punishment strategy was not subgame perfect because, in the subgame beginning in the period just after a defection, the minimax choices did not constitute a Nash equilibrium.

Both Nash reversion and Abreu's simple penal codes are subgame perfect equilibrium strategies and so satisfy this criterion of credibility. The former does so because a strategy of playing Nash equilibrium in every constituent game is also a Nash equilibrium of an entire repeated game. In the case of the simple penal code, the essential reason it is in the interest of a firm in this case to carry out the threat of punishment is that it believes that if it does not it itself will be punished. This in turn is credible because if any other firm does not join in this punishment it will be punished, and so on. Thus belief in the credibility of punishment is sustained by the expectation that each firm will prefer to be the punisher than the punished. This can be put in its least intuitively reasonable light if we assume just two firms. If firm 1 reneges, firm 2 in the next period must punish it. If firm 2 reneges on punishment, then in the following period firm 1 must punish firm 2 for not having punished it in the previous period, and so on.

This reliance on 'self-lacerating' punishment strategies has led a number of authors to propose an alternative criterion of credibility, known as 'renegotiation proofness'. Here we shall discuss that formulation due to Farrell and Maskin (1989). They begin by asking the question: in the period immediately following a defection, what would stop the firms getting together and, instead of actually carrying out the punishment, agreeing to reinstitute the collusive agreement? The game from that period looks just as it did when the original agreement was concluded—because of the infinite horizon assumption every subgame is identical to the original game—and so if it was in the firms' interests to negotiate that agreement initially it will be in their interests now to renegotiate that agreement. But if firms perceive that a deviation will be followed by renegotiation rather than punishment this means that punishment would never be carried out, and so agreement to collude could not be reached in the first place. Abreu's strategies appear to assume away such renegotiation possibilities—an agreement is made once and for all and can never be reopened.

This argument leads to the *renegotiation proofness* criterion of credibility of threats. Punishment strategies are credible only if they are not only subgame perfect but also not capable of being pre-empted by renegotiation of the agreement if the occasion arises that they must be implemented. Informally put, in the case of an oligopolistic market this can be achieved by an agreement which specifies that the punishing firms choose outputs or prices which yield them higher profit than at the collusive allocation, so that they would actually gain in the punishment phase. This ensures that they would not be prepared to renegotiate back to the original agreement.

These theories suggest that collusion may or may not be successful in a particular market: that depends on the values taken by a set of market or firm-specific parameters. The assumption that the same constituent game is repeated period after period also implies that collusion, if achieved, is perfectly stable and never breaks down. Although the non-co-operative collusive equilibrium is sustained by threats, those threats never have to be implemented because they are successful. Thus we would never observe price wars. Given that price wars *are* observed, the question arises of how to explain them within this type of approach. A great insight of George J. Stigler provides one basis for an answer, which has been further developed by Green and Porter (1984), Rotemberg and Saloner (1986), and Rees (1985), among others.[6] Here we focus on the first of these.

Stigler's insight was that randomness in demand provides scope for cheating on a collusive agreement, and creates a problem of statistical inference in enforcing that agreement. In Green and Porter's model it is assumed that a firm's choice of output cannot be observed by another firm, and the sum of all outputs determines market price according to a demand function which is subject to unobservable random shocks. Then, when price is low firms do not know for sure whether it was because someone cheated (produced a larger than agreed output), or because demand was low. The strategy for maintaining collusion consists of choosing a critical level of price such that, if market price falls below that level, firms infer cheating and enter a punishment phase, a price war. It is always possible (for some set of discount rates) to find a critical price level that will fully enforce adherence to the agreement—no one cheats. There is now, however, a non-zero probability that in any time period a price war will break out, and in an infinitely repeated market it is virtually certain that one will be observed. The

interesting, though not necessarily plausible, feature of this result is that firms know that when the price falls below the critical level this is due to a random shock, because they know it pays no one to cheat, but nevertheless they must still go into the punishment phase to enforce the collusive agreement. This is clearly very much open to the critique based upon renegotiation-proofness, even more so than in the case without uncertainty. From the point of view of this paper, an important aspect of the model is that it shows the costs that can be imposed (in the form of probable price wars) when firms' outputs are unknown to each other and demand is stochastic. We return to this point when we consider the subject of information agreements later.

This concludes our brief survey of equilibrium concepts and the models of oligopoly in which they are embedded. We now consider what they imply for the analysis of tacit collusion.

III. Facilitating tacit collusion

Many theorists see the models surveyed in the previous section as giving analytical precision to the idea of tacit collusion. For example, Fudenberg and Tirole (1989) take a simple example of homogeneous output-setting duopoly with identical (non-decreasing) costs, and note that:

patient, identical Cournot duopolists can implicitly collude by each producing one-half the monopoly output, with any deviation triggering a switch to the Cournot outcome. This would be 'collusive' in yielding the monopoly price. The collusion is 'implicit' (or 'tacit') in that the firms would not need to enter into binding contracts to enforce their co-operation. (p. 280)

In this quotation, however, both the words 'collusion' and 'tacit' are being interpreted in a different sense to that adopted in this paper. 'Collusion' should, certainly for antitrust purposes, refer to a form of conduct, not the value of an outcome: collusive behaviour might well result in less than monopoly profits. It is tacit not simply because of the absence of a binding (legally enforceable) agreement, but because of the absence of any explicit agreement whatsoever. Explicit collusion would involve the firms in talking to each other, explicitly agreeing to produce half the monopoly output each, and, quite possibly, agreeing also that deviation by one would be punished by a price war. The fact that the agreement is sustained by threats of market sanctions rather than a binding contract makes it no less

---

[6] Abreu *et al.* (1986) in particular show how the Green and Porter model can be extended by replacing Nash reversion punishments with Abreu's simple penal code.

explicit,[7] at least in the eyes of antitrust law. Tacit collusion, on the other hand, would involve no explicit agreement but simply the unspoken acceptance by the two firms that it was in their best interests each to produce half the monopoly output on the understanding that failure to do so would provoke a price war.

As with non-co-operative playing of the one-shot game, the tacitly collusive equilibrium still requires information. In the simple model above each firm must know that the other's costs are identical to its own, and must know that they have the same beliefs about the market demand function as well as in the credibility of the punishment that would result from a deviation. It is easy to see that these information requirements expand considerably with the number of firms, product heterogeneity, spatial dispersion of markets, uncertainty about future demands and costs, rate of technological change, and the extent of threats from entry of new firms. If firms are to collude tacitly, they must somehow choose prices and outputs which are sustainable by a credible punishment strategy that also has to be tacitly agreed upon. We have seen that there may be many punishment strategies, and relative to any one of them there may be a very large set of sustainable price–output configurations. The firms must somehow define the set of feasible agreements, reach a point within it, preserve stability of the agreement, and make the threat of punishment as effective and credible as possible.

It is, therefore, natural that in real-world markets many so-called 'facilitating devices' would have been developed. These are arrangements or practices which can be construed as helping firms in at least one of the four steps to stable, successful tacit collusion: defining the possible agreements; focusing upon one; preserving it; and providing for credible effective punishment. It should also be noted that in many cases they would also facilitate explicit collusion, and so their use does not rule out the (possibly concealed) existence of this. We shall consider them in order of increasing specificity.

Information exchange: a flow of information among firms is clearly essential for all four aspects of successful collusion. Firms may enter into formal information agreements, under which they undertake to exchange information on costs, outputs, prices, and discounts. Exchange of cost information is clearly important in defining the set of possible agreements and arriving at one. Exchange of price and output data is important in detecting deviation: the shorter the lag between cheating and detection, the smaller the incentive to cheat. Such exchange of information is, of course, possible in the absence of a formal information agreement.

Trade associations: many industries have a central organization which may function fairly innocuously, handling public relations at the industry-wide level and organizing conventions, trade fairs, etc. However, they may also act as facilitating devices, collecting and disseminating information on costs, outputs, and prices, suggesting price lists (for example, the professional associations for lawyers, doctors, and architects publish 'recommended fee scales') and policing the (tacit) agreement. For example, the trade association in the UK nut and bolt industry actually employed individuals who posed as buyers and tried to obtain discounts on prices from sellers suspected of cheating. Trade associations may also carry out services such as demand forecasting and capacity planning for the market as a whole. This can be important both in achieving agreement on prices in the short run, and in preventing the development of excess capacity, which can pose a serious threat to collusion in the long run. At the very least, trade associations often provide the opportunities for the 'meetings of merriment and diversion' mentioned in Adam Smith's famous remark.

Price leadership: it is usual to distinguish between 'dominant firm' and 'barometric' price leadership. In the former, the largest firm first announces price changes and the other firms then follow within a short space of time; in the latter, some non-dominant firm, which presumably is considered the best at judging the market conditions, plays this role. In many markets, however, the identity of the firm initiating a price change may vary over time, possibly to avoid the impression that there *is* a price leader, or to spread more equitably the unpopularity of being the first firm to raise prices. Clearly, the practice of price leadership is a way of solving the problem of choosing one price agreement in the set of possible agreements. If the leader is good at finding mutually acceptable prices, or has the market power to punish deviants from its prices sufficiently, agreement can be entirely tacit. For many writers the 'conscious parallelism' in prices associated with price leadership is the very essence of tacit collusion.[8]

Collaborative research and cross-licensing of patents: for sound reasons—high fixed costs, economies of scale, and risk-sharing—firms may pool research and development (R & D) resources and set up a common R & D agency. This obviously limits competition in

---

[7] One may speak of a 'legal' or 'formal' cartel to cover this latter case.

[8] At the same time, price leadership may also be a way of implementing an agreement arrived at by explicit, though secret, negotiations. Colluding firms may well choose to announce price increases in a non-simultaneous way.

product design and innovation and facilitates uniform pricing of the resulting products. In the case of cross-licensing on the other hand, firms license use of the results of their own research out to their competitors. It is legal under the terms of these licenses to specify selling prices and to place other restrictions on sale, for example geographical area. Thus what may at first sight appear to be something that facilitates competition can actually be a form of legal collusion.

MFN and MC clauses in buyer–seller contracts: Salop (1986) pointed out that 'most favoured nation' (MFN) and 'meeting competition' (MC) clauses in contracts between buyers and sellers can act to facilitate collusion among sellers. A MFN clause guarantees to a buyer that if, when the contract is concluded or within some specified time period later, the seller makes a sale to another buyer at a lower price, then the buyer in question will also receive that lower price. A MC clause guarantees that if the buyer can find another seller offering a lower price, then the seller in question will match that price upon presentation of appropriate evidence. Salop argues convincingly that both these types of clauses help sustain collusion. Note first that since they form part of a contract between buyer and seller they are legally enforceable and that in itself is an important advantage because it reduces the cost of enforcing collusion. Moreover, the buyer has an incentive to detect and report deviations from the price agreement, either by the seller in question (under MFN) or by other sellers (under MC). A MFN clause sustains collusion because it makes it costly for a seller to reduce price in a discriminatory way, which is how secret cheating on a price agreement often takes place. If price cuts have to be paid to all buyers this reduces their profitability as well as increasing their detectability. A MC clause obviously sustains collusion by creating an incentive for a buyer to report to a seller keeping to the agreement the prices of a seller who may be cheating on the agreement, at the same time nullifying the effect of the latter.

Resale price maintenance: this is a system under which manufacturers contractually control the minimum level of prices charged by retailers. This obviously stops collusion at the manufacturing stage being undone by price competition at the point of sale to the ultimate buyer.

Basing point pricing: this is a pricing system often encountered in industries, such as steel and cement, where transport costs are high relative to production costs and buyers and sellers are spatially dispersed. In one variant, manufacturing plants of each seller are designated as bases, and a 'base price' is set at each of them. There is also a standard table of transport charges.

Then, a buyer at any given location will be quoted a price by each seller, equal to the base price at the nearest base plus the standard charge for transporting the product from the base to the buyer's location. The result is then that *delivered* prices to any buyer are always uniform across sellers, and there is no price competition. Clearly sellers must exchange information—the list of bases and base prices, the standard transport charges—but no *explicit* agreement to collude on prices need be made.

Common costing books: in some industries where there may be variation in the form of the finished product because of variation in the buyer's specifications (for example, industrial engines, building services) a book may be circulated by a trade association which shows how the overall cost of the specific product variant can be calculated. This encourages price uniformity among sellers and makes it less easy to label price-cutting a computational mistake.

This list covers the most generally encountered facilitating devices. Particular markets may provide examples of practices specific to them. For example, if airlines share a computerized reservation system this makes it easy to monitor and collude on prices. Insurance companies may collaborate in working out loss probabilities and this leads to uniformity in premium rates.[9] It should also be noted that there are many opportunities for company representatives to make their views known to each other on the state of the market and the direction prices should take, for example, in after-dinner speeches, newspaper interviews, articles in trade publications as well as while doing lunch.

IV. Policy implications

We now turn to the relation between tacit collusion and antitrust policy in the US, UK, and the EC. In all three jurisdictions explicit collusion is clearly dealt with.[10] In respect of tacit collusion there is far less clarity. In the US explicit collusion is, with a few exceptions,[11] *per se* illegal, and so it is simply necessary in a given case to establish whether or not collusion has existed. In the UK the Restrictive Trade Practices Court and the Monopolies and Mergers Commission (MMC) exist to investigate whether collusive agreements exist or

---

[9] See, for example, the discussion of the *Concordato Incendio* case in the paper by Sapir *et al.* (1993).

[10] For much fuller discussion of policy in these three jurisdictions, see the papers by Sapir *et al.* (1993), Williams (1993), and White (1993), and the references given there.

[11] For discussion of these see White (1993).

collusive conduct has taken place and, if so, whether they have operated against the public interest. For the EC, Article 85 of the Treaty of Rome prohibits agreements designed to prevent, restrict, or distort competition within the common market, though specific agreements may be exempted by the European Commission if they are found to have overall net benefits. In a 1989 White Paper and 1992 Green Paper (DTI, 1989, 1992) the UK government declared an intention to revise UK law in the direction of consistency with Articles 85 and 86 of the Treaty of Rome.[12]

In relation to tacit collusion the US legislation is, to use White's term, 'sloppy'.[13] Price leadership is not illegal, and 'conscious parallelism' does not amount to collusion. Thus, to quote Scherer:[14]

Oligopolists refraining from price competition merely because they recognize the likelihood of rival retaliation do not violate the law as long as their decisions are taken independently. And by avoiding any suggestion of encouraging or compelling rivals to co-operate, they may also facilitate uniform and non-aggressive pricing through such devices as price leadership and open price-reporting systems.

At the same time, there have been cases[15] in which 'the inference of illegal conspiracy' has been drawn from 'detailed similarity of behaviour'. From the economic point of view, the problem is that in most cases the US antitrust process is concerned with deciding whether *conduct* has been illegal, rather than with the appraisal of the economic consequences of whatever conduct may have taken place. In this respect the UK system, though it also has substantial defects, is superior, as I shall now try to establish.

In theoretical language, we could state the core of the problem as being that tacit collusion is a form of non-co-operative equilibrium, just as is Nash equilibrium in a one-shot oligopoly game (which, as we argued earlier, would never be regarded as collusive). The equilibrium results from rational pursuit of individual self-interest in a situation of perceived mutual interdependence. The behaviour of firms need not be conspiratorial in the legal sense. Therefore a conduct-based approach such as that underlying US antitrust law inevitably encounters difficulties.

To bring out the contrast with UK policy, we can consider a specific case, that of the MMC inquiry into the White Salt Market.[16] Two firms supplied virtually the entire UK salt market and, over the 13-year period

taken by the MMC, their prices had been identical and had changed identically within a few weeks of each other. The identity of the price leader had changed from time to time with no obvious pattern. One firm would inform the other of its proposed price increases by letter, usually a month before they came into effect, and the other would usually respond within that period. The firms argued that this was because they bought quantities of salt from each other (usually small), and it was usual to notify important buyers in advance of price changes. They also pointed out that in a competitive market for a homogeneous product it was to be expected that prices would be identical and follow each other closely. The firms denied collusion. It is also clear that they understood the logic of tacit collusion, put very clearly by one firm:[17]

if [we] raised prices to a lesser amount than [our competitor] and [it] failed to lower its own prices to the same level, there would be an immediate transfer of business [to us] . . . This would lead to a long-term retaliation by [our competitor].

I would contend that it is a major strength of the British legislation that the MMC *did not have to decide* whether the firms had 'really colluded'. By examining the costs, prices, and profits of the two firms they were able to conclude that the outcome of the conduct of the firms, however that conduct may be described, was against the public interest or, in economic terms, highly distortive of economic efficiency. It is hard to disagree with that decision.

Under a prohibition system such as that of the EEC, it *would* have to be established that the firms had colluded. In the absence of any concrete evidence of an agreement it is unlikely that this could have been done. In fact, the 1992 Green Paper explicitly recognizes (p. 27) that under a prohibition system in the case of price leadership or parallel pricing it is 'unlikely that breach of the prohibition would be established in the absence of anti-competitive behaviour'. I take this to mean that price leadership or parallel pricing are not in themselves regarded as anti-competitive: the firms would have to have followed some specifically anti-competitive course of conduct, for example exclusive dealing or discriminatory discounting, to fall foul of the law.

It would appear, then, that since many of the facilitating devices listed in the previous section are not subject to prohibition (information agreements are the only type of device that are, although Resale Price Maintenance is also usually excluded by law), a move to a purely prohibition system would make the British system as helpless in the face of tacit collusion as the

---

[12] Williams (1993) gives a very thorough discussion of these proposals.
[13] See also Scherer (1980), chs. 19 and 20.
[14] Scherer (1980), p. 525.
[15] For discussion of these see Scherer (1980).
[16] For a more extensive treatment of this fascinating case, see Rees (1993).

[17] MMC (1986), para 28.11.

American.[18] Given that there are advantages in other aspects to be derived from introducing a prohibition system (especially with the attendant threats of fines and private action for damages and injunctive relief), this argues for adopting the Green Paper's proposal for a dual system (option 3). Under this, prohibition replaces the Competition Act 1980 provisions on anti-competitive practices, but the provisions of the Fair Trading Act 1973 remain in force, thus allowing tacit collusion to be dealt with by the MMC.

V. Conclusions

In this concluding section I shall try to pull together the preceding discussions of the theory, practice, and policy relating to tacit collusion. The theoretical models reflect the strengths and weaknesses of modern game theory: they provide a rigorous characterization of what 'credible punishment' might mean, and a formal analysis of the way in which discount rates and demand, capacity, and cost parameters interact to determine the sustainability of tacit collusion. At the same time nothing is said about the way in which firms will converge on one of the large set of possible equilibrium agreements (given that collusion is sustainable). Firms are assumed to have unbounded capacity for working out strategies and payoffs, and for working through the abstract chains of reasoning which lead them to non-co-operative equilibrium strategies. Do firms 'really do' all that?

In practice it is very probable that they do not. Firms clearly do share the intuition underlying the idea of collusion sustained by punishment threats (recall the quotation given above from the White Salt report) and it seems very obvious to them. Moreover, numerical examples, experimental games, and such empirical case studies as have been carried out (see, for example, Rees, 1993) seem to suggest that typically punishments far outweigh the gains to short-run deviation for empirically reasonable discount rates and so it is really not hard to explain collusion. Not only may firms be unable, for reasons of bounded rationality, to work through the complex mathematics of these models, they may not have to because the answer is to them so obvious. It has been shown in the experimental literature on the prisoners' dilemma game that the strategy of 'tit for tat' is a very effective and frequently chosen way of sustaining co-operation even though it is far simpler than Abreu's strategies (and neither subgame

perfect nor renegotiation-proof). Moreover, as we have seen, firms have developed facilitating devices such as information agreements, trade associations, and price leadership to help them solve the problem of achieving and maintaining agreements. These can be seen as practical methods of resolving the kinds of problems identified by the theory.[19]

Turning now to policy, it seems clear that a prohibitions-based or *per se* illegality form of legislation cannot effectively deal with tacit collusion. This is because that kind of approach is aimed at conduct which is explicitly conspiratorial. Tacit collusion is a form of non-co-operative equilibrium: it results from the rational, independent pursuit of self-interest, which courts tend to find not nearly as reprehensible, to say the least, as conspiratorial conduct. Further complications are created by the fact that secret explicit collusion may be observationally equivalent to tacit collusion given surveillance methods constrained by considerations of 'liberty and justice'. There will always be the problem of trying to infer whether apparently tacit collusion really was well-concealed explicit collusion.

These problems are avoided by an effects-based approach such as that underlying the UK legislation. Whether firms 'really' colluded is not a central issue. What matters is the appraisal of the outcomes of their behaviour from the point of view of economic efficiency. To eliminate the possibility of this would seem to be a retrograde step. Indeed, there is every argument for strengthening it by introducing penalties and allowing MMC findings on the outcomes of firms' behaviour to form the basis for private actions for damages. This is all the more necessary because, although some facilitating devices such as information agreements may be made the subject of prohibitions, the majority of them appear to escape these.

References

Abreu, D., Pearce, D., and Stacchetti, E. (1986), 'Optimal Cartel Equilibria with Imperfect Monitoring', *Journal of Economic Theory*, **39**, 251–69.

DTI (1989), 'Opening Markets: New Policy on Restrictive Trade Practices', Cm 727, London, HMSO.

---

[18] This seems, in fact, to be fully recognized in paras 3.14 and 3.15 of the Green Paper.

[19] In this author's opinion, the major contribution of the models surveyed in section II has been to liberate the literature of oligopoly theory from almost exclusive concern with one-shot models, in which collusion cannot be rationalized, and to extend rigorous analysis to a wide and important set of economic phenomena. It has re-focused theoretical attention on the right questions even if all of them have not yet been answered.

—— (1992), 'Abuse of Market Power', Cm 2100, London, HMSO.

Farrell, J., and Maskin, E. (1989), 'Renegotiation in Repeated Games', *Games and Economic Behaviour*, **1**, 327–60.

Friedman, J. (1986), *Game Theory with Applications to Economics*, Oxford, Oxford University Press.

Fudenberg, D., and Tirole, J. (1989), 'Noncooperative Game Theory for Industrial Organisation: An Introduction and Overview', ch. 5 in R. Schmalensee and R. Willig (eds.), *Handbook of Industrial Organisation*, Vol. 1, Amsterdam, North-Holland.

Gravelle, H. S. E., and Rees, R. (1992), *Microeconomics*, London, Longman.

Green, E., and Porter, R. (1984), 'Noncooperative Collusion under Imperfect Price Information', *Econometrica*, **52**, 87–100.

Kreps, D., Milgrom, P., Roberts, J., and Wilson, R. (1982), 'Rational Cooperation in the Finitely Repeated Prisoners' Dilemma', *Journal of Economic Theory*, **27**, 245–52.

Martin, S. (1992), *Advanced Industrial Economics*, Oxford, Blackwell.

MMC (1986), 'White Salt: A Report on the Supply of White Salt in the United Kingdom by Producers of Such Salt', London, HMSO.

Rees, R. (1985), 'Cheating in a Duopoly Supergame', *Journal of Industrial Economics*.

—— (1993), 'Collusive Equilibrium in the Great Salt Duopoly', *The Economic Journal*, **103**, 883–48.

Rotemberg, J., and Saloner, G. (1986), 'A Supergame-theoretic Model of Business Cycles and Price Wars during Booms', *American Economic Review*, **76**, 390–407.

Salop, S. C. (1986), 'Practices that (Credibly) Facilitate Oligopoly Coordination', ch. 9 in J. E. Stiglitz and G. F. Matthewson (eds.), *New Developments in the Analysis of Market Structure*, London, MacMillan Press.

Sapir, A., Buigues, P., and Jacquemin, A. (1993), 'European Competition Policy in Manufacturing and Services: A Two-speed Approach?', *Oxford Review of Economic Policy*, **9**(2), 113–32.

Scherer, F. M. (1980), *Industrial Market Structure and Economic Performance* (2nd edn.), Chicago, Rand McNally.

Shapiro, C. (1989), 'Theories of Oligopoly Behavior', ch. 6 of R. Schmalensee and R. Willig (eds.), *Handbook of Industrial Organization*, Vol. 1, Amsterdam, North-Holland.

Tirole, J. (1988) *The Theory of Industrial Organization*, Cambridge MA, MIT Press.

White, L. J. (1993), 'Competition Policy in the United States: An Overview', *Oxford Review of Economic Policy*, **9**(2), 133–53.

Williams, M. E. (1993), 'The Effectiveness of Competition Policy in the United Kingdom', *Oxford Review of Economic Policy*, **9**(2), 94–112.

3

Vertical integration and vertical restraints

MICHAEL WATERSON

University of Warwick

I. Introduction

'Cut out middleman's profits—buy direct from the manufacturer' is a phrase often seen in newspaper advertisements, implying that the retailing and whole-saling functions are otiose, or at least inefficient. On the other hand, certain of our major retailers (e.g. Marks and Spencer) are commonly thought of as models of efficiency, and their 'own brands' command widespread respect—the typical consumer does not think twice about which factory or by whom they are made. Manufacturers of complex products such as cars seldom make a feature of the source of their inputs—whose brake system, whose gearbox (perhaps a competitor's), or whatever ('Intel inside' computers is a striking exception here). There is also a certain amount of secrecy, or lack of communication, about vertical arrangements more generally. Is Specsavers a chain of opticians or not? Is MacDonalds a vertically integrated firm? Why do tyre retailers not say they are (on the whole) owned by tyre manufacturers, and why then do they sell competitors' products? Why will aluminium producers agree to pay for electricity even if they do not use it? How 'free' is a free public house?

Clearly, vertical arrangements take a variety of forms, and they are an important feature of industrial society, indeed have been so since the Industrial Revolution. Two quite directly opposing views on their policy significance prevail. One views unusual vertical arrangements with suspicion, presuming that they are made so as to prevent others entering the industry, to raise margins and thereby increase profits at the expense of consumers. The alternative benign view is that all contracts are made, broadly speaking, to ease the flow of product. Thus, according to Bork (1978, p. 245) 'in the absence of a most unlikely proved predatory power and purpose, anti-trust should never object to the verticality of any merger' and, much more straightforward, 'every vertical restraint should be completely lawful' (p. 288).

As we shall see, the hostile view is linked to some extent with strategic theories about the existence of vertical links, whereas the benign view relates to a contractarian approach. Unusually, explanations from more than one school of thought constitute the mainstream view here. However, the match between theoretical school and policy implication is by no means exact. In later sections, the major theoretical contributions aimed at understanding vertical linkages will be outlined, and subsequently policy implications will be drawn from them. Before that, the legal position in the UK will be outlined in brief, and issues raised by recent investigations will be considered.

Definitions: For simplicity, throughout the theoretical and policy section the world will be taken to have only two vertical stages below final consumers—called manufacturers and retailers—rather than many.

Vertical integration will be taken to mean the complete interlinkage of a manufacturer and a retailer under one owner or organizer. Conceptually at least, this is reasonably straightforward.

Vertical restraints come under a number of guises. There is retail price maintenance by the manufacturer, both maximum price and minimum price. Or a manufacturer could specify minimum quantity (quantity forcing), or details of service and demonstration

First published in *Oxford Review of Economic Policy*, vol. 9, no. 2 (1993). This version has been updated and revised to incorporate recent developments.

facilities, or quality criteria (e.g. no hamburger to be sold more than two minutes after being cooked). The manufacturer could impose full-line forcing, obliging the retailer to take a whole range of its products if it takes one, or tie-in sales, no X sold without Y. It could impose exclusive purchasing (no products of a certain description to be bought from anywhere but itself), and may offer selective and exclusive distribution agreements (suppliers have to meet certain criteria in order to be selected to distribute a product, and may be offered an exclusive territory or even absolute territorial protection). It may package a number of these restraints as a business format franchise, and charge a fee or a royalty, or some combination. Retailers with power will, perhaps less commonly, use it to invoke restraints such as slotting allowances for the right of a manufacturer's product to be on the shelves of a supermarket.

II. The policy framework

1. The law

This short section does not purport to be a complete statement of the legal position regarding vertical activity. It is at best an outline of the main points in a rather complex field. For a more authoritative view, a book such as Whish (1993) is helpful.

Vertical *mergers* are treated little differently from horizontal mergers by the law. They are covered by the Fair Trading Act 1973 (FTA), under which mergers involving the takeover of assets worth (currently) £70m or more may be referred to the Monopolies and Mergers Commission (MMC). However, it is widely known that only a small proportion of such qualifying mergers are referred, and further that vertical mergers are a small proportion of the total. Moreover, the current rules or guidelines focus on the impact on competition as the ground for referral by the Secretary of State. Hence few vertical mergers are investigated. Vertical mergers having a Community dimension can be investigated under the various provisions in EC law, principally the Merger Regulation.

Vertical integration which does not come about through merger but which has anticompetitive consequences is a potential concern of the FTA if it involves a monopoly situation. Thus the MMC could produce a monopoly report. But the main use of this act in relation to present concerns is regarding *exploitation* of monopoly situations. Similarly, 'abuse of a dominant position' in Article 86 of EC law is likely to relate to

advantage taken of monopolistic power in imposing terms. Hence we turn to such matters and therefore to the question of vertical restraints.

A vertical restraint may take one of two forms: one is unilateral imposition of substantive conditions for supply, for example a manufacturer saying 'you may not take my product X unless you also take my product Y'. The second is a mutual agreement that substantive conditions of supply will hold, for example 'in exchange for you granting me an exclusive territory, I promise to sell only your products in that territory'.

At first sight, the latter would seem to come under the framework of the Restrictive Trade Practices Act 1976 (RTP). However, for a variety of reasons such agreements are unlikely to require registration, as matters stand. First, schedule 3 to the Act exempts some exclusive dealing arrangements. Second, it is usually not difficult to write an agreement in such a manner that it does not take a form which is registrable. For example, only one party may accept restrictions of the designated form. A series of bipartite agreements, each allocating a particular territory to a retailer would be treated entirely differently from a (registrable) multipartite agreement regarding exclusivity, though it may have the same effect.

Neither will most mutual agreements of the second type be caught by EC law under Article 85(1), because they can commonly benefit either from block exemption or individual exemption under 85(3). Thus, there are block exemptions for exclusive distribution, exclusive purchasing including special provisions for beer and petrol, motor vehicle distribution arrangements, and franchise agreements, also concerning intellectual property matters. This does not mean that all such arrangements are exempted (particularly in service industries), for they have to satisfy various conditions. The block exemptions are subject to review, since they have expiry dates written in, but no substantial change is imminent. Reviews are planned by 1997.

The imposition of vertical resale price maintenance (RPM) is in almost all cases illegal, in the UK through the Resale Prices Act 1976, and through Article 85(1) concerning cross-border trades. This contrasts fairly sharply with other vertical restraints either unilaterally imposed or, as we have seen, mutually agreed. In addition to exclusive purchasing, distribution, and franchise arrangements, selective distribution may be held not to infringe Article 85(1). It is unlikely to be caught by the RTP Act either. Franchising can be, but is commonly allowed on registration.

Thus the applicable legal framework on such vertical restraints in the UK comes essentially from the FTA and the Competition Act 1980. The same goes for tie-in sales and full-line forcing, and for refusal to supply. But these Acts do not proscribe activities, they simply provide for investigation in appropriate cases. Hence the UK framework is far more lenient with regard to non-price than price restraints. (Tie-in sales and full-line forcing could be caught by Article 85(1) but there have been few cases; Article 86 is the more likely to be relevant.)

It is worth mentioning that the anticompetitive practice provisions of the Competition Act 1980, which enable the Office of Fair Trading (OFT) to investigate particular practices and produce a report which may then lead to an MMC reference, have often involved vertical restraints. These include selective distribution and exclusionary tactics. For example, exclusive dealing has been condemned in anticompetitive practice reports on several occasions. But these have mostly been of rather limited significance (one concerned the supply of taxi cabs at Brighton station); see Utton (1994) for a review. Much more important are the monopoly investigations under the FTA, like those discussed below.

Lastly, it should not be forgotten that the common law, through the restraint of trade doctrine, has a potential role to play. Some vertical agreements, such as exclusive distribution and exclusive purchasing, have been examined under this framework.

2. Some important cases

In a remarkable series of investigations, the MMC examined the practices in beer, petroleum, and motor vehicle supply. These are the three main areas in which the relationship between manufacturer and final consumer is affected by vertical restraints, covering perhaps 30 per cent of UK retail trade by value. Thus together they amount to a concerted attempt to investigate whether or not any form of vertical behaviour is to be allowed. Because of the high profile of the industries, the reports have aroused considerable interest.

The Supply of Beer (MMC, 1989), the first of these reports, is in some ways also the most noteworthy. It set the tone for the others by being massive—500 pages in A4 format. Included are appendices containing a certain amount of relatively sophisticated economic analysis—diagrams and algebra. The Commission found that the various vertical practices, including brewers' imposition of exclusive-purchase obligations for a range of products including beer (the 'tied house'), and connected with this, the use of loans at preferential rates of interest, 'prevent, restrict and distort competition from the point of view of both suppliers and consumers' (p. 250, para 11.21). As a result of these and other factors, a number of detriments to the public interest resulted, including (*a*) real increases in beer prices of 15 per cent in the six years ending December 1986; (*b*) raised margins on lager above cost compared with beer; (*c*) a restricted choice of beers and other drinks; (*d*) limited independence of tenants, and (*e*) a restricted role for independent wholesalers.

Unusually the MMC (or rather a majority of its serving members) proposed a structural remedy. Only on a few occasions have they gone this far; where they suggest changes they will often be limited to 'undertakings' or promises. (This was the case for example with the report (MMC, 1986) into the vertical merger of BT with Mitel, an equipment maker.) The major recommendation was that brewers be prevented from owning or leasing, or having an interest in, or an exclusive relationship with any more than 2,000 on-licensed outlets in the UK. This implied structural changes for all the big brewers. In addition there were behavioural remedies proposed in order to reduce the extent of the product tie. Following the report, although the then Secretary of State at first indicated he would implement its recommendations in full, they were subsequently modified to make them less swingeing. The brewers' various structural responses, which have included vertical disintegration as well as sales of tied estate, have now been completed but have been replaced in part by exclusive dealing relationships (on which, see below).

Another feature of interest in this report concerns the relationship between UK and EC law. The Brewers' Society contended that arrangements with their outlets fell within the block exemption of exclusive purchasing agreements 1984/83, and therefore that the UK would be in breach of its obligations under the Treaty of Rome if it prohibited such arrangements. The MMC pointed out that the block exemption only applied if there were no effective competition, no refusal to supply, or if it were not true that less favourable conditions were imposed on those with an exclusive purchasing obligation. They argued that these conditions were not satisfied and, therefore, that there was no legal difficulty in remedying adverse effects in the UK.

The Supply of Petrol (MMC, 1990) came to quite different conclusions regarding the superficially similar vertical arrangements in that industry. The MMC found no grounds to suggest that the pattern of ownership, 'solus' ties or pricing arrangements in the industry, operated against the public interest. They therefore recommended no structural or behavioural changes, though they did feel that continued monitoring of the industry by the OFT was necessary.

New Motor Cars (MMC, 1992*a*) is the longest of all,

and almost certainly the longest MMC report ever, at nearly 850 pages including appendices. Again, there are complex vertical linkages in the industry and, again, there is a block exemption which covers distribution arrangements within the industry, provided they remain within certain parameters (which the European Community's DG IV believe they do not in some respects). The MMC found that restrictions in the selective and exclusive distribution agreements prevent efficient dealers from growing strong, promoting outside their territory, obtaining competing franchises and gaining bargaining power, thereby bargaining for better terms and obtaining more customers by passing some of these benefits on to final consumers. Therefore these features operate against the public interest. The MMC proposed a behavioural remedy, that in their agreements with manufacturers, franchised dealers be allowed to advertise outside their designated territories and to acquire dealerships outside that territory, and not be limited as to the number of cars they may sell. They also proposed that dealers may hold competing dealerships in an area and provide other services outside their territories. However, no changes have resulted to date.

Accompanying this report was a related, less extensive inquiry into motor car parts (MMC, 1992b), in which industry there are also substantial vertical interlinkages. However, the MMC, although finding areas of potential concern, did not propose any remedies.

There are cases in quite different spheres which suggest a perceived considerable importance in vertical arrangements. Prime amongst these is the electricity industry in England and Wales. In 1990 the industry, which was both vertically and horizontally integrated, became separated into different units (for fuller details, see e.g. Vickers and Yarrow, 1991). Generation was initially in the hands of two main concerns, National Power and PowerGen, together with input from Nuclear Electric, imports from Scotland and France, but, in due course, competition from independent producers is anticipated. The generators have to bid for the right to supply electricity to the National Grid, the central player in the system. It operates on behalf of the regional electricity companies (RECs) in buying and transmitting power to them. They then distribute (and supply) electricity to final consumers, except the largest ones. The RECs can generate electricity on their own account but are strictly limited in the extent to which they can do so.

One major concern in creating this structure seems to have been the recognition that competition in generation was feasible and capable in principle of producing cost reductions, but that the structure of the interrelationship between generation and distribution had to be carefully designed. Electricity is essentially non-storable, so total generated supply has to equal total demand at every point in time. Hence there is a regulated market system organized by the Grid interposed between the two, determining prices and supply for each half-hour period. (Previously there had been a shadow market, based upon operating-cost information.) The system as a whole is overseen by the Director General of Electricity Supply, who has a duty to promote competition in generation and supply. Currently moves are in train to reduce the extent of vertical integration in gas supply, also with the aim of aiding the development of competition.

Finally, in devising structures for essentially new but potentially problematic industries (problematic as a result of natural monopoly issues) such as cable TV and cordless telephone communication, the government has experimented with a variety of vertical systems and restraints. Clearly, vertical arrangements are not matters which can be left to chance in all circumstances.

III. Theoretical analyses of vertical linkages

1. Technological economies

The first set of factors leading to close vertical linkages is fairly straightforward-technological interdependence. The classic example concerns various stages of the steelmaking process, where unnecessary cooling and reheating is avoided by siting these activities in close proximity to each other, usually under common ownership. However, there are certainly other industries where it is normal to group activities in this way.

A rather different example is newspapers, where typesetting, printing, and publishing are all commonly carried out on the same premises by one company. This is quite different from the case with books where the activities are very often carried out in different locations. But with newspapers, speed is essential for economic production, hence the proximity to minimize delay. The example also illustrates the influence of technology—now that data is easily transferred electronically, typesetting and printing of newspapers is often carried out in different places, with printing taking place at several locations.

Nor need the activities necessarily be performed by the same firm. Electricity generation is quite often carried out at coal-mine mouths, but (as Joskow, 1985, has documented) under a variety of contractual relationships. Vertical linkages can be used rather than vertical integration. The same is true of relationships between aluminium smelters and electricity suppliers. Contractual arrangements between the parties can lead to disputes, but it is not clear that these are the concern of competition policy authorities.

2. The transactions cost approach

From one point of view, the theory of vertical integration and vertical restraints is but a special case of the theory of the firm. The employment relation or contract, which characterizes all firms larger than sole proprietorships and certain partnerships, is a form of vertical integration. Thus a second approach is to look at vertical linkages as a way of minimizing transaction costs, or reducing them below market transaction levels.

The approach originates from the insights of Coase (1937) but has largely been developed by Williamson (e.g. 1971, 1975, and 1985). For reasons which will become apparent, I will not provide more than a brief overview of this approach.

A major element in this analysis is the concept of asset specificity. Assets are specific to a transaction to the extent to which their costs are sunk. If I, a plastics factory owner, decide to make a rear-lamp cluster for a particular car, either I or the car assembler will have to invest in the specific mould to produce it. The subsequent bargaining position between me and the assembler will depend a great deal on the nature of the ownership structure regarding this asset, and may be subject to dispute, especially if I acquire some knowledge as a result of using it.

This first element interacts with the second, uncertainty. If we knew what the future would bring, our contract regarding the specific asset (and other matters) could be well and completely thought out. But what if demand is lower than expected—must I keep to my quoted price? If demand is higher than expected, can I object if the manufacturer asks another producer also to make the same product? If there was no asset specificity, then there would be no commitment on either side, and hence no problem.

Frequency of exchange is also important. Suppose the same sort of bargain will have to be concluded quite often, then it may make sense to devise a framework, or 'governance structure' or protocol, to facilitate it.

Thus market exchange has its weaknesses, as well as its strengths (competition, anonymity, flexibility). It is noteworthy that General Motors and Toyota developed quite different responses to the problem exemplified, the former specializing in vertical integration,

the latter in vertical linkages well short of that, but both some distance from anonymous market exchange.

3. A contractual rights approach

A more recent outgrowth of the transactions cost approach stems from the work of Grossman, Hart, and Moore (GHM) (Grossman and Hart, 1986; Hart and Moore, e.g. 1990). This accepts that integration provides benefits identified by Coase, Williamson, and others, but is critical of their analysis of the costs. In caricatures of the Coase–Williamson view, one might expect the firm to grow without limit, in the absence of the costs of overburdening bureaucracy. But what, more precisely, are these costs?

To answer this question, GHM define ownership as control over the (residual rights in the) firm's assets, the firm itself being viewed as a collection of assets. Naturally, the firm has employees but, in the absence of slavery, the workers have inalienable rights. A manager can order an employee to carry out a specific task. If the employee refuses then, in an extreme case, he or she will be fired. The manager is no better off, seemingly, than if the employee were a sub-contractor, whose contract could be rescinded for poor performance. Thus control over employees, and the incentives of employees, come indirectly through management's ownership of assets, which in turn defines the status quo, within this framework.

An example from Hart (1989) will illustrate the costs as well as benefits of ownership of two successive stages of production. The example involves a car assembler and a car-body manufacturer. Suppose the two are separate. Then if the assembler wants to make changes to the contract, the body-maker is in a strong position because it can threaten to keep both employees and assets working to the original contracts. However, if the two are integrated, those running the body-making division are in a weaker position if asked to make changes, since they have no independent control rights over the assets they manage. This is a benefit of integration. On the other hand, those running the body-making division of an integrated firm would have a dulled incentive to come up with cost-saving or quality-enhancing innovations for producing bodies than would an independent body-maker. Management in the latter would appropriate a surplus created by the innovation to a far greater extent than in the integrated firm, assuming that the innovation is asset-specific. This dulled incentive to enhance productivity is a cost of integration that must be borne in mind when amalgamation is contemplated. Integration does not yield the outcome which would arise under complete contracts. The example sketched out above concerns those relatively high up in the hierarchy, but it can be extended to cover other employees of the body-maker.

These ideas can be developed into a theory of the boundaries of the firm. The first result is that complementary assets should be owned by a single firm. If a product may only be realized by the use of two sets of assets, and each set has no alternative use, then when both sets are under common control, fewer parties can hold up any non-contracted changes to the production process. On the other hand, when assets are economically independent, integration would bring in outside control which would dilute incentives in the division being controlled. Hence the second result, that independent assets should be separately owned. Less polar cases will depend upon a balance of forces. Thus there are, in principle, limits to the scope of a firm based upon the technology and transactions involved in its production and output processes.

This theory builds upon transactions cost theory but, its proponents would argue, provides clearer predictions. In both frameworks, firms are in a second-best world; first-best contractual arrangements are not available *ex ante* (and the Coase theorem, therefore, does not apply). Firms have an incentive to opt for particular levels or types of integration. Whether in practice they act in this way has not been established convincingly.

The main gap in the theoretical analysis in both cases is any consideration of whether or when there is likely to be a divergence between the private and socially desirable directions of vertical integration for contractual reasons. The fact that firms find it in their mutual interests to combine, or to develop lasting links, does not mean that such links are socially desirable in the wider sense (as Williamson, for example, would agree). Thus whilst transactions cost and contractual rights approaches are capable of considerable insights, and have strong links with delegation and strategic issues which will be discussed later, they do not yet lend themselves very readily to propositions in welfare economics. This is the reason for comparative neglect in the material that follows.

4. Monopolistic motives for integration

The third main set of arguments will be the most extensively covered, under a number of sub-headings. First, there are a number of standard arguments regarding integration which, although widely available in texts, should be briefly reviewed.

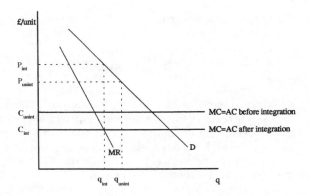

Figure 3.1. Cost and price changes on vertical integration

Following Vernon and Graham (1971), if variable proportions may be used in production, but one input is monopolized and priced above marginal cost whereas the other is not, then merger between the upstream monopolized input supplier and the final producer(s) can remove the inefficiency caused by the factor distortion in production. However, it simultaneously increases the monopolist's market, since possibilities of substitution away from the monopolized input are eliminated. Hence final price may rise (particularly if the downstream stage was competitive) and social welfare could fall—see Schmalensee (1973). The possibility is illustrated in Figure 3.1.

If (with Greenhut and Ohta, 1976) the upstream and downstream stages were connected by fixed proportions, with upstream being a monopoly and downstream an oligopoly, then integration would remove successive mark-ups at different stages in favour of a single mark-up. Monopoly power would not increase, but price would fall and a welfare gain would ensue.

Clearly these two effects can be combined (Waterson, 1982). Thus, if the elasticity of substitution is fairly low (high), and numbers at the downstream stage prior to integration are low (high), social welfare is likely to rise (fall) on integration. This modelling framework can also be extended to include oligopoly at each level and firm by firm integration, at the cost of some complexity.

Two comments on this analysis are in order. First, it assumes there are no contractual means to eliminate the problems of successive mark-ups/input pricing distortions in the absence of complete integration despite potential benefits to the parties involved. Second, it is sometimes said that the pure vertical effects of integration are always positive in a welfare sense—they only become negative because of associated horizontal effects, for example as a result of a reduction in the number of downstream firms. But this is of little comfort, since the two are commonly inextricably intertwined.

From the point of view of policy, there is a substantial difference between horizontal mergers and vertical mergers, based upon this analysis. In the absence of scale economy benefits, horizontal mergers are likely to be socially undesirable. The presumption with a vertical merger is that unless a substantial horizontal impact is involved, it will be socially beneficial on balance. Of course some parties will be adversely affected, but the overall effect takes this into account.

One particular element of concern here is what is known as the foreclosure issue. If one of the few upstream firms integrates with a downstream firm, then its previous customers may find their supply of input dries up, or is subject to onerous terms. This was a factor in the merger between BMC and Pressed Steel Fisher some years ago (Monopolies Commission, 1966). In this particular case, there seems to have been no question of halting supply, but undertakings were sought that, in times of high demand, outside customers (Rootes, etc.) would receive fair attention to their orders.

More recently, the question has been raised analytically by Salinger (1988). He argues that in the absence of diminishing returns to production of the intermediate or final good, or some element of product differentiation at intermediate or final levels, or the need for a firm's intermediate product division to be held to being competitive, then vertically integrated firms will not participate in the intermediate good market. Thus, under certain circumstances intermediate good prices in the unintegrated sector can rise as a result of integration, and vertical merger can thereby cause a rise in final good prices. However, it will be noted that the list of qualifications under which participation in the intermediate market will not take place is extensive. As a matter of fact, such participation often takes place. And some recent work (Abiru *et al.*, 1992) questions this analysis in any case. Therefore the importance of the foreclosure issue as regards overall welfare is rather unclear.

A further element may enter here to complicate the picture. Suppose upstream scale economies are extensive. A downstream firm may wish to integrate backwards despite the scale economies in order to value (shadow price) additional units of input at marginal cost. But this will have adverse effects on remaining upstream firms, who will be faced with a thinner market over which to cover their costs, and may harm overall welfare. Again this assumes there is no contractual means, for example a two-part tariff, by which to

enable the intending integrator to obtain additional units at or near marginal cost.

Finally, suppose that the upstream firm's product has two uses with very different elasticities of demand. In order to sustain price discrimination between the two sets of purchasers, it may decide to integrate into the area of relatively elastic demand and charge a high price to the other. Of course we must remember that the welfare implications of price discrimination are not clear-cut.

5. Vertical restraints and the 'externality problem'

At first sight, it might be thought that a manufacturer would be keen on retailing being as competitive as possible. This argument goes as follows: There is a demand by consumers for the product of manufacturer X. But the manufacturer faces a derived demand from dealers/retailers in the product. If the retail sector is competitive, the derived demand curve will be the same shape as the final demand curve, and below it by a distance representing the marginal cost of retailing. If the retail sector were imperfectly competitive, the derived demand curve would be steeper in slope, and if it were inefficient the derived demand curve would be a greater distance below. Neither possibility would be in the manufacturer's interest. All other things being equal, the smaller the retailing mark-up, the greater the profit share for the manufacturer. So what is wrong with this argument?

In essence, the complication is that retailers provide 'much more than mere warehousing' (Marvel and McCafferty, 1984, p. 348). They provide both specific and general services to customers and potential customers—demonstration facilities, information, stocks, and so on. But these do not come free. Retailers incur fixed costs, many of which contain a sunk element, for example fixtures and fittings. Manufacturers gain through having their product demonstrated, or even through having it present in a store (or else they would be unwilling to pay 'slotting allowances' to supermarkets), so that demand is not exogenous to retailing. The fact that there are fixed costs means perfect competition is an unattainable ideal framework for retailing. Moreover, for many goods, competition is localized due to the spatial nature of retailing. When modelling vertical restraints, it becomes important to incorporate these features (see e.g. Dixit, 1983; Mathewson and Winter, 1984).

Once a model incorporating a manufacturer with some monopoly power and (say) a monopolistically competitive retail sector has been set up, it becomes apparent that manufacturer and retailer interests diverge; the retailers may want more or less margin than the manufacturer would like to impose. For example, Gallini and Winter (1983) show that a typical retailer would want a margin [(price − input cost)/price] of $1/\varepsilon_r$, whereas the manufacturer would want the retail margin to be $\varepsilon_n/\varepsilon_R$, ε_r being the elasticity of demand when one retailer changes price, ε_R the elasticity when all retailers do likewise and ε_n, the elasticity of demand with respect to changes in the number of retailers. Moreover, the numbers entering retailing may be suboptimal from the manufacturer's point of view. This divergence of views can be seen (following Mathewson and Winter, 1984) as arising out of a set of externalities.

(i) Retailers do not gain all the benefits of action taken to improve sales; some goes to manufacturers. For every extra unit a retailer sells by modifying pricing or advertising strategies, the manufacturer gains an amount given by the difference between the wholesale price and marginal production costs. Thus, there is a positive externality bestowed on the manufacturer by such retailers' actions, which in turn means that retailers will tend to set prices too high and advertising too low from the manufacturer's point of view (i.e. high prices are a negative vertical externality).

(ii) On the other hand, retailers when raising price confer benefits on neighbouring retailers, by increasing demand for their products. This is a positive horizontal externality created by one retailer on others; in attempting to gain a greater margin for itself, it drives some custom away. It will tend to mean retailers will keep prices lower than they would be in the absence of rivals.

Clearly, these two opposing effects imply that it is unlikely there will be a dominant direction to the outcome over all modelling variants.

(iii) Each retailer confers a positive externality on other retailers and on the manufacturer by engaging in advertising of the product, unless the advertising is very specifically targeted. There is a similar effect regarding other services—demonstration facilities and so on. Because the horizontal and vertical externalities here operate in the same direction, the clear prediction is that, in the absence of any agreements, too little promotional and demonstration activity will take place. Some retailers will attempt to 'free ride' on others, perhaps offering low prices and a warehouse-type *ambiance*, once customers have had a product demonstrated elsewhere.

(iv) Retailers left to themselves would be likely to set location sufficiently distant from rivals to permit supernormal returns to their location but not sufficient to make entry worthwhile. This assumes an element of sunkness about location (which Mathewson and Winter did not), so that potential entrants believe they are unlikely to be able to push established firms out of current locations. In this case, the retailers' locational choices confer a negative externality on the manufacturer leading to a suboptimal density of suppliers from the manufacturer's point of view.

Vertical restraints imposed by the manufacturer can in principle control all these problems or deal with the externalities involved. Resale price maintenance, quantity forcing, specification of demonstration service and promotional facilities, franchise fees, allocation of territories, and so on, can all be used to this end, assuming the manufacturer has sufficient information regarding the underlying cost and demand parameters, and assuming all are legal.

To call something an externality is potentially emotive. In welfare economics we are taught that to internalize externalities by appropriate contracts is socially desirable. But that should not lead us to assume that the same holds for the externalities identified here. Internalization will be in the manufacturer's interest, but the manufacturer and society do not have the same set of preferences. The manufacturer's interest in a high price, for example, may be in opposition to the social desirability of a low price.

The positive analysis of vertical restraints within this framework can be taken a little further, with implications for normative issues. Still assuming a deterministic setting, and given sufficient mathematical regularity in the underlying functions, the number of instruments needed might be expected to equal the number of variables to be controlled. (Uncertainty will be introduced later.) Thus in the absence of the fourth externality discussed above, it is price and advertising levels (and thereby quantity, as well) set by retailers which the manufacturer wishes to control. Two instruments are sufficient. Depending on the framework, it can be shown that alternative pairs of instruments can be used.

Moving to policy issues, if two alternative pairs with the same properties exist, then if one set is deemed socially (un)desirable, so should the other set be. Mathewson and Winter note an asymmetry between the treatment of RPM and various territorial and franchise restrictions in the law of the US (and the same is true of the UK). Pricing restraints are treated much more harshly than non-price restraints. If it is true that they are simply used as substitutes, the law is making an economically illegitimate distinction.

In fact, I have argued (Waterson, 1988) that things are not as straightforward as this. Cases are documented where what are seen in Mathewson and Winter as potential substitutes (territory distribution and RPM) were used together. There are, I believe, two reasons, first that closed territory distribution (sales outside an area being prohibited) is normally infeasible and second that the fourth externality may be of importance. Hence to ban one but not the other may not be as ridiculous as a simple interpretation of their model would suggest. Moreover, there are circumstances under which simple vertical restraints do not perform as Mathewson and Winter suggest (see Bolton and Bonanno, 1988; O'Brien and Shaffer, 1992). There is also the question of the relationship between maximum and minimum RPM (see Perry and Besanko, 1991).

But there is one important general point which holds regardless of these specific criticisms. For economists, a focus on the effects of a set of practices is what matters. Whether they take one particular legal form or another, whether they involve particular instruments or another set, is not of first importance. Thus the idea that instruments are substitutes at all is rather damning for a restrictive practices policy which, like that currently in operation in the UK, is based upon form rather than effect.

Finally, one general feature of the framework of this subsection is worthy of note, in order to facilitate comparisons between models. The manufacturer's ideal would be complete vertical control—vertical integration. The restraints are imposed in an attempt to mimic this. But then there is no rationale within the model for restraints per se. Perhaps restraints are imposed because the history of the industry precludes vertical integration. Perhaps the manufacturer lacks sufficient capital to build the network. It cannot be a lack of expertise, given the framework. Other models soon to be discussed have more fundamental reasons for vertical restraints, as opposed to vertical integration.

6. Interbrand v. intrabrand competition

In almost every purchase one makes, from a butter substitute to a bathroom suite, there are two forms of competition. Do I want Flora or St Ivel Gold, is one form; do I buy from Tesco or Sainsbury is the other. (With some products, like the bathroom suite, there is a further question—within the Armitage Shanks range, do I want the Sandringham-Envoy with Silverspa taps, or some higher specification? I will not consider this issue any further in the present context.) The models of

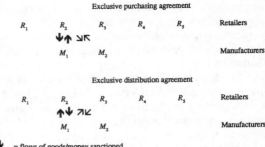

Figure 3.2. Exclusive purchasing and exclusive distribution

the previous section, by assuming a monopoly manufacturer, neglected interbrand competition and the role of exclusive purchasing agreements.

An exclusive purchasing agreement obliges a retailer to purchase its supply of a particular good or set of goods solely from one manufacturer. In Figure 3.2, R_2 must buy from M_1 not M_2, but M_1 is unconstrained. This gives the manufacturer some immunity from interbrand competition and, as a first-order effect, increases the manufacturer's margin, which is privately but not socially desirable.

In practice (as, for example, in car retailing, and commonly in franchising) it is often coupled with an exclusive distribution agreement. Again in Figure 3.2, M_1 says it will sell to R_2 but not to R_3, a neighbour of R_2. R_2 will often be given a 'territory', although this will not normally mean that R_2 makes all sales of M_1's product inside the territory. However, other retailers of the product will normally be under some obligation not to seek customers actively in R_2's industry. Thus it gives the retailer some immunity from intrabrand competition, as discussed above, and as a first-order effect increases the retailer's margin.

There will be additional effects as a result of these marketing agreements. For example, the exclusive purchasing agreement by itself raises the manufacturer's margin, but may lower the retail margin. If retailers are spread around the country, in some places it will transpire that there is room for only one seller of both manufacturer M_1's and manufacturer M_2's product. If exclusive purchasing is then instituted, there may be enough custom for one retailer of each product. This increases competition at the retail level, all other things being equal, compared with the no-restraint position, and so reduces retail margins (see Waterson, 1990). Therefore the effects of exclusive purchasing agreements on social welfare are not clear; sometimes restrictions will be desirable, sometimes not, dependent upon particular parameters of the model. However, it appears that the higher the cross-elasticity of demand between rival goods or brands, the more likely are exclusive purchasing agreements to be socially desirable, and vice versa (see Besanko and Perry, 1994; Dobson and Waterson, 1994). Also, there is a greater private than social incentive for manufacturers to impose exclusive purchasing. There are similar considerations related to exclusive distribution, as the preamble to the legislation on the block exemption suggests (see also Rey and Stiglitz, 1995).

7. Strategic effects and vertical separation

So far, much of the analysis has implied that firms are likely to want vertical integration and that, though in many cases it would be socially desirable, in some it may not be. A rather different type of argument suggests there may be strategic advantages in manufacturers remaining separate from retailers, whilst having distinct linkages.

Suppose two manufacturers produce goods which are partial substitutes, and (for whatever reason) competition in the market is through price. Suppose they are each integrated with their retailing operation. If the goods are close substitutes, competition between them will drive price down near to marginal cost. Now let the retailing operations be separate. In order to avoid successive mark-up problems, the manufacturers may each decide to charge input at marginal cost, but gain benefits by imposing a positive franchise fee. However, if the products are very close, the price mark-up retailers can charge above marginal cost will be low, so the level at which the franchise fee can be set will not prove very rewarding to the manufacturers.

Therefore, let us consider an alternative scenario, in which one manufacturer decides to raise its input price (possibly at the same time reducing the franchise fee). This will raise its retailer's costs, so causing an increase in price and reduction in output. Provided the manufacturer can claw back the benefits, this will increase its profitability. In fact, Bonanno and Vickers (1988, p. 260) show the following proposition: 'if franchise fees can be used to extract the retailers' profits, it is in the individual interest of each manufacturer to choose vertical separation and charge his retailer a wholesale price in excess of unit production cost' whether the other is integrated or separated.

The point may be illustrated in a reaction function diagram. Because the products' prices are strategic complements (in the Bulow et al., 1985 sense) their

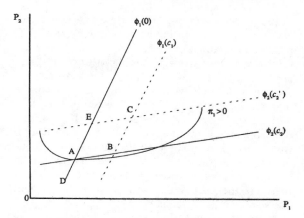

Figure 3.3. Reaction functions with vertical integration

reaction functions will be upward sloping—see Figure 3.3. The line $\phi_1(0)$ is the reaction function of manufacturer 1 whilst $\phi_2(c_2)$ is the reaction function of the retailer of 2's product when charged an input price $c_2 \geq 0$ (costs are assumed here to equal zero). When charged an input price of 0, $\phi_1(0)$ is also the reaction function of the retailer of good 1. The franchise fee will determine the point D, below which the retailer would make losses. When the manufacturer charges a unit price c_1 somewhat above zero, the retailer sets a higher price for any given price of retailer 2, leading to the reaction function $\phi_1(c_1)$ and equilibrium at B. The same argument can be made for manufacturer 2. Hence the eventual position will be at a point like C.

Intuitively, what is happening here is that the force which argues for an increase in output (fall in prices) from the double marginalization position in monopoly is being outweighed by a force which argues for a decrease in output (increase in price) from the duopoly position. This increases manufacturer profits, as long as the surplus can be captured. But notice that position A is socially preferred to B or C, involving as it does lower prices and greater output for both products. Therefore, from the social point of view, vertical integration would be preferable to vertical separation.

This model can be extended to compare vertical separation with the complete absence of vertical linkages, through an adaptation of the model of Ordover et al. (1990); see also Rey and Stiglitz (1988, 1995). Here there are two manufacturers and two retailers. The manufacturers produce identical products (say, for simplicity). Therefore price competition between them for the right to sell to the retailers would drive price to marginal cost. The retailers' products are somewhat differentiated, so that price competition would still leave a mark-up above costs.

Suppose now that manufacturer 1 signs a selective and exclusive distribution agreement with retailer 1, promising not to supply retailer 2. Manufacturer 2 can then raise its price to retailer 2 above cost, because there is no alternative source of supply. Hence, by signing the agreement, retailer 1 has raised rival's costs in the manner suggested by Salop and Scheffman (1987). In terms of the figure, $\phi_2(c_2)$ shifts up to $\phi_2(c_2')$, so that if the original outcome was point A it now moves to E (or if the original outcome were B, it moves to C). Thus manufacturer 1 and retailer 1 have some surplus to share. Once manufacturer 1 and retailer 1 have signed their agreement, it may pay manufacturer 2 and retailer 2 to sign a similar agreement.

Again it appears that vertical separation (here vertical restraints, of the exclusive distribution kind) are socially less desirable than the alternative, in this case complete absence of vertical links. Obviously the result is dependent on there being not too much differentiation at the upstream stage, or the double marginalization effect of no linkage would dominate. Also important is the limited availability of alternative sources for retailer 2 once the first agreement is signed. This harks back to the foreclosure issue. But the general point is that vertical restraints should not be thought of, in social welfare terms, as intermediate between no linkage and complete integration.

8. Risk, uncertainty, and agency

Discussion of the benefits to the manufacturer of vertical separation and of imposing restraints on downstream firms reminds us that one way the whole issue can be thought of is as a principal–agent problem of delegation. The manufacturer delegates to the agent the task of setting final price (usually), output, presale services, and so on, but is rather careful about the construction of the award schedule. Still in this vein, one element not so far introduced is risk and uncertainty and its impact on the modelling of frameworks and outcomes. It is once these are introduced that traditional agency factors come into play.

Rey and Tirole (1986) have a model in which a manufacturer supplies a number of retailers, but cannot observe a retailer's profit or quantity sold. There is the possibility of demand uncertainty and cost uncertainty in the retail markets. Also retailers may be risk-averse. They show that in general RPM and exclusive territories are not equivalent (they would be in their model without uncertainty). The manufacturer is likely to prefer one or the other depending upon the nature of uncertainty and the risk preferences of retailers. Gal

Or (1991b) in a development of this model, finds some relative strengths of RPM. Social and private preferences may also diverge.

Moreover, agency considerations may conflict with strategic considerations. The following example developed from Slade (1993) will illustrate the point. Suppose some retailers are more risk-averse than others. Traditional agency theory then suggests that the more risk-averse be given contracts which force them to bear less of the risk involved in the venture. The outcome will be influenced by their effort, but they need to be heavily compensated for bearing risks. This may be tackled for example by paying them a relatively higher fixed salary with less dependent upon the outcome. In other words, they are more vertically integrated. Thereby, they work hard. In the context of a petrol station, the risk-averse are offered a salary plus a small performance bonus for running the station, whereas the less risk-averse are offered petrol at wholesale price and are free to decide how to behave.

Suppose also that there are two groups of petrol stations. Those which offer petrol alone have relatively higher cross elasticities of demand between them than those which have additional facilities (carwash, repairs, retailing, and so on). In other words, in the former price and profits are more likely to be affected by price wars. Thus it is in the former that the manufacturer has the greater strategic motive for vertical separation, setting wholesale prices and charging franchise fees.

However, if the typical person running the latter group of stations (those with additional facilities) is also less risk-averse than the typical person running the former, then there is a conflict. Strategic motives would imply vertical separation for the petrol-only stations; agency motives would imply the opposite (see also Gal Or, 1991a). Clearly, whether this is an important issue or conflict can only be answered empirically. In her paper, Slade finds that strategic motives are important in determining contract choice. This is comforting for applications to policy questions of previously discussed results of the vertical separation literature.

IV. Policy implications

A nihilistic view about the policy implications of recent theoretical work in the area of vertical restraints would be that, since almost anything can happen, nothing can be said about policy. In fact, although there is an element of truth to this position, the previous theoretical analysis is arguably of substantial assistance in commenting upon the current framework of the law. A number of points may be made.

(i)   The element of truth certainly resides in the point that there is no direct link between competition and social welfare in the area of vertical relationships. One arrangement (e.g. vertical integration) may involve less competition in some sense but may be socially more desirable than another. This is rather unlike horizontal competition. But this point is already clearly recognized in the legal framework through such elements as the block exemptions. Thus the general lessons are that a concentrated vertical market structure is not necessarily undesirable, and that freely negotiated contractual relationships are not necessarily benign. The theory gives little support to Bork's (1978) position. Moreover, combinations of factors can conspire to turn vertical effects into horizontal effects, for example the combination of vertical linkages and the necessity for licences at the retail stage (as in the supply of beer) or the general use of exclusive territories to facilitate collusion.

(ii)   Moving on to more specific issues, theory gives comparatively little support to the legal position that resale price maintenance should be treated differently from other vertical restraints. There is some justification, in that RPM may be the most direct method of maintaining high prices. But combinations of other controls which are viewed benignly may very easily lead to similar effects. Indeed, some people would argue they are worse, if anything. What is, unfortunately, not clear as a general proposition is whether the controls on RPM should be relaxed, or whether exclusive dealing and so on should be viewed with greater suspicion.

(iii)   There is another factor which arises in this connection. If one set of instruments can substitute for another, policy is in any case badly served by a legal framework which focuses on form rather than effect, as the UK restrictive practice legislation does. (Kay, 1990, extends this argument to say that effect should be valued over intent as well.) Two sets of words may amount to the same thing, but one set may be caught by the Act and another set not. Those formulating agreements are obviously better advised to avoid the particular frameworks captured by the Act. But then the Act loses its utility. This lesson appears to have been accepted in principle (Department of Trade and Industry, 1988, 1989) but moves to implement changes seem remarkably dilatory.

(iv)   The case for block exemption of franchising does not appear clear in economic theory. It is perhaps implicitly assumed that each franchise chain has little market power. Otherwise the fact that RPM is disallowed but that franchisors can 'recommend' selling prices to franchisees would be quite remarkable. Alternatively, it is perhaps assumed that without franchises there would be a vertically integrated chain, which would be less socially desirable. But neither is this necessarily the case. This leads to a more general point.

(v)   The law appears so far to have almost entirely failed to rise to the challenge of the vertical separation literature. Vertical integration is not strongly controlled, but vertical (non-price) restraints are actively smiled upon. Clearly this is likely to encourage development of the latter, including franchising. But we have seen that vertical separation with restraints may well be more socially undesirable than vertical integration. This is not a curiosum: the types of arrangements in the beer and petrol industries in which tied retailers face a higher unit price and possibly subsidised fixed costs (i.e. a negative franchise fee) seem to accord quite closely with the predictions of some theoretical models. Admittedly in the beer industry the MMC took the position that, although there were block exemptions, they could be negated under certain circumstances if the agreements were detrimental. But the point was not very forcefully made, and vertical restraints did in some cases replace vertical integration.

References

Abiru, M., Nahata, B., and Waterson, M. (1992), 'On the Profitability of Vertical Integration', Working Paper No. 9255, Department of Economics, University of Warwick.

Besanko, D., and Perry, M. K. (1994), 'Exclusive Dealing in a Spatial Model of Retail Competition', *International Journal of Industrial Organization*, **12**, 299–329.

Bolton, P., and Bonanno, G. (1988), 'Vertical Restraints in a Model of Vertical Differentiation', *Quarterly Journal of Economics*, **103**, 555–70.

Bonanno, G., and Vickers, J. (1988), 'Vertical Separation', *Journal of Industrial Economics*, **36**, 257–65.

Bork, R. H. (1978), *The Antitrust Paradox*, New York, Basic Books.

Bulow, J., Geanakoplos, J., and Klemperer, P. (1985), 'Multimarket Oligopoly: Strategic Substitutes and Complements', *Journal of Political Economy*, **93**, 488–511.

Coase, R. M. (1937), 'The Nature of the Firm', *Economica*, NS4, 386–405.

Department of Trade and Industry (1988), *Review of Restrictive Trade Practices Policy*, Cm 331, London, HMSO.

—— (1989), *Opening Markets: New Policy on Restrictive Trade Practices*, Cm 727, London, HMSO.

Dixit, A. K. (1983), 'Vertical Integration in a Monopolistically Competitive Industry', *International Journal of Industrial Organization*, **1**, 63–78.

Dobson, P. W., and Waterson, M. (1994), 'The Effects of Exclusive Purchasing on Interbrand and Intrabrand Rivalry', Warwick Economics Working Paper no. 94–15, University of Warwick.

Gallini, N. T., and Winter, R. A. (1983), 'On Vertical Control in Monopolistic Competition', *International Journal of Industrial Organisation*, **1**, 275–86.

Gal Or, E. (1991a), 'Optimal Franchising in Oligopolistic Markets with Uncertain Demand', *International Journal of Industrial Organisation*, **9**, 343–64.

—— (1991b), 'Vertical Restraints with Incomplete Information', *Journal of Industrial Economics*, **39**, 503–16.

Greenhut, M., and Ohta, H. (1976), 'Related Market Conditions and Interindustrial Margins', *American Economic Review*, **66**, 267–77.

Grossman, S. J., and Hart, O. D. (1986), 'The Costs and Benefits of Ownership: A Theory of Vertical and Lateral Integration', *Journal of Political Economy*, **94**, 691–719.

Hart, O. D. (1989), 'An Economist's Perspective on the Theory of the Firm', *Columbia Law Review*, **89**, 1757–74.

—— Moore, J. (1990), 'Property Rights and the Nature of the Firm', *Journal of Political Economy*, **98**, 1119–58.

Joskow, P. (1985), 'Vertical Integration and Long-Term Contracts: The Case of Coal-burning Electric Utilities', *Journal of Law, Economics and Organisation*, **1**, 33–80.

Kay, J. (1990), 'Vertical Restraints in European Competition Policy', *European Economic Review*, **34**, 551–61.

Marvel, H. R., and McCafferty, S. (1984), 'Resale Price Maintenance and Quality Certification', *Rand Journal of Economics*, **15**, 346–59.

Mathewson, G. F., and Winter, R. A. (1984), 'An Economic Theory of Vertical Restraints', *Rand Journal of Economics*, **15**, 27–38.

Monopolies Commission (1966), *The British Motor Corporation Ltd. and the Pressed Steel Company Ltd: A Report on the Merger*, HCP 46, London, HMSO.

Monopolies and Mergers Commission (1986), *British Telecommunications plc/Mitel Corporation*, Cmnd 9715, London, HMSO.

—— (1989), *The Supply of Beer*, Cm 651, London, HMSO.

—— (1990), *The Supply of Petrol*, Cm 972, London, HMSO.

—— (1992a), *New Motor Cars*, Cm 1808, London, HMSO.

—— (1992b), *Motor Car Parts*, Cm 1818, London, HMSO.

O'Brien, D. P., and Shaffer, G. (1992), 'Vertical Control with Bilateral Contracts', *Rand Journal of Economics*, **23**, 299–308.

Ordover, J. A., Saloner, G., and Salop, S. C. (1990), 'Equilibrium Vertical Foreclosure', *American Economic Review*, **86**, 137–41.

Perry, M. K., and Besanko, D. (1991), 'Resale Price Maintenance and Manufacturer Competition for Exclusive Dealerships', *Journal of Industrial Economics*, **39**, 517–44.

Rey, P., and Stiglitz, J. (1988), 'Vertical Restraints and Producers' Competition', *European Economic Review*, **32**, 561–8.

——, and —— (1995), 'The Role of Exclusive Territories in Producers' Competition', *Rand Jouranl of Economics*, **26**, 431–51.

—— Tirole, J. (1986), 'The Logic of Vertical Restraints', *American Economic Review*, **76**, 921–39.

Salinger, M. A. (1988), 'Vertical Merger and Market Foreclosure', *Quarterly Journal of Economics*, **103**, 345–56.

Salop, S. C., and Scheffman, D. (1987), 'Cost-raising Strategies', *Journal of Industrial Economics*, **36**, 19–34.

Schmalensee, R. (1973), 'A Note on the Theory of Vertical Integration', *Journal of Political Economy*, **81**, 442–9.

Slade, M. (1993), 'Strategic Motives for Vertical Separation: Evidence from Retail Gasoline', Economic Discussion Paper #93:12, University of British Columbia.

Utton, M. (1994), 'Anti-competitive Practices and the UK Competition Act 1980', *Antitrust Bulletin*, **39**, 485–539.

Vernon, J., and Graham, D. (1971), 'Profitability of Monopolisation by Vertical Integration', *Journal of Political Economy*, **79**, 924–5.

Vickers, J., and Yarrow, G. (1991), 'The British Electricity Experiment', *Economic Policy*, **12**, 187–232.

Waterson, M. (1982), 'Vertical Integration, Variable Proportions and Oligopoly', *Economic Journal*, **92**, 129–44.

—— (1988), 'On Vertical Restraints and the Law: A Note', *Rand Journal of Economics*, **19**, 293–7.

—— (1990), 'Some Economics of Exclusive Purchasing Obligations', University of Reading Discussion Papers in Industrial Economics No. 22.

Whish, R. (1993), *Competition Law*, (3rd edn.), London, Butterworths.

Williamson, O. E. (1971), 'The Vertical Integration of Production: Market Failure Considerations', *American Economic Review*, **61**, 112–23.

—— (1975), *Markets and Hierarchies: Analysis and Antitrust Implications*, New York, Free Press.

—— (1985), *The Economic Institutions of Capitalism*, New York, Free Press.

PART II

RESEARCH AND DEVELOPMENT

4

The economics of technology policy

PAUL STONEMAN

University of Warwick

JOHN VICKERS[1]

All Souls College, Oxford

The Government has ... a general responsibility to support science and technology because this is fundamental to the social and economic well-being of the country.

House of Lords Select Committee on Science and Technology (1986)

Firms themselves are best able to assess their own markets and to balance the commercial risks and rewards of financing R & D and innovation. The Government should not take on responsibilities which are principally those of industry.

Department of Trade and Industry (1988)

The long-run performance of any economy depends upon its success in innovating new products and processes. Few would doubt that the spectacular post-war economic record of Japan, as compared to that of the US or the UK, has had much to do with its superior achievements in developing and applying new technologies. However, it is much harder to agree on what factors, let alone which government policies, promote good technological performance. In this paper we do not claim to have reached definitive conclusions on these major questions. Rather, the aim is to clarify and examine—both theoretically and empirically—a number of economic issues in technology policy, in the hope of contributing to recent debates. In the final section of the paper, however, we attempt to illustrate how the lessons learnt from the discussion can illuminate the arguments, as illustrated in the two contradictory quotes above, over an appropriate technology policy for the UK.

It is useful to begin with some basic definitions. First we define technological change, following Schumpeter, as changes in products, processes of production, raw materials, and management methods. A classic trilogy that has informed and conditioned many of the debates on technology and technology policy, again attributed to Schumpeter, is that which characterizes three stages in the process of technological change: *invention*—the generation of new ideas; *innovation*—the transformation of those ideas into, for example, new marketable products and processes; and *diffusion*—the spread of use and ownership of new technology. Implicit in this trilogy is the knowledge base which underlies technological change and which is itself continually changing and evolving. The trilogy should not be taken to be unidirectional or lacking in feedback, but it is a useful organizing framework. It should also be realized that a country's technology does not always have to be produced at home: new technology can be and is often imported from overseas. Moreover, technology does not necessarily come from a formal Research and Development effort: phenomena such as learning-by-doing can be important sources of technology. It is also worth noting that it is only at the diffusion stage that the economy obtains benefit from and is affected by new technology. Nevertheless much of the literature and technology policy debate tends to focus upon R & D spending although this is in fact more related to invention and innovation than diffusion.

A distinction often made is that between Science and Technology. At a general level it is common to associate science with the knowledge base and technology with invention, innovation, and diffusion. However, Dasgupta and David (1986) argue persuasively that the

First published in *Oxford Review of Economic Policy*, vol. 4, no. 4 (1988).

[1] We are grateful to Chris Allsopp, Tim Jenkinson, and Colin Mayer for their comments on an earlier version of this paper.

difference between the two lies in the respective goals of the scientific and technological communities. For the former, knowledge is a public good, and scientists compete to be first to publish new ideas. For technologists, however, the value of being first to innovate lies not in public esteem but in private return. The distinction is not hard and fast, and it would be a serious mistake to think that science policy and technology policy can be considered in isolation from one another. Scientists and technologists have different incentive systems—for reasons that will become more apparent below—but they are intimately connected in the process of technological change. For example, science is the main source of technological labour.

What then exactly does 'technology policy' mean? In the present context technology policy is defined as a set of policies involving government intervention in the economy with the *intent* of affecting the process of technological change. However, even with this definition the economics of technology policy is a complex subject. Some of the reasons for this are that, first, the incentives that firms have to invest in new technology are influenced by such diverse factors as the nature of product market competition (including international competition), the degree of 'spillover' from one firm's technological change to the technological capability of another, the availability of skilled personnel, the extent of public subsidy (direct or via procurement policy), and the availability of finance for technological change. Some of those factors, for example market structure, are in turn influenced by the outcome of technological competition, and hence the reciprocal interactions become yet more complicated.

Second, technological change and thus technology policy proceed in an environment of uncertainty and often very incomplete information. This not only complicates analysis but makes the design of policy subject to such problems as informational poverty, adverse selection, and moral hazard. Moreover, attitudes to risk and uncertainty greatly influence the funding of technological activity and thus bring issues of finance to the fore of technology policy discussions.

Third, as will already be apparent, several government policy instruments have interacting effects on incentives to advance technology. As well as direct instruments of technology policy, enforcement of property rights over information, subsidies, public R & D, etc., it is essential to consider the impact of other microeconomic policies, notably competition policy (see Baumol and Ordover (1988)), trade policy (see Hausman and Mackie-Mason (1988)), and education and training policies.

Fourth, there are severe difficulties of measurement.

Neither input measures (e.g. R & D expenditure) nor output measures (e.g. patents filed) are perfect indicators of innovative activity. Nevertheless, measurements have to be made, and data problems overcome, for empirical analysis to proceed (see Pavitt and Patel (1988)).

Fifth, there are problems of evaluation. It is hard enough for firms themselves to make sensible assessments of the private return to technological activity, and it is harder still to assess social returns. Quite apart from difficulties in gauging the (probabilities of) future returns, there is the question of what discount rate to apply to them, and in particular how to take risk into account.

Sixth, assessment of the national return from technology policy is complicated by international rivalry. For example there may be dangers of countries attempting to 'free-ride' on each others' R & D efforts, or, on the other hand, governments might compete in a zero sum game to support their 'national champions' in the hope of gaining them strategic advantages in international markets.

Easy answers, therefore, are not to be had. However, that is no excuse for agnosticism and inaction, because one fact is clear: unassisted market forces cannot be relied upon to secure an efficient allocation of resources to technological activity—market failure is pervasive (see the paper by Dasgupta in this volume). The 'invisible hand' may be tolerably good at achieving static efficiency in many circumstances, though with notable exceptions and probably with undesirable distributional consequences, but dynamic efficiency is quite another matter. A *laissez-faire* technology policy would therefore be a dangerous thing but, on the other hand, the problems facing policy design in practice are quite daunting.

The purpose of this paper is to give an overview of the economics of technology policy (see Stoneman, 1987, for a fuller account). Our focus will be on microeconomic analysis, notwithstanding the importance of technology policy for macroeconomic performance, and we shall discuss UK technology policy in particular. We begin, in section 1, with a discussion of various types of technological activity in the UK and an outline of the current pattern of R & D expenditure by government and industry, including international comparisons. Some broad 'stylized facts' will be derived from the data. Section 2 examines why unassisted market forces are unlikely to produce socially desirable rates and directions of innovative activity, and establishes the general case for government intervention. The pros and cons of various policy instruments are considered in section 3. Section 4 discusses recent debates and government policy statements on technology policy in the UK. Section 5 contains conclusions.

I. Technological activity in the UK

We have discussed above the problems associated with measuring technological activity. Of the several imperfect measures available we have most data on R & D expenditure, and this section mainly concentrates on R & D data (Pavitt and Patel (1988) consider others) although we shall make one or two comments on diffusion as well. R & D is an aggregate measure and can be disaggregated in several ways. One division is between basic, strategic, and applied research, and development, which were defined by the House of Lords Select Committee (1986, p. 13) as

'basic (pure or fundamental) research—research undertaken primarily to acquire new knowledge and with no specific applications in mind;

strategic research—research undertaken with eventual practical applications in mind even though these cannot be clearly specified;

applied research—research directed primarily towards specific practical aims or objectives;

development—systematic work drawing on existing knowledge to produce new products, processes, etc.'

R & D activity can also be characterized according to who pays for it and who carries it out. The bulk of publicly funded R & D is conducted either intramurally (within government institutions), or by universities and research councils, or by public and private industry. Most industry R & D is performed intramurally and may be funded by industry itself, by government, or from overseas. The nature of the explicit or implicit 'research contracts' associated with these relationships create particular difficulties where R & D is concerned, partly because inputs and outputs are hard to measure. That is one reason why reward is often accorded to priority of discovery, both in the scientific and technological communities—priority is easier to observe than effort. Dasgupta's paper in this volume provides a fuller discussion of these issues.

In Tables 4.1 to 4.6 below we present some data on R & D spending in the major OECD economies. Table 4.1 illustrates that UK R & D as a percentage of GDP is broadly in line with, although generally somewhat lower than, the spending of its main international competitors. More striking, however, is the decline of the UK from a position of international preeminence in 1965 to a much lower status in 1985. Moreover, given

Table 4.1. R & D as percentage of GDP 1963–1985

Country	R & D/GDP %	
	1963	1985
UK	2.2	2.3
Japan	1.4	2.6
Sweden	1.2	2.8
W. Germany	1.5	2.7
Italy	n.a.	1.1
France	n.a.	2.3
USA	3.1	2.8

Source: OECD (1984) and Cabinet Office (1988), Table 4.10.

Table 4.2. Government finance of R & D

Country	Government finance as percentage of gross expenditure on R & D 1985
Italy	51.7
France	52.9
W. Germany	36.7
Japan	19.1
Sweden	34.0
USA	50.3
UK	43.1

Source: Cabinet Office (1988), Table 4.10.

Table 4.3. Government funding of R & D 1986

Country	Defence R & D (£m)	Civil R & D (£m)	Total R&D (£m)	Defence as % of Total
Italy	229	2,465	2,695	8.5
France	1,775	3,667	5,421	32.7
W. Germany	596	4,324	4,920	12.1
Sweden	199	566	764	26.0
USA	21,159	9,320	30,479	69.4
UK	2,259	2,330	4,589	49.2

Source: Cabinet Office (1988), Table 4.8.

Table 4.4. UK government spending on R & D 1987/8 by type (percentage of totals)

	Civil	Defence	Total
Basic	36.7	—	18.2
Strategic	27.6	1.7	14.5
Applied	24.8	14.9	19.8
Development	10.9	83.5	47.5
Total	100.0	100.0	100.0

Source: Cabinet Office (1988), Table 1.23

Table 4.5. Industrial R & D in the UK (£m)

Year	R & D at current prices	R & D at 1975 prices
1986	5,673	1,883
1985	5,146	1,752
1983	4,163	1,564
1981	3,792	1,661
1978	2,324	1,566
1975	1,340	1,340
1972	830	1,418
1969	680	1,513
1968	639	1,506
1967	604	1,514
1966	580	1,504
1964	489	1,400

Source: Survey of Industrial R & D, British Business, various dates.

Table 4.6. UK industrial R & D by sector (percentage of total industrial R & D)

Industry	1975	1981	1986
Chemicals	16.9	16.3	18.3
Mech. Engineering	7.3	6.9	4.7
Electronic Engineering	21.2	32.6	34.1
Other Electrical	5.4	3.2	2.9
Motor Vehicles	6.6	4.8	6.9
Aerospace	21.7	20.1	16.9
Other Manufactures	15.8	8.8	7.7
Non Manufactures	4.8	7.4	8.4
Total	100.0	100.0	100.0

Source: as Table 4.5.

the relatively poor GDP growth performance in the UK in international terms over these last twenty years, total R & D expenditure in the UK is now below that of many other nations and this may be a more relevant statistic.

The proportion of total R & D financed from public sources is lower in the UK than in the USA, France, and Italy but is higher than in Germany and much higher than in Japan (Table 4.2). As can be seen from the data in Table 4.3, the proportion of government funded R & D that is defence related is high in the UK. This pattern is repeated in the USA and France, but in Germany and Japan only a limited amount of government funded R & D is defence related. The overall result of this pattern and level of government funding is that in the UK a high proportion of total R & D is defence related. As a proportion of total R & D approximately 22 per cent is devoted to defence in the UK, this is far greater than in Germany (4.4 per cent), France (16.5 per cent), Italy (5.1 per cent), and Japan (no accurate

figures) but less than in the USA (34 per cent). The obvious corollary of this when combined with the data on R & D spent as a proportion of GDP is that the UK devotes proportionately less of its GDP to civil R & D than do its major international competitors.

In Table 4.4 we show the composition of government spending—civil and defence—as between basic, strategic and applied research, and development. It should be noted that defence R & D is never classed as basic in the UK. These and other data illustrate that the UK Government allocates a relatively high proportion of its R & D expenditure to development, but this spending is predominantly defence related. Civil spending is directed away from development and towards basic, applied, and strategic research. Current government policy is to increase the emphasis in civil spending away from the 'near market' end.

R & D performed in UK industry recovered in the 1980s (with a hiccup in 1983) after a prolonged decline between the mid-sixties and the mid- to late seventies (see Table 4.5). The sectoral breakdown of industrial R & D in the UK (see Table 4.6) illustrates, however, that it is concentrated, with the exception of chemicals, in defence-related sectors. Further data in Cabinet Office (1988), not presented here, also illustrates certain patterns in the finance of industrial R & D. One trend is the increasing proportion of funding for UK industrial R & D that comes from overseas. This has risen secularly from 4 per cent in 1967 to 13 per cent in 1986. This finance is concentrated in the chemicals and electronics sectors. Government finance of industrial R & D rose from 29 per cent of the total spent in 1967 to peak at 33 per cent in 1972, but fell back to 23 per cent in 1985 and 1986. In particular this proportion fell from 30 per cent in 1983 to 23 per cent in 1985. The share of finance for industrial R & D in the UK provided by industry itself (i.e. 1 minus the government share) is relatively low in international terms (OECD figures not strictly comparable to those above put the UK share at 48 per cent in 1985 compared with the USA at 65 per cent, Germany 80 per cent, and Japan 100 per cent). To some degree the high contribution of government in the UK could be attributed to the high level of defence contracts placed with UK industry. However, the support for *civil* R & D in industry by the UK Government may well be quite low, although accurate data on this are not available.

The overall picture as described above can thus be summarized as a decline in the UK's share of GDP devoted to R & D relative to that in other countries and an excessive emphasis on defence. Recently there has been a rise in industrial R & D expenditure, but this expenditure has been biased towards defence. There has been an increasing reliance on overseas funds to finance industrial R & D in the UK and a decline in the government's contribution to industrial R & D. The government contribution is planned to be cut further as the government moves away from the support of near-market R & D. This is, however, occurring at a time when the private funding of industrial R & D in the UK is relatively low in international terms.

Non-R & D-based indicators of technological activity are more difficult to locate. Pavitt and Patel (1988) discuss patent data with conclusions that reinforce those above. Work on citation indices has similarly shown a decline in the status of UK science over the last twenty years. Diffusion indicators are very sparse. However, some work (e.g. Northcott *et al.*, 1985, and Nabseth and Ray, 1984), has shown that UK industry has not been particularly laggard in adopting new process technologies, but, on the other hand, a common observation on the UK economy is that it displays a very high incremental capital output ratio (i.e. for any given investment spending it achieves very little extra output). This may imply that UK industry invests in new technology but obtains, for various reasons, only limited effectiveness in its use.

In our view, taking the indicators as a whole, there is cause for concern about technological activity in the UK.

II. Why have technology policies?

There would be little point in having technology policies if unassisted market forces could be expected to lead to the efficient allocation of resources to technological activity. Unfortunately that is not the case. The purpose of this section is to explain the nature of 'market failures' in technological activity, and the next section considers policies to help remedy them.

Technological change is concerned with the production of new information. Information is unlike ordinary commodities (Arrow 1962, and Dasgupta, this volume). Once discovered, a piece of information can usually be made widely available at very little (social) cost. This is an extreme kind of scale economy, it costs virtually no more to produce a given piece of information many times over once the first unit has been produced. Other things being equal it is generally beneficial from the social point of view for information to be widely disseminated. For example, in commercial situations, it allows firms to compete more intensively and resulting benefits are passed on to the consuming public. From the private viewpoint of the innovating firm,

however, dissemination of that information is likely to be very costly. Indeed, the private value of information tends to diminish the more widely it is known. The more that other firms benefit from, or 'free ride' on, the R & D efforts of the first firm, the less incentive is there to engage in R & D activity in the first place. This conflict between the public interest in dissemination and the private interest in exercising exclusive property rights over information—and the tension between static and dynamic efficiency that results—is known as the *appropriability problem*. It is central to the economics of technology policy.

Even where there is perfect appropriability, e.g. watertight and long-lived patents, there are often reasons to expect the private reward from technological activity to be less than the social benefit. For example, a monopolist or oligopolist will have less incentive to cut unit costs than would a benign public enterprise manager setting price equal to marginal cost, because the private firm supplies fewer units of output on which to achieve unit cost savings. (Even in reasonably competitive settings, price typically exceeds marginal cost in R & D intensive industries because a considerable mark-up is needed to recoup R & D expenditures. This is another source of allocative inefficiency.) Furthermore, successful R & D is generally of net benefit to consumers over and above the gain in profits to the innovator. This positive 'externality' to consumers will not be part of private calculations of the marginal benefit of R & D, and is hence another reason why its provision may be socially suboptimal. Mansfield (1977) has actually provided some estimates of the difference between social and private rates of return. Yet another reason is that private discount rates may exceed social discount rates, a point that we shall return to later.

Externalities between firms must also be considered. If there are 'spillovers', so that firm B benefits from the technological activities undertaken by firm A (e.g. because it learns or can partly imitate) then each firm will hold back its technological efforts to some extent, and hope to benefit from the efforts of others. This is the free-rider problem mentioned above.

However, although each firm may have less incentive than socially desirable to engage in technological activity, it is possible that there will be too many firms engaging in such activity. This is the potential problem of *duplication* of, for example, research efforts. It is straightforward to show analytically (see, e.g. Dasgupta and Stiglitz, 1980) that industry R & D expenditure might exceed the socially desirably level of R & D, with too many firms each individually doing too little. In that case there is too much R & D input and too little R & D output, a double inefficiency.

Similarly, in some cases there may be a 'common pool' problem in which the first-past-the-post-takes-all nature of the race to invent induces excessive speed in the process. It is natural to think of policies to promote co-operative R & D in these contexts (see the next section). On the other hand, rivalry in R & D can have advantages. First, it is desirable when independent, as opposed to completely parallel, research strategies are being pursued. Then there is advantage in diversity (though it is questionable whether the market will produce the right type of diversity, see Dasgupta and Maskin, 1987). Second, as noted before, competition between researchers, whether they are in academic or commercial environments, allows reward to be based on priority of discovery. With research inputs and outputs being hard to observe, and the relation between them being unknown, it is difficult to provide incentives for effort in the absence of some rivalry.

As discussed above, technological activity is taking place in an environment of incomplete information and uncertainty. In view of the difficulties of measuring R & D inputs and prospective returns, R & D funding is beset with acute problems of asymmetric information, and the market for R & D finance is likely to be highly imperfect. The problems include ones of adverse selection, moral hazard, performance monitoring, and information flows. The nature of financial institutions can influence how well such problems are overcome, and it has been argued that financing via long-term relationships with banks may be more effective than stock-market financing due to closer monitoring arrangements and better information flows (see Mayer, 1987). Moreover, given asymmetric information, managers anxious to satisfy stock-market opinion may divert resources towards visible signals of corporate health (e.g. high dividends) and away from less tangible activities (e.g. R & D). Such imperfections in the capital market reduce opportunities for risk-shifting, and risk-aversion may become a dominant influence in R & D investment decisions. Problems of this kind are part of what is described as excessive 'short-termism' in financial markets. It is worth noting that only recently has it become a convention in the UK for publicly quoted companies to detail their R & D spending in Annual Reports. Without such information it is difficult to see how capital markets could optimally allocate resources for technological activity across alternative uses. Pavitt and Patel (1988) lay considerable emphasis on the shortcomings of the market for R & D finance in the UK.

Thus there are several reasons— including externalities, scale economies, market power, attitudes to risk, and information asymmetries—to expect that market forces will not result in desirable levels of technological activity and dynamic efficiency if left to themselves. Policy intervention is likely to be necessary to remedy some of these defects. Moreover, there may be other reasons that motivate technology policies by national governments in the context of international competition (see Lyons, 1987 and Yarrow, 1985 for surveys). For example, it is often claimed that Japanese technology policies, in conjunction with trade policies, have been designed to put Japanese firms at a strategic advantage over their international competitors in world markets. It can indeed be shown analytically that a country may have a unilateral incentive to subsidize the technological efforts of its domestic firm or firms in order to shift the 'equilibrium' of oligopolistic international markets to expand their market share and profits. Strategic industrial and trade policies may be used similarly to attempt to influence entry and exit decisions. Competition in the civil aircraft industry between the European Airbus and Boeing and McDonnell-Douglas is often cited as an example of this. Thus, not only are unassisted market forces unlikely to lead to levels and directions of innovative activity that are in the general interest, but governments may also seek to influence the position of their national firms in world markets. This discussion is already complex enough. It is now time to consider what technology policies can do to help.

III. Policy instruments

Many branches of government policy have an influence —actual or potential—on R & D activity. We saw in the last section that externalities between firms, and between firms and consumers, are the principal source of market failure in technological activity, and we highlighted in particular the problem of appropriability. There are four general approaches to externality problems in economics: private property rights, public provision, subsidies/taxes, and co-operation. All four are used in technology policy.

1. The patent system

The patent system and related laws are designed to give discoverers property rights over their new information, at least for a period of years. The advantages of such systems are obvious, they promote dynamic efficiency by providing incentives for R & D effort. The disadvantages are twofold. First, patents do not always succeed in ensuring appropriability of rewards. Other firms may learn a great deal from the filing of a patent, and may be able to innovate by 'inventing around' it. Indeed, it is said that firms sometimes refrain from patenting because of the loss of secrecy that it entails. In addition, there are considerable enforcement costs. Hausman and Mackie-Mason (1988) discuss many of the issues that arise, in the context of international competition. In short patents do not invariably contain spillovers of information to rival firms.

The second difficulty is that, even where patents give appropriability, they do so at a cost. If a patent gives the private reward of market power, then it brings with it the social cost of allocative, and possibly also productive, inefficiency. This is of course the trade-off between static and dynamic efficiency. Furthermore, the competition for that reward may encourage inefficient duplication of effort, also as discussed above. Thus while the enforcement of patents and other intellectual property rights is an important element of overall technology policy, it is usually a very imperfect system even where it is practicable.

2. Public provision

At the other extreme from private property rights lies the public provision of R & D through institutions such as government research labs, research councils, and universities. Public provision overcomes free-rider problems in R & D, avoids competitive duplication of effort, and allows researchers to be motivated other than by the prospective market power conveyed by patents. (The difference in reward schemes between scientists and technologists was discussed above.) However, the difficulties of public provision include the relative lack of commercial information and incentive that firms in industry are more likely to possess. For these reasons, public R & D activity is more appropriate to basic research than near-market research.

3. R & D subsidies

Subsidies to R & D are a way of attempting to improve the terms of the trade-off between static and dynamic efficiency that is at the heart of the appropriability problem. In principle a combination of R & D subsidies and relatively *high* spillovers between firms could promote both kinds of efficiency (Spence, 1984). Innovative efforts would be encouraged by the subsidies, and spillovers would allow the competitive and widespread application of improved technology. The main

problem, however, is knowing the appropriate rate and direction of subsidy. Which activities should be subsidized? Should particular firms be singled out for support, or should subsidies be generally available (e.g. via favourable tax treatment of R & D expenditure)? How large should subsidies be? These key questions are enormously difficult to answer. The costs and benefits of R & D are hard enough to measure *ex post*, let alone *ex ante*. And the public authorities who give subsidies are invariably less well-informed about the costs and benefits than those who seek them. (A recent institutional innovation in the UK is designed to overcome this problem, the Centre for the Exploitation of Science and Technology (CEST) has been charged with the formidably difficult task of reporting on those areas of Science and Technology in which the UK should specialize.) In addition, of course, there is the cost of subsidies to public funds. Properly speaking, that cost is the marginal distortion elsewhere in the economy arising from the extra taxation needed to pay for the subsidies. The question of subsidies will be pursued further in the policy discussion in the next section.

4. Co-operative R & D

Like all the other policies considered here, co-operative R & D—in the form of joint ventures or mergers in high technology industries—has pros and cons (see Dasgupta, this volume and Baumol and Ordover, 1988). It 'internalizes' the externalities between firms, and can in principle overcome both free-rider problems and duplication problems in R & D, while also being consistent with product market competition in the case of research joint ventures. However, in practice there is the obvious danger that collaboration in R & D will lead to anticompetitive collaboration in the product market. That necessarily happens in the case of merger (and this was a key issue in the proposed merger between GEC and Plessey, which was stopped on competition grounds). (See Monopolies and Mergers Commission, 1986.)

In addition, there is an equally serious problem when R & D collaboration does not lead to product market collaboration. A research joint venture can greatly diminish the incentive to innovate. For example, if all firms in a competitive industry succeeded in achieving a common cost reduction, they would not enhance their profits much by introducing the same because prices would fall in line with costs; consumers, and not the innovating firms, would be the main beneficiaries from innovation. This point needs to be modified if only a subset of firms in the industry are engaged in

R & D co-operation, but it serves to highlight an important consideration. Market failure in R & D occurs not only because of externalities between firms, but also because of externalities between firms and consumers. This is another awkward tension between the desire to promote innovation and consumer benefit, which requires some competitive stimulus between firms, and the desire to avoid wasteful duplication.

5. Other policy instruments

Many other policies have important effects on technological performance, including the following.

Risk-Sharing: In the absence of perfect markets for shifting risk the Government may intervene as a risk bearer. Also in a world where the Government may be less risk averse than the private sector, the carrying of risk by government is an appropriate policy. In the UK such arguments have been used to support government involvement in for example, Aerospace R & D, via Launch Aid. It is clear, however, that risk carrying policies are subject to problems of adverse selection and moral hazard that makes their design difficult. It should also be made clear that if the risk argument is used to justify government funding of R & D then such policies are bound, on occasion, to involve failures and losses.

Diffusion Policies: We have stressed that diffusion is the stage when new technology affects economic activity and when the benefits arise. It is clear, however, that diffusion policy is the poor relation in technology policy. What diffusion policies there are tend to be of two types—information provision or dissemination policies, and subsidy policies. Information dissemination policies, programmes to promote the awareness of new technologies, are particularly important for diffusion. Increasing returns to scale in information—the one-off cost of information collection and the low marginal cost of its transmission—make centralized policies very appropriate in this context. Subsidy policies are designed to extend the use of or speed the adoption of particular new technologies (past examples include computers, fibre optics, and robotics) by reducing the post subsidy cost of acquisition. Research in this area (see Stoneman, 1987), has explored the welfare consequences of subsidizing the use of new technology in this way. By making comparison with the welfare optimal diffusion path, it is argued that, depending on the price expectations of potential users of the new technology and the market structure of the industry supplying the new technology, the actual diffusion path may be too fast or too slow from a welfare point of view. Thus only in a particular circumstance is a subsidy desirable. Moreover, it is also argued that, with a monopolist supplier of new technology, some of the effects of the subsidy will be offset by compensatory changes in the prices set by the monopolist. Thus the need for and the effectiveness of a subsidy policy is not a simple issue.

Competition Policy: The discussion above on co-operative R & D has indicated the role of competition policy, especially policy on mergers and agreements between firms. Mergers in high technology industries may permit the realization of scale economies and the pooling of incentives in R & D, and avoid duplication of efforts. But, as we have argued above, competition in R & D can have major beneficial consequences. Moreover, even where R & D collaboration is desirable, it should ideally be achieved without undermining product market competition (proper account being taken of international competition) even in high-technology industries. This is consistent with a permissive attitude to many types of R & D agreement in restrictive trade practices policy, provided that such agreements do not lead to product market competition being undermined, and do not blunt the incentive to innovate (see above). R & D agreements are most likely to be beneficial when they involve a subset of firms in the industry. A much fuller account of these and other competition issues is given by Baumol and Ordover (1988).

Trade Policy: We discussed above how R & D policies, e.g. subsidies to R & D, can be used to affect the positions of domestic firms in world markets, including their international rivals. Conversely, trade policies can be used as instruments of technology policy. For example, where there are important learning effects, i.e. technological capability depends on the cumulative output of a firm or industry, measures such as export subsidies or protection from import competition can enhance the output, and hence technological performance of domestic firm(s), and put them at an advantage over foreign rivals (see, for example, Krugman, 1984). This strategy, protection to achieve learning effects followed by aggressive international competition, has sometimes been attributed to the Japanese, for example in the market for TV apparatus. Hausman and MacKie-Mason (1988) examine another aspect of the relationship between R & D and international trade policy—the enforcement of intellectual property rights against foreign competitors, and the emphasis placed in the USA on the protection of industries as against the enforcement of property rights.

Education and Training Policy: Perhaps the most important 'input' to technological activity is trained personnel. An adequate resource of appropriately trained 'human capital' is therefore a prerequisite for successful technology policies. If, for example, there is a restricted supply of scientists and technologists, then the main effect of R & D subsidies could be to drive up their salaries rather than lead to much greater R & D output. (The outcome depends on the elasticity of substitution between labour and other inputs in R & D activity, as well as the elasticity of supply of trained personnel, see Dixit and Grossman, 1986.)

Procurement Policies: These can be oriented towards technological objectives as ways of hidden protectionism (see above), R & D finance, or information dissemination via demonstration effects. However, the costs of deflecting procurement policy from the straightforward objective of cost minimization can be high, albeit hidden from view, and it may often be dominated by other more direct policy instruments.

Defence Policies: Similar comments apply here. Although the technological 'spin-offs' from military projects can be considerable, there is a danger that they will be exaggerated, especially given the large vested interests typically involved. Moreover, the nature of military projects is sometimes such that the technological information gained cannot be made generally available. Another influence of defence policy on civil R & D concerns the supply of scientists and technologists. Depending on the size and flexibility of that supply, defence policy can have undesirable crowding-out effects on the civil sector. If, as seems plausible, the salaries of the individuals involved do not fully reflect their 'shadow values', i.e. potential value added of their contributions elsewhere, then the cost of defence policy to civil R & D is understated by the accounting cost of defence R & D. Any additional cost should be set against the potential value of spin-offs from that R & D.

Policy on Standards and Compatibility: The issue of standards and compatibility arises in many high-technology industries, including telecommunications and electronic data processing. Software and hardware must be able to work together, and complementary pieces of apparatus (e.g. disk drive and processor) must be readily connectable. Standardization, for example of telecommunications protocols, is desirable for two reasons. By minimizing consumer switching costs, it breaks down market segmentation and enhances competition. Second, it allows the full exploitation of scale economies. On the other hand, standardization can have costs. Co-ordination on a suboptimal standard (e.g. the QWERTY typewriter keyboard) has obvious

costs and may be virtually irreversible given the enormous difficulty of changing standards. Moreover, a standard may itself be an object of innovation. The requirement of a given standard could stifle the introduction of new and better standards. There is no guarantee that the market will produce a desirable outcome regarding standards. (Typically there are multiple market equilibria anyway.) The Government can intervene effectively, and at a relatively low direct cost, by laying down requirements on standards. Its ability to influence events is greatest when a new technology is in its infancy, but that is when it is least informed. No general maxims for intervention can be laid down, but standards and compatibility are issues for technology and competition policies that cannot be ignored.

This list of policies could easily be extended, but we shall stop here. To summarize, we have shown how the four direct approaches to externality problems in R & D— intellectual property rights, public provision, subsidies, and co-operation—all have disadvantages as well as advantages. In particular, we hope to have indicated where and why one form of intervention has advantages over another. Several other branches of policy with a bearing on R & D performance have also been discussed. It should, however, be noted that although very thin, the literature on the evaluation of technology policies does not suggest that the use of the various policy instruments in the past has met with particular success. On this point we now turn to consider the recent debates on how, and to what extent, the instruments of technology policy should be used, with particular reference to the UK.

IV. UK technology policy

It is widely believed that the UK's technological performance in the post-war period has fallen short of that of most other industrialized countries, and that this is an important factor in explaining the UK's relatively poor record of economic growth. While it is impossible to draw conclusions from aggregate data the statistical evidence reviewed in section 1 above does suggest a number of problems in the UK, the prime one being the continuing low level of civil R & D, but the overall failure of UK R & D to match the growth of R & D elsewhere and the small share of private finance in industrial R & D are symptomatic of related problems.

It would be natural to consider that the poor R & D performance in the UK is related to the market failures detailed above. However, when basing judgements on international comparisons this raises a problem, for surely those failures also apply in other economies. Differences in the technological performance of economies thus cannot be attributed to the market failures *per se* but must be traced back to the institutional and environmental factors that underlie market conditions. Pursuing this line of argument the poor UK performance could be attributed to several factors, including (a) the economic structure, for example, the UK economy is very different from the US economy in terms of size and external trade relations ('1992' may have important consequences for the UK and EC economies in this regard), (b) entrepreneurial attitudes, e.g. attitudes to risk taking or 'animal spirits' and the nature of the labour market, (c) UK institutions, especially financial institutions that may be excessively short-termist, and (d) UK government policies. It is not our intention here to try to separate out the role of these several different factors in explaining the poor UK performance. Rather we intend to explore here the reaction of the UK government to the problem and the nature of the technology policy that it is currently pursuing.

A useful starting-point is to consider the classification of technology policies as presented by Ergas (1987). He distinguishes between:

(i) 'mission-orientated' countries (UK, US, France) in which science and high technology is applied to big problems (e.g. the space programme, Concorde, and especially defence projects) in the search for international strategic leadership;
(ii) diffusion-orientated countries (e.g. Germany, Switzerland, Sweden) whose policies aim to promote a capacity for adjustment to technological change throughout the industrial structure by the provision of R & D-related public goods, notably in education, product standardization, and co-operative research;
(iii) Japan, where vigorous policies to promote national technological goals have been pursued in tandem with diffusion-oriented policies.

This character of UK policy with its orientation towards high technology and defence is seen by many as the basis of the problem in the UK, the argument often being pursued by comparison with the success of Japan with its much more broadly based policy of intervention. However, the pattern of publicly funded R & D as a whole in the UK is open to question. One can enquire into (a) the level of government R & D spending, (b) its distribution between basic research, applied research and development, (c) its distribution between civil and military, (d) its distribution across industrial sectors and technological opportunities, and (e) its division between in-house and external research. Some information on these issues was presented in section 1 above. In addition, there are questions about policy on research and training in higher education, which are vital to the long-run availability of scientists and technologists. Although it would be possible to discuss in great detail these issues and their relationships to the institutional structure of UK technology policy, we shall approach here what is at one and the same time both a more general and a more specific question. We will address the philosophy that conditions the policy rather than the policies *per se*, and within this we concentrate upon how that philosophy impacts upon government support for private sector industrial R & D.

The philosophy behind current UK government policy can be neatly illustrated by comparing the attitudes of the House of Lords Select Committee on Science and Technology (1986) with the government attitudes as detailed in two policy statements (Department of Trade and Industry,1988 and HM Government, 1987). In its report on *Civil Research and Development* the House of Lords Select Committee observed 'the gravity of the United Kingdom's prospects in R & D' (p. 66), argued that UK R & D was badly underfunded, and expressed the need for a recognized policy for the public support of R & D. On industrial R & D, the Lords Committee recommended, among other things:

- that more attention, including some public support, be given to the development phase in R & D (para. 7.21);
- that the total amount of DTI support for industrial R & D be increased (7.23);
- that tax incentives for R & D in the UK should be examined (7.24);
- that public purchasing be used more to stimulate R & D in the private sector (7.26);
- that the Government take steps to increase awareness and knowledge of R & D results from overseas (7.27);
- that the provision of information about public and private R & D be greatly improved (7.25 and 7.28); and
- that the Government should do more to meet the R & D needs of small firms (7.29).

The Committee also recommended that a process should be introduced for funding strategic research of particular significance to the country's economic future. It also made recommendations about the research councils and higher education, the civil implications of defence R & D, and administrative structures.

The Government responded to the Lords Committee in a White Paper, *Civil Research and Development* (HM Government, 1987). The conclusions of a review of the DTI's role in technology policy were presented in a White Paper, *DTI—the Department for Enterprise* (Department of Trade and Industry, 1988, chapter 8). In the former document, the Government stated its view that 'the primary problem . . . is the low level of industry's investment in R & D' (para. 4). As to remedying that low level of investment, the Government pointed to the improved economic climate, especially the recovery in corporate profitability, and said that firms were now better placed to invest in R & D than in the past. As to the Government's role, the 1987 White Paper (para. 24) states:

Industry must take the initiative for its R & D programmes. This requires commercial decisions reflecting market forces. Government support is only considered where a worthwhile and viable project is at risk through failure of the market mechanism.

The 1987 White Paper agreed with a number of recommendations of the Lords Committee, and said that its policies (e.g. on helping R & D in small firms) were already in line with them. However, the idea of tax incentives for R & D was rejected, mainly on grounds of cost effectiveness (for a survey of the evidence see Inland Revenue, 1987), and no comment was made on the proposal to increase substantially DTI support for industrial R & D (it is in fact due to decrease through to 1991 in real terms).

The 1988 White Paper announced some changes in the direction, rather than the scale, of DTI support for innovation. The scheme for innovation grant assistance to individual companies is to be ended, as are programmes of support for the microelectronics industry, software products, and fibreoptics. A general move away from 'near-market' R & D support is proposed. Instead, greater emphasis is to be given to collaborative R & D programmes and technology transfer. International collaboration within Europe is highlighted, including programmes such as ESPRIT, RACE, and EUREKA. Research collaboration between industry and institutions of higher education is also emphasized (by, for example, the LINK project). The measures on technology transfer are aimed at improving the transfer of scientific capability into commercial application, which is seen as one of the sources of the UK's weakness in industrial innovation.

Overall, the crux of the Government's strategy is to withdraw from near-market decisions and to try to make the market work better by facilitating collaboration and information provision. The possibility of market failure in R & D is recognized, but seems to be regarded as the exception rather than the rule. Thus: 'There may be exceptional cases of single company projects which offer significant national benefits but which would not be undertaken without financial assistance from the Government' (para. 8.28). As in other areas of economic policy, the Government sees its role primarily as one of creating an appropriate climate, and leaving firms to take the initiative.

However, as was argued in section 2, market failure in R & D is the rule rather than the exception. A number of the Government's policy proposals, for example on dissemination, are welcome so far as they go, but it is partly an act of faith to suppose that the poor record of investment in R & D by UK firms will be radically altered by those proposals (for example, Pavitt and Patel (1988) argue that it is the share of profits devoted to R & D that is the problem in the UK, not total profitability; an improvement in the latter is not the same as an improvement in the former). There is some sense of frustration in the Government's attitude to R & D, and a possible tension between the view that R & D investment decisions should be entirely up to participants in the market, and the evident belief that they continue to underinvest. Better informed and more collaborative *laissez-faire* may work somewhat better than before, but it is far from clear that the Government's response is adequate to the task.

In international terms, as well as in terms of economic theory, one might argue that the UK government with its *laissez-faire* philosophy is somewhat out of step. To give just a few examples, the Australian Government has recently introduced large-scale tax incentives to R & D, the Japanese have for many years helped the development of the technological base of their industries, and the involvement of the French Government in certain civilian high-technology products (e.g. in rail transport and telecommunications) is well known.

V. Conclusions

In this assessment we have examined both the theory and practice of technology policy. It has been argued on theoretical grounds that for numerous reasons one should not expect a free market economy to allocate a socially optimal amount of resources to technological advance and as such there is a role for government to play in correcting such market failures. We have illustrated that, in international terms, the technological performance of the UK economy is not impressive and we have explored the policy stance of the UK government in reaction to this. We find that the Government's relatively *laissez-faire* attitude towards civil R & D is seriously open to question. Theoretical analysis reveals that market failure in R & D is likely to be the norm rather than the exception. The existing institutional and policy framework in the UK is not in practice delivering a technological performance that compares well with that achieved elsewhere, and governments in competitor nations are generally pursuing more active policies. The concerns expressed by the House of Lords Select Committee on Science and Technology appear to be well-founded, and the government's response involves a greater degree of faith in unassisted market forces than we would be prepared to make.

References

Arrow, K. (1962), 'Economic Welfare and the Allocation of Resources for Inventions', in Nelson, R. R. (ed.), *The Rate and Direction of Inventive Activity*, Princeton, Princeton University Press.

Baumol, W., and Ordover, J. (1988), 'Antitrust Policy and High-Technology Industries', *Oxford Review of Economic Policy*, Vol. 4, No. 4, 13–34.

Cabinet Office (1988), *Annual Review of Government Funded Research and Development*, London, HMSO.

Dasgupta, P., and David, P. (1986), 'Information Disclosure and the Economics of Science and Technology', in Feiwel, G. (ed.), *Arrow and the Foundations of the Theory of Economic Policy*, London, Macmillan.

Dasgupta, P., and Maskin, E. (1987), 'The Simple Economics of Research Portfolios', *Economic Journal*, **97**, 581–95.

—— and Stiglitz, J. (1980), 'Industrial Structure and the Nature of Innovative Activity', *Economic Journal*, **90**, 266–93.

—— and Stoneman, P. (eds.) (1987), *Economic Policy and Technological Performance*, Cambridge, Cambridge University Press.

Department of Trade and Industry (1988), *DTI—the department for enterprise*, Cmnd. 278, London, HMSO.

Dixit, A., and Grossman, G. (1986), 'Targeted Export Promotion with Several Oligopolistic Industries', *Journal of International Economics*, **21**, 233–49.

Ergas, H. (1987), 'The Importance of Technology Policy' in Dasgupta, P., and Stoneman, P. (eds.), op. cit.

Hausman, J., and MacKie-Mason, J. (1988), 'Innovation and International Trade Policy: Some Lessons from the US', *Oxford Review of Economic Policy*, Vol. 4, No. 4, 56–72.

HM Government (1987), *Civil Research and Development*, Cmnd. 185, London, HMSO.

House of Lords Select Committee on Science and Technology (1986), *Civil Research and Development*, HL 20 London, HMSO.

Inland Revenue (1987), *Fiscal Incentives for R & D Spending*, London, HM Treasury.

Krugman, P. (1984), 'Import Protection as Export Promotion: International Competition in the Presence of Oligopoly and Economies of Scale', in Kierzkowski, H. (ed.), *Monopolistic Competition and International Trade*, Oxford, Oxford University Press.

Lyons, B. (1987), 'International Trade and Technology Policy', in Dasgupta, P., and Stoneman, P. (eds.), op. cit.

Mansfield, E. (1977), *The Production and Application of New Industrial Technology*, New York, Norton.

Mayer, C. (1987), 'The Assessment: Financial Systems and Corporate Investment', *Oxford Review of Economic Policy*, Vol. 3, No. 4, i–xvi.

Monopolies and Mergers Commission (1986), *The General Electric Company plc and Plessey plc—A Report on the Proposed Merger*, Cmnd. 9867, London, HMSO.

Nabseth, L., and Ray, G. (1984), *The Diffusion of New Industrial Processes: An International Study*, London, Cambridge University Press.

Northcott, J. *et al.* (1985), *Microelectronics in Industry*, London, Policy Studies Institute.

Organization for Economic Co-operation and Development (1984), *OECD Science and Technology Indicators*, Paris, OECD.

Pavitt, K., and Patel, P. (1988), 'The International Distribution and Determinants of Technological Activities', *Oxford Review of Economic Policy*, Vol. 4, No. 4, 35–55.

Spence, M. (1984), 'Cost Reduction, Competition and Industry Performance', *Econometrica*, **52**, 101–21.

Stoneman, P. (1987), *The Economic Analysis of Technology Policy*, Oxford, Oxford University Press.

Yarrow, G. (1985), 'Strategic Issues in Industrial Policy', *Oxford Review of Economic Policy*, Vol. 1, No. 3, 95–109.

5

The welfare economics of knowledge production

PARTHA DASGUPTA[1]

University of Cambridge

I. Introduction

Carl Christian von Weizsäcker begins his excellent book on entry barriers by classifying economic activity into three classes, or levels as he calls them: the exchange of goods, the production of material commodities, and the creation of knowledge. (See von Weizsäcker, 1980.) He is prompted into developing this classification, rather than some other, because these three levels are on the whole easy to distinguish, and because they are in an order of increasing distance from the consumption of material goods and services. Von Weizsäcker in fact proceeds to demonstrate in his book that this distance has a marked influence on the organization of the economic activity in question.

Von Weizsäcker's classification is time honoured. But until recently much of the focus of analytical economics had been on the first two levels: those of exchange and production of material goods and services. The analytical economics of knowledge had been on the whole an impoverished sibling. All this has changed over the past decade or so, and the microeconomic analysis of technological change is today an active field of research. But as in all other types of enquiry it would appear rapidly to have acquired an internal history. A number of the early papers in the field (e.g. Kamien and Schwartz, 1978; Levin, 1978; Loury, 1979; Dasgupta and Stiglitz, 1980*a,b*) analysed the characteristics of

strategic behaviour on the part of profit-maximizing firms when they compete not only in the production of goods and services, but also in the development of new products and new ways of manufacturing old products; what one would want to call technological competition. Now, for reasons that are well understood today, the theory of perfect competition is of no use here.[2] Even if technological competition were fierce, the resulting industrial structure would be oligopolistic, as the recent literature on these matters has made clear. Moreover, in order to understand the structure of industries we must trace back to the possibilities facing inventors and developers, to their underlying motivation, and to the background incentive structure. The recent literature on the microeconomics of technological change has clarified a number of these issues. Nevertheless, it is unfortunate that the literature has been dominated by matters concerning patent races, at the expense of pretty much all else.

In this essay I want to redress the balance, even if only by a tiny bit, and talk of other matters. Specifically, I want to study the sorts of social institutions which can, at least in principle, sustain an efficient level of inventive and innovative activity. Plainly, the characteristics of such institutions will depend upon the nature of the produced commodity in question, namely knowledge. It is best then to start with that.

First published in *Oxford Review of Economic Policy*, vol. 4, no. 4 (1988).

[1] Over the years I have gained much from discussions on the matters covered in this essay with Paul David, Eric Maskin, and Joseph Stiglitz, with each of whom I have collaborated on several occasions. The material in Section II is based largely on Dasgupta and David (1988), which

also develops a thesis concerning the historical origins of science and technology as social institutions. In writing this essay I have also benefited greatly from the instructions that John Vickers has given me.

[2] See Schumpeter (1976) for an early elaboration of this viewpoint.

II. Knowledge-producing institutions: an argument by design

Knowledge is not a homogeneous commodity. There are different kinds of knowledge and no obvious natural units in which they can be measured. Indeed, each piece of knowledge is a separate commodity. It is indivisible, in the sense that once a certain piece of knowledge has been acquired there is no value to acquiring it again: the wheel does not need to be invented twice. The same piece of information can be used over and over again, at no cost (Marx, 1970; Arrow, 1962). For my purpose here it does not matter whether we think that certain kinds of knowledge possess intrinsic worth in the Aristotelian sense, or whether we value knowledge solely in functional terms.[3] What is of critical importance is that knowledge, and more specifically information, can be jointly consumed and used by as many as care to. Thus, if one person gives another person a piece of information this does not reduce the amount of information held by the first possessor, although of course the benefit to each typically will depend upon whether and in what manner the other makes use of this piece of knowledge. In short, knowledge has the hallmark of a public good, a durable public good.

In what follows I shall for simplicity of exposition assume that the cost of transmitting knowledge is negligible when compared to its production cost. This is not as wild an assumption as it might appear at first blush, especially today, because transmission costs are to be distinguished from the costs incurred in educating people to interpret the knowledge and to make use of it. This latter is what one would call the cost of education, of learning, of absorption, of processing and so forth. Plainly, the greater the number of people who can make use of transmitted knowledge the greater is the social value of that knowledge.[4] Plainly also, not all knowledge can be communicated, especially problem-solving skills, more generally knowledge that is acquired through practice on the part of the researcher.

I am not considering this kind of knowledge here, for they are embodied in the researcher. We would call such knowledge the researcher's skill, or acquired ability. Models of learning (by doing) with incomplete spillover capture this kind of person-specific knowledge. (See Dasgupta and Stiglitz, 1988.)

Given this, one seeks to identify resource allocation mechanisms, more grandly socio-economic institutions, which can *in principle* produce and allocate knowledge in an efficient manner. The qualification should be noted. As in all theories of institutional design, I am here interested in a thought-experiment. So I assume that it is possible costlessly to design and establish an entire socio-economic institution, supporting it with a background of attendant rules, norms, rights, and backing them with the force of the law. As it happens, modern resource-allocation theory suggests that there are three possible institutions. As it also happens, there are analogues of each in the world as we know it. I shall elaborate upon them in turn.

1. The Samuelsonian contrivance

The first consists in the government engaging itself directly in the production of knowledge, allowing free use of it (recall that transmission costs are assumed negligible) and financing the production cost from general taxation. This was at the heart of Professor Samuelson's classic analysis of the efficient production and allocation of public goods (Samuelson, 1954).[5] Government research and development (R & D) laboratories which publicly disclose their findings, such as for example agricultural research establishments, are an approximation of such an arrangement. It is as well to note that the volume of public expenditure for the production of knowledge and the allocation of this expenditure for different kinds of knowledge are in this institutional set-up public decisions.

2. Pigovian public finance

The second resource-allocation mechanism which in principle can produce knowledge in an efficient manner is one where production is undertaken by private agents, who in turn are subsidized for their effort by the public purse. Thus, the subsidies are financed by general taxation. A crucial feature of this arrangement

---

[3] In the context of education policy such a distinction matters greatly, and the education literature has consistently displayed a tension between these two aspects, most especially in debates over the choice of course curricula. This tension has on occasion been diffused, as in the writings of John Dewey, who in his philosophy tried to fuse the two by appealing to a sort of Aristotelian view of the development of a person. Nevertheless, the tension is a real one. But for the most part this distinction does not affect the arguments in this essay.

[4] Throughout, I am thinking of knowledge as a 'good', unlike pollution. Thus I am ignoring the kinds of knowledge that are used for purposes of waging war. This would involve a different set of considerations regarding public policy.

[5] The social cost-benefit rule, it will be recalled, is the equality of the marginal rate of transformation between the public good and a numeraire private good and the *sum* of the private marginal rates of indifferent substitution between these two goods.

is that private producers are denied exclusive rights to the knowledge they produce. Once knowledge is produced under this arrangement it is freely available to all. This is the Pigovian solution to the problem posed by public goods, and more generally, by externalities (see Pigou, 1932; Baumol and Oates, 1975; Dasgupta and Heal, 1979). In albeit imperfect forms this arrangement characterizes much research in public entities, such as state-funded universities, where a good deal of the research output is prohibited from being patented, and where salaries and promotions—the production subsidies—are paid out of public funds.

These two resource allocation mechanisms resemble one another greatly, but there are important differences, at least in theory. I am thinking of the Pigovian solution as a decentralized mechanism, one where production decisions are made by private agents, and whose work is subsidized by the government. (The subsidies are the shadow costs of production.) And I am characterizing the Samuelsonian solution as a command mode of planning: the decision of what to produce and how much to produce is made by the government. Of course, where the second fundamental theorem of welfare economics holds there is no serious difference in the implementability of these two resource allocation mechanisms. Nevertheless, they represent different methods of planning.

3. The Lindahl market mechanism

Each of these institutions reflects a non-market mechanism for resource allocation. The third and final institution to consider is therefore the market mechanism itself. Admittedly, we are discussing the production of a public good, a commodity which can be consumed jointly. But this does not mean that private appropriation of benefits is necessarily impossible. For some types of knowledge, what one might call the output of basic research (see Section III), private appropriation may prove difficult. For other types it may to a large extent be possible. I want to think now of those sorts of knowledge to which private ownership can be legally assigned and whose ownership can be enforced. By ownership I mean the right to control the use of the public good. Suppose then that society grants producers of new knowledge property rights to discoveries and inventions, and allows them to engage in trade should they wish to, via licensing or outright sale. In the world as we know it, patents, trademarks, and copyrights are an embodiment of such ownership.

Clearly, the value of a given piece of knowledge is different for different people. Therefore, if production under the market mechanism is to be efficient the owner must set different prices for different buyers, since efficiency demands that the marginal cost of production of this knowledge equals the sum of the fees charged by the producer to all buyers. At an efficient market equilibrium the quantity demanded by each buyer equals the total amount which is produced and is on offer. This was Lindahl's proposal for the supply of public goods; to establish a competitive market mechanism for it. (See Musgrave and Peacock, 1968.)

One problem with the suggestion, as Arrow (1971) noted, is this. Since Lindahl prices are 'named' prices, one for each buyer, each of the Lindahl markets for a given piece of knowledge is thin, essentially a bilateral monopoly. This is scarcely a propitious environment for the emergence of efficiency prices. Furthermore, the enforcement of property rights is difficult, particularly on the output of fundamental research, for the findings of such research have possible applications in wide varieties of fields, and it can be exceptionally difficult to detect a violation of property rights. In other words, the economic benefits of knowledge are often difficult to appropriate privately, and therefore to market efficiently. This is so even when patent and copyright protection gives one transferable legal rights to exclude others from using that knowledge. Matters are easier in the case of more narrowly restricted knowledge of new technical processes and practical devices. This partly explains why it is a commonplace today to see A paying B a licence fee for using B's patent on the manufacture of a new product, or on a new process for manufacturing an old product.[6]

There is in fact an additional difficulty in applying Lindahl's theory of public goods directly to the case of knowledge. As we noted earlier each piece of knowledge is a distinct entity. Producing the same piece of knowledge more than once is of no use.[7] Different pieces of knowledge differ from one another in their detailed characteristics, and each piece can be thought of as a unit of the commodity with that characteristic. We are then in the realm of product differentiation, and unless strong assumptions are made, such as for example that the space of product characteristics is closed and bounded, we cannot in general ensure that competitive equilibria with full appropriability is

[6] Private firms often do not rely on patents, which involves disclosure of their discoveries, and they rely instead on secrecy. This involves a different type of risk, in that a rival may at a future date discover the same thing and exploit it with the backing of a patent. I am ignoring the practice of secrecy here only because I am considering Lindahl markets, which by definition cannot be established if firms keep their discoveries secret.

[7] By this I don't of course mean that repeating an experiment to confirm one's own or others' findings is useless. That is a different matter altogether.

efficient.[8] The point is a familiar one, that firms can locate themselves in the 'neighbourhood' of other firms in terms of the characteristics of the knowledge they produce, or more accurately, the characteristics of the research programmes they pursue. We would then expect that firms face downward-sloping demand curves in the market for knowledge, even in a large economy; unless, of course, fairly strong assumptions are made regarding the potential size of firms. I conclude that on *a-priori* grounds there are inefficiencies associated with the market mechanism, even when appropriability poses no problems.[9]

But this is only one side of the ledger. The other side is the fact that if they are to function well the two non-market mechanisms we noted earlier require an enormous quantity of centralized information, not only about private demand for knowledge but also about research possibilities open to individuals and firms. This tension, induced by the fact that the market mechanism and each of the various non-market planning mechanisms suffers from different types of weaknesses, has been a pervasive feature of the literature on science and technology policy.

As noted earlier, each of the three allocation mechanisms we have outlined is to be found in economies we know. They have developed over a long period, traceable in the European context at least, to the Renaissance patronage system. (For a development of this historical thesis, see Dasgupta and David, 1988.) They work in imperfect ways, as the foregoing discussion predicts they would, but they try and capture the essential features of the idealized social constructs. They have not risen and grown out of pure design, they have instead evolved over several hundred years.[10] Nevertheless, it is a useful exercise to study the argument by design, as we have done. It makes clear the central features of the organizations that have evolved over time, and are to be found today. Moreover, the fact that they co-exist requires explanation, and the argument by design gives us a lead as to why they do; why in fact we do not see the dominance of one of them. It has to do with differing characteristics of different kinds of knowledge.[11] I argue this next.

III. Basic and applied research

The analysis of Section II suggests that von Weizsäcker's three-level classification of economic activity is too coarse. One would want to classify knowledge into types to see whether there is at least a tendency for the market and non-market mechanisms to produce specific types. As it happens there is a classification which is of use for this purpose: basic and applied knowledge. In his classic article, Arrow (1962), thought of basic research as that kind of activity, the output of which is used only as an informational input into other inventive activities. By way of contrast, applied research is the kind of activity whose informational output is an input in the production of commodities—von Weizsäcker's intermediate level.

There are, of course, other classification schemes that are similar in spirit, though some are misleading. Thus it is a commonplace to think of science as being concerned with basic research and technology with applied research. On occasion one distinguishes abstract from concrete knowledge, and on other occasions the search for principles from the seeking of applications. And so forth. It would be out of place here to discuss connections between these classification schemes. The basic-applied research distinction is adequate enough for my purposes.

The distinction is an analytical one and in actual practice it is not clear cut. Moreover, the intention of a researcher is often quite different from his actual performance. Much basic knowledge has been acquired as an accidental outcome of what is applied research. For example, the immediate motivation behind Pasteur's research around 1870 was to solve certain practical problems connected with fermentation in the local wine industry. He was successful in this. But the by-product of his research is what made him immortal. The history of science and technology is littered with instances of this.

These are happy accidents, a bonus as it were, and although they are not rare, the immediate target of the researcher is in such cases the solution to an applied problem. The fact that there are happy accidents does not rule out the desirability of conducting basic research, that is, where the goal itself is basic knowledge. In his oft-cited essay Arrow (1962) advanced the argument that the more basic the character of the research the more in need it is of public funding. He argued this from two observations. First, the intended output of

[8] Even in a large economy. For an analysis of the efficiency properties of monopolistic competitive industries, see e.g. Hart, (1979).

[9] There are a number of other problems with this mechanism in the market for knowledge. I do not go into them here. But see Dasgupta, (1988).

[10] For example, the first systematic use of patents began in Venice in 1474, when the Republic promised privileges of ten years to inventors of new arts and machines. The rule of priority in science was institutionalized in the seventeenth century, with the rise of parliaments of scientists, specifically the Royal Society of England (1662).

[11] In an early discussion the late Michael Polanyi, (Polanyi, 1943–4), suggested that the patent system should be abolished, that it should be replaced by a system where inventors are rewarded out of public funds and that potential users should have unrestricted access to the inventions. Polanyi was thus arguing (by design) that an imperfect Pigovian solution is superior to an imperfect Lindahl solution.

basic research (we are calling it basic knowledge) is more difficult to appropriate than applied knowledge (which is to be taken to mean knowledge applicable directly to the production of material commodities). We have already touched upon this.

The second observation is more controversial. Arrow argued that the value of basic research is more conjectural than that of applied research and is therefore more likely to be undervalued by private individuals and firms. The idea here is that private firms and individuals are likely to be more risk averse than they would be if acting collectively through the government, and so may avoid undertaking basic research to any large extent because of its greater uncertainty. A related idea is that basic research involves on average a longer gestation lag than applied research. If private rates of discount exceed social rates, either because of myopia or because of imperfect capital markets, there is a case for the provision of public assistance to basic research.

These arguments have had an influence on public policy towards basic research, both in Western Europe and in the United States.[12] While the share of basic research expenditure incurred by the Federal Government in the United States has been declining in recent years, it is still about two-thirds of the total. (See National Science Foundation, 1986.) In a recent interesting essay Rosenberg (1988) provides evidence to indicate that these arguments are also correct. For example, he notes that the most successful basic research laboratories in the private sector have been in firms that have strong market positions, such as Bell Labs., IBM, Dupont, Dow Chemical, Eastman Kodak, etc. Being large and enduring they can absorb risk and take the long view. Their research success has been to a large extent due to the close intellectual proximity maintained between the basic research laboratories and the development and production wings of these firms.

It was noted earlier that even though the transmission cost of knowledge may be low, the cost of absorbing the information, of interpreting it and using it fruitfully may well be very high. This is often the case with research output at the frontiers of science and technology. Firms wishing to make use of the latest findings that are publicly available need to have scientists who can make it possible for them to do so. A good portion of the 'technology' of their being able to do so consists in their pursuing basic research! This provides one reason why private firms conduct basic research.[13]

All this is to see basic knowledge as an accidental outcome of applied research, or as being tied to applied research. In fact, of course, many of the most creative leaps that humankind has made have been made by thinkers chasing an intellectual problem thrown up internally by their subjects of specialization. If one had asked the late Professor Paul Dirac what he was doing when attempting to write down the relativistic quantum field equation for the electron, he would have answered that he was attempting just that. The avenues along which basic knowledge grows are many and varied, and typically unpredictable. It is for this reason one hears the argument that a part of the public subsidy for research ought to be earmarked for creative persons rather than projects. Creative people can be relied upon to choose promising problems. That is what makes them creative. One reason behind the astonishing success of the Cavendish Laboratory at Cambridge immediately after the Second World War was that its then Director pursued this policy.

The direction which these considerations point at then is this. Centralized information about promising avenues of research, both applied and basic, is by the nature of things necessarily sparse. Such diverse and specialized knowledge is dispersed among professionals in their fields; scientists, technologists, market analysts, and so on. R & D decisions have to be decentralized. For reasons that we have explored, much basic research needs to be funded publicly, along Pigovian lines, where persons and teams are funded but where the choice of research programmes and strategies are left to the researchers themselves. Of course, the detailed organization of decisions that ought to be established is a complex matter, as current discussion on the subject in the United Kingdom shows. Here I have for obvious reasons been painting the organizational structures in broad strokes, in terms of prototypes.

The matter is different for applied research. Appropriability of applied knowledge is easier. Moreover, a good deal of applied research addresses the development of products and manufacturing processes, involving less in the way of an advancement of one's understanding of basic principles. There is then a supposition that on average applied research, as we have defined it here, is intellectually less enticing. Thus for example the oft-made claim that many scientists hanker after knowledge for its own sake is one made about those who are attracted to basic research. For these reasons as well there is an *a-priori* case for relying in the main on the private sector for applied research by

---

[12] See Mowery (1983) for a good discussion of the influence these arguments have had on public policy towards basic research in the United States.

[13] A related reason is the large demand of governments for equipment connected with warfare. Private firms conduct basic research in these fields so as to be able to compete against one another for government contracts.

instituting intellectual property rights, such as patents, copyrights, and trademarks.[14] There is then the question of efficient property rights and the desirability of preventing excessive duplication of R & D in the private sector. In the next two sections I go into these issues.

IV. Efficient property rights

At first blush the structure of efficient property rights is obvious. The Arrow-Debreu theory tells us that if it is costless to establish markets, each and every commodity ought to be supported by a competitive market in a private ownership economy. There is then an immediate problem in using the theory when knowledge is treated as a commodity.[15] For suppose that given any knowledge base there are constant returns to scale in the production of commodities. Since R & D involves the expenditure of resources, production of commodities, including knowledge, must involve increasing returns to scale. Thus in particular firms must be allowed to earn profits from their production activities in order to recoup their R & D expenditure. Patents are designed to allow that to happen, to prevent competition in the producer market. But the problem is that it is not clear what a patent means.

We noted in Section II that the right way to think of the production of knowledge is to think about the economics of product differentiation. Inventions and discoveries differ by way of the characteristics of the information associated with them. A statement made with 95 per cent confidence is different from what is verbally the same statement made with 90 per cent confidence. Not by much perhaps, but they are by no means the same. A patent provides a protected sphere around the characteristics of the invention made by the patent holder. We should therefore be interested not only in the optimal *duration* of patents, but we should also be interested in the optimal *tightness* of patents, or in other words, the size of the protected sphere. In addressing this question I shall elaborate upon an argument put to me by Professor Carl Shapiro of Princeton University.

Purely for the sake of expositional ease I suppose that knowledge characteristics can be aggregated adequately into a scalar number. We then have a natural metric, providing us with a distance measure between any two pieces of information. Without loss of generality I suppose that the state of knowledge at the initial date $(t = 0)$ is zero. For simplicity I assume that the cost of producing knowledge of measure y $(y \geq 0)$ is $k(y)$. (This cost can be thought of as being the expenditure of a numeraire commodity, say income.) The greater the extent of the invention, the greater is the cost. Thus $k'(y) > 0$.[16] We may think of y as the extent of a cost reducing invention, or an index of the quality improvement of an existing product.

Denote by x the size of the protected sphere around the discovery. The interpretation is that when a discovery is made the discoverer is protected from entry by rivals into the region consisting of points within a distance x from the discovery, y. (It should be remembered that when the discoverer of y announces it rivals can, unless prevented by law, make use of y without having to incur $k(y)$.) Let T be the duration of this protection, the patent length. Let $B(x,y)$ denote the flow of social benefits and $P(x,y)$ the flow of private profits to the discoverer. Making standard assumptions we would conclude that $B_x(x,y) < 0$, $B_y(x,y) > 0$, $P_x(x,y) > 0$, $P_y(x,y) > 0$, and $P(0,y) = 0$ for all y. In what follows I ignore income effects. The government is to choose x, y and T with a view to maximizing the present value of social benefits, subject to the constraint that the present value of profits earned by the inventor is non-negative.[17] Let r (>0) be the social rate of discount, assumed without loss of generality to be equal to the discount rate of the private sector. It follows that the government's problem is: Choose x (≥ 0), y (≥ 0) and T (≥ 0) so as to maximize

$$\int_0^T B(x,y)e^{-rt}dt + (B(o,y)/r)e^{-rT} - k(y) \qquad (1)$$

---

[14] It should be noted that English and American patent laws, as forerunners of modern patent laws elsewhere, expressly forbade patenting a 'fact of nature'. The problem is that it is not clear what is a fact of nature. This was illustrated recently in the litigation over the Stanford University and the University of California at Berkeley patents on recombinant DNA. Under United States Law, a patent can be awarded to cover '. . . any new and useful process, machine, manufacture, or composition of matter, or any new and useful improvement thereof'. The duration of a US patent is 17 years from the date of issue.

[15] I am ignoring oft-cited problems connected with the fact that research often throws up unthought of possibilities, more specifically surprise events, so that the information partition not only becomes finer with discoveries, it contains elements not included previously. These issues are pertinent not only to the Arrow-Debreu theory but to decision theory in particular and economics in general.

[16] As usual, for simplicity of exposition I assume that the discovery is made instantaneously. I ignore uncertainty in the R & D process since this will raise additional matters. For an analysis of this last see Dasgupta (1989). See also Section V.

[17] Thus, the government is a Stackleberg leader. I suppose for simplicity of exposition that competition among potential inventors leads in equilibrium to a single agent carrying out the R & D at a pace which the government can choose so long as it does not yield negative present value profits.

Subject to the constraint

$$\int_0^T P(x,y)e^{-rt}dt \ge k(y).$$

To have a non-trivial problem suppose that it is socially beneficial to have some discovery. It is then a trivial matter to confirm that the optimal values of x and y satisfy the pair of conditions

$$P(x,y) = rk(y) \qquad (2)$$

and

$$P_x(x,y) \, [B_y(x,y) - rk'(y) \,] \\ = B_x(x,y) \, [P_y(x,y) - rk'(y) \,]; \qquad (3)$$

and that the optimal value of T is infinity. In other words, the patent issued should be a permanent one, but the protected sphere defining the patent on y should be of the smallest size consistent with the researcher being willing to undertake the research (condition [2]). Putting it slightly differently, the intellectual property should be a free-hold, but the property should be defined as narrowly as is compatible with incentives on the part of the private sector to produce the property.

An immediate implication of conditions (2) and (3) is that the size of the optimum protected sphere is not invariant to the kind of discovery we are studying. This follows at once from the fact that both the social benefit function, B, and the private profit function, P, depend upon the type of knowledge production we are considering. What is invariant is the optimum length of the patent. This invariance result should be contrasted with the results in Nordhaus (1969), Dasgupta and Stiglitz (1980b), Stoneman (1987) and Dasgupta (1989), which argue that the optimum patent length is finite and that it is dependent upon the type of discovery being studied. I shall presently try and explain why we are obtaining such strikingly different results.

Why do we not see the policy implied by (1) put into practice? There are several reasons. Here I want to concentrate on one which brings out quite sharply a feature of knowledge production which is not captured in (1). It has to do with private learning and it carries with it the implication that the solution of (1) is not implementable; in short, it is inconsistent with incentives.

Let x* and y* denote the solution to (1). By hypothesis, the initial state of knowledge is zero. (This, as we noted, is merely a normalization, of no significance.) But y* > 0. Thus the optimum solution envisages a discrete change in the state variable, namely the state of knowledge. Consider the agent who has made the discovery. Assume for the moment that the agent does not disclose his finding. Thus, the state of knowledge of this agent is y*, that of all others is still nil. But now the cost of discovering all pieces of knowledge in the neigh-

bourhood of y* is tiny for the agent in question and is approximately k(y*) for each of the others. The knowledgeable person has a great advantage over the rest. So then when the discoverer applies for a patent he will seek a patent not only on y*, but on all pieces of knowledge in the neighbourhood of y*, the size of the neighbourhood depending upon how easy it is for the discoverer to scan around the discovery y*. In general when this learning effect is large, the neighbourhood the discoverer can scan pretty much costlessly exceeds x*. One concludes that when a discoverer applies for a patent he applies for a patent on an entire region in the space of knowledge characteristics. It follows that in general x* is not implementable: the protected sphere cannot be made as small as the government might ideally like. From this it follows at once that the optimum patent length is finite.[18]

V. Joint ventures

Research projects have uncertain yields. No one who launches a programme of research can be certain of the outcome. Each project possesses an irreducible element which is specific to the team conducting it; which is another way of saying that in characterizing a project one must include the minds that are directing and conducting it. Thus, a part of the uncertainty concerning output is what one might call 'team-specific'. It follows from this that the uncertainties faced by two research teams can never be fully and positively correlated.[19] They would not be fully and positively correlated even if, acting as separate teams, they were to pursue what is otherwise the same programme of research.

It can be argued that private firms competing for a patent pursue overly correlated projects (Dasgupta and Maskin, 1987). This they tend to do even when they are neutral to risk. The intuition behind this result makes clearer the effect of the institution of patents on R & D races. As we noted earlier, patents aim at awarding all

[18] Nordhaus (1969) and Stoneman (1987) explored the optimum lengths of patents when, as in (1) above, the R & D process involves no uncertainty. This enabled them to postulate that in equilibrium there is a single agent engaged in R & D. Dasgupta and Stiglitz (1980b) explored some of the additional problems that arise if firms face independent uncertainties regarding their R & D technologies. In equilibrium the number of firms in this sort of situation is not unity and one has to correct for the fact that the number of active firms is also affected by the patent length. The result in Dasgupta and Stiglitz (1980b) concerning the length of optimum patents is valid only if the patent holder is a perfectly discriminating monopolist. Dasgupta (1989) corrects the erroneous statement in the earlier paper that it does not depend upon this assumption.

[19] They can, of course, be fully and negatively correlated if they are involved in, say, testing mutually exclusive hypotheses.

private profits to the winner of the race, the more comprehensive a patent the greater is the flow of profits to the winner. If a firm were to choose a research project which is less correlated with the project chosen by its rival, it would bestow a positive externality on the rival. Specifically, the likelihood that the rival is successful when the firm in question is not, would increase. This is socially desirable (because *cet. par.* society does not care who wins the patent, so long as a good discovery is made), but it is not picked up in the firm's private calculation. As our intuitions about externalities would suggest, this means that there is excessive similarity among the research projects pursued by private firms engaged in a patent race.

Entry into patent races can be a cause of waste. If entry is relatively costless there can be a dissipation of expected rents from inventions, as firms chase an invention knowing that there is *some* chance of winning the patent. It is possible to show that under a wide class of cases, patent competition results in firms pursuing an excessive number of parallel research projects. (Loury, 1979; Dasgupta and Stiglitz, 1980*a*,*b*.) This is another way of saying that the market can sustain excessive duplication.[20]

This is a special kind of market failure, and it is not easy to see how it can be corrected for by R & D taxes. In order to impose such corrective taxes the government needs to be able to monitor a firm's R & D programme in specific details. (How else is the government to judge that it has chosen an overly duplicative programme?) This the firm rightly will not wish to allow, because this would disclose information and would dilute the firm's prospects of appropriating the benefits from its R & D effort. The discussion of Section II is relevant again. Disclosure (of one's R & D project) dilutes the incentives for undertaking R & D in the first place. One concludes that the prescription of an externality tax is incompatible with incentives.

I would argue that these possibilities on their own provide some justification for the encouragement of joint R & D ventures among private firms. They are different from the argument that is most often put forward in popular writings, that joint ventures enable firms to pool their R & D risks and thereby enable them to undertake projects which otherwise would not be undertaken.[21]

The distinction between basic and applied research is somewhat blurred in a joint venture, for the reason that such programmes are highly targeted towards commercial goals. But in principle one can ask about the appropriate mix of co-operation and competition, even at the R & D stage. For example, one can imagine firms co-operating in basic research; that is, pooling their research laboratories and sharing the output of basic research, and then competing at the development stage once the basic research is completed. On the other hand, one often sees in practice an agreement to share the costs and output of R & D (both basic and developmental), to be followed by competition in commodity production. Then there are examples, such as EUREKA, where the venture is joint all the way from research and development to the product market, what I shall call a vertically integrated joint venture.

In a closed economy an analysis of a vertically integrated joint venture may seem in effect an analysis of pure monopoly. But this would not be correct. When firms enter a joint venture they do not become a single firm. Their R & D laboratories will co-operate but they will not become a single laboratory. This makes the analysis of joint ventures difficult even when they are vertically integrated. Nevertheless, many of the ingredients of any such analysis are embedded in the discussions of Sections II and III.

Within joint ventures a distinction should be made between two polar cases: (i) those where the venture not only allows firms to co-ordinate their policies, it also commits them to share their newly discovered knowledge; and (ii) those where the only gain is a co-ordination of policies. The key feature underlying (ii) is that the extent to which knowledge is shared is not subject to control: a certain 'fraction' of each firm's R & D output spills over to the rival firm whether or not they agree on a joint venture. The distinction therefore is based on the extent to which the firms' R & D laboratories are combined by the venture. Underlying (i) is the assumption that the laboratory outputs are common property. Underlying (ii) is the hypothesis that they are kept separate, but that their funding is determined by a joint policy.

Our earlier discussion is directly applicable to (i), and in fact it is (i) which is most often alluded to in the literature. A central gain, both to the firms involved and to society, is the sharing of knowledge. As against this is a possible loss to society, occasioned by the fact that a joint venture implies greater monopoly power. The gain from shared knowledge is absent from (ii), because

---

[20] We emphasize the use of the term 'excessive' because it is often desirable socially to have several parallel research projects in operation, just as it is desirable to hold a diversified financial portfolio.

[21] Within the European Economic Community members are engaged in large-scale operations, such as RACE (Research in Advanced Telecommunication Technology for Europe Programme), EUREKA (European Research Coordination Agency), ESPRIT (European Strategic Pro-

gramme for R & D in Information Technologies); and in the United States by MCC (Microelectronics and Computer Technology Corporation).

by hypothesis the extent to which knowledge is made common is unaffected by the venture, although of course the amount of knowledge each firm produces *is* affected.[22]

In a recent interesting note d'Aspremont and Jacquemin (1987) have analysed the implications of joint ventures with (ii) as the background situation. There is no uncertainty postulated, R & D is directed at process innovations, and the R & D technology is assumed to enjoy no scale economies. It is supposed that a certain amount of knowledge spills across the firms' R & D laboratories in an exogenous manner. (This last is what makes the venture one of pure co-ordination; case [ii].)

Knowledge spillovers are a form of positive externality. So it might be thought that a joint venture must necessarily involve greater R & D expenditure: the venture after all internalizes the externality. But this would be wrong. The point is that if the joint venture were to be restricted to a co-ordination of R & D expenditure, the firms would expect to compete in the product market once R & D were completed. The firms would know in advance that after the completion of R & D there will be no jointly agreed production policy. Given this, they may well choose to agree on a lower R & D expenditure level, lower than, that is, the level that would emerge if they were not to have a joint venture.

Clearly then the answer depends upon the extent of knowledge spillover. If this is large a joint R & D venture would be expected to result in greater R & D expenditure and, indeed, even greater output production. This can be shown to be the case. (See d'Aspremont and Jacquemin, 1987.) In fact it can be shown that if knowledge spillovers are large a vertically integrated joint venture would be expected to sustain even greater R & D expenditure than a mere R & D joint venture. Where a vertically integrated joint venture is restrictive is at the production stage, and consumers can end up paying a higher product price even though production costs are lower because of the integrated nature of the venture. The greater surplus is captured by what is in effect a monopolist and distributed to shareholders. A joint venture, whether restricted to the R & D stage or whether integrated fully, does not produce the first-best efficient outcome. But if spillovers are large an R & D joint venture can be closer to it than unbridled competition.

These results are congenial to intuition. They also indicate that our broad-brush discussion of the welfare economics of knowledge production has probably been along the right lines. The tension we noted earlier in this essay, between the need for co-ordination and sharing of produced knowledge, the paucity of centralized information about R & D possibilities, and dilution of private incentives to produce knowledge if it is to be shared, is at the heart of the basis upon which public policy has to be geared.

References

Arrow, K. J. (1962), 'Economic Welfare and the Allocation of Resources for Inventions', in Nelson, R. R. (ed.), *The Rate and Direction of Inventive Activity: Economic and Social Factors*, Princeton University Press.

—— (1971), 'Political and Economic Evaluation of Social Effects and Externalities', in Intriligator, M. (ed.), *Frontiers of Quantitative Economics*, Vol. I, Amsterdam, North Holland.

d'Aspremont, C., and Jacquemin, A. (1987), 'A Note on Cooperative and Non Cooperative R & D in Duopoly', *American Economic Review*.

Baumol, W. J., and Oates, W. E. (1975), *The Theory of Environmental Policy: Externalities, Public Outlays and the Quality of Life*, Englewood Cliffs, NJ, Prentice Hall.

Dasgupta, P. (1988), 'Patents, Priority and Imitation or, The Economics of Races and Waiting Games', *Economic Journal*, 98.

—— (1989), 'The Economics of Parallel Research', in Hahn, F. (ed.), *The Economic Theory of Information, Games, and Missing Markets*, Oxford University Press.

—— and David, P. (1988), 'Priority, Secrecy, Patents and the Socio-Economics of Science and Technology', CEPR Publication No. 127, Stanford University.

—— and Heal, G. (1979), *Economic Theory and Exhaustible Resources*, Cambridge University Press.

—— and Maskin, E. (1987), 'The Simple Economics of Research Portfolios', *Economic Journal*, 97.

—— and Stiglitz, J. E. (1980a), 'Market Structure and the Nature of Innovative Activity', *Economic Journal*, 90.

—— (1980b), 'Uncertainty, Industrial Structure and the Speed of R & D', *Bell Journal of Economics*, Spring.

—— (1988), 'Learning-by-Doing, Market Structure and Industrial and Trade Policies', *Oxford Economic Papers*, 40.

Hart, O. (1979), 'Monopolistic Competition in a Large Economy with Differentiated Commodities', *Review of Economic Studies*, 46.

Kamien, M., and Schwartz, N. (1978), 'Potential Rivalry, Monopoly Profits and the Pace of Inventive Activity', *Review of Economic Studies*, 45.

Levin, R. (1978), 'Technical Change, Barriers to Entry and Market Structure', *Economica*, 45.

---

[22] A good deal of the urgency expressed within the EEC and the USA about having joint ventures in R & D, especially in high-technology industries, is the competitive threat from Japan. In the text I shall ignore such gains from joint ventures and ask whether there are gains to a society in having R & D ventures *even* if it were to face no competitive threat from outside.

Loury, G. (1979), 'Market Structure and Innovation', *Quarterly Journal of Economics*, 93.

Marx, K. (1970), *Capital*, London, Lawrence and Wisehart.

Mowery, D. C. (1983), 'Economic Theory and Government Technology Policy', *Policy Sciences*, 16.

Musgrave, R. A., and Peacock, A. T. (eds.) (1968), *Classics in the Theory of Public Finance*, London, Macmillan.

National Science Foundation (1986), 'National Patterns of Science and Technology Resources', NSF, 86–309, Washington DC.

Nordhaus, W. (1969), *Invention, Growth and Welfare*, Cambridge, Mass., MIT Press.

Pigou, A. C. (1932), *The Economics of Welfare*, London, Macmillan.

Polanyi, M. (1943–4), 'Patent Reform', *Review of Economic Studies*.

Rosenberg, N. (1988), 'Why Do Companies Do Basic Research (with their own Money)?', mimeo. Department of Economics, Stanford University.

Samuelson, P. A. (1954), 'The Pure Theory of Public Expenditure', *Review of Economics and Statistics*, 36.

Schumpeter, J. (1976), *Capitalism, Socialism and Democracy*, 5th edn., London, Allen and Unwin.

Stoneman, P. (1987), *The Economic Analysis of Technology Policy*, Oxford, Oxford University Press.

von Weizsäcker, C. C. (1980), *Barriers to Entry: A Theoretical Treatment*, Berlin, Springer-Verlag.

PART III

COMPETITION AND INDUSTRIAL POLICY

6

Competition policy

DONALD HAY

Jesus College and Institute of Economics and Statistics, Oxford[1]

I. Introduction

A precondition for a successful market economy is the existence of an effective competition policy. The need for such a policy was recognized by Adam Smith when he wrote in the *Wealth of Nations* in 1776: 'People of the same trade seldom meet together, even for merriment and diversion, but the conversation ends in a conspiracy against the public, or in some instances to raise prices.'

The problem, as many writers since Adam Smith have recognized, is that a market can be manipulated to give some of those involved greater economic power so that competition is distorted and economic efficiency impaired. There may also be ethical and social objections to the absence of competition: it is simply not fair that large firms or cartels should be able to oppress smaller competitors and/or customers by charging prices that greatly exceed the costs of supply. It is perhaps notable that a key piece of UK legislation is called the Fair Trading Act and the main UK competition policy institution is the Office of Fair Trading. Alternatively there may be a commitment to competition as the appropriate form of economic organization, either because competition is a good in itself, or because it delivers the goods. The objective of this paper is to advance four propositions about the purpose, scope, and implementation of competition policy, to measure existing policies against these theses, and to identify the directions in which reform might go. Particular attention will be devoted to recent proposals to reform UK competition policy.

First published in *Oxford Review of Economic Policy*, vol. 9, no. 2 (1993). This version has been updated and revised to incorporate recent developments.

[1] I am very grateful to Paul Geroski, Hans Liesner, Derek Morris, and John Vickers, and to my co-editor Colin Mayer, for detailed comments on previous drafts of this paper. None of these is responsible for the defects which remain, or for the judgements which are expressed.

The first proposition, that *the role of competition policy should be to promote economic efficiency*, is explored in section II. Alternative views of the matter are that competition policy should be guided by some broader notion of the public interest, including perhaps non-economic social objectives, or that competition, *per se*, should be promoted. There is evidence that despite differing objectives at the origination of policy in the US, EU, and UK, the growing consensus is that the focus should be on economic efficiency. Papers on policy themes by economists generally make the assumption that economic efficiency is the goal.

The second proposition, discussed in section III, is that *economic analysis is generally ambiguous, a priori, about the efficiency effects of particular market structures and conduct*. This proposition builds on the considerable advances in industrial organization of the past 15 years, which have enabled theorists to identify the policy issues raised by a wide range of market phenomena. However, the problem for competition policy is that trade-offs are more or less ubiquitous, and only in a few cases (price fixing or market sharing are examples) is it possible to reach an unambiguous verdict.

The third proposition, in section IV, builds on the first two. It is that *the appropriate design of policy and policy institutions is crucial to a successful competition policy*. In particular, given the ambiguity of economic analysis, policy has to identify rules or presumptions to indicate the boundaries between acceptable and unacceptable market conduct and structure, but it has to offer at least some scope for the parties involved in such cases to argue countervailing efficiency benefits. Institutionally, implementation of policy requires a public procedure. We identify an ideal where there is a public competition policy institution empowered to identify, investigate, and propose remedies for failures of competition, with a competition tribunal to review cases where the institution is proposing fines for abuses, or where the firms are unwilling to accept the initial findings.

The final thesis is that *international harmonization of competition policies is essential, and probably a supranational competition authority is needed as well.* This proposition is the subject of section V of the paper, and reflects the growing internationalization of economic activity with multinational enterprises supplying markets that extend beyond the boundaries of particular states (and therefore the jurisdiction of competition authorities). A particular example is the development of EU competition policy, and its relation to policies of member states. Another concern is that national governments may use competition policy as an instrument to protect domestic markets against overseas entrants, or to promote the interests of domestic producers in world markets; this suggests the need to harmonize policy in different economies, and to seek international agreements to desist from using policy in a protectionist manner.

The last section of the paper will apply these four propositions to the reform of competition policy in the UK and the EU.

II. First proposition

The role of competition policy should be to promote economic efficiency.

There are at least three schools of thought about what competition policy is seeking to achieve. Mainstream industrial organization argues that the purpose of the policy is to promote economic efficiency. Competition is not an end in itself. Rather it is to be encouraged as a means to improving economic efficiency, where 'efficiency' is defined in terms of partial equilibrium welfare economics, that is the maximization of the sum of the discounted present value of consumer and producer surpluses (Hay and Morris, 1991, chs. 16 and 17). This definition encompasses the trade-off between static and dynamic efficiency: current welfare losses may be acceptable, if the market structure or conduct which gives rise to the losses will also generate efficiencies in the long run, so long as the prospective benefits are not too delayed in realization and the social discount rate is not too high.

It is important to define quite carefully what is meant by 'competition'. Traditionally, competition has been understood in terms of price competition, with firms pursuing their own self-interest in the setting of prices, not colluding with each other. However, it has been shown that, under a variety of assumptions about in-formation conditions, collusive outcomes are supportable as Nash perfect equilibria in repeated games (see Tirole, 1989, ch. 6 for a convenient summary). Furthermore, price-cutting can in some circumstances be anti-competitive: predatory pricing to drive out a rival or an entrant, or low prices seeking to mislead entrants about the efficiency of the incumbent firms are cases in point (Milgrom and Roberts, 1982; Phlips, 1995, chapter IV). Competition can, of course, come in other forms. In differentiated goods markets firms may compete on the number of brands they put on the market, in quality and in marketing (including advertising). It is not always the case that a partial equilibrium welfare analysis will show unequivocally that more 'competition' in this form is better. For example, brand proliferation may generate a welfare loss through excessive expenditure on fixed costs associated with each brand (Schmalensee, 1978; Salop, 1979). At least some competitive advertising may be wasteful, as firms seek to duplicate each other's expenditures in order to avoid market-share losses (Lambin, 1976; Dixit and Norman, 1978). In the long run firms may compete in physical investment or in R&D, leading to duplication of capacity or innovation expenditures. The outcome of such competition may be that one firm emerges as the 'winner', able to dominate the market and earn monopoly rents (Gilbert and Newbery, 1982). The sunk costs involved in building a strong market position may additionally become a barrier to entry, even if the intention was 'innocent' competition rather than a deliberate strategy to exclude potential competitors. The welfare evaluation of such competition is far from unequivocal. The conclusion is that 'promoting competition' is not sufficient in itself, if the objective of competition policy is to improve economic efficiency. We need to be clear what is meant by competition, and different kinds of competitive behaviour need to be separately evaluated.

A second, smaller but nevertheless vociferous, school of thought argues that competition, in and of itself, *is* the appropriate objective: this neo-Austrian approach is more concerned with process than with outcomes, and in its extreme statement is not concerned with evaluation of economic efficiency at all. A moderate exposition is that of Littlechild (1986) who argues that it is the *process* of competition which matters, and that the concept of economic efficiency which emerges from static welfare analysis is at best misleading. The competitive process arises out of disequilibrium in markets giving opportunities for entrepreneurs to exploit their superior information and earn profits. Equilibrium is never achieved, because the market is always changing due to new information, innovation, and shocks.

Monopoly profits are (or should be) eroded by the entry of new firms and products, which are able to displace the incumbent firms by offering lower prices or a better product. So monopoly profits are a reward to innovation and entrepreneurship and a signal to competitors rather than a 'welfare loss'. For Littlechild, therefore, the objectives of competition policy should be the promotion of competition, by acting against market conduct designed to inhibit it.

Both the economic efficiency and neo-Austrian schools of thought express concerns about the views of a third school, which either has some fairly broad concept of the public interest as its stated objective, or in practice is motivated by more than a single-minded pursuit of economic efficiency and/or competition.

UK competition policy, for example, does not focus solely on economic efficiency.[2] Section 84 of the Fair Trading Act 1973 lists five criteria in determining the public interest. The first refers to effective competition between suppliers, the third makes reference to long-run competition through new products, processes, and entry to the market, and the fifth relates to maintaining and promoting competitive activity in markets outside the United Kingdom. The second criterion refers to the promotion of the interests of consumers and purchasers of goods and services via quality and variety. The fourth criterion is 'maintaining and promoting the balanced distribution of industry and employment in the United Kingdom'. This last criterion was applied in the Charter Consolidated Ltd/Anderson Strathclyde Ltd Report (1982), where the concern was for the effects of the merger on employment in an area of Scotland which already had high unemployment. Similarly, in Swedish Match AB/Alleghany International Inc. (1987) one reason adduced for permitting the merger was that a factory in a high unemployment area of Liverpool would thereby be saved from closure. It is important to note that these criteria are not intended to be an exhaustive definition of the public interest. Indeed, the MMC has on numerous occasions addressed other public-interest issues. For example, in Lonrho/House of Fraser (1979), it concerned itself with the managerial capacity of a particular individual. In a number of cases it has raised a question about a UK company passing into the control of an overseas company. Thus the issue in Shanghai Banking Corporation/Royal Bank of Scotland (1982) was whether it was acceptable for a major UK clearing bank to be controlled from outside the UK, and the

likely consequences for the conduct of UK monetary policy. In Government of Kuwait/British Petroleum (1988) the MMC concluded that control of BP by the Kuwaiti government would operate against the public interest. More recently, the question has been raised as to whether it is contrary to the public interest for a private company to be taken over by a foreign state-owned company, given the privatization objectives of the UK government. In Elders IXL/Allied Lyons (1986) the MMC concerned itself with the method by which Elders' bid was to be financed, but came to the view that the issue of leveraged bids was not one on which it should pronounce.

The other major arm of UK competition policy is the Restrictive Trades Practices Act, 1976. Agreements between two or more firms that involve certain types of restrictions must be registered with the Director General of Fair Trading, and defended in the Restrictive Practices Court. The presumption is that such agreements are contrary to the public interest, and the onus is on the parties to the agreement to demonstrate that a particular agreement is not. The Act lays down criteria, known as 'gateways', by which restrictions may be justified. These include the effect on exports from the UK, and regional unemployment, as well as a 'catch-all' gateway (b): restrictions may be permitted which would confer on the public as purchasers, consumers or users of any goods or services, other specific and substantial benefits or advantages enjoyed or likely to be enjoyed by them as such. This gateway was pleaded successfully in the Net Book Agreement (1957). The argument was that the agreement kept a larger number of booksellers in business and maintained the number of books published, particularly those of literary and scholarly merit. (The validity of these assertions has been seriously questioned since: the agreement collapsed in 1995 when a number of leading publishers decided that it was no longer in their interests to continue it.) In Permanent Magnets (1962), the benefit identified was that the absence of price competition had encouraged technical collaboration between the firms, giving purchasers the benefits of both lower costs *and* a range of suppliers. Improved ability to compete with overseas competitors was also claimed. The regional unemployment gateway was successfully pleaded in Yarn Spinners (1959), the impact on employment in Lancashire being the issue. (However, the Court concluded that this benefit was outweighed by the detriment of perpetuating excess capacity in a declining industry, and the agreement was therefore struck down under the 'tailpiece' which is appended to the gateways.)

By contrast, competition law in the USA and the EU

---

[2] The text by Whish (1993) gives an excellent summary and evaluation of UK and EC Law, and has been used extensively in the preparation of this paper. Note that all cases are referred to by date of the report or judgement of the relevant competition authority.

is ostensibly more focused on competition and economic efficiency. However, historically at least, the origins of US antitrust were somewhat different. Neale (1970, p. 459), for example, noted that:

the rationale for antitrust is essentially a device to provide legal checks to economic power, and is not a pursuit of economic efficiency as such. Consequently the question asked is not whether antitrust decisions lead to the greatest economic efficiency but whether it can be said, given the non-economic reasons for antitrust policy, that these decisions do any serious harm.

According to Neale, the origin of US antitrust legislation, beginning with the Sherman Act in 1890, was a desire to limit the power of big business and trusts, and in particular to protect small business and consumers against their predatory behaviour. George Hay (1987) has shown how this approach to antitrust survived into the post Second World War period with the adverse judgements in the Alcoa and United Shoe Machinery cases, where the companies concerned were condemned for 'monopolization' of their respective markets, despite the fact that they had only employed normal competitive means to acquire and maintain their dominant positions. However, from 1975 economic efficiency became the primary focus of antitrust cases in parallel with an increasing involvement of professional economists in antitrust institutions, and economists began to be used widely as expert witnesses. This was particularly evident in the IBM case where several academic economists were drafted in to prepare IBM's defence (Fisher et al., 1983).

Despite these developments, White (1993) still describes US competition policy as 'sloppy', referring particularly to American populism that favours small firms against big business, to a contradictory respect for scale economies, and to the capture of governmental processes by rent-seeking special interests. In his review of the content of US antitrust, he indicates some areas of policy where the decisions are now largely driven by sound economic analysis (horizontal agreements and mergers) and others where the basis for judgements is less satisfactory and the practice sometimes inconsistent (vertical restraints and price discrimination). White also points to conflicts of antitrust policy with other areas of governmental regulation, notably utilities regulation, health–safety–environmental regulations, and incipient import protectionism.

EU competition law is based on Articles 85 and 86 of the Treaty of Rome, which respectively prohibit restrictive agreements between firms, and the abuse of dominant positions. Until 1990, anticompetitive mergers could only be attacked under Article 86, on the basis of the precedent created by the Continental Can judgment in 1972. In 1989, after years of discussion within the EU, a specific merger regulation was introduced. Sapir et al. (1993) note that the context of EU competition policy has always been the promotion of competition within a single European market, despite arguments that have sometimes been expressed in favour of industrial policies designed to improve the competitiveness of European firms in international markets. The stress on competition has led the competition Directorate of the European Commission (DGIV) to place a particular emphasis on attacking any behaviour which might appear to segment the European market into national markets. Thus in United Brands Co. v. Commission (1978), the Court held that United Brands had abused its dominant position by charging different prices for bananas according to the member state of their destination, where these prices could not be justified on the basis of transport costs. The implication was that only the retailers in each destination market would be permitted to vary prices according to local conditions. It was as if the Commission was seeking to *impose* a common market with common prices, rather than to ensure that competition prevailed. The result was that United Brands had to abandon what was generally acknowledged to be a highly efficient distribution system, arguably to the detriment of consumer welfare. While EU competition law has nothing equivalent to the wide 'public-interest' test of UK law, Article 85(3) does permit the granting of exemptions for agreements between firms that can be shown to produce beneficial effects. Thus exemptions have been made available for R&D agreements, specialization agreements, and other agreements which seek to improve efficiency in production (Sapir et al. 1993 give examples). There is considerable debate as to whether this category of 'beneficial effects' can be extended to take social objectives into account, for example in the treatment of recession cartels. Article 86, by contrast, has no section 3 to permit exemptions, which has sometimes been thought to be a weakness. Similarly, as Sapir et al. note, there is no provision within the 1989 Merger Regulation for the Commission to consider tradeoffs between productive efficiency and reduced competition in assessing mergers.

The thinking behind EU competition law has particular significance currently for the UK where there have been proposals to reform UK competition law to bring it into line with Articles 85 and 86. After consultations with interested parties, the government published a White Paper in 1989, *Opening Markets: New Policies on Restrictive Trades Practices*, which proposed the replacement of existing legislation on restrictive trades practices with legislation along the lines of Article 85 . Key features of the proposal included: (*a*) an Article 85-type prohibition of anticompetitive agreements, including an illustrative, but not exhaustive, list of banned practices such as price fixing, collusive tendering, resale price maintenance (RPM), market sharing, and collective boycotts: the focus of the prohibition is to be on the effects of agreements rather than the specific form that they take; (*b*) provision for both block and individual exemptions from the prohibition, following the example of Article 85(3); the test to be applied is that of technical or economic improvement; a general public-interest criterion is specifically excluded, despite being asked for by, among others, the professions which are to be included in the scope of the legislation, unlike the existing Restrictive Trades Practices Act 1976; (*c*) fines of up to 10 per cent of UK turnover for firms found to be in breach of the prohibitions.

In 1992 this White Paper was followed up by a consultation document from the Department of Trade and Industry, *Abuse of Market Power*, which set out options for reform in the areas currently covered by the Fair Trading Act 1973 and the Competition Act 1980. While the document listed a number of legislative options, it made a powerful case for the introduction of a prohibition system, along the lines of Article 86, to complement the proposals for restrictive trades practices previously put forward, and operating in a broadly similar manner. It was noted that an Article 86 law, on its own, would not be sufficient: the scope of the legislation would need to be widened to include 'complex monopolies', and the remedies available should include structural remedies (e.g. divestment) and regulatory remedies (e.g. price controls). Williams (1993) argued that there should be scope for a third verdict (in addition to 'guilty' or 'not guilty' of abusing market power), where the market situation, though not the firms' conduct, is not conducive to competition or economic efficiency, and on this basis is to be declared to be against the public interest. But the appropriate remedies might be divestment, regulation, or removal of entry barriers rather than fines. A key feature of the proposals in the consultation document was, once again, that the main focus of policy should be on the economic effects of market structure and conduct, and not on *general* public interest considerations. Unfortunately, as we will explain below in section VI, the Government decided in April 1993 not to proceed with these proposals.

The comparison of the philosophy of competition policy in the three jurisdictions should serve as a warning against ignoring completely the 'public-interest'

dimension. Whatever economists might like to think, economic efficiency is not the only consideration that is motivating policy. A solution might be to accept that while public policy in general cannot be confined to considerations of economic efficiency, it is inappropriate for competition policy to examine wider social costs and benefits. First, a wide definition of the public interest leads to policy implementation that is lacking in transparency: a firm and its advisers will be unable to judge whether or not a proposed course of conduct will be acceptable to the authorities. (This criticism has been particularly levelled at the workings of the MMC in the UK.) A second reason is that wider economic consequences may be better dealt with by other branches of economic policy: for example, regional policy can be designed specifically to deal with localized unemployment problems, R & D policy to deal with the promotion of R & D and the protection of intellectual property rights. But this doctrine of matching policy instruments to policy variables is unlikely to be effective in all cases: for example, a desire for strategic reasons to protect a domestic defence industry from foreign takeovers, or a desire to maintain a diversity of ownership in the newspaper industry.

III. Second proposition

Economic analysis is often ambiguous, a priori, about the efficiency effects of particular market structures and conduct.

Despite major differences of approach in different competition policy jurisdictions, the policy agenda is remarkably similar. Competition policy is concerned with agreements between firms, and with monopoly. In respect of monopoly, the concern is generally with the abuse of dominant positions in markets, including charging excessive prices, the practice of price discrimination and vertical restraints, and with the means by which dominant positions are acquired (including mergers) and maintained. The difficulty with all these policy areas is that the effect on economic efficiency is by no means clear cut: there are nearly always benefits and losses that have to be weighed. In this section we will briefly indicate the nature of the trade-offs involved before turning, in the next section, to the implications for the design of competition policy.

1. Agreements between firms

Competition policy in respect of agreements between firms is based on the standard economic analysis of cartels and other collusive agreements (Jacquemin and Slade, 1989; Phlips, 1995, chapter I). The objective of such agreements is to raise prices and reduce output. How this is achieved by the colluding firms varies depending on the circumstances of the market, and the product. In fairly simple markets, agreements may focus on the price of a standardized product (including agreement on exactly what constitutes a standard product, e.g. terms and conditions of sale), or on production quotas for the participating firms. In more complex markets, the agreements may take the form of dividing up the market geographically or according to product type. Where the market is allocated on the basis of tenders, more intricate measures may be needed to ensure that the contracts are shared out, including perhaps 'allocation' of each contract to a particular firm and agreement on how the other firms will rig their bids to ensure that they are not awarded the contract 'by mistake'. The static welfare analysis of such practices is straightforward: price is higher and output lower than it would otherwise have been, so there is a welfare triangle loss. (This, of course, ignores the theory of the second best, where the existence of price distortions in related markets may require a price which exceeds marginal cost in the market under consideration. A counter to that argument is that an effective competition policy will seek to deal with related market price distortions at the same time.) Furthermore, there may also be an X-efficiency loss: high prices and the absence of competition may make firms slack in their use of resources, generating higher costs than would otherwise be the case. Note, however, that if the slack only takes the form of paying out some of the monopoly rents as higher remuneration to factors of production, then there is no efficiency loss implied.

A possible exception to this general conclusion of welfare loss from collusion was provided by Richardson (1965). He argued that in some markets the lumpy nature of demand made it essential that contracts be shared out, to ensure that the competitors were not exposed to the risk of alternating 'feast and famine' in their order books. A similar argument applies to cases where investment is lumpy (e.g. large processing plants): agreements to take turns in investing may be necessary to avoid excess capacity being built (or to avoid insufficient capacity being built as firms are afraid of excess capacity!). In sectors that are suffering long-term or cyclical decline, arguments are often made for 'crisis' or 'recession' cartels, to prevent the scrapping of capacity that will remain viable in the longer term, and to ensure that contraction of the industry occurs in an orderly manner. A sector which faces a monopoly buyer may wish to organize itself to increase its bargaining power: the welfare effects of such a move are ambiguous. Finally, it should be noted that export cartels (to exploit monopoly rents in overseas markets), and import cartels (to increase bargaining power vis-à-vis overseas suppliers) improve the terms of trade for the domestic economy and can generate (like optimal tariffs) welfare gains. In practice, export cartels are not pursued by competition authorities in any of the three jurisdictions discussed above, though in the UK export agreements are supposed to be notified to the Office of Fair Trading.

If overt collusion is not permitted, then firms may be able to replicate its effect via tacit collusion (Tirole, 1989, ch. 6; Phlips 1995, chapter II), which may take the form of 'conscious parallelism' with firms making identical price changes more or less at the same time. This feature of concentrated markets is discussed in the paper by Rees in this volume. He notes that successful collusion requires communication between the firms and that this is made much easier if they are able to exchange information about prices, outputs, and costs. Hence, in most competition policy jurisdictions, agreements to exchange information are frowned upon. Unfortunately, as Phlips (1987) has pointed out, exchange of information may be needed to facilitate the establishment of non-co-operative equilibria, in a situation where demands and costs are changing rapidly. The alternative may be prices that tend to be sticky, unresponsive to shifts in the market. Furthermore, certain commercial practices such as 'meeting competition clauses', 'most favoured nation' (MFN) clauses, and tie-ins that release the buyer if she can find a lower price supplier elsewhere can serve both to ensure information-sharing about discounts and price-cutting and to give (in the case of MFN clauses) an incentive not to cut price (see Salop, 1985). However, Rees also notes that collusion requires a mechanism to enforce agreements. Without such a mechanism, all communication is just 'cheap talk': there is no reason for a firm to believe what the others say. But theoretical analysis suggests that credible punishment strategies may need to be quite subtle and sophisticated, which leads to the conclusion that so-called 'tacit' collusion may in practice turn out to be 'secret' collusion. The implication, according to Rees, is that competition policy in this area should focus on outcomes rather than on market conduct.

As soon as the discussion extends to agreements between firms on other aspects of competition, the welfare analysis becomes even more ambiguous. The seminal analysis of Dixit and Norman (1978) suggested that competitive advertising by oligopolists (which the evidence suggests is mutually cancelling) generates a welfare loss, and that agreements to limit competitive advertising would therefore be beneficial. The difficulty with this result is that advertising is usually only one part of a marketing strategy, and that agreements on advertising are likely to spill over into other elements of that strategy including prices. A similar difficulty arises with R&D agreements (see the paper by Geroski in this volume). The case for R&D agreements is partly that they avoid wasteful duplication of research, and allow complementary skills and risks to be pooled, but mainly that they internalize the information spillovers which mean that a single firm is unable to appropriate all the returns to its R & D efforts. Geroski's review of empirical studies suggests that the effectiveness of patents in ensuring appropriability is generally quite weak, that imitation lags are short, and imitation costs low compared to innovation costs. However, the evidence also suggests that information spillovers are more important in research than in development, and that a firm has to do quite a lot of its own R & D, if it is to be able to absorb information spillovers effectively. These results suggest that R & D agreements will generate the highest social benefits where they concentrate on R rather than D, which will in addition reduce the perceived risk that competition in the markets created by the innovations will be blunted. This risk will also be lessened where the firms involved produce complementary products rather than substitutes, where there are several R & D joint ventures in the industry, and where joint marketing arrangements are not part of the agreements (joint production may be required for productive efficiency in exploiting the R & D results).

2. Abuse of dominant positions

The most obvious abuses of a dominant position are thought to be excessive pricing, price discrimination, predatory pricing, and vertical restraints. If a firm charges an excessive price, it generates a welfare triangle loss (as in the cartel case). The difficulty is to identify what might be an 'excessive price'. The point is raised most acutely in R & D intensive sectors. The prices of pharmaceutical products have frequently been reviewed by competition authorities, and at first sight the mark-ups appear to be very large. The response of the companies is that such prices are necessary to recoup the costs of R & D, and to compensate for risk, since only a small proportion of R & D generates innovations that are commercially viable.

Price discrimination can take a number of forms (Phlips, 1983; Varian, 1989). First, it may be spatial in that prices are set to reflect demand conditions in different geographical markets, those prices not reflecting different costs of supply. Second, it may be competitive or 'predatory'—a lower price being charged in markets where actual or potential competition is more active. Third, price discrimination may appear in the guise of loyalty bonuses, rebates, and discounts. Fourth, discounts for 'full line' ordering and commodity bundling are best interpreted as forms of price discrimination. Each of these cases merits a separate welfare analysis. In principle, price discrimination *is* required for optimal resource allocation: for example, a monopolist practising perfect price discrimination will produce more output than a non-discriminating monopolist. However, Schmalensee (1981) has shown that discrimination allocates output inefficiently across consumers, which is undesirable unless offset by higher total output, e.g. where the discrimination permits additional markets to be served.

So-called 'predatory pricing' has provided a major conundrum for competition authorities. The concern of the authorities is that a dominant firm will price aggressively in those markets where it faces actual or potential competition with the intention of seeing off the competition. There has been much theoretical discussion of this possibility (see Tirole, 1989, ch. 9; Ordover and Saloner, 1989). The argument has to rely either on imperfect information about the predator's costs, so that price cutting is a means of building a reputation for being efficient, or on a 'deep pocket' story where the predator has access to either internal or external funds to finance its activities (Bolton and Scharfstein, 1990). The defence of a firm accused of predatory pricing is often that it is merely responding to competition: so evidence of its *intentions* may be quite important in deciding whether a firm's conduct is predatory or not. Unfortunately for competition policy, such evidence will invariably be lacking, and actual conduct is all that the authorities have to go on. The welfare analysis of predatory pricing is also generally ambiguous. It is necessary to weigh the short-run gains from lower prices against the long-run detriment if the predator does succeed in establishing a monopoly position.

Bonuses, rebates, and discounts related to the buyers' *past* purchases from the supplier have also been frowned upon by the authorities. These 'loyalty discounts' give rise to switching costs, since a consumer who switches to another supplier loses the discount. Such switching costs can serve to facilitate collusion and to deter competitive entry (Klemperer, 1987). Once again there is a trade-off between lower effective prices in the short run, against the loss of more active price competition in the long run.

The issue of commodity bundling has been central

to a number of celebrated competition policy cases, including those involving IBM in both the United States and Europe. The argument against commodity bundling is that by offering a bundle of goods at a lower price than the sum of the prices for the components of the bundle the supplier is able to prevent competition from producers of individual goods within the bundle. (The situation is even more acute if the existence of intellectual property rights or product design by a dominant firm excludes rivals from supplying products that are compatible with its equipment (Whinston, 1990).) However, Adams and Yellen (1976) have shown that commodity bundling can be a form of price discrimination, which serves to sort consumers into groups with different demand characteristics and thereby to extend the market.

One unresolved issue is the extent to which price discriminatory practices can be taken as *evidence* of market dominance, since one view is that the authorities should only be concerned about such practices if the firm has a dominant position. Neven and Phlips (1985) show that price discrimination can occur in oligopoly, but that it disappears as the number of competitors increases. However, in a differentiated goods market even a small supplier might use price discrimination as a marketing strategy in its niche of the market, though the adverse effects on welfare will probably be slight.

Before leaving the subject of price discrimination, it is worth noting again that actual competition policies on price discrimination are sometimes motivated by a concern to protect small businesses *vis-à-vis* large ones, even though the competitive effects of price discrimination may be beneficial (lower prices to consumers). This is certainly the case with the Robinson Patman Act 1936 in the USA. The same concern was expressed in the investigations of discounts to retailers in the UK (MMC Report on Discounts to Retailers, 1981; Office of Fair Trading, 1985), though these reports argued against a general prohibition of price discriminatory practices in favour of a case-by-case evaluation, and the focus was as much on the monopsony power of the larger retail chains.

Another area of firm behaviour that has attracted the attention of competition authorities concerned with the abuse of dominant positions is vertical restraints (Katz, 1989; Waterson, this volume). Examples of such restraints are exclusive distribution agreements, exclusive purchasing agreements, selective distribution systems and exclusive franchises, tie-ins and full-line forcing, refusal to supply, and attempts at resale price maintenance. As Waterson shows, economic analysis has made considerable advances in the past ten years

in developing a framework within which this type of behaviour can be explained. But he also comments that the welfare analysis of restraints is quite equivocal. They will often combine both pro-competitive and anti-competitive effects, and the net welfare effect is unclear. His analysis also shows that Bork's (1978) position, that there is no reason to interfere with contractual relationships since different firms may adopt different marketing strategies, is not sustainable. He is also critical of UK policy that prohibits one form of vertical restraint, namely resale price maintenance, while taking a more relaxed view of other restraints.

3. The acquisition and maintenance of dominant positions

The acquisition of dominant positions in markets has long been a concern of US antitrust, where section 2 of the Sherman Act 1890 outlaws behaviour to 'monopolize or attempt to monopolize' a market. Article 86 of EU Law is *prima facie* only concerned with the abuse of a monopoly position, though the Continental Can judgment implied that an attempt by a firm, which was already dominant, to increase its dominance (e.g. by merger) could be interpreted as an abuse. The UK legislation allows for the scrutiny of mergers, but is generally silent on the acquisition of dominant positions as opposed to the behaviour of firms in maintaining and exploiting these positions once achieved.

These are four means by which firms may achieve dominant positions in markets (Hay and Vickers, 1987):

(i)   The firm is granted market power by a public authority. This is most common in the utility industries—power, water, and telecommunications. In the US these have always been private-sector firms, but subject to regulation. In the UK the process of privatization over the past eleven years has moved utilities from public to private ownership, again under a regime of regulation (Vickers and Yarrow, 1988; Armstrong, Cowan and Vickers, 1994). The rationale for retaining at least part of these industries as single units is that they are 'natural monopolies' with subadditive costs, especially where networks are concerned. Regulation is an indication that competition policy cannot provide a solution to the monopolistic behaviour of these sectors.

(ii)   Achieving dominance by 'skill, foresight, and industry'. The problem for competition policy, as stated by Judge Learned Hand in the Alcoa decision (1945) in the US, is that 'The successful competitor, having been urged to compete, must not be turned upon when he wins' (quoted in Schmalensee (1987)). The problem for competition policy is once again a trade-off. Dynamic competition to establish a dominant position may involve reducing costs, process innovation, and product innovation, which are welfare-enhancing. The resulting market power will generate static welfare losses. The problem is particularly acute where the dynamic competition involves investment in risky R & D: the market power it confers is the incentive for undertaking the investment.

(iii) There is a further problem of distinguishing fair competition (lower prices, better quality) from anticompetitive behaviour, such as predatory pricing, which is the third means by which firms may come to dominate a market (Ordover and Saloner, 1989; Phlips, 1995, ch. IV). Predatory behaviour was discussed above, in the context of a firm abusing a dominant position. The same problems of interpretation of market behaviour apply in this case.

(iv) Acquiring a dominant position by merger has been one of the major routes to achieving dominance in recent experience in the UK and US. Given that merger is the ultimate form of collusion, it might be asked why policy should not take an equally tough stance (Willig, 1991). One reason is that there may be efficiency gains from merger, e.g. due to scale economies. Williamson (1968) showed that quite modest gains in efficiency could offset a substantial increase in monopoly power. The reason is that efficiency gains accrue across the whole range of a firm's output: the welfare losses only arise from the marginal loss in output as monopoly prices are changed. A second reason is that the market for corporate control is thought to be an important disciplining device particularly in those circumstances where competition in product markets is absent. An inefficient management must either improve its performance, or face the consequences of the shareholders selling out to an alternative managerial team. The efficiency of this mechanism has been challenged on both theoretical and empirical grounds. The theoretical argument, stated by Grossman and Hart (1980) (see also Yarrow, 1985), is that shareholders will attempt to free ride on post-merger improvements in performance by not selling their (small) individual holdings. The consequence is that merger bids aimed at improving performance will tend to fail. The empirical grounds are that studies of post-merger performance are far from unanimous in identifying improved performance. For examples, Jensen and Ruback (1983) and Franks and Harris (1989) report substantial gains to shareholders of target firms, but Meeks (1977) and Ravenscraft and Scherer (1987) fail to identify merger gains from accounting data.

Having acquired a dominant position in a market, a firm will presumably seek to exploit that position, unless it is constrained by the threat of potential competition. The constraint of potential entry on the behaviour of dominant firms lies at the heart of the concept of contestable markets (see Baumol, 1982). In a contestable market, existing firms are vulnerable to entry if they attempt to exploit their market power; there are no sunk costs, and hence exit is costless; and entrants have access to the same technology and factor prices as incumbents. While it may be doubted whether contestability theory is an appropriate benchmark for assessing markets, as claimed by its protagonists (for sceptical views see Schwarz, 1986, and Shepherd, 1984), it has performed a useful role by underlining the significance of sunk costs in the analysis of entry.

The literature on strategic entry deterrence has analysed how firms may be able to use sunk costs to maintain dominant positions (Gilbert, 1989; Sutton, 1991). The basic idea is that sunk costs shift profit outcomes in the post-entry game so that a potential entrant will be deterred. The costs must be sunk, otherwise the threat would not be credible and, faced with entry, it would be in the incumbent's interest to reverse the decision. Examples of strategic variables that might be used for entry deterrence include physical capital investment or R & D to reduce costs, pre-emptive patenting, and manipulation of demand conditions by advertising or brand proliferation (for a sceptical analysis see Smiley, 1988). The analytic problem, for competition policy, is that these strategies involve both welfare gains and losses. Thus lower costs and prices arising from R & D or physical investment are beneficial: the loss is that prices might have been even lower had entry not been deterred. Similarly, an increase in the number of brands on offer may be a consumer gain, even though it reduces the probability of new suppliers entering the market in the long run. If we take the robust view that it is long-run competition which is important, and therefore entry-deterring strategies are to be frowned upon, there is the considerable difficulty of distinguishing 'innocent' from 'strategic' behaviour. A firm which innocently seeks to lower costs and improve product quality may simultaneously be making it harder for entry to occur. If it passes on lower costs to its customers in the form of lower prices it may be open to the accusation of behaving in a predatory fashion.

There are other means which firms may use to exclude potential rivals from the market. One literature focuses attention on 'foreclosure': an incumbent may seek to bar entry by entering into exclusive contracts with suppliers or customers (Aghion and Bolton,

1987), or by vertical integration upstream or downstream (Ordover *et al.*, 1990; Hart and Tirole, 1990; Ordover and Saloner, 1989). A similar strategy, explored by Salop and Scheffman (1987), is where integration or contracts entered into by the incumbent have the effect of raising rivals costs, e.g. where a contract with a supplier specifies that an input will only be supplied to an entrant at a higher price than that enjoyed by the incumbent.

In practice, firms may be protected from entry by regulation, and therefore have no need to take steps to deter potential competitors. White (1993) notes that while much has been achieved by deregulation in the US since the 1970s, regulation with anticompetitive effects remains common in the services sector, and much health–safety–environmental regulation is designed in a manner which gives an advantage to incumbent firms. Sapir *et al.* (1993) and Williams (1993), also note the adverse consequences for competition of regulation in the European economies, especially in services.

Finally, there is the possibility of 'excessive entry' (Mankiw and Whinston, 1986), when firms compete in quantities rather than prices, or where products are differentiated. If firms incur fixed costs, a free-entry zero-profit equilibrium may result in too many firms operating with high average costs. Entry deterrence may then be socially optimal, the social costs of higher prices being offset by lower average costs (for an example, see Hay and Morris, 1991, pp. 590–2).

The discussion of this section points to the ubiquity of welfare trade-offs in competition policy issues. This does, of course, greatly complicate the design of policy —both the substance of competition law, and the institutional framework for implementing that law. It is to these questions that we turn in the next section.

IV. Third proposition

The appropriate design of policy and policy institutions is crucial to a successful competition policy.

The design of policy has to take into account the ambiguity of the welfare analysis outlined in the previous section. However, it is clearly infeasible to treat every market situation or example of firm behaviour as being in principle open to investigation and decision by the competition authorities. For one thing, it could absorb a lot of expert resources and the policy gains might not outweigh the costs of investigation in many cases: it could also encourage rent-seeking behaviour.

For another, the main virtue of a market economy is that firms are able to pursue their objectives and allocate resources without being constantly subject to scrutiny. If the advantages of decentralization of decision making are to be preserved, firms must be able to operate within a set of rules for competition that enable them to identify what strategies are likely to attract scrutiny, and what strategies they can pursue without hindrance. It is, therefore, essential that competition policy provides such a set of rules or guidelines.

Hay and Vickers (1987) identified the following general principles for the design of policy:

(i)   There are two types of error that competition policy might make. The first is that desirable behaviour may be condemned or discouraged; the second is the risk of promoting or permitting undesirable behaviour. Policy should, therefore, be framed with a view to minimizing these costs, together with the costs of administering the policy (Hay, 1981). In practice, this means that rules and guidelines are essential. Two examples will be briefly reviewed here. The first example is the EU procedure of providing for block exemptions from Articles 85 and 86 (Whish, 1993, ch. 13). Thus Regulation 418/85 provides exemption for R&D agreements from the effects of Article 85, making it clear that exemptions only apply to agreements that do not extend to joint marketing and selling. Article 4 of the Regulation provides a list of permitted restrictions in such agreements. Similarly, franchise agreements are granted block exemption under Regulation 4087/88. The 1989 White Paper *Opening Markets: New Policy on Restrictive Trade Practices* proposed a similar approach in the revision of UK law. A second example is the US Justice Department Merger Guidelines, the latest version of which was published in 1992 (see White (1993) for a description). One issue is the effect of 'ease of entry' in the post-merger situation, where there are potential anticompetitive effects. Anticipated entry must be probable, rapid, and sufficient to counteract these effects. A second issue is the increase in concentration anticipated in relevant markets, which may be quite narrowly defined. The guidelines are delineated in terms of the Herfindahl–Hirschman Index (HHI), which is the sum of the squares of the market shares, where the shares are expressed in percentages. A merger with a resulting index between 1,000 and 1,800, and an increase in the index of 100 'potentially' will raise competition concerns; a merger with a resulting index which exceeds 1,800, and an increase over 100, will be presumed anticompetitive, though there is an option for the parties to argue otherwise. The Guidelines also spell out in some detail what anticompetitive effects the

Department is concerned about. While the Guidelines are merely informative of how the Justice Department approaches merger situations, and do not bind the Department, the Federal Trade Commission, or private litigants, they are helpful to firms and their advisers in assessing whether a particular merger is likely to be acceptable to the competition authorities. The Justice Department has similar Guidelines setting out the situations in which vertical restraints are likely to attract attention from the authorities.

(ii) Some rules are likely to generate cases where desirable behaviour is discouraged or condemned. If this is a difficulty, the solution is to allow firms to present a case for exemption from those rules if they can demonstrate that the public interest will be furthered thereby. The reason for putting the onus of proof on the firms is that they have both the incentive to make the case, and access to the detailed information on which the case is to be based. This procedure is quite common in competition policy, but by no means universal. For example, it is possible for firms to apply for exemption for agreements under Article 85(3), even where the agreement is not covered by the block exemptions described above. Similarly, it is open to firms to argue for a restrictive agreement before the Restrictive Trade Practices Court, citing one or more of the 'gateways' contained in the Act. This contrasts oddly with the MMC procedure in the case of a merger, where the MMC has to conduct an open inquiry. Obviously it will be in the interests of the firms involved to present evidence favourable to their case. But they do not have to demonstrate that there will be *gains*. The MMC simply has to be satisfied that the merger is not contrary to the public interest.

(iii) The competition authorities should concern themselves with firms' conduct only when there is reason to believe that competition is absent (or would be absent were the conduct permitted). This dictum applies particularly to price discrimination and vertical restraints. As we saw in section III, in the US and EU jurisdictions price discrimination is more or less *per se* illegal: resale price maintenance is also *per se* illegal in all jurisdictions, though it is difficult to justify separating out RPM from other vertical restraints on the basis of economic analysis. The treatment of other vertical restraints—tie-ins, full-line forcing, and rebates— is more variable, though the general drift of policy is antagonistic. However, it is difficult to see how they might generate significant welfare losses (and, indeed, may involve some welfare gains—see Waterson in this volume), unless practised by firms that have significant market power, in which case they may be used to exploit and sustain a dominant position. There can be no objection in principle to a firm in a competitive environment seeking to differentiate its marketing from its rivals, and this may involve vertical restraints such as exclusive distribution or exclusive purchasing, as well as a package of rebates, loyalty bonuses, and discounts to retailers. It is this type of thinking that lies behind the US Justice Department's Vertical Restraints Guidelines mentioned above, though White (1993) remarks that these 1985 Guidelines have not been particularly successful in clarifying the issues, and vertical restraints remain an unsatisfactory area of US antitrust policy. In principle, applications of Article 86, and the investigation of 'anticompetitive practices' under the Competition Act 1980 in the UK are predicated on the existence of market power.

(iv) It ought to be obvious, but is far from universally acknowledged in competition law, that where policy towards market dominance is in question, prevention is better than seeking remedies after a dominant position has been achieved. Short of drastic action, to split up a major firm (as in the AT&T case in the US (Evans, 1983) or to order divestment (as in *Supply of Beer*, 1989), the remedies that can be applied are invariably weak. A major firm has probably sunk cost in such a way that it is unlikely to be successfully challenged by an entrant. Attacks on its conduct (e.g. vertical restraints, price discrimination, etc.) may serve only to decrease its efficiency in extracting monopoly rents, rather than to increase economic efficiency or consumer welfare. Regulation is an option, but creates additional problems of its own, which are unlikely to commend it to the authorities except in exceptional circumstances (e.g. as part of a privatization programme involving natural monopolies). Given these difficulties in dealing with established monopolies it is surprising that only US antitrust identifies 'attempts to monopolize' a market as a breach of the rules (under the Sherman Act). Article 86 of EU law only deals directly with the abuse of a dominant position, presumably once the firm has achieved that position, and until recently the scope for dealing with mergers which create dominant positions was severely limited. In the UK, too, it is conduct to exploit a monopoly position which is attacked under the Fair Trade Act 1973 and the Competition Act 1980, rather than the process of acquiring that position. Mergers that create dominant positions can be referred to the MMC, but there is no presumption against mergers (if anything, the reverse) and general public-interest criteria are applied in their evaluation.

One reason for this reluctance to take action against the process of monopolization is the difficulty of distinguishing acceptable and unacceptable behaviour. As we saw in the previous section, there is an understandable reluctance to move against firms that have competed successfully and won market share. The case history of US antitrust (Alcoa, United Shoe, AT&T, and IBM) in the postwar period is a witness to the difficulties that competition authorities face in this area. In both Alcoa and United Shoe the courts acknowledged that the defendants had built their market shares by legal means, but none the less found them guilty because their respective dominant positions were due to conscious choice. In the IBM case, an additional key feature was the question of the relevant market. The Justice Department, and a number of private litigants, argued that attention should be focused on sub-markets of the computer industry, in many of which IBM did indeed have high market shares. IBM argued that the market should be analysed as a whole, in which the IBM share was considerably less (Brock, 1975; Fisher *et al.*, 1983).

(v) the competition authorities should have powers to impose punishments on firms that engage in anticompetitive practices (e.g. price fixing, and exclusionary or predatory practices), to require firms to enter into binding commitments to desist from conduct that is demonstrably prejudicial to competition, and to propose structural remedies where firms have established a dominant position in a market. The lack of 'teeth' in UK restrictive trades practices policy is in stark contrast to both the US (where executives of colluding companies have been gaoled for conspiracy, in addition to the levying of substantial fines on companies), and the EU (where a firm can be fined up to 10 per cent of its worldwide turnover). Thus an agreement to fix prices or share out markets will be declared unlawful by the Restrictive Trades Practices Court, and struck down. But the Court has no power to impose penalties unless the agreement is a renewing of an agreement that has previously been judged illegal. In all three jurisdictions the authorities can, and do, seek binding undertakings from firms in respect of their market conduct, and can order structural remedies (either formally or as a result of negotiations with the firms involved). Examples are the splitting up of AT&T in the US, referred to above, the more stringent conditions put on the BA/BCal merger by the EU authorities, and the MMC recommendation that the major UK brewers should divest themselves of most of their public houses (*Supply of Beer*, 1989).

A remaining issue is the shape of institutions that should be given the task of enforcing/applying competition law. First, it clearly requires a public institution that is empowered to seek out and to evaluate possible failures of competition (including powers to collect evidence). Private actions, even class actions, are unlikely to prove effective on their own, because of the free-rider problem, given the costs involved. However, White (1993) argues that private actions have played an important role in the development of more effective antitrust in the US, and that the recent decline in the number of cases has allayed the fears, expressed in the 1980s, of excessive litigation. Second, it would be appropriate for this institution to emphasize economic analysis of market dominance and conduct, rather than conformity to legal definitions of anticompetitive market situations and/or conduct. However, as explained above, too much emphasis on economic analysis of each situation generates an impossible situation for firms who wish to know what is or is not permitted. Hence it is important for the legislation to spell out the situations and conduct that will be presumed to be anticompetitive, and to provide for the competition policy institution to publish guidelines as to how it proposes to apply the legislation. Furthermore, the institution should be required to listen to representations from the parties as to why the presumption of the legislation should not apply in a particular case, and to evaluate these representations. Having completed its analysis, the institution should then be required to publish a judgment of the matter under consideration, together with a statement of its arguments in arriving at that judgment.

Third, there should be a competition tribunal, which would be brought in in two circumstances. The first is where the firms are unwilling to accept the judgment of the competition policy institution, and wish to have the case reviewed. The second is where the institution is proposing the imposition of penalties on the firm for particularly outstanding violations of competition law rules without any mitigating circumstances (e.g. persistent involvement in price-fixing cartels). Then the institution should be required to present the matter before the tribunal: an important role of the tribunal would be to prevent arbitrary exercise of power by the competition policy institution. A further right of appeal to higher Courts on interpretation of the law would also be desirable.

The diversity of the actual institutions in the UK, USA, and EU, at first sight, is very great. In the US there are two agencies entrusted with the enforcement of antitrust legislation—the Antitrust Division of the Justice Department, and the Federal Trade Commission. The division of labour between them is not entirely clear, but their overall task is to bring actions against infringement of the provisions of the relevant Acts. There are criminal penalties, including fines and imprisonment, for violations. There is also provision for private litigation, whereby private parties can sue for three times the damages inflicted upon them by violations of the law. In the EU responsibility for competition matters rests with Directorate-General IV of the European Commission (DGIV). They are empowered to investigate breaches of Articles 85 and 86, which deal with competition matters, and where an infringement is identified, to require the parties to desist. Fines of up to 10 per cent of the worldwide turnover of the guilty parties may be imposed. The European Court has powers of judicial review over Commission decisions, and there have been many appeals to the Court against the decisions of DGIV. The Court, therefore, has had a considerable impact on the development of policy. As in the US, there is scope for private parties to bring actions for damages (though not multiple damages) where their interests have been harmed by violations of Articles 85 and 86.

By comparison with the US and the EU, UK competition-policy institutions are a muddle. As far as agreements between firms are concerned the Restrictive Trades Practices Act 1976 requires all agreements to be notified to the Director General of Fair Trading who is then required to refer these to the Restrictive Practices Court. The Court is able to hear arguments from the parties for the exemption of the agreement from the provision of the Act. The precise form of the agreement is very significant: indeed, careful drafting can take an agreement outside the provisions of the Act even when the economic effects are identical to an agreement which is caught by the Act. Other competition matters are handled in the first place by the Office of Fair Trading, which can, under the Competition Act, seek undertakings from firms to desist from certain anticompetitive practices. In merger cases, the Director General of Fair Trading advises the Secretary of State on a reference to the Monopolies and Mergers Commission (MMC). In monopoly cases, either the Director General or the Secretary of State can make the reference. In practice it is almost invariably the Director General who acts, though the Secretary of State initiated the reference of British Gas to the MMC in 1992. The MMC then investigates, and if there is an adverse finding, it makes recommendations to the Secretary of State who is free to accept or reject the recommendations, in whole or in part. The Secretary of State cannot, however, overrule a finding by the MMC that a merger, for example, is not contrary to the public interest. The key feature is that the procedure is administrative (and discretionary): there is no concept of a breach or violation of the relevant competition law, and there is no 'plaintiff' or 'defendant'.

It is evident that US and EU competition policy conform much more closely to the desired shape for competition policy institutions than does current UK policy. However, in practice, the EU system has attracted considerable criticism from competition lawyers. One problem is that appeals to the European Court from decisions of DGIV tend to take a very long time, and there is also some doubt as to whether the Court is an appropriately constituted body to act as a review tribunal in the sense described above. The criticism is that these problems have left DGIV with far too much power to act as both prosecutor and judge in the cases it has pursued. An obvious reform would be to institute a competition tribunal. At least some of these criticisms seem to have been taken on board in the 1992 consultation proposals for reform of UK competition policy described in section II above. The proposals would have given the Office of Fair Trading extensive powers to investigate market conduct, along the lines of the powers exercised by DGIV, and to reach conclusions about fines or remedies. However, the parties would have had access to a specialized competition policy tribunal (a restructured MMC), if they were unhappy with the conclusions of the Office of Fair Trading, and further rights of appeal to the High Court on points of law, on the interpretation of evidence, and on the level of fines.

V. Fourth proposition

International harmonization of competition policies is essential and probably a supranational competition authority as well.

Two further issues for competition policy are becoming increasingly important. One concerns the geographical level at which competition policy should operate, an issue that is arising in the context of EU policy in relation to policy of member states of the EU. The second is the potential for conflict between competition policy and other microeconomic policies, which are often loosely termed 'industrial policies'.

1. The level at which competition policy should operate

The issue to be analysed in this section takes a number of different forms in practice. The most straightforward example is where a firm has a dominant position in the

UK national market, but argues before the competition authorities that the relevant market definition is not national, but, for example, the whole EU. A more complex case is where the supplier in the UK national market is a branch of a multinational company, which has made an agreement with other multinationals to share out world markets by allocating different economies to different suppliers. How can the national competition authorities take action against the suppliers? Similarly, the UK national market may be supplied by a group of firms, say American firms, that have (legally) formed an export cartel. Alternatively, consider a case where a UK firm merges with an overseas firm, which was not currently serving the UK market, but which had the potential to enter the UK market. Obviously, potential competition is reduced though current supplies are not affected. Should the UK competition authorities seek to block the merger?

In principle, once the market has been defined, then it is appropriate to apply competition policy to that market. A sensible division of labour then suggests itself. If a particular market is 'national' in the sense that the good in question is strictly non-tradable, then it is appropriate for the issue to be considered by a national authority. If, however, the market is international, and the good in question widely traded, then a higher level authority is required (or full collaboration between the national authorities affected). The relationship between UK and EU competition policy approximates to this division of labour. Thus UK competition policy is very clearly directed at market behaviour and conduct that affects the supply of goods and services *within the United Kingdom*. So the behaviour of an overseas firm is not investigated unless its actions and the consequent effects are felt in the domestic market. EU competition policy, by contrast, applies when trade between member states is affected, or potentially affected, by the conduct which is being scrutinized. The rule is that EU competition law takes precedence over UK law, though this has not prevented merger cases being examined by both jurisdictions (e.g. British Airways/British Caledonian, 1987). The 1989 EU Regulation on mergers should help to allocate jurisdiction in these cases.

However, this neat division of labour is predicated on being able to distinguish traded and non-traded goods in a precise fashion. In practice, the problem of market definition remains. Because of transport costs one might expect heavy building materials, such as cement, to be non-traded. However, as UK cement manufacturers discovered to their cost, high prices in the UK market made it worthwhile for low cost EU and third country suppliers, located at deep water ports, to begin supplying the UK market. The basic point is that, in the absence of major tariff or non-tariff barriers to trade, a good becomes more 'traded' (i.e. attracting import competition) the higher the domestic price. Obviously the potential for entry via imports needs to be considered carefully by domestic competition authorities in assessing whether a firm is dominant and whether it is abusing its monopoly position. This emphasizes a further point to which domestic competition authorities need to apply their minds. It is quite possible that a good is in principle tradable, but that the domestic distribution system has been 'captured' by a single supplier in such a way that entry by trade is difficult. But a national authority may find it (politically) difficult to pursue a domestic firm with a view to enabling foreign firms to achieve a greater market share. The EU authorities will need to intervene on the grounds that potential trade is being stifled. However, the EU authorities should not be over zealous in this matter to the extent of arguing that any territorial division of the EU market, especially the charging of different prices in different countries, is a sign of non-competitive behaviour. Thus in the United Brands (1978) case, the company was not permitted to charge (in Rotterdam/Bremerhaven) different prices for bananas depending on where they were to be sold (lowest price in Eire, highest price in Germany). As noted above, the welfare effects of price discrimination can be positive, and it should not be treated automatically as an abuse of a dominant position.

There remains the case where a group of firms in a third country form an export cartel (e.g. a group of United States firms forming an export cartel as permitted by the Webb–Pomerene Act of 1918). The UK maintains a strong doctrine of extraterritoriality which means that UK competition policy cannot be applied in such cases, any more than US antitrust policy would be permitted to pursue a cartel of UK firms exporting to the US. The EU position remains unclear. In the Wood Pulp case (1985) the Commission held that a concerted practice by non-EU firms fell within the jurisdiction of EU law because of the *effects* on the EU market. The Court avoided this doctrine by finding that the agreement had been *implemented* within the EU, and hence fell within the jurisdiction of EU law. Such cases do, however, point to the need for international collaboration to promote competition in global markets.

The issue of jurisdiction in competition policy is discussed by Neven and Siotis (1993), in the context of an analysis of foreign direct investment (FDI). They note that some explanations of FDI appeal to the existence of market failures and imperfect competition, and hence imply the need for careful scrutiny by competition authorities. In particular, a firm undertaking FDI needs a firm-specific advantage (e.g. a brand name of a patent), which it prefers to exploit itself rather than license to an existing domestic producer. Furthermore, there must be country-specific advantages in producing there rather than exporting. These advantages may relate to factor supplies, technology spillovers from domestic firms that can only be captured by locating there, the need to jump over trade barriers, or simply the opportunity to exploit a potential monopoly position. The competition policy issues follow from this analysis. Intangible assets may give rise to market power rents in addition to pure rents on specific attributes, where the asset is used strategically to prevent entry by a competitor. On the other hand, FDI with superior technology could generate net welfare gains, despite monopoly rents, especially if there are spillovers to host-country producers (e.g. where FDI is subject to local content rules). But this latter argument can be reversed if the motivation for FDI is to source technology from domestic suppliers. The issue of jurisdiction is raised most acutely where FDI is by means of acquisition. As noted above, acquisition may *indirectly* affect competition in the domestic market by eliminating a potential alternative supplier, even though the market structure is unchanged. An FDI acquisition may also affect competition in a third market to which both the acquirer and the acquired firms were actual or potential suppliers.

2. Competition policy and industrial policies

The discussion of export cartels in the previous section has pointed to the possibility that competition policy might be designed and applied to protect domestic markets and to promote domestic producers in export markets (Hay, 1994). Indeed, it is not unusual for business groups to argue that competition policy should be used in this way.

There are a number of ways in which competition policy might be applied (or fail to be applied!) to protect the domestic market. One route is to take a hostile view of takeovers involving the absorption of a domestic firm by a foreign buyer, since takeover is often the best method for a potential competitor to get an initial share in the domestic market. In practice, the MMC has sometimes reported against foreign takeovers as contrary to the public interest, but the reasoning has been other than a desire to stifle competition (e.g. the report on Government of Kuwait/British Petroleum, 1988, which decided that it was contrary to the public

interest for the Government of Kuwait to gain a major shareholding in BP). A second route might be to allow domestic producers to agree on predatory responses to attempts by foreign suppliers to enter the national market. A third route could be to permit vertical relationships and restraints between domestic producers, or domestic producers and distributors, which made it difficult either for a foreign firm to set up production and gain essential supplies, or for a foreign firm to get access to existing distribution networks. None of these possibilities is countenanced by competition policy in any of the three jurisdictions previously discussed, though there have been calls for a more protectionist approach in the US.

We should also note that there are some trade measures that are protectionist in effect, and have strong links with competition policy. A sector which is under pressure from imports may seek voluntary export restraints on the part of the foreign suppliers (a wide range of Japanese exports to the United States and the EU have been affected by such agreements). Alternatively, a hard-pressed sector may seek to persuade its government to invoke anti-dumping measures. The parallel is with the treatment of predatory pricing in competition policy. Anti-dumping measures are supposed to be a response to 'unfair' competition, but it is difficult to distinguish genuine low-cost entry from predatory entry by foreign suppliers. If all else fails, a sector which is being undermined by imports may successfully apply for exemption from restrictions on the formation of a cartel to enable the decline of the sector to proceed in an orderly manner. A number of such cartels have been permitted, indeed promoted, by the EU authorities.

Industrial policy is usually linked to promotion of exports rather than the protection of the domestic market *per se*. The key insights were provided by Krugman (1984): protection of a market enables domestic producers to realize economies of scale or learning by doing, and to recoup R & D costs, so that when protection is removed, and the firms begin to export they have cost advantages over foreign producers and can capture larger market shares. Itoh *et al.* (1991) have analysed various industrial policy measures that may achieve these ends, including direct and indirect subsidies to producers as well as standard protectionist measures such as tariffs, quotas, and non-tariff barriers. Our focus here is on the use of competition policy to achieve the same ends.

There are three ways in which competition policy might be used to promote the interests of domestic producers. The first is permitting the creation of 'national champions'. Thus firms may be allowed to grow to dominate their domestic market, by internal growth or by merger, on the pretext of creating firms that will be able to compete on 'equal terms' in world markets. If these world markets are themselves genuinely competitive, and if the domestic market is open to imports, then there may be little direct harm resulting from the pursuit of large scale (though ideally one would wish there to be some scrutiny of the dominant firm in the context of the world market by a supra-national competition authority). However, the domestic competition authorities should satisfy themselves that the domestic market *is* genuinely open. Arguments for 'national champions' have sometimes appeared in MMC reports, notably the BA/BCal (1987) Report. Sapir *et al.* (1993) identify a 1990 decision of the European Commission to permit a co-operation agreement on R&D, production, and marketing of electronic components for satellites, on the grounds that the companies otherwise would find it difficult to compete with non-European suppliers.

A second method of promoting the interests of domestic producers is by permitting them to enter into collaborations of various kinds. One kind is the establishment of joint ventures for exporting: the justification is that they can share the fixed costs, and pool expertise, in penetrating foreign markets, and that they can avoid competing against each other for foreign orders. Export cartels are permitted under both UK and US competition law. The justification is that it is undesirable for domestic firms to compete against each other in overseas markets: national welfare is enhanced if they maximize their joint rents. As we have seen, this gain is a loss to the welfare of consumers in the country to which they are exporting, and the cartel would, therefore, presumably be disallowed by an international competition authority.

Other joint ventures are in R & D: once again the gain is the sharing of fixed costs and the avoidance of costly duplication of activities. Another type of collaboration is a specialization agreement where firms agree to specialize in production so that they can achieve scale economies, with commitments to supply each other (on favourable terms) with the products that the other is not producing. All these possibilities are recognized in EU competition policy, and are given exemption from Article 85 so long as certain safeguards are in place. R & D agreements and specialization agreements between UK firms can be drafted in such a way as to fall outside the Restrictive Trade Practices Act 1976: otherwise firms might be able to appeal to the permissive stance of EU law to override any difficulties with the UK rules. The Director General of Fair Trading has indicated that joint ventures can be made the subject of a direction (under section 21(2) of the Act) by the Secretary of State to the Director General not to take proceedings before the Restrictive Practices Court.

3. Implications for competition policy jurisdiction

It will be evident that the two issues raised in this section—the appropriate level for competition policy, and the use of competition policy as a tool of industrial policy (whether protectionist or promotional)—are two sides of the same question. The question is whether competition policy is seeking to raise the welfare of a particular economy, or whether it should be used as an instrument to promote economic efficiency at a supranational (or even international) level. In respect of UK membership of the EU it should be recalled that Article 3(f) of the Treaty of Rome provides for 'the institution of a system ensuring that competition in the common market is not distorted'. In principle that must imply the abandonment of any attempt by member governments to use competition policy to protect or promote their domestic industry (just as other industrial and trade policy measures have had to be progressively abandoned). It also implies the need to harmonize UK and EU competition policies, and to make clear the division of labour between them: this will almost certainly imply a greater role for EU policy, and a diminution of the authority of UK policy and institutions. At the international level much will depend on whether the OECD countries continue to pursue free trade, or whether protectionist tendencies proliferate. If free trade remains the objective then agreements on international aspects of competition policy to collaborate in the implementation of competition policy, where more than one economy is affected, will be required.

Neven and Siotis (1993) contrast decentralization of policy to competition authorities in member states with centralization in a strengthened DGIV in Brussels. In favour of decentralization, they appeal to the doctrine of subsidiarity, and additionally argue that a supranational authority is likely to be unduly prone to capture by interest groups. But they recognize that decentralization will only work if there is agreement on the fundamental competition rules to be applied (with little or no discretion), and if there are clear rules for allocating cases across jurisdictions (e.g. where a particular merger will have competition implications in several member states of the EU). There is a particular danger that national competition policies might be used in a protectionist or promotional manner as described above to give advantage to domestic producers. The experience of the EU with member state aids to attract foreign direct investment should serve as a warning that EU rules are not always sufficient to prevent member states from taking unilateral steps to improve their national economies at the expense of others.

VI. Conclusions: what should be done about competition policy in the UK and EU?

The paper has argued four propositions concerning competition policy. The first three relate to the objectives and design of policy and institutions and form a logical sequence; the fourth looks at international aspects of policy, particularly the issue of policy jurisdiction between, for example, the member states of the EU and the European Commission in Brussels. We began in section II with the proposition that competition policy should seek to promote economic efficiency. The alternatives are that it should promote competition, *per se*, or that it should operate with fairly broadly defined public-interest criteria. We rejected the former alternative on the grounds that competition can, paradoxically, sometimes be inimical to economic efficiency. The public-interest objective is harder to reject, because it is eminently reasonable that public policy should be concerned with more than just economic efficiency, though it clearly generates considerable uncertainty for firms about what they may and may not do. However, we suggested that this point can be met substantially by the traditional argument about economic policy making, that it is best to assign separate instruments to different targets. If there is, for example, an active regional policy, then regional issues need not be on the competition policy agenda.

If the first proposition is accepted, it is then necessary to identify market situations and conduct, which are, or are not, conducive to economic efficiency. In section III of the paper, the common policy agenda across different competition policy jurisdictions was identified as (i) agreements between firms, (ii) abuse of dominant positions, and (iii) the acquisition and maintenance of dominant positions. Developments in industrial organization theory in the last fifteen years have shown that the effects on economic efficiency in these three areas are seldom entirely clear cut: usually there is a trade-off involved with ambiguous net effects on welfare (price-fixing cartels are one exception, where it is extremely difficult to identify offsetting efficiency gains). This judgement gives rise to our second proposition: economic analysis is often ambiguous, a priori, about the efficiency effects of particular market structures and conduct.

The second proposition generates a considerable difficulty for the design of competition policy. A policy which requires a case-by-case approach would not only be extremely expensive, but would also completely fail to provide firms with a well-defined framework within which to pursue their activities. The third proposition is, therefore, that institutional design is crucial for competition policy. In particular, policy rules and guidelines are necessary to spell out the presumptions of policy, but there should generally be a procedure by which firms can present a case for exemption if they can demonstrate offsetting efficiency gains (an exception might be price-fixing cartels). Furthermore, the rules and guidelines should identify situations where there is good reason to believe that competition might be absent, before any investigation of supposed 'anticompetitive practices' such as price discrimination or vertical restraints. The US Justice Department's Merger Guidelines and Vertical Restraints Guidelines are examples of rules designed to give an initial screen, and are obviously extremely helpful to firms and their advisers. Not least, they serve as a warning to firms that are building dominant positions in markets that their conduct is likely to be scrutinized if their market share crosses a given threshold. Finally, we have argued that an appropriate institutional design must involve giving the competition authorities real 'teeth' to fine firms for abuses of market power, and to order structural remedies or regulation where the circumstances warrant such action.

There remains the question of the optimal shape of the competition policy institutions. We have argued that such institutions should be public (though not ruling out the possibility of a role, even an important role, for private actions, as an additional deterrent to abuses of market power); that there should be a single investigating institution with powers to identify and to investigate cases, and to propose remedies, within a clearly stated framework of rules and guidelines; that firms should be given an opportunity to make representations as to why the competition policy presumptions should not apply in a particular case; and that there should be a competition tribunal with the task of reviewing and monitoring the recommendations of the competition policy institution.

(i) UK competition policy

By the standards of these three propositions, UK competition policy is in need of a radical reform. First, it is evident that the broad public interest criteria which are identified in the Fair Trading Act 1973 and the Competition Act 1980, and the existence of the 'gateways' in the Restrictive Trades Practices Act 1976, potentially (and in practice) permit issues to be considered that either have little or nothing to do with economic efficiency, or are more properly the concern of other areas of policy. Second, this lack of focus not only renders policy less effective, but crucially the absence of clearly stated rules and guidelines introduces great uncertainty for firms. It is notable that in recent years, the 'Tebbit doctrine' has sought to narrow the scope of monopoly and merger references to cases that raise clear issues of competition. It is, however, unsatisfactory to have the general content of policy dependent on the whims of the Secretary of State.[3] In the area of restrictive trades practices, the problem is not so much the absence of rules, as the form the rules take. In particular, the focus on the form of restrictive agreements, rather than on their effects, means that careful drafting can take some agreements between firms outside the scope of the legislation.

Third, the institutional arrangements in the UK are a mess. There is a multiplicity of competition-policy institutions—notably the Office of Fair Trading, the Monopolies and Mergers Commission, and the Restrictive Trades Court—which are entrusted with different responsibilities under the relevant legislation. There is no justification in economic analysis for giving different institutional treatment to different competition policy areas. Fourth, the absence of penalties for abuses, such as involvement in price-fixing, means that firms have every incentive to engage in anticompetitive behaviour until they are discovered. (The lack of teeth in terms of penalties is compounded by a lack of powers to search for evidence of abuses.)

Much of this critique of current policy was taken into account in the White Paper outlining new policy on restrictive trades practices (Department of Trade and Industry, 1989), and the consultation document on options to tighten up the legislation and policy implementation in the area of abuse of market power (Department of Trade and Industry, 1992).[4] As explained

above, the main feature of these proposals was that the UK should adopt an Article 85-type law on restrictive trade practices, and an Article 86-type law on abuse of market power (though this is only one of the options put forward), while retaining the present UK arrangements for mergers policy. There is no doubt that such a reform would represent a decisive shift in the direction of the 'best practice' competition policy and institutions outlined previously. Policy would focus on economic efficiency, there would be explicit rules and guidelines (including exemptions from the rules), there would be a relatively unified set of competition-policy institutions (a strengthened OFT, and a reformed MMC to act as a tribunal to review the analysis and proposals for fines or remedies made by the OFT), and there would be penalties for abuses.

However, although we believe that a reform along these lines does offer the best way forward, it is appropriate to note some of the possible drawbacks. One is the loss of flexibility: there is a tension between the objective of promoting economic efficiency in different market situations, and the need to provide rules or guidelines to indicate to firms the boundaries between acceptable and unacceptable market structures or conduct. Rules, and the policy institutions that apply them, are inevitably less flexible than a discretionary policy. Another drawback is that a rules-based policy, especially where this is drafted in terms of prohibitions with penalties for non-compliance, may be less than appropriate for dealing with problems of uncompetitive market structures. For example, as noted previously, a market situation may not be conducive to economic efficiency, but the conduct of the firms that make up the market may be 'innocent'. Therefore, we would wish to maintain the scope for competition policy authorities to propose structural remedies, e.g. divestment, or regulation, or to seek undertakings from firms, even where there is no identifiable abuse.

To conclude, our analysis suggests that the 1989 White Paper and the 1992 consultation document proposals for the reform of UK competition policy were broadly consistent with the goal of improving economic efficiency in the market place. It is therefore very disappointing that those proposals have been taken no further. The promised legislation on restrictive practices policy has not found a place in the governments legislative programme, and a decision was taken in 1993 not to proceed with the proposals for an Article 86-type reform of policy on the abuse of market power, when the government announced its conclusions on the

---

[3] It is probably infeasible to rule out entirely political 'interference' in particular cases (e.g. takeovers in the defence industry or the media), where wider public interest issues are involved. It would be best if such decisions were taken *after* the MMC had reported on competition issues. The Secretary of State would then have to justify to Parliament any decision on public-interest grounds.

[4] An earlier review of mergers policy (Department of Trade and Industry, 1988) had concluded that the general thrust of policy in this area was satisfactory, but made a number of recommendations, which were subsequently implemented, including arrangements for the pre-

notification of mergers, and for the OFT to accept statutory undertakings from the parties to avoid a reference to the MMC.

consultations that had followed publication of the document on *Abuse of Market Power*. The document had asked for comments on three legislative options: (i) strengthening existing competition legislation; (ii) a prohibition system based on Article 86; and (iii) a hybrid option combining (i) and (ii). The decision was to pursue the first option with some changes to current legislation: stronger investigative powers for the Director General of Fair Trading; permitting the Director General to accept enforceable undertakings from companies before an investigation under the Competition Act, or in lieu of a monopoly reference under the Fair Trading Act; and scope for interim orders under the Competition Act to prohibit specific activities by a firm where there is a risk of serious damage to a competitor, supplier, or customer during the period of the MMC's investigation.

While these measures to strengthen existing legislation are generally to be welcomed, the unwillingness of the government to pursue reform along the lines of Article 86 was very disappointing, given the case for a more radical reform made in the main text of the document. The reasons for not pursuing a more radical course were given by the government as the increased burden of compliance placed on companies, the absence of clear criteria for what constitutes an abuse of market power giving rise to uncertainty for business (and the possible consequent 'chilling effect' on competitive behaviour), and the suggestion that a prohibition system would bite on fewer market situations than present legislation.

In response to this first reason, it should be noted that major UK companies with involvement in European markets already have to maintain sophisticated compliance programmes with respect to EU Article 86: parallel UK legislation might, therefore, be expected to reduce the total costs of compliance for these companies as it would cut out some duplication. Compliance with new legislation might, however, be more costly for firms that are dominant in UK markets alone, and do not currently regard the powers of the OFT and MMC as sufficient of a threat to require them to take competition policy particularly seriously. The difference, of course, is that under Article 86-type legislation there would be a prospect of fines for abuse of market power, giving rise to potential costs much greater than those incurred by an MMC inquiry. The second reason given seems a little odd at first: a specific list of prohibited practices can only decrease the degree of uncertainty for firms compared to the current arrangements, where *nothing* is specified. But the presence or absence of specificity may not matter much where the most serious penalty is an OFT or MMC

inquiry. Matters are quite different if substantial fines are in prospect. The argument is that:

It can be very difficult to assess in advance what will be regarded as anticompetitive and what is acceptable business behaviour. This inherent uncertainty, coupled with the possibility of fines and private actions, could risk inhibiting rather than promoting competition. (Neil Hamilton, Minister of State for Corporate Affairs, in a statement to the House of Commons, 14 April 1993.)

This concern could, however, be easily met if it were made clear that fines would only be recommended by the OFT as a matter of course where a company had evidently breached one of the prohibitions. In 'grey' areas it would be appropriate for no fines to be levied initially, until some cases had established whether a particular practice was generally an abuse of market power. Summing up on the first and second reasons, it is evident that the main objection to Article 86 legislation is that business does not relish the prospect of fines for abuse of monopoly power, because it would have to take competition policy more seriously in future. But that is precisely what *is* needed, and it is disappointing that for this reason the government has drawn back from attempting reform. The third reason given for not pursuing a more radical reform is that a prohibition system would bite on fewer market situations than present legislation. The thought is presumably that, whereas at present any monopoly or complex monopoly situation can in principle be referred to the MMC, under an Article 86-type policy there would have to be *prima facie* evidence of abuse. But in practice past references to the MMC have been linked, implicitly at least, to some suspicion that firms have been acting anticompetitively. In any case, this concern about Article 86 legislation could be met relatively easily by retaining monopoly references to the MMC, with the OFT proposing behavioural or structural remedies, where a market situation was not in the public interest but there was no evidence of abuse by the firms involved.

Some further consequences of the government's decision should be noted. The first is that however the decision is presented, one suspects that it represents a reversal of the previous commitment of the government to strengthening competition. A second consequence is that UK competition law will remain out of line with EU law. The EU Commission is, therefore, less likely to be willing to leave Article 86-type competition cases to the UK competition authorities, and disputes over jurisdiction are, therefore, more likely. Third, a soft UK policy on abuse of market power will make it more difficult for the UK to argue that the EU should strengthen its merger policy (see below).

This decision represents a disappointing failure to embark on a much needed set of reforms. The UK has had an inadequate competition policy framework for far too long.

(ii) EU competition policy

Given our endorsement of an Article 85 and Article 86 reform for UK competition policy, it is unsurprising that our evaluation of EU policy has been positive. However, there are a number of areas that are a cause for concern. The first is that while Article 85 has a section 3, which permits both block and individual exemptions to be granted on the basis of beneficial affects of particular agreements, there are no corresponding sections in either Article 86 or the Merger Regulation. This denies market participants the opportunity to argue that a particular merger or dominant firm practice does offer efficiency gains. One danger in giving such an opportunity might be that it would give greater scope for industrial policy ('European champions') proponents, not least within the European Commission: however, that is not a reason for preventing DGIV from considering the point in a particular case, however sceptically. There is, however, a second concern, as noted by Sapir *et al.* (1993) and by Neven *et al.* (1993) that EU merger policy, even since the introduction of the Merger Regulation, has been seen to be ineffective. Tougher policy rules, and tougher implementation are required. A third concern, expressed above in relation to the proposals for UK policy, is that Article 86 does not provide for remedies where a market situation is not conducive to economic efficiency but the actual conduct of dominant firms is 'innocent'. A fourth concern is that the rules on price discrimination and vertical restraints, for example, do not reflect the ambiguity of economic analysis with respect to the welfare consequences of these practices. The lists of prohibited practices need revision, and a section 3 procedure for individual exceptions needs to be introduced, as previously argued. A fifth concern is the absence of a specialized competition tribunal to review the decisions of DGIV. The European Court procedure is too slow and cumbersome. The effect has been to leave DGIV acting as both prosecutor and judge in competition cases, which is unacceptable. Finally, as Sapir *et al.* argue European policy should give more emphasis to the supply of services, and particularly to the detrimental effects of regulation on competition.

The fourth proposition in the paper is that harmonization of national competition policies, and possibly a supranational competition policy authority, are essential. The obvious application of this proposition is to relationships between European policy and DGIV on the one hand, and policy and institutions in the UK (or any other member state of the EU) on the other hand. This is not just for administrative tidiness: lack of co-ordination generates significant problems. The first is where the relevant market or markets being examined in a competition case are genuinely multinational, and the issue of extraterritoriality is raised. A particular example is where a merger wholly overseas affects the level of competition, or potential competition, in a domestic market. The question is whether domestic competition-policy authorities have the capacity to pursue the issue. Either there have to be bilateral agreements between the competition-policy authorities in different economies, or they have to cede the authority to act to a supranational body. Obviously there will have to be agreements on the division of labour between national authorities and the supranational agency. The EU Merger Regulation spells out some rules, mainly relating to the degree to which the parties are operating in more than one member state, and the overall size of the merger. In other policy areas, as noted previously, all EU policy rules take precedence over national policy, though DGIV is unlikely to get involved with competition in national domestic markets unless trade within the Union is potentially affected.

The second problem is that a lax competition policy might be used by a member state as a substitute for trade policy or industrial policy, to protect domestic producers or to promote export sectors. The solution here, as in trade policy (the GATT), is for international agreements to harmonize policies. It is a moot point whether a supranational authority is also required. Obviously, consistency in competition policy is going to be easier to achieve with a central authority. In the EU context, the ability of DGIV to override member-state interests is probably crucial for full integration of the European market.

If this fourth proposition is accepted, it is an additional reason to argue for a reform of UK competition policy to bring it into line with European policy. At the same time, the UK should press for reform of EU policy to deal with the weaknesses identified above. The major practical difficulty is decisions on whether the EU or UK authorities should handle a particular case. As in the case of the EU Merger Regulation, published rules for assignment are probably the best method with negotiation between the authorities to decide borderline cases.

References

Adams, W. J., and Yellen, J. (1976), 'Commodity Bundling and the Burden of Monopoly', *Quarterly Journal of Economics*, **90**, 475–98.

Aghion, P., and Bolton, P. (1987), 'Contracts as a Barrier to Entry', *American Economic Review*, 77, 388–401.

Armstrong, M., Cowan, S., and Vickers, J. S. (1994), *Regulatory Reform: Economic Analysis and British Experience*, Cambridge Mass., MIT Press.

Baumol, W. J. (1982), 'Contestable Markets: An Uprising in the Theory of Industry Structure', *American Economic Review*, 72, 1–15.

Bolton, P., and Scharfstein, D. (1990), 'A Theory of Predation Based on Agency Problems in Financial Contracting', *American Economic Review*, **80**, 93–106.

Bork, R. H. (1978), *The Antitrust Paradox*, New York, Basic Books.

Brock, G. W. (1975), *The US Computer Industry: A Study of Market Power*, Cambridge MA, Harvard University Press.

Department of Trade and Industry (1988), *Mergers Policy*, London, HMSO.

—— (1989), *Opening Markets: New Policy on Restrictive Trade Practices*, Cm 727, London, HMSO.

—— (1992), *Abuse of Market Power: A Consultation Document on Possible Legislative Options*, CM 2100, London, HMSO.

Dixit, A. K., and Norman, V. (1978), 'Advertising and Welfare', *Bell Journal*, 9, 1–17.

Evans, D. S. (ed.) (1983), *Breaking up Bell*, New York, North Holland.

Fisher, F., McGowan, J., and Greenwood, J. (1983), *Folded, Spindled and Mutilated: Economic Analysis and US vs. IBM*, Cambridge MA, MIT Press.

Franks, J., and Harris, R. (1989), 'Shareholder Wealth Effects of UK Takeovers', in J. A. Fairburn and J. A. Kay (eds.), *Mergers and Merger Policy*, 148–74, Oxford, Oxford University Press.

Geroski, P. A. (1993), 'Antitrust policy towards cooperative R & D ventures', *Oxford Review of Economic Policy*, 9(2), 58–71.

Gilbert, R. J. (1989), 'Mobility Barriers and the Value of Incumbency', ch. 8 in R. Schmalensee and R. Willig (eds.), *Handbook of Industrial Organisation*, Amsterdam, North Holland.

—— Newbery, D. M. G. (1982), 'Pre-emptive Patenting and the Persistence of Monopoly', *American Economic Review*, 72, 514–25.

Grossman, S., and Hart, O. D. (1980), 'Takeover Bids, the Free-rider Problem and the Theory of the Corporation', *Bell Journal*, 11, 42–64.

Hart, O., and Tirole, J. (1990), 'Vertical Integration and Market Foreclosure', *Brookings Papers on Economic Activity, Microeconomics*, 205–86.

Hay, D. A. (1994), 'International aspects of competition policy in the United Kingdom', University of Oxford Institute of Economics and Statistics Applied Economics Discussion Paper Series no. 160.

Hay, D. A., and Vickers, J. S. (1987), 'The Economics of Market Dominance', ch. of D. A. Hay and J. S. Vickers (eds.), *The Economics of Market Dominance*, Oxford, Blackwell.

—— Morris, D. J. (1991), *Industrial Economics and Organization*, Oxford, Oxford University Press.

Hay, G. A. (1981), 'A Confused Lawyer's Guide to the Predatory Pricing Literature' in S. Salop (ed.), *Strategy, Predation and Antitrust Analysis*, Washington DC, Federal Trade Commission.

—— (1987), 'The Interaction of Market Structure and Conduct', ch. 4 in D. A. Hay and J. S. Vickers (eds.), *The Economics of Market Dominance*, Oxford, Blackwell.

Itoh, M., Kiyono, K., Okuno-Fugiwara, M., and Suzumura, K. (1991), *Economic Analysis of Industrial Policy*, San Diego, Academic Press.

Jacquemin, A., and Slade, M. E. (1989), 'Cartels, Collusion and Horizontal Merger', ch. 7 in R. Schmalensee and R. Willig (eds.), *Handbook of Industrial Organisation*, Amsterdam, North Holland.

Jensen, M. C., and Ruback, R. (1983), 'The Market for Corporate Control: The Scientific Evidence', *Journal of Financial Economics*, 11, 5–50.

Katz, M. L. (1989), 'Vertical Contractual Relations', ch. 11 in R. Schmalensee and R. Willig (eds.), *Handbook of Industrial Organisation*, Amsterdam, North Holland.

Klemperer, P. (1987), 'The Competitiveness of Markets with Switching Costs', *Rand Journal of Economics*, 18, 138–50.

Krugman, P. R. (1984), 'Import Protection as Export Promotion: International Competition in the Presence of Oligopoly and Scale Economies', in H. Kierzkowski (ed.), *Monopolistic Competition and International Trade*, Oxford, Oxford University Press.

Lambin, J. J. (1976), *Advertising, Competition and Market Conduct in Oligopoly over Time*, Amsterdam, North-Holland.

Littlechild, S. C. (1986), *The Fallacy of the Mixed Economy*, 2nd edn., London, IEA.

Mankiw, N. G., and Whinston, M. D. (1986), 'Free Entry and Social Inefficiency', *Rand Journal of Economics*, 17, 48–58.

Meeks, G. (1977), *Disappointing Marriage: A Study of the Gains from Merger*, Cambridge, Cambridge University Press.

Milgrom, P., and Roberts, J. (1982), 'Limit Pricing and Entry under Incomplete Information', *Econometrica*, 50, 443–60.

Neale, A. D. (1970), *The Antitrust Laws of the USA: A Study of Competition Enforced by Law*, 2nd edn., Cambridge, Cambridge University Press (a third edition with D. G. Goyder as an additional author, was published in 1980).

Neven, D., Nuttall, R., and Seabright, P. (1993), *Merger in Daylight*, London, CEPR.

Neven, D., and Phlips, L. (1985), 'Discriminating Oligopolists and Common Markets', *Journal of Industrial Economics*, 34, 133–50.

Neven, D., and Siotis, G. (1993), 'Foreign direct investment in the European Community: some policy issues', *Oxford Review of Economic Policy*, 9(2), 72–93.

Office of Fair Trading (1985), *Competition and Retailing*, London, Office of Fair Trading.

Ordover, J. A., and Saloner, G. (1989), 'Predation, monopolization and antitrust', ch. 9 in R. Schmalensee and R. Willig (eds.), *Handbook of Industrial Organisation*, Amsterdam, North Holland.

—— and Salop, S. (1990), 'Equilibrium vertical foreclosure', *American Economic Review*, 80, 127–42.

Phlips, L. (1983), *The Economics of Price Discrimination*, Cambridge, Cambridge University Press.

—— (1987), 'Information and Collusion', ch. 4 of D. A. Hay and J. S. Vickers (eds.), *The Economics of Market Dominance*, Oxford, Blackwell.

—— (1995), *Competition Policy: A Game Theoretic Perspective*, Cambridge, Cambridge University Press.

Ravenscraft, D., and Scherer, F. M. (1987), *Mergers, Sell-Offs and Economic Efficiency*, Washington, The Brookings Institution.

Rees, R. (1993), 'Tacit collusion', *Oxford Review of Economic Policy*, 9(2), 27–40.

Richardson, G. B. (1965), 'The Theory of Restrictive Practices', *Oxford Economic Papers*, 19, 432–49.

Salop, S. (1979), 'Monopolistic Competition with Outside Goods', *Bell Journal*, 10, 141–56.

—— (1985), 'Practices that (Credibly) Facilitate Oligopoly Coordination', in F. Mathewson and J. E. Stiglitz (eds.), *New Developments in the Analysis of Market Structure*, London, Macmillan.

—— Scheffman, D. (1987), 'Cost Raising Strategies', *Journal of Industrial Economics*, 36, 19–34.

Sapir, A., Buigues, P., and Jacquemin, A. (1993), 'European Competition Policy in Manufacturing and Services: a two speed approach?', *Oxford Review of Economic Policy*, 9(2), 113–32.

Schmalensee, R. (1978), 'Entry Deterrence in the Ready to Eat Breakfast Cereal Industry', *Bell Journal*, 9, 305–27.

—— (1981), 'Output and Welfare Implications of Monopolistic Third Degree Price Discrimination', *American Economic Review*, 71, 242–7.

—— (1987), 'Standards for Dominant Firms' Conduct: What can Economics Contribute?', ch. 2 of D. A. Hay and J. S. Vickers (eds.), *The Economics of Market Dominance*, Oxford, Blackwell.

Schwarz, M. (1986), 'The Nature and Scope of Contestability Theory', *Oxford Economic Papers*, 38, 37–57.

Shepherd, W. (1984), 'Contestability vs. Competition', *American Economic Review*, 74, 572–87.

Smiley, R. (1988), 'Empirical Evidence on Strategic Entry Deterrence', *International Journal of Industrial Organisation*, 16, 167–80.

Smith, A. (1776), *The Wealth of Nations* (available in a Penguin Classics edition, 1986).

Sutton, J. (1991), *Sunk Costs and Market Structure*, London, MIT Press.

Tirole, J. (1989), *The Theory of Industrial Organization*, Cambridge, MA, MIT Press.

US Department of Justice and Federal Trade Commission (1992), *Horizontal Merger Guidelines*, Washington DC.

Varian, H. (1989), 'Price discrimination', ch. 10 in R. Schmalensee and R. Willig (eds.), *Handbook of Industrial Organisation*, Amsterdam, North Holland.

Vickers, J. S., and Yarrow, G. K. (1988), *Privatization: An Economic Analysis*, Cambridge, MA, MIT Press.

Waterson, M. (1993), 'Vertical integration and vertical restraints', *Oxford Review of Economic Policy*, 9(2), 41–57.

Whinston, M. D. (1990), 'Tying, foreclosure and exclusion', *American Economic Review*, 80, 837–59.

Whish, R. (1993), *Competition Law*, 3rd edn., London, Butterworths.

White, L. J. (1993), 'Competition policy in the United States: an overview', *Oxford Review of Economic Policy*, 9(2), 133–53.

Williams, M. E. (1993), 'The effectiveness of competition policy in the United Kingdom', *Oxford Review of Economic Policy*, 9(2), 94–112.

Williamson, O. E. (1968), 'Economies as an Antitrust Defence', *American Economic Review*, 58, 18–31.

Willig, R. D. (1991), 'Merger Analysis, Industrial Organisation Theory and Merger Guidelines', *Brookings Papers on Economic Activity*, 281–331.

Yarrow, G. K. (1985), 'Shareholder Protection, Compulsory Acquisition and the Efficiency of the Takeover Process', *Journal of Industrial Economics*, 34, 3–16.

7

European industrial policy and industrial policy in Europe

PAUL GEROSKI

London Business School[1]

I. Introduction

Among the most vexing problems facing those concerned with the formation and implementation of industrial policy is deciding what it is, why it exists, and whether there ought to be more or less of it than exists at present. Any random collection of six economists is sure to produce at least a dozen different opinions on the subject, not least because many economists have trouble in reconciling their gut reaction that industrial policy should not exist with the obvious fact that it does. The vigorous debate that now rages between those who believe that industrial policy should and those that believe that it should not be consciously pursued by governments is but a pale reflection of the true diversity of opinion that exists on the subject. Even amongst that group of economists who are enthusiastic about industrial policy, the range of specific policy proposals that have been put forth is enormous, and the debate within this group is no less active (and acrimonious) than that between the pros and antis.

Following what is a clear, if unintended, characteristic of many of the contributions to this debate, this paper is devoted to complicating rather than simplifying the issues. In particular, the question that we shall explore is whether there might be a type of industrial policy which should be applied at a supra-national level. Although this question has been actively discussed in Europe since the signing of the Treaty of Rome (at least), the revival of free market ideologies, 1992 and recent discussions of European political union have all added a good deal of fuel to the fire. More than a few ambitious European politicians have launched initiatives that apparently usurp national policy prerogatives, and the response by many national governments has become increasingly angry and strident. Traditional liberalism struggled for years to define the boundaries of the state in terms of the rights and responsibilities of its individual members; tomorrow's liberals are likely to be concerned with the boundaries of the European Commission in terms of the rights and responsibilities of individual member states.

Our exploration of the subject will proceed through four stages. In section II, we shall briefly touch upon the questions of what industrial policy is and why it ought to exist (in some form or another), at least at a national level. Section III extends the argument to a supra-national level by asking whether there exists scope for a European industrial policy to complement national policies. With these discussions in hand, we shall turn to discuss the content of policy by examining what is certainly the most extensively hyped European initiative in this policy area, the 1992 programme to unify the internal European market. In section IV, we discuss the 1992 proposals and assess their likely effects, turning in section V to a broader, more speculative evaluation of European industrial policies post-1992.

II. The industrial policy problem

'Industrial policy' is the label that has come to be used to describe a wide-ranging, ill-assorted collection of

First published in *Oxford Review of Economic Policy*, vol. 5, no. 2 (1989).

[1] I am obliged to Dieter Helm, Keith Cowling, Alexis Jacquemin, Hiro Odagiri, John Kay, Roger Sugden, and Jonathan Aylen for helpful comments. The usual disclaimer applies, however.

micro-based supply-side initiatives which are designed to improve market performance in a variety of occasionally mutually inconsistent ways. The performance criteria typically used include productive and allocative efficiency, equity of market outcomes, progressivity of firms, and flexibility of production structures, and action is typically demanded in cases of egregious 'market failure' involving public goods or externalities, or where major changes need to be effected quickly.

One's view about the desirability of industrial policy is conditioned at base on one's evaluation of market processes. Popular discussions of the virtues of market processes have, of late, displayed a depressing tendency to substitute adulation for analysis, and this has led many commentators to make rather exaggerated claims for the efficacy of markets. What markets are good at is allocating resources between producers, and goods between consumers in very simple, very static settings. Much of the power of markets in these circumstances emerges because prices convey all the information needed by participants in the market, and this enables them to act independently without explicit co-ordination and yet still reach a collectively efficient decision. Although the possibility that markets can (in principle) solve simple, static allocation problems efficiently is remarkable, it is not very surprising to discover that markets fare less well in more demanding circumstances. Situations in which elements of monopoly are present, in which the actions of agents have unintended (and unpriced) effects on others, in which product quality as well as quantity is the subject of choice, in which risk and uncertainty have a major effect on decisions and in which economies of scale in supply or inappropriability in sale exist are all circumstances where information on marginal decisions by consumers or producers (which is what prices convey) is not sufficient to ensure that an efficient outcome is realized. Some degree of explicit co-ordination between agents is necessary in these circumstances, either to ensure that an adequate flow of information is made available for individuals to make appropriate decisions, or because it is impossible for isolated, independent decision-makers to make a sensible decision in almost any circumstances. Many of these types of problem emerge in industries where R & D is an important element of competitive strategy and where large investments in infrastructure are necessary if efficient production is to be realized, and there is no reason to rule out consideration of various types of policy initiatives that might supplement market processes in these sectors.

Industrial policy is not, of course, the only type of micro-economic supply-side policy that can be devised and it is, therefore, often further distinguished as being directed (in the main) at firms. This qualification has two effects. First, it makes plain that the application of industrial policy is largely directed at realizing micro-economic goals (like growth in industry exports, or stimulating the rate of product or process innovation) rather than macro-economic goals (like full employment or zero inflation). Of course, systematic and repeated applications of successful micro-based supply-side policies will, sooner or later, ease major macro-economic constraints, but this is, at best, a long-run target to aim at. Second, the qualification has the effect of distinguishing industrial policy from education or taxation policy, although not necessarily from trade or regional policy (which are occasionally considered to be perfect substitutes for industrial policy). Conversely, identifying industrial policy in terms of such a broad target means that it covers a wide range of policies that are directed at specific activities undertaken by firms. Thus, industrial policy understood in these terms encompasses R & D policy, competition policy, and so on.

The fact that one can encompass a range of types of policy under the heading 'industrial policy' does not, of course, mean that the resulting collection necessarily has much coherence. Indeed, the complexity of industrial policy programmes often arises from the need to reconcile the various conflicting effects that different types of policy create, and, occasionally, to reconcile conflicting policy targets. Instruments generally cannot be narrowly targeted at specific goals because they often have many unintended (and usually unanticipated) effects. For example, R & D joint ventures (or, in the limit, mergers) initiated by otherwise competing firms may be essential to the development of technology in certain sectors, but may also facilitate collusion over prices (for a good discussion, see Jacquemin, 1987). The consequence is that any technology policy designed to solve problems associated with scale economies in R & D may create a monopoly problem as an unintended side effect. This, in turn, is likely to require the application of some form of competitive policy lest the potential gains from co-operation in technology development fail to materialize for consumers because of co-operation in pricing. Indeed, one of the central dilemmas in policy design is that of reconciling many industrial policy initiatives (ranging from crisis cartels to R & D joint ventures to the current privatization programme) with the need to preserve a fairly active degree of competition in markets. This is a conundrum that emerged (to take just one example) in the September, 1983, French memorandum to the European Council (see Pearce and

Table 7.1. Industrial policy support in the UK (in £M, 1980 prices)

	1974	1975	1976	1977	1978	1979	1980	1981
Regional	878	1,032	1,011	660	731	566	624	773
R & D	308	333	360	306	299	313	354	300
Employment	280	449	720	922	943	945	1,280	1,539
Investment Grants	199	94	31	7	3	2	1	—
Selective spending through various schemes & NEB	47	533	115	117	177	170	168	188
Selective spending directed to Aerospace, Ship-Building, Steel & Vehicles	450	363	427	565	393	391	513	858
Trade	313	264	330	175	279	399	498	529
Redundancy	257	269	252	246	243	259	445	688
R & D (Defence & Other)	1,400	1,640	2,093	1,962	1,954	2,026	na	na
Capital Allowances & Stock Relief	5,875	6,900	6,025	7,125	8,125	7,300	na	7,650

Source: NEDC (1982).

Sutton, 1986). Taking the view that increasing competitiveness in Europe required reducing intra-European trade barriers and stimulating intra-European co-operation, it argued that the need for co-operation to create European 'superfirms' was so pressing as to override standard competition policy worries about market dominance. Amongst other things, it suggested that member states use the Community-wide market and not national markets as the relevant market for assessing the extent of monopolization. The issue came to a head with the (French Government inspired) merger proposed between Grundig (Germany) and Thomson-Brandt (France) which the West German cartel office would not approve (the merged firm's market share in the German market would have exceeded 55 per cent). Similar issues are involved in the recent GEC–Siemans proposed takeover of Plessey.

That industrial policy is 'industrial' in the sense of being directed at firms does not, of course, mean that it must necessarily be directed at specific firms or industries, and it is perfectly possible to imagine general forms of assistance that are made available to all firms on a non-discriminating basis. Indeed, one of the more contentious issues that features in debates on the subject is the extent to which industrial policy ought to be targeted at specific sectors or firms. Various debates on the subject have generated a good deal more heat than light, not least because targeting is usually discussed as a policy of 'picking winners' and then promptly dismissed as something that politicians and civil servants are congenitally incapable of doing properly. The problem is, however, both simpler and more challenging than this. In principle, the choice between sectors that one might consider supporting hinges on identifying market failures, and, in practice, most lists of poten-

tial 'winners' are generally pretty similar. The difficult questions are those concerned with how to go about 'creating winners' from what are merely possibilities that may fail to materialize if left on their own. General, non-discretionary assistance has the sole virtue of being (relatively) administratively simple to provide, but this is achieved at the cost of providing support that is not necessarily well-tailored to the needs of most recipients, that can (in the case of subsidies) undermine the incentives of most recipients and that provides support for (perhaps many) firms that do not need it. Although it is by no means certain, it is hard to believe that more discretionary, better-targeted, and more carefully custom-designed policies cannot provide more satisfactory results for the same input.

Tables 7.1–7.3 give some feel for both the range of policies that one might gather together under the heading of industrial policy, and the pattern of support that was typically available under these headings in various European countries at the end of the 1970s. Table 7.1 shows UK spending on a range of functions directed at (non-nationalized) manufacturing industry. By far the most important type of support offered was general (non-discretionary) rather than sector-specific, taking the form of tax allowances largely granted through provisions for accelerated depreciation. Regional and employment (including redundancy) spending also was substantial, with the former decreasing in importance over time and the latter increasing both absolutely and relatively. Neither type of spending is sector-specific in principle, although, in practice, the uneven regional distribution and cyclical instability of different sectors ensures that aid is not evenly distributed throughout the manufacturing sector. Trade- and defence-related R & D are also sector-specific in

Table 7.2. Expenditure on industrial support in Europe (for 1978, 1979, or 1980)

	UK	Belgium	France	Italy	Netherlands	Norway	Sweden	West Germany
Total expenditure in £M	1,505	1,654	3,003	2,183	495	2,309	6,146	2,380
Total expenditure as a % of GDP	3.0	0.7	2.3	3.2	2.0	4.6	1.7	1.2
% allocated to:								
Regional	19.0	4	—	—	43	8	33	356
R & D	2.5	16	—	9	2	6	15	3
Small Business	4.5	3	—			2	2	
Sectoral, Structural	12.0	29	—	42	17	18	22	40
Employment, Training	44.0	26	—	42	17	18	22	40

Source: NEDC (1981).

application (although not necessarily in conception), and the latter is a substantive source of R & D support provided by the UK government. Selective intervention schemes have generally been directed at crisis sectors (even the spending channelled through the National Enterprise Board had this character), and this explicitly targeted spending has accounted for a very modest share of spending. In so far as the UK had a sector or firm specific set of targeted industrial policies in the late 1970s (which is not far), Table 7.1 suggests that they were partly administered by the Department of Employment and the Ministry of Defence.

Tables 7.2 and 7.3 provide two complementary comparisons of types of industrial policy spending across a range of European countries. Table 7.2 reveals Sweden, the Netherlands, and Belgium to be high-spenders (in terms of GNP). Norway, West Germany, and the UK have a heavy regional emphasis on their spending (in contrast to France and Sweden), France and West Germany tend to emphasize support to R & D (in contrast to the UK and Norway) and Norway, France, and Sweden all have strong sectoral support policies (in contrast to the UK and the Netherlands). Focusing only on subsidy programmes, Table 7.3 shows a similar ranking across countries by per cent of GNP spent on subsidies: from high to low, the ranking on Tables 7.2 and 7.3 is Sweden, Italy, Norway, West Germany, and the UK. As on Table 7.2, Table 7.3 shows the UK and Norway to have a heavy regional bias in their subsidies, West Germany to have an R & D bias, and the UK to have a bias towards employment subsidies. Table 7.3 also shows most countries to have fairly high levels of general rather than sectoral support (especially West Germany and the UK), but what it does not fully convey is the high concentrations of such sector specific support in a few 'crisis' sectors (like coal, cars, shipbuilding, and steel).

Thus, there is a case for a positive, activist industrial policy in principle. The major policy dilemmas arise from the fact that the instruments typically used have multiple effects, that policy targets can conflict, and that, to be effective, policy must often be selectively applied and custom-designed. In practice, all of this means that industrial policies must be carefully crafted if they are to succeed in realizing their stated goals, much less in realizing a net positive benefit over all effects, intended and unintended. That the job is difficult does not, of course, mean that it cannot or should not be done.

III. European industrial policy

It is one thing to argue the case for national industrial policies, and quite another to argue that there exists a case for formulating industrial policies at a European level. While one must accept the case for national industrial policies before one will find a European industrial policy attractive, acceptance of the former does not automatically imply acceptance of the latter. In fact, there is a respectable case to be made for a European industrial policy, and it hinges on a mismatch between national and 'economic' markets. Since there is very little reason to extend the jurisdiction of any economic policy beyond the domains of the activity it is designed to effect, European policies will only ever make sense when markets spill over national boundaries in so fundamental a manner as to make national policies unviable. Despite the almost hysterical conviction of many business analysts that markets in the 1980s and beyond are inherently global, the fact is that most of them are not even national, much less pan-European. It follows, then, that however respectable the case for a European industry policy is, it is quite a limited one.

The first step in the argument is the assertion that policy ought to be conducted at as local a level as possible. There are perhaps three arguments to be made

Table 7.3. An international comparison of subsidy programmes

	UK	Italy	Norway	Sweden	West Germany
General Support (percentage):					
Export Subsidies	19.4	31.3	3.2	9.8	8.0
R & D Subsidies	13.8	1.4	12.8	10.7	20.3
Investment Subsidies	0.1	4.4	8.2	—	—
Employment Subsidies	10.8	—	2.6	2.6	—
Regional, Small Firms	20.0	13.4	25.2	20.3	54.8
Rescue Operations	1.0	2.5	2.0	3.5	1.65
Sector Specific	4.0	—	23.1	8.1	12.1
Firm Specific	31.9	49.5	24.9	48.5	1.8
Total Subsidies as a % of GDP	1.0	2.6	2.0	3.5	1.65

Source: Carlsson (1983).

in support of this proposition. First, any policy worthy of consideration requires a good deal of highly detailed information if it is to be properly designed, and this is particularly so for any policy that is targeted at specific firms or sectors. There is no doubt that local policy-making units which operate close to the targeted firm or sector will have a substantial advantage in gathering such information, and thus should be better placed to design and implement policies suited to its needs. Second, there is some reason to think that the complexities of policies rises more than proportionately in the number of parties involved. Even if every participant had similar preferences, the costs of establishing and maintaining a system of communications between them rises exponentially in the number involved. Since increasing the numbers involved is likely to increase the diversity among and conflicts between the preferences of participants, costs are, in fact, likely to rise even faster than this. More modest policies applied in situations where informal communication channels supplement existing ones are likely to be far easier to manage than large, grandiose schemes, and thus stand a better chance of succeeding. Third and finally, applying policies at a local level is attractive because they can be tailored to suit local preferences, and choices can be made in (potentially) a more democratic fashion. For all these reasons, then, policy ought to be designed and applied at as low a level as possible, subject to the constraint that it is viable.

Purely national policies will not be viable whenever the domains of the activity—the 'economic' market—being regulated spills over national boundaries in such a way as to make it impossible to realize effects within national borders using policies that apply only to agents located within those borders. To appreciate what constraints this puts on the effectiveness of national policies, it is necessary to define 'economic markets' in an operationally useful way. Markets are conventionally defined from the point of view of both supply and demand, and such definitions usually run in terms of elasticities of supply and cross elasticities of demand. The relevant market for some good W produced and sold in some country X at time Y by some firm Z depends on the alternatives to W available to consumers in country X at time Y, on whether W represents a viable consumption alternative for consumers in countries outside X, or whether there are alternatives to W at other times before or after Y, and on the number of potential suppliers of W or similar products. It is natural to define the economic market of a good as the minimum region in which production and sale are viable. From the point of view of a firm, the minimum area in which production and sale are viable is of importance since it defines where the firm must (at least) compete if it is to survive. No firm is viable unless its activities span the domain of the economic market. From the point of view of policy, the minimum area of viability is crucial. Any policy whose domain is less than that of the economic market will not span the activities of those to whom the policy is applied, and any attempt to restrict their activities and bring them within the boundaries of policy application will, of necessity, be doomed to failure.

To bring the definition of the economic market into bolder relief, consider the market for some homogeneous good W that is desired by consumers in several countries. If scale economies in production dictate the existence of minimum efficient plants rather larger than total demand in country X, then no firm could viably produce good W for country X alone and not be undercut by suppliers from outside X. Similarly, if the production of W requires costly prior investment in, say, R & D which is substantial (on a per unit basis) relative to the price of W, then any producer that produces for country X alone may not be able to survive in the face of competition from multi-national suppliers. Indeed, it may not even be able to cover its costs even if such competition is blocked and it is allowed to operate in X alone. Both situations correspond to cases where the economic market for W exceeds the boundary of nation X, and it is clear that both turn on non-convexities in supply coupled with cross-regional homogeneities in demand. It follows, then, that goods for which there exist marked national preferences in demand, no major economies of scale, and little need for large scale creation of or adjustment in the infrastructure supporting its supply are goods for which national production and sale is viable. The economic markets in which they are sold are comfortably contained within national boundaries, and the need for supra-national industrial policy does not exist.

The fact that the economic market for a good is comfortably contained within national boundaries does not, of course, mean that the firms which operate in that market need necessarily restrict their activities to a single national market. Indeed, from the point of view of a firm, multi-national operations may be attractive simply because they enable the firm to escape from national controls, and, perhaps, to play different national policy bodies off against each other. However, the mere existence of multi-national firms does not provide any justification for a multi-national industry policy. If the economic market in which such firms operate is contained within national boundaries, then restrictions on multi-national activity that give national policies some bite do not give rise to substantial costs. The fact that such firms exist does not mean that the domain of policy must expand *pari passu* since, as we have seen, this is likely to impose real costs in a way that restricting the operations of such firms will not. If, on the other hand, the economic market exceeds national boundaries, or if the expansion of multi-nationals is facilitated by national subsidies, then some form of supra-national policy may be worth consideration. Certainly, rent-seeking behaviour by footloose multi-nationals should not be allowed to develop into a bidding free-for-all amongst nation states.

At a practical level, the use of the concept of an economic market to help define the appropriate domain of European industrial policy suggests that there are two broad areas where such a supra-national policy may be warranted. The first concerns trade barriers. Clearly, if national and economic markets do not coincide and if, in addition, barriers to trade impede the movement of goods and services across national boundaries, then market performance will suffer. When significant scale economies exist, then such barriers to trade limit both the diversity of products that can be viably produced and sold on the market, and the efficiency with which they can be produced (see Helpman and Krugman, 1986). Further, in so far as such barriers to trade limit the degree of competition in national markets, they weaken the incentives which encourage firms to produce efficiently, to innovate, to respond flexibly to market events, and to produce a range of products closely tailored to consumers' needs. It follows, then, that a case for European industrial policy exists whenever barriers to trade inhibit the flow of goods and services between national markets within the same economic market, and the form that policy ought to take is that of removing those barriers.

Externalities and other forms of market failure are the second broad area where a supra-national policy may be warranted. These phenomena create market failures because they drive a wedge between private and social rates of return, and, when they spill over national boundaries, this wedge is affected by the scale of the market. It follows that when economic and national markets do not coincide, the appropriate solution to these problems may take on a supra-national character. Thus, for example, large-scale investment in R & D or other infrastructure projects may be far more efficiently carried out if the resources of several small national economies are pooled, and supra-national supervision may be necessary to prevent national free-riding. In fact, many of the important barriers to trade that exist have been created by national governments' implementing industrial policies which seek to favour national contractors on such projects. The need to co-ordinate on a supra-national level, then, is often a logical extension of the need to remove trade barriers in these markets.

In practice, European industrial policy has, in the main, focused on opening up the internal European market by removing various types of barriers between national states (see Swann, 1983; Hesselman, 1983; and Wilkinson, 1984). The principles of this policy were enshrined in the Treaty of Rome, and have maintained a high profile in official Community rhetoric since then. Actions, however, speak louder than words, and, throughout the 1960s, a range of other issues (such as the Common Agricultural Policy) preoccupied policy makers in Brussels. As a consequence, little in the way of substantive policy initiatives addressed to the internal market emerged. The major changes were ushered in by the so-called Colonna Report in 1970 which urged an active initiation of policies to unify the internal European Market, to encourage (or enable) firms to organize on a European scale, to encourage the Community to catch up in areas where it was technologically lagging, to encourage the emergence of new industries, and to ensure that Community enterprises were able to compete fairly in other markets. The Report reflected a growing chorus of worry about what was perceived to be the uncompetitively small size of most European enterprises, and the apparently slow speed at which these enterprises reacted to opportunities and developments in new markets. Although cause and consequence are not easy to disentangle, it is nevertheless the case that Community industrial policies became more activist and were more actively pursued throughout the 1970s and into the 1980s. In the process, the stress in policy towards opening up the internal market has gradually expanded to include a large element of co-ordination as the EEC Commission has struggled to bring a pan-European coherence to national industrial policies applied to particular sectors. Although it is not difficult to see an intellectual coherence in this shift in emphasis, it must also be said that the shift is due partly to the fact that many of the more important barriers to trade that the Commission has struggled to eliminate have been imposed either by or with the connivance of national governments.

Perhaps the most famous manifestations of these policies have been in various 'crisis' sectors. European policies towards steel are unusual in that the EEC Commission was given powers in the Treaty of Paris to raise levies on steel production, vet the investment plans of firms, set mandatory minimum prices, and establish quotas. These powers were little used until the crisis of 1974 which provoked the first substantial intervention in this sector, and eventually culminated in the Davignon Plan of 1977. This proposed a new series of voluntary and mandatory minimum prices and production quotas, a series of voluntary export restrictions, it controlled national subsidies, provided social aids to assist closure, and, finally, it introduced controls on the investment decisions of European firms. A further crisis in 1980 saw these voluntary agreements break down, and ushered in stronger, mandatory measures. While most commentators believe that the European steel policy has been a success, it is worth noting how much of that success depended upon the support and co-operation of particular national governments. In particular, adjustment was very uneven between countries: the UK made cuts of 67 per cent of its labour costs, and France made cuts of 43 per cent, while West Germany uncharacteristically subsidized sections of its industry, and Italy continued to increase its productive capacity into 1982 (see Swann, 1983; Tsoukakis and Strauss, 1985).

Another major crisis sector policy, that in synthetic fibres, was rather less successful. In contrast to steel, synthetic fibres is an example where the limited legal powers of the Commission inhibited action, and where policy conflicts (in particular, with competition policy) eventually killed the proposed course of action. Here a slowdown in market growth in the early 1970s was not matched by capacity reduction, resulting in an average level of capacity utilization of 68 per cent, and losses for virtually all firms in the industry between 1974 and 1980. Various national industrial policies emerged in response to the crisis. Belgium nationalized its major producer, Fabelta, as an alternative to closure early in 1976, and, more spectacularly, the Italian government rained assistance on ailing firms (e.g. the state refused to allow plants to close, and picked up the tab for employing 6,000 workers). All of this intervention activity produced a classically sub-optimal outcome, and the Commission was approached for assistance in organizing an orderly reduction in European capacity. In particular, non-Italian firms (and their governments) were concerned not to retire capacity while the Italians were extending theirs. A provisional cartel was organized by the Commission in June 1978 which involved a planned capacity reduction of 16.5 per cent over two years, and a rough maintenance of market shares (some small increase in the Italian share was allowed). The interesting point here is that the market-sharing agreement was deemed to be anti-competitive, and the whole 'crisis cartel' had to be abandoned in 1980. Even had the conflict with competition policy not created difficulties, it was clear that many national governments were intent on intervention regardless of the cartel agreement (see Shaw and Shaw, 1983, and more generally on textiles, see Swann, 1983; Shepherd, 1984; de la Torre and Bacchetta, 1980; and others).

Although they have been much in the headlines, European industrial policy initiatives have not been confined to crisis sectors. One area where the Commission has begun to enjoy some success is in the setting of standards in high technology sectors. By helping to reduce uncertainty about product specifications and ensuring the compatability of different components in complex systems, the erection of standards enables a division of labour to emerge in supply. Firms are able to specialize in parts of the standardized system that reflect their comparative advantage in research, product development, or production. Further, the erection of a Europe-wide standard essentially homogenizes demand and so creates a market that is likely to be large enough to exhaust scale economies in any or all individual components. Thus, the recent establishment of a common (narrow band) standard for a digital cellular phone network has led to the emergence of a number of cross-country consortia formed between firms with different skills, as well as to the appearance of a number of specialist producers. The results seem likely to lead to a far more efficient outcome than has been observed for analog systems where a failure to agree on a common standard led to the Balkanization of the European market into national markets each controlled by national producers (see Geroski and Toker, 1989).

Policies have also been devised in various other high-tech or 'sunrise' sectors. The European Strategic Programme for R & D in Information Technology (ESPRIT), for example, is a joint Community–private sector programme in which larger European firms undertake projects (in micro-electronics, software, information-processing, office systems, and computer manufacturing technology) singly or partly financed by the EEC. The policy initiative emerged from fears that national markets in Europe were too small to support a full range of research in information technology, and that specialization would only work if common standards were erected at a European level (and not set by major non-EEC competitors). The amount of money spent has been fairly modest, but most of it has been in basic R & D, and much effort has been expended in promoting alliances within Europe among European firms, and to erecting standards which will help create a division of labour among these firms within the Community (see Pearce and Sutton, 1986; Mytelka and Delapierre, 1987; Woolcock, 1984; Cameron and Georghiou, 1987; and others).

The particular types of consortium structure that one notices in the ESPRIT programme are not unlike that in Airbus Industries, which is composed of a group of leading European firms who have combined together (and with their national governments) to challenge the dominance of US aerospace companies. What is interesting about this type of structure is that it reflects the lack of power that the EEC Commission itself has, and the fact that its policies have largely relied on the voluntary support of independent national governments. Like the structure of the EEC Commission, these consortia generally tend to allocate planning and control to national hands, leaving the Commission to co-ordinate efforts. A good illustration of why this may actually be the only currently feasible structure for these types of initiatives can be found in the European aerospace industry. While Airbus now forms the nucleus of the Community's aerospace industry, the Commission floated a proposal in 1975 called the Action Programme for Aerospace (APA) which was far more ambitious. The APA proposed a consolidation of national industries into a single Community-controlled system, taking the sponsorship of aerospace completely out of national control. By 1980, this initiative was clearly perceived to have failed. The main causes for its demise appear to have been inefficiencies induced by national employment practices, the APA's inability to raise itself above 'buy national' policies, and a waning in enthusiasm for European political unification (on aerospace, see Rallo, 1984, and, on joint defence procurement in aerospace, see Hartley, 1983, Chapter 8; Hartley, 1987; and others).

This last observation on the practice of European industrial policy leads one back to one final issue of principle. That the kinds of policies which have been pursued at a European level have been concerned with opening up markets and co-ordinating pan-European efforts in markets (like aerospace and information technology) whose economic boundaries exceed those of nations does not imply that they are a substitute for national policies. Rather, they should be (and often have been) designed as complements, enabling national policy to have its maximum domestic effect subject to the constraint that it does not adversely affect other nations. At its best, a European industrial policy can do no more than enable individual nations collectively to pursue policies in Europe-wide markets and achieve results that they could not reach alone. For every ESPRIT, there ought to be a range of national Alvey programmes that encourage the formation of industry and university links and disseminate technical information to the countless smaller national producers and users who could never join a Europe-wide initiative without making it unwieldy and unworkable (see also Cameron and Georghiou, 1987). As was noted above, policy ought to be as local and as custom-built as possible. When economic markets spill over the borders of local policy jurisdiction, then a higher level of policy action may be called for. However, as one moves up the policy hierarchy from local to national policy and then to supra-national policy, the appropriate policy stance must shift from policy design to policy co-ordination to reflect the comparative advantages of policy makers at each level. Policy at a European level can never be as well informed, as capably executed, and as sensitive to local preferences as national policies, and should, therefore, never be allowed to override national policies. However, when economic markets spill over national boundaries, national policies are liable to conflict and, in any case, their viability is likely to be undermined. In this situation, there is a role for a supra-national policy to play in co-ordinating national programmes, enabling them to achieve as many of their goals as possible. In short, supra-national policy stands to national policy as a complement and not a substitute.

IV. 1992 as European industrial policy

The most recent and by far most dramatically publicized European initiative is the set of proposals to complete the unification of the internal European Market by 1992 (see EEC, 1988, or its popularization in Cecchini, 1988; Kay, 1988; Geroski, 1988, and Davis *et al.*, 1989, are critical overviews of many of the proposals). The philosophy behind this initiative mirrors the continually recurring fear of many European policy-makers that the small size of the individual national markets in Europe restricts both the degree of competition that national firms face and their ability to achieve the benefits of scale economies. The 1992 initiative aspires to reducing the remaining barriers that separate European markets, and looks forward to what it sees as an inevitable restructuring of European industry, one that will facilitate the growth of large pan-European firms able to compete on a par with their US or Japanese rivals. The two major sets of barriers that are thought to have inhibited such restructuring are customs procedures that impose unnecessary costs on the internal Community flow of goods, and national technical regulations or standards and restrictive national procurement policies that unfairly favour national suppliers.

Customs procedures within the EEC are often unbelievably complex and burdensome, and have become increasingly so over the years. This has been the result of a growing need to handle problems of tax adjustment arising from national differences in VAT, to deal with increasing and increasingly complex health and transport regulations, and to monitor various bilateral trade quota regimes (such as those relating to the import of cars). Various estimates suggest that most of these costs are administrative, and these are thought by the Commission to total about 7.5 billion ECU. Costs associated with frontier delays are thought to add between 1 and 2 billion further ECU to this total. More important, these costs seem to be very unevenly divided between firms, and can apparently be as much as 30–40 per cent higher for small firms than for large firms. A survey of businesses conducted for the Commission found that frontier costs were ranked as being the most important of all barriers to trade in textiles, footwear and clothing, paper, mineral oil refining, rubber products, precision engineering and food (see EEC, 1988, pp. 44–9).

Technical regulations, standards, and testing/certification procedures govern the specifications of goods which can be sold in the various national markets. There is no doubt that they are ubiquitous, and that they are often designed to satisfy strictly protectionist purposes. Typical of these regulations is that in Italy prohibiting the use of common (as opposed to durum) wheat in pasta. The removal of these is thought likely to generate savings of between 35 and 100 million ECU per year. Purity standards for beer in Germany are cited as a typical example of how such obstacles lead to inefficient production, with too many producers (75 per cent of all Community brewers apparently) crowded into an over-protected market. Cost savings of 3–7 per cent of beer value added are anticipated from a restructuring of the industry into a smaller number of large producers. Similarly, public procurement policies in the various member states often systematically favour domestic over foreign suppliers, as national governments attempt to build up or support 'national champions', particularly in defence-related areas. Needless to say, evidence on the extent of such practices is difficult to come by, but the Commission examined procurement practices for 40 goods frequently purchased by public sector bodies, and argued that open tendering might save 3 billion ECU in aggregate. More important, open tendering was thought likely to lead to a major restructuring of the industries concerned, producing perhaps a further 8 billion ECU by way of efficiency gains. In telecommunications, for example, the gains from standardizing technical specifications are thought to be in the region of 0.58–1.1 billion ECU, while those resulting from a more competitive procurement regime are thought to be in the range of 2.2–3.7 billion ECU (EEC, 1988, pp. 49–59.)

The basic policy proposal at the core of the 1992 programme is to eliminate frontier controls and border checks, and this, in turn, requires the removal of the various different national standards and the harmonization of taxes. A major plank in this programme is, of course, the harmonization of VAT and excise duties, but no less important are a variety of other policies that will attempt to harmonize national technical regulations and improve the functioning of European standardization bodies. Last but by no means least, a serious attempt will be made to open up national public procurement decisions to Community-wide competition. In addition, a range of further policies will be pursued to ensure that the full benefits of the basic programme are realized. Chief amongst these is competition policy. Firms that currently enjoy dominant positions in national markets will not be allowed to block new competitors and, although there are proposals to encourage the formation of intra-European co-operative R & D projects, these will not be allowed to extend co-operation into other dimensions. State aids and

Table 7.4. The distribution of MES as a percentage of the European markets

	Number of industries where MES is between x and y%	Distribution of MES as a percentage of the European market for 68 industries
0–<1	20	29
1–<2.5	17	25
2.5–<5	13	19
5–<10	11	16
1–<20	5	7
20–<50	2	3
50–<100	1	1
100 and over	—	—
Total	69	100

Source: EEC (1988).

subsidies to promote national champions or to protect domestic producers will, as before, be carefully monitored, and the practice of applying sanctions against unfair support schemes will continue unabated. Finally, since industries will almost certainly expand in some countries and contract or disappear in others as a consequence of the 1992 programme, a system of compensation will be introduced to prevent the emergence of intra-Community tensions.

What long-run consequences is the 1992 programme likely to have on European industry? The view of many senior European politicians is that economies of scale are present and unexploited in most sectors, and thus that large-scale rationalization ought to occur as a consequence of completing the internal market, leaving a small number of mass producers operating in Community-wide markets. Proponents of this view tend to cite estimates made by the Commission suggesting that the potential gains from restructuring are so large that more than half of the savings of 5.8–6.4 per cent of Community GDP that are claimed to be within reach are associated with restructuring (EEC, 1988, pp. 155–6). The major problem with this view is that the evidence hardly supports the weight that has been put on it. As we have seen, the classic example of a market whose economic boundaries exceed national boudaries is one where tastes are homogeneous and production is subject to substantial economies of scale. In fact, the evidence on scale economies and price dispersion within the EEC suggests that very few European markets fit this bill.

The evidence on scale economies amassed by the Commission takes the form of a range of estimates of best practice techniques based on engineering assessments of the potential productivity of new plants designed on state-of-the-art principles. The Commission gathered together a number of estimates of this type that have been made over the last decade or so, and expressed them in terms of the minimum efficient scale (MES) that must be realized to avoid cost penalties. As Table 7. 4 shows, most of the industries surveyed (89 per cent of them) exhibited levels of minimum efficient scale less than 10 per cent of the Community market, and three-quarters were less than 5 per cent. What is more, the cost penalty on sub-minimum efficient scale production was found to be fairly modest in most sectors, leading one to suspect that most markets could sustain at least twenty efficient producers, and often considerably more. Table 7.5 shows a range of sectors

Table 7.5. UK industries in which MES exceeds 20% of the UK market

Industry UK	MES as % of UK product	MES as % of EEC product	Number of firms, 1983
221: iron and steel	72	10	148
223: steel wire	20	4	442
224: aluminium	114	15	591
251: chemicals	23–100	3–50	827
256: fertilizers	23	4	644
321: tractors	98	19	667
326: ball-bearings	20	2	1,140
342: electrical equipment	60	6	1,228
344: telecommunications equipment	50	10	1,603
345: TV sets, etc.	40	9	736
346: domestic appliances	57–85	10–11	234
351: motor vehicles	200	20	187
361: marine engines	30	5	1,105
364: aircraft	100+	?	312
429: tobacco	24	6	19

Source: EEC (1988).

in which the minimum efficient size of the best practice plants is thought to exceed 20 per cent of the UK market. It is clear that virtually all of these appear to require only a very modest fraction of the European market to be viable, suggesting that the necessary extent of restructuring at the European level will require only very modest levels of Europe-wide concentration.

In fact, the numbers in tables 7.4 and 7.5 considerably overestimate the importance of scale economies in the total population of industries, largely because they were collected from studies directed at large MES industries. Further, this type of estimate of scale economies overstates the cost savings realizable in practice because it focuses on what is technologically possible without considering organizational or managerial constraints. In fact, large plants are difficult to manage and are noticeably more strike prone than smaller establishments. There are many problems in managing large plants, and, indeed, comparative productivity studies generally fail to find plant size to be an important factor in explaining productivity differences between countries (e.g. see the case studies discussed in Prais, 1981). In fact, UK performance, to take one example, appears to be inferior in those sectors where its plants are largest, particularly because of the poor performance of the large plants in those sectors (Caves and Davies, 1987, p. 68). The experience of the 1960s has shown that mergers which are designed to exploit scale economies often fail, leaving unmanageable and inefficient enterprises in their wake (see Cowling *et al.*, 1980, and the papers in Fairburn and Kay, 1989). Table 7.5 also shows that an enormous number of firms populate industries in the UK where MES is high, and it is well known that the distribution of plant sizes in virtually all industries is extremely large. It is inconceivable that such an enormous range of plant sizes would exist were scale economies large and the penalty on sub-optimal production great. Similarly, even if there were big cost advantages to operating large-scale establishments and enterprises, the high failure rate of mergers indicates that only a relatively small number of managers can handle the organization problems which hinder their realization.

It is also more than clear that tastes are not homogeneous across Europe, and that the wide diversity of preferences that exists means that the internal European market will never be more than a collection of distinct market niches. One slightly indirect way to see the importance of this point is to examine the variation in prices for similar goods across Europe. All the evidence suggests that prices vary enormously within the Community. In 1983, for example, UK car prices were nearly 44 per cent higher (before and after taxes),

prices in Germany were 23 per cent and 11 per cent higher, prices in France were 19 per cent and 25 per cent higher, and those in Italy were 32 per cent and 29 per cent higher than prices in Belgium (Mertens and Ginsburgh, 1985). Washing machines in France, Germany, and Italy are extremely expensive relative to Belgium and the UK. A machine that cost £270 in the UK in 1986, for example, cost £362 in France, £292 in the FRG in 1985, £305 in Belgium in 1985, and £390 in Italy in 1987 (see Nicolaides and Baden-Fuller, 1987). Prices net of tax for men's sporting outfits were 64 per cent higher in France than in the UK, 25 per cent higher in Italy, and 1 per cent lower in Germany; woollen skirts were twice as expensive in Denmark as in the UK, but slightly cheaper still in Greece (Rossini, 1988). Finally, the price of pharmaceuticals can differ by as much as a factor of 10 across countries: exclusive of taxes, prices were, on average, 24 per cent higher in Germany than in Ireland, 39 per cent higher in Ireland than Belgium, and 19 per cent higher in Belgium than in France in 1983 (EEC, 1988, pp. 67–70).

More broadly the Commission examined prices for about 90 goods sold throughout the Community, and found that the standard deviation of price dispersion was about 27 per cent of the average level of prices (EEC, 1988, p. 118). What is more, only a small part of this observed dispersion was attributed to taxes and high non-tariff barriers (perhaps about a quarter according to Commission estimates). This is also true in the specific industries cited above. In cars, much of the observed variation in prices was sustained by the selective distribution system authorized by the Commission in 1985, VAT rates on washing machines were virtually identical across countries and the price differences that were created by VAT differences were more than dwarfed by differences in retail prices; trade barriers in textiles were thought to affect unit costs by less than 1 per cent in general and much the same applies in pharmaceuticals. The obvious implication to draw is that there is something much more important than trade barriers which drives a wedge between the prices of similar goods in different national markets, and it is hard to avoid the conclusion that a large percentage of the variation in intra-Community prices reflects both subtle differences in product specifications that cater to local tastes and monopolistic pricing to exploit differences in demand elasticities.

These observations make it very difficult to believe that 1992 will have much impact on industry performance, since very few markets extend beyond national borders in any meaningful way. The one exception to this rule seems to be those sectors whose output is mainly sold to large government procurement departments. Industries like construction, telecommunications, and various defence areas typically require major investments in R & D and production facilities, and the gains to scale that exist in these sectors are unlikely to be exhausted at the national level. Indeed, plenty of evidence suggests that there exists a significant amount of excess capacity Europe-wide in these sectors. Telecommunications is a case in point. Trade in telecommunications is only a fraction of production and most of that takes the form of extra-Community trade. It is widely agreed that there are major scale economies in production that have not been fully exploited in European plants (which are rather small by world standards). Further, extensive duplication of software development across a number of protected national markets raises costs unnecessarily (to some degree). The evidence suggests that much the most important source of gains is likely to occur in the central office switching area: transmissions are thought likely to benefit from rationalization, but not to the same degree. However, this said, the evidence also suggests that only a fraction of the gains likely to be realized by opening up procurement practices will emerge from realizing latent scale economies. Much more important is the fact that open procurement practices will mean more competition and, therefore, will provide incentives to increase efficiency that current protectionist policies lack (see Muller, 1988). Thus, while these sectors are possible exceptions to the general rule that the 1992 initiative promises only modest gains (if that) in many sectors, they are not an exception to the general rule that the restructuring associated with 1992 should be far more modest than 1992 enthusiasts have asserted.

V. European industrial policy beyond 1992

Markets often work, but they do not always work well or produce outcomes that suit social preferences. Markets make choices that effectively determine the efficiency, progressivity, flexibility, and diversity of production, and do so on the basis of rather limited information (e.g. prices). That reasonably coherent choices are made at all in this fashion is something of a minor miracle, but that should not blind one into thinking that alternative choices do not exist. There are a range of 'market failures' which are generally associated with the provision of infrastructure or other public goods which markets often fail to provide, or do so

only slowly and incompletely, and there is no reason to think that a carefully crafted industrial policy cannot improve upon market forces in these sectors. In fact, many of these situations are ones where market forces will never be allowed free rein. There is a strong, built-in bias in the political system which encourages politicians and civil servants to lavish attention (and money) on crisis sectors (which have well-established constituencies). Such interventions invariably slow market processes, and rarely allocate aid to new sunrise sectors. For this reason alone, then, there is at the very least a strong case to be made for at least formulating positive industrial policy programmes. In practice, a policy of 'leaving it to the market' often means leaving it to the short-term self-interested actions of politicians and civil servants.

The role of a European industrial policy is far more limited than this, for two reasons. First, there is no case whatsoever for European decisions to override those made on the basis of national preferences for particular types of market outcome, even in markets whose borders cross national boundaries. Second, and no less important, policies at a European level only make sense when economic markets exceed national boundaries, and there are few markets in which this is true in any real sense. It is, therefore, hard to see any reason why the EEC should get involved in regulating drinking water quality throughout Europe (however comforting it is to see someone prodding the Department of the Environment into action) or in determining the appropriate wheat content of pasta. On the other hand, there is a good case to be made for European action to open up a range of public procurement practices in sectors (like defence) where substantial excess capacity exists at a European level, and where the size of national purchasing is insufficient to support an efficient and competitive industry structure.

It is worth summarizing the argument by developing a metaphor to describe the appropriate role of industrial policy at a European level (e.g. Hampden-Turner, 1989). Competition has many of the features of a game, and the actions of national firms in the international competitive arena are often aided and abetted by national governments. Despite many years of pious utterances on European solidarity, such competition occurs no less within Europe than between European nation states and non-Europeans. There are three types of stance that European policy makers can take towards this competitive game, that of spectator, team captain, or referee. The argument that local preferences should matter and the local policy-makers have a major comparative advantage in designing and implementing policy, rules out the role of team captain.

The observations that economic markets occasionally spill over national boundaries, and that national governments often abuse these boundaries in their own interests both suggest that a spectator is likely to be quite dissatisfied with the outcome of the game. It follows, then, that the appropriate role for European industrial policy is that of referee. With individual European countries initiating different types of industrial policy geared to producing market outcomes that suit national preferences, there is a clear need for supra-national policies to harmonize the various initiatives, particularly in economic markets that are fundamentally pan-European in operation.

In fact, the 1992 policy programme is, in some ways, a classic illustration of how European industrial policy can, in principle, be used to enhance European economic performance. It is focused on removing barriers to trade within Europe—particularly those that have been thrown up by national policies pursuing national self-interest—and on harmonizing standards and opening up procurement programmes to European competition. However, in practice, there appears to be rather more to the 1992 agenda than this, and the willingness and enthusiasm of a number of European leaders to adopt the mantle of team captain threatens the modest but genuine gains promised by the basic 1992 programme. It is, for example, a splendid idea to remove technical standards that do no more than protect local firms against competition, but it is also the case that many of these regulations were designed to cater to legitimate local needs and preferences. In cases like this, there is little to be gained and much to be lost in erecting some kind of pan-European standard that reflects no one's preferences.

More fundamentally, one of the major limitations of the 1992 programme is that it has been used to encourage a restructuring of European industry that, at best, is unnecessary. Minimum efficient scale in most markets is small and national tastes for product diversity are strong and quite diverse. Most national markets are more than large enough to enable viable production strategies to be pursued, and free trade provides a useful way of increasing both diversity and efficiency at little real cost, and with little need for increased market concentration. The case for building large pan-European enterprises—much less for building them rapidly through a policy of pan-European merger—is almost wholly imaginary (not least because the often superior performance of Japanese rivals cannot be attributed to size), and, in fact, runs strongly against the spirit of the type of European industrial policy that has proved successful in the past (see Geroski and Jacquemin, 1984, 1985). What has always been both

laudable and fairly successful has been the policy of encouraging and maintaining alliances amongst firms and, on occasions, national policy-makers to jointly solve specific policies. Projects like ESPRIT and Airbus on the one hand, and various crisis cartels on the other show how the role of referee can be effectively used. Alliances, however, need not be permanent, and they need not be bought at the cost of reducing competition. If 1992 sees the emergence of a European industrial policy promoting the rise of large scale pan-European firms determined to standardize tastes and exploit economies of large-scale production, then one might legitimately see European industrial policy as part of Europe's problem and not as an element of its solution.

References

Cameron, H., and Georghiou, L. (1987), 'The ESPRIT Programme and the UK', mimeo, PREST, University of Manchester.

Carlsson, B. (1983), 'Industrial Subsidies in Sweden: Macro-Economic Effects and an International Comparison', *Journal of Industrial Economics*, **32**, 1–24.

Caves, R., and Davies, S. (1987), *Britain's Productivity Gap*, Cambridge, Cambridge University Press.

Cecchini, P. (1988), *1992: The European Challenge*, Aldershot, Wildwood House.

Cowling, K. *et al.* (1980), *Mergers and Economic Performance*, Cambridge, Cambridge University Press.

Davis, E. *et al.* (1989), *1992: Myths & Realities*, Report for the Centre for Business Strategy, London Business School.

EEC (1988), *The Economics of 1992*, EEC Commission, Brussels.

Fairburn, J., and Kay, J. (1989), *Mergers and Merger Policy*, Oxford, Oxford University Press.

Geroski, P. (1988), '1992 and European Industrial Structure in the Twenty-first Century', mimeo, London Business School.

—— and Jacquemin, A. (1984), 'Large Firms in the European Corporate Economy and Industrial Policy in the 1980s', in Jacquemin, A. (ed.), *European Industry: Public Policy and Corporate Strategy*, Oxford, Oxford University Press.

—— and —— (1985), 'Industrial Change, Barriers to Mobility, and European Industrial Policy', *Economic Policy*, **1**, 170–205.

—— and Toker, S. (1988), 'Setting Standards in the Pan-European Digital Cellular Phone Market', mimeo, London Business School.

Hampden-Turner, C. (1989), 'Three Images of Government: The Referee, the Coach, and the Abolitionist', mimeo, London Business School.

Hartley, K. (1983), *NATO Arms Co-operation: A Study in Economics and Politics*, London, George Allen & Unwin.

—— (1987), 'Public Procurement and Competitiveness: A Community Market for Military Hardware and Technology?', *Journal of Common Market Studies*, **25**, 237–47.

Helpman, E., and Krugman, P. (1986), *Market Structure and Foreign Trade*, Cambridge, Mass., MIT Press.

Hesselman, L. (1983), 'Trends in European Industrial Intervention', *Cambridge Journal of Economics*, **7**, 197–208.

Jacquemin, A. (1987), 'Collusive Behaviour, R & D and European Policy', mimeo, EEC DG II, Brussels.

Kay, N. (1988), 'Competition, Technological Change and 1992', mimeo, Heriot-Watt University.

Mertens, Y., and Ginsburgh, V. (1985), 'Product Differentiation and Price Discrimination in the European Community', *Journal of Industrial Economics*, **34**, 151–66.

Müller, J. (1988), 'The Benefits of Completing the Internal Market for Telecommunications Services in the Community', mimeo, INSEAD

Mytelka, L., and Delapierre, M. (1987), 'The Alliance Strategies of European Firms in the Information Technology Industry and the Role of ESPRIT', *Journal of Common Market Studies*, **26**, 231–53.

NEDC (1981), *Industrial Policies in Europe*, National Economic Development Office, London.

—— (1982), *Industrial Policy in the UK*, National Economic Development Office, London.

Nicolaides, P., and Baden-Fuller, C. (1987), 'Price Discrimination and Product Differentiation in the European Domestic Appliances Market', mimeo, London Business School.

Pearce, J., and Sutton, J. (1986), *Protection and Industrial Policy*, London, Routledge & Kegan Paul.

Prais, S. (1981), *Productivity and Industrial Structure*, Cambridge, Cambridge University Press.

Rallo, J. (1984), 'The European Communities Industrial Policy Revisited: The Case of Aerospace', *Journal of Common Market Studies*, **22**, 245–67.

Rossini, G. (1988), 'Price Discrimination in the European Clothing Sector', mimeo, University of Bologna.

Shaw, R., and Shaw, S. (1983), 'Excess Capacity and Rationalisation in the West European Synthetic Fibres Industry', *Journal of Industrial Economics*, **32**, 149–66.

Shepherd, G. (1984), 'Industrial Change in European Countries: The Experience of Six Sectors', in Jacquemin, A. (ed.), *European Industry: Public Policy and Corporate Strategy*, Oxford, Oxford University Press.

Swann, D. (1983), *Competition and Industrial Policy in the European Community*, New York, Methuen.

de la Torre, J., and Bacchetta, M. (1980), 'The Uncommon Market: European Policies towards the Clothing Industry in the 1970s', *Journal of Common Market Studies*, **18**, 95–122.

Tsoukakis, L., and Strauss, R. (1985), 'Crisis and Adjustment in European Steel: Beyond Laisser-Faire', *Journal of Common Market Studies*, **23**, 207–28.

Wilkinson, C. (1984), 'Trends in Industrial Policy in the EC: Theory and Practice', in Jacquemin, A. (ed.), *European Industry: Public Policy and Corporate Strategy*, Oxford, Oxford University Press.

Woolcock, S. (1984), 'Information Technology: The Challenge to Europe', *Journal of Common Market Studies*, **22**, 315–31.

8

British utility regulation: theory, practice, and reform

DIETER HELM

New College, Oxford[1]

I. Introduction

The incoming Conservative government in 1979 was committed to rolling back the economic borders of the state. Gradually, but with increasing confidence, the policy gathered pace. First, industries in competitive markets were privatized. Then, after the Conservatives' election victory in 1983, a process of privatizing utilities was initiated with British Telecom, followed by British Gas. Further election success in 1987 paved the way for airports, water, and electricity to complete the main utility privatization programme. After almost 15 years, all that remain are a number of hard industry cases: postal services, nuclear power, railways, and Scottish water—all of which are currently under consideration for privatization.

As a result of the privatization programme, the state has made a major retreat in its functions. The conventional wisdom has changed, too. It is no longer obvious why the state should *produce* anything. Almost any activity can be contracted out to the private sector.

Yet this retreat from production, illustrated in Table 8.1, with the transfer of what is now over 12 per cent of the total UK stock market value, has not brought with it a corresponding decline in the state's interventions. As witnessed particularly in the energy and water industries, privatization has, if anything, raised the political profile. The utilities are rarely out of the news. Most spectacularly, the coal crisis was a critical juncture for regulation, but, more generally, water and electricity prices have had a significant impact on voter behaviour. The demands for intervention have not

decreased with privatization: they have, in fact, probably increased.

The paradox—private ownership but greater public intervention—is more apparent than real. Once it is recognized that ownership and control are not synonymous, then the impact of different forms of ownership on mechanisms of control becomes the relevant issue. It turns out that it is often easier to control firms which the state does not own, since the consequences of the exercise of control typically do not fall directly on government and the public purse. Public ownership has given way to public rather than private control.

The exercise of control is through regulation. As privatization has proceeded, it is natural for the state to shift from being a *producing state* to become a *regulating state*. The features of the regulatory state, and especially the institutions it has developed for utilities, are the subject of this paper. There has been an extensive debate over regulatory reform. Critics have challenged its design on a variety of grounds, both procedural and in terms of its outcomes. These have included Veljanovski (1993*a*,*b*), Helm (1993*b*, 1994), Souter (1994), and Waterson (1994). Foster (1992, 1993) has defended the new system, supported by comments from most of the incumbent regulators. This paper analyses the key features of the new regulatory regime, and considers the merits of the case for reform. Now that the period of experiment is largely over, it will be argued that, after more than a decade of regulatory experience, reform is needed.

The paper is structured as follows. Section II focuses on the economic principles of regulatory design and, in particular, on the regulatory failures which the new institutions are designed to minimize. Section III sets out the British approach to utility regulation and shows how it has attempted to address the core regulatory

First published in *Oxford Review of Economic Policy*, vol. 10, no. 3 (1994).

[1] I am grateful for research assistance from Emily Clark and Ian Alexander, and for comments from Colin Mayer, Gerald Holtham, Tim Jenkinson, and an anonymous referee. All errors remain mine.

Table 8.1. The retreat from the productive state in utilities

	Privatization date	Current market value (1/9/94) (£ billion)
British Telecom	November 1984	24.2
British Airports Authority (BAA)	July 1987	5.2
British Gas	December 1987	12.9
Water and sewerage companies	November 1989	13.3
Regional electricity companies	December 1990	17.3
National Power and PowerGen	March 1991	11.3
Scottish electricity companies	June 1991	4.9
Utilities total		89.1
Total market value		742.3
Utilities as percentage of total market value		12%

Source: Oxford Economic Research Associates and Datastream.

failures. It demonstrates that the British system has not uniquely overcome the generic problems confronting all major regulatory systems. Section IV sets out the case for reform, focusing on the additional costs of the British system and its failure to minimize the scope for regulatory failures. Section V proposes a series of pragmatic reforms. Section VI concludes.

II. Regulatory failures: incentives and information

Intervention by government is only efficient if the costs of the market failures which it addresses exceed the costs of intervention. Market failures must exceed regulatory failures. The attention of those who favour intervention is typically focused on the former; those who favour *laissez-faire* typically stress the latter. To some—on the Left and the Right—there is no trade-off at all. Socialist planners have argued that markets are inherently less efficient than the state; while those of the Austrian School have argued that markets are inherently more efficient than the state. Among the latter, Hayek (1948) claimed an informational superiority for markets over planning, helping to spawn a vast literature associated with the New Right in the 1980s. Others argue that empirical evidence of experience under nationalization supports a general presumption in favour of markets.

However, given that both markets and regulators fail, and given the prevalence of natural monopoly in utilities, it is assumed here that there is a significant domain within utilities for which a degree of pragmatism is required and, hence, regulation.[2] The focus of this analysis will therefore be the problems of regulatory failure which are relevant to the design of

regulation. At the heart of this issue is the question to which regulatory systems have been designed as an answer—how to intervene to minimize cost, rather than whether to intervene at all. In attempting to provide an answer, three theoretical problems need to be addressed—the incentives of the regulator, the information monopoly, and the incentives of the regulatee.

1. The incentives of the regulator

It has been fashionable to assume that regulators pursue a set of social objectives; that there is no difference between what they ought to do and what they actually do. With this assumption in mind, theoretical analysis has focused on the normative rather than the positive aspects of the regulatory behaviour: how regulators ought to behave, rather than how they actually behave.

Such an assumption sits ill with modern political and economic thought. Economists, in analysing firms' behaviour, assume that managers pursue self-interest rather than that of shareholders: they must be constrained from exercising their discretion over business decisions in order to bring about a coincidence of their own interests and those of owners. In nationalized industries, economists have developed models of managerial behaviour—focusing on the maximization of the scale of the business, i.e. output rather than the profit maximization (Rees, 1989). In political science, politicians are readily assumed to pursue power and office, rather than altruistic objectives. The literature on voting theory and social choice develops these insights into a general theory of self-interest. In the regulation literature, two schools of thought have developed this approach—the Chicago School and the Virginian School.[3]

---

[2]   The grounds for this assumption are set out in Helm (1986).

[3]   The seminal works are Kahn (1971), and Stigler (1971) and Buchanan (1972), respectively.

The task of institutional design for both the political and the economic analyst is to come up with ways in which constraints on discretion can be imposed to realign conduct. Managers' pay may be linked to profits or the share price, and competition between firms weeds out those who deviate too far from the profit-maximizing path. The threat of takeovers limits managerial security. Similarly, constitutions and elections play analogous roles in constraining the exercise of political self-interest.

But while it is natural to think in these terms in considering politicians and managers, it has not yet been widely applied to regulators of privatized utilities in the British context. We do not, as yet, describe the objectives of the regulators as rent-seeking, and analyse their behaviour in terms of their own self-interest. This is a mistake. Although 'good' regulators may be selected, this will not necessarily always be so. Regulatory institutions should not be built on the assumptions that a 'good chap' will be found.[4]

The assumption of rent-seeking regulators provides the starting point for an analysis of regulatory failure. The identification of incentives sets up one of the problems to which regulating institutions are supposed to provide answers. The incentives of regulators can be divided into two categories: direct and indirect rewards.

The direct rewards—the maximization of income (the Chicago assumption)—are typically low in the short run, but not necessarily in the long run.[5] The indirect, non-pecuniary rewards can also be considerable (the assumption in public-choice literature). Regulators presumably find their jobs interesting, especially when they have already invested much intellectual capital in the relevant industries.[6] Some of them will have their own economic theories and will no doubt relish the opportunity to apply them. Where there is considerable scope for discretion and powers to alter the structures of the industries, this may have a strong appeal for them.

2. Regulatory capture: the monopoly of information

Rent-seeking objectives do not, however, automatically translate into results: regulators operate in contexts where the course of action which maximizes their returns is typically far from obvious. Regulatory offences are often poorly defined, and the evidence to prove their occurrence is not usually readily available (Foster, 1992, p. 258). Information—access to it, and its interpretation—is critical. It is rarely independent of the regulatee and, in consequence, its provision provides opportunities for the utility to manipulate it to gain favourable outcomes—i.e. to capture the regulator.

Regulators make their decisions on the basis of the information available to them. Their main source is typically the regulatee. Since the regulatee's objective is to maximize profits and therefore to be confronted with the weakest constraints, and since the regulatee has an element of control or even monopoly over the information provided to the regulator, there is an incentive to present information selectively. In the case of utilities, this takes the form of providing business plans which may overstate costs and understate demand, and in selectively fitting the information to suit their interests.[7] A regulatory game in information takes place between the regulatee and regulators, from which an equilibrium may arise.[8]

Regulatory capture is an extreme theoretical case (Stigler, 1971).[9] It arises when the control of information is complete, such that *de facto* the regulator acts in the interests of the regulatee. In practice, there are almost always methods by which the regulator can weaken the utilities' informational grip. As we shall see below in section III.1, these include the use of comparative data from other similar companies, either domestically or abroad, and the application of reductions in costs based on the difference between past predictions and subsequent performance.

---

[4] Foster (1992), in defending 'independent' regulators, stresses the importance of appointing the right individuals and provides much exhortation about how they should conduct themselves. The utilities themselves expend considerable efforts to try to track the views and opinions of their particular regulators.

[5] Where regulators leave office before retirement they can often, like politicians, claim high private-sector salaries. Lord Tebbit and Lord Walker joined the boards of the companies they were responsible for privatizing (British Telecom and British Gas respectively). The only utility regulator to leave the public sector so far has collected private-sector posts. In environmental regulation, the practice of regulators joining the regulatees is widespread: experience in Her Majesty's Inspectorate of Pollution is, for example, very valuable to the polluting firms.

[6] Academics are heavily represented in regulation. Only the first Director General of Gas Supply and the current Director General of Telecommunications are strictly non-economist businessmen. In the main regulatory bodies, the current Director General of Electricity Supply is a professor, as was the first Director General of Telecommunications. The Directors General of Water Services and now Gas Supply are professional economists, both ex-Treasury.

[7] A good example is provided by the Office of Electricity Regulation (OFFER, 1994, para 5.22) which reports that, in preparing its case for the distribution review, one regional electricity company projected a fall of 17 per cent in unit costs by the year 2000, but another anticipated a rise of 33 per cent.

[8] Kahn (1971). See Sappington and Stiglitz (1986) and Vickers and Yarrow (1988, ch. 4) for surveys of the literature on information and regulation.

[9] See Stigler and Friedland (1962) for supporting evidence on US electricity regulation.

The information monopoly can be formally addressed through yardstick competition.[10] Here, the regulator sets price (or rate of return) not on the regulatee's own cost forecasts and past performance, but rather on those of its competitors. For example, a water company's prices could be determined by a basket of other companies' costs.[11] The most general form of yardstick competition is to base the regulatee's allowed prices on the performance of industry as a whole. Again, using the water example, the Director General (DG) of the Office of Water Services (OFWAT) has argued that this indicates a base of RPI — 2 for the 10-year period starting in 1995 (OFWAT, 1994a).

These exogenous information sources, however, only provide a partial solution. There are always 'special' features which tie the regulator to a regulatee's information. The information game therefore, in practice, remains heavily biased towards the utilities, as was best witnessed at the time of privatization. It is widely acknowledged that the initial cost estimates were over-generous and, in practice, regulators, at each successive review of prices (and sometimes between the reviews), have attempted gradually to claw back the excessive returns built into the initial prices.

3. The incentives of the regulatee: cost inflation and rate-of-return regulation

In a competitive market, firms seek to maximize longer-term profits through product innovation and the creation of monopoly, and shorter-term profits through the minimization of costs. Deviations from cost-minimization encourage entry, with rivals stealing market share in the absence of entry barriers. The firm finds itself constrained to the role of a price-taker. In regulated utilities, the regulator acts as a substitute for the market, taking on some of the functions of a competitor, attempting to provide a similar incentive to reduce costs by setting prices.

The extent to which the regulatory process can in practice mimic the competitive process turns on the relationship between the prices set by regulators and the regulatee's costs. All regulators set price: the question is the basis upon which price is set. The key components are: the operating expenditure (OPEX); the capital expenditure (CAPEX); the asset valuation; and the cost of capital. In *all* regulatory systems, the

regulators are required to adjudicate—implicitly or explicitly—on *all* of these items. The difference between the British price cap and the US rate-of-return regulation is not one of kind, but of degree. In this regard, price-cap regulation does not escape the informational problems of regulatory capture, as some have argued.[12]

It follows from the above that, to the extent that higher expected costs lead to higher prices, a utility has an incentive at price-setting to inflate the asset base, to inflate CAPEX, and to argue for a high OPEX. It will also want to maximize the assumed cost of capital. The higher the expected costs, the higher the added value to shareholders, provided the allowed rate of return exceeds the actual cost of capital. These are the key components of utility regulatory strategy towards price-setting.

The US system is widely misinterpreted to focus exclusively on the rate of return and to permit full cost pass-through, thereby providing little incentive for efficiency or the avoidance of gold-plating. It is, however, both forward- and backward-looking. It inevitably has an element of prediction over the required revenues to sustain the business and these predictions are not simply based on what the utility claims are its costs. But it also corrects its mistakes, clawing back excess returns. The British system was designed not only to overcome the informational problem at price-setting, but also that of the incentives on utilities between price-settings. The question to which we now turn is the extent to which it has, in practice, overcome these regulatory failures.

III. The British approach: contracts and discretion

The British approach to utility regulation has been innovative: it deliberately set out to break new ground in overcoming the traditional elements of regulatory failure. In designing the new regulatory regime, three cardinal principles were adopted: the rejection of rate-of-return regulation; the rejection of direct government control; and the rejection of the assumption of monopoly as a permanent feature. Thus was born RPI − X price-cap regulation; the 'independent' regulatory

---

[10] The theory of yardstick competition is set out in Shleifer (1985).

[11] Littlechild (1988), in advising on the appropriate regulation for the water industry, considers this approach.

[12] Foster (1993) makes this fundamental mistake. As we shall see below in section IV.2, in many respects it is more, rather than less, vulnerable to capture, given the degree of freedom open to individual regulators, because the procedure for establishing the price is only loosely defined under the British system.

offices headed by Directors General (DGs); and the promotion of competition as a primary duty for regulators. Regulation was to mimic the competitive market by setting prices to price-taking utilities, while competition was encouraged to take over as much of the regulatory function as possible. Politics, and particularly civil servants in government ministries, were to be kept out. Regulatory failures, in terms of government incentives and cost inflation, were to be minimized, while the monopoly of information was to be gradually broken down through the development of competition.

This optimistic approach was first applied in the case of British Telecom (now BT). Privatization would, it was argued, provide a spur to efficiency, technical change, and investment, but in the transition to the competitive market, temporary regulation was required for a 7-year initial period.[13] That temporary regulation has now become, in effect, permanent. Indeed, the domain has been extended: more of BT's activities are now subject to regulation than at privatization, despite the growth of competition. The framework hastily put in place for BT has become the blueprint for all subsequent utility regulation. Creeping regulation has similarly occurred in the electricity industry, with the extension of price capping to the generators, and there have been major interventions in gas. The detail of water regulation has been extensive. Thus, regulation is not only permanent, but growing.

There have been various interpretations of the new regulatory regime. One approach is to view it as analogous to a *contract*. The shareholders in the utility are given the right to operate a monopoly through a licence. The price is fixed in relation to the retail price index (RPI) plus or minus some number, X, to represent the expected future efficiency savings. The utility can then maximize profits by minimizing costs during the period over which prices are set. Then, at a periodic review (usually between 3 and 5 years afterwards), the prices are again reset. The customers are issued a price; the shareholders a cash-flow.

This more formal part of the contract is then bolstered by an informal part. While monitoring and enforcing the price cap, the regulator pursues general duties enshrined in legislation, in particular, to promote competition. Thus the regulation of monopoly (the price cap) is augmented by regulatory intervention to promote competition. This later aspect of the framework has proved very intrusive: regulation *for*

competition has turned out to be much more onerous than that *of* monopoly.

The contract approach to regulation focuses on the relative position of the parties. To the extent that the contract is well defined, it encourages efficiency and thereby avoids some of the problems associated with cost inflation. The balance of interests within the contract becomes a distributional matter. However, the incentives remain clear only to the extent that regulators have access to independent information, and refrain from interference between the periods. In other words, the regulatory failure associated with cost inflation can be overcome only if the monopoly of information is also overcome and the scope for *ad hoc* regulatory intervention is constrained. As we shall now see, the former (the information monopoly) is largely unaltered, while the latter (intervention) has proved a considerable temptation, given the objectives of regulators and the discretion they have—via their informal general duties—to pursue them.

The contractual approach derives from a more general attempt to inject precision and clarification into government intervention. It follows the earlier trends to improve the efficiency of the regulating state by *contracting out* public services, particularly at the local government level, subjecting government activities to formal tendering procedures, and introducing individual contracts for public employees. This wider tendency to formalism through contract development is in contrast to the British administrative tradition, which has shied away from legal rules and formalism, towards more piecemeal and discretionary types of intervention. The contract approach ultimately lends itself to an increasing reliance on courts and legal enforcement, as property rights are more clearly defined. Yet, as we shall see, the logical consequence of such an approach, notably legal accountability through judicial review, the publication of reasons for decisions, and the curtailment of discretion, have not been a feature of British utility regulation. Indeed, apologists for the new regime positively welcome the discretionary element.[14] The contract approach is therefore one-sided: a formalization of the obligations on the regulatees' side, but not for their regulators.

We now examine the three key characteristics of the new system, identified above: the price limits, the new independent regulators and offices, and the promotion of competition.

---

[13] 'Competition is by far the most effective means of protection against monopoly. Vigilance against anti-competitive practices is also important. Profit regulation is merely a 'stop-gap' until sufficient competition develops.' (Littlechild, 1985).

[14] Foster (1992) is most explicit, stating, 'to be effective, history suggests, regulators need ample discretion, that is, power to act as they see fit' (p. 268). But see Sherman (1989, ch. 7) who argues that discretion is at the heart of the problems with rate-of-return regulation in the US.

1. RPI–X price caps

The informational requirements

In a competitive market, prices are set by the inter-action of supply and demand. Monopoly pricing is cur-tailed through competitive entry: supernormal profits attract new entry, until profits return to normal. In regulated markets, the regulator must choose a price which mimics this process. Too high a price leads to monopoly profits; too low a price leads to under-investment. The regulator therefore attempts to set prices such that *expected* profits are sufficient to yield a normal rate of return (the cost of capital) on assets em-ployed (asset valuation), to remunerate efficient levels of OPEX, and to finance efficient levels of CAPEX. The business must have sufficient cash to finance all its functions.[15]

In evaluating these components, British and US regulators (and indeed European and Japanese as well) rarely face pure monopoly and, to that extent, they therefore rarely face a complete monopoly of infor-mation. As noted in section II, all regulators seek exogenous information in order to evaluate the com-ponents of the price-setting process. The information sources vary from case to case, but broadly fall under the following headings: yardstick information from other comparator utilities, domestic and overseas (OPEX); cost trends in the economy generally (OPEX and CAPEX); expert engineering appraisals (particu-larly CAPEX); equity and debt market valuations of risk (cost of capital); and utilization tests and system com-parisons (asset valuation).

Although this search for exogenous information is not unique to Britain, recent work by the main regula-tory offices has made a number of advances. On com-parative efficiency, major exercises by OFWAT have provided the basis for the eventual development of a more formal cost linkage between water companies (OFWAT, 1994*b*,*c*). The Office of Electricity Regula-tion (OFFER), by contrast, has taken a much less trans-parent approach and fallen back on 'judgement' (OFFER, 1994). On cost trends more generally, most regulatory offices have been active in data gathering. For example, OFWAT has suggested a going rate of RPI–2 as the norm (OFWAT, 1994*a*). Expert engineer-ing appraisals have been formalized through the requirement for CAPEX certification in the water in-dustry, and consultants have been required to appraise required CAPEX for the regional electricity companies

(RECs), though there is as yet little consensus on how this should be conducted.

On asset valuation, there has been a major contro-versy in British regulation due to the fact that most util-ities were privatized at a discount to their current-cost accounting (CCA) valuations, in some cases substan-tially so.[16]

Regulators, faced with the problem of setting prices at periodic reviews, have had to set implicitly or explic-itly a value for the assets to which the cost of capital is applied, to derive a required cash-stream to remuner-ate existing shareholders. The problem was particularly important in the case of British Gas, where the Mono-polies and Mergers Commission (MMC) decided that a recent market value was appropriate. In water, the DG of OFWAT has favoured a market value established over the first 200 days (but compensated by a higher rate of return for the future period on existing assets, gradually reducing to the cost of capital (OFWAT, 1994). In electricity, the DG appears to have taken the flotation value, rolled forward, for Scottish transmis-sion, but then opted for a quasi-market-related value for the RECs (OFFER, 1994).

There has been an intense debate on the appropri-ate methodology and, although it is still much disput-ed, a degree of consensus appears to be slowly emerging (Mayer, 1994). This comprises a rejection of both CCA values for existing assets and of the initial flotation value. There is thus a measure of agreement that the correct value lies between the two, though the degree of divergence still possible within these boundaries is significant.

This has resulted in regulators making judgements on market values given by capital markets, to the ex-tent that, in effect, regulated asset valuations are set at periodic reviews. This necessity has brought the Brit-ish system close to the concept of the rate base in US regulation. Furthermore, in beginning to question the CCA valuations themselves, the British system is im-porting another US feature, the prudence review. This considers whether assets which have been created should be allowed to earn a return (i.e. enter the rate base), on the basis of their use.[17]

A further distortion relates to differential treatment of depreciation. The two extremes are full CCA depre-ciation, which amounts to funding on an accruals basis, and pay-as-you-go. The former ensures that the business is *sustained*, in the sense that reserves are

---

[15] The cash approach was explicitly endorsed in the MMC gas case (MMC, 1993). See also OFFER (1994).

[16] In the case of British Gas and the electricity generators, the CCA value was about twice the flotation value; in the case of water, almost ten times. See OFWAT (1992 and 1994*c*, Section 8) and MMC (1993).

[17] This prospect of assessing the assets in the CCA valuation is men-tioned in OFGAS (1994).

created to meet future liabilities. The latter relies on the promise that future regulators will honour commitments made by current regulators—that, in effect, current regulators can fetter the discretion of future regulators.

The cost of capital affects *future* investment decisions. It will vary between utilities and over time as investors value the non-diversifiable risks of shares, the risk-free rate, and the equity premium. By fixing at periodic reviews the cost of capital at a particular point in time for the next period, it will not reflect reassessments by investors and is certain, therefore, to be wrong. There is no explicit revision mechanism between periods.

The regulators have used various methods for estimating the cost of capital. The DG of OFWAT has been most explicit, initially favouring the dividend growth model (DGM) over the capital asset pricing model (CAPM) (OFWAT, 1991).[18] The DG of OFFER has rather vaguely expressed concern about the CAPM, but then appears to have used its framework (OFFER, 1994), while the MMC in the gas case stressed the subjectivity of the judgement and, therefore, took a variety of measures (MMC, 1993, Vol. 2, chs 7 and 8). In consequence, investors do not know *ex ante* the basis of cost-of-capital estimates over the lifetime of investments and, therefore, are constrained in project appraisal to estimates made within the regulatory period. At the next periodic review, the method may change and, hence, if investors are risk-averse, a lower value will be assumed, creating an investment distortion.[19]

The RPI–X price-cap approach has not, therefore, overcome the problems of information monopoly, although the British regulators have been creative in addressing them. Advances that have been made in overcoming the information monopoly could equally be applied to the US. The periodic nature of price-setting is, however, distinct, and it is to this that we now turn.

Fixed periods and refraining from intervention: the temptation to chisel

At first sight, a regime of fixed prices for periods of around 5 years is not what one would expect to characterize a competitive market. On the contrary, in competitive markets, prices move frequently to reflect new information about demand and cost changes. There is, then, nothing *natural* about fixed-price periods, and *even if* the regulator sets the right price at a periodic review, it is to be expected that, as the period advances, the gap between what would have been dictated by the market and the actual prices under RPI–X will widen. Given that other (unregulated) prices are moving, the pressure from customers and industry for intervention is likely to grow.[20] This may be reinforced by the desire of regulators to fulfil their own objectives —the problem of rent-seeking by regulators identified in section II above—and by governments sensitive to the politics of utility pricing.[21]

But before considering how these pressures are reflected in regulatory practice, the impact of fixed periods on regulatees should be explored. As noted above, the central idea is extremely simple. When the price cap is set, the utility has a degree of security over income. Profits are maximized by minimizing costs—both OPEX and CAPEX—provided the regulator does not intervene or claw back excess returns.

This may still leave volume risk, if the formula sets the price per unit sold, in which case the utility also enhances profits by sales maximization. However, because environmental concerns indicate that the public interest may not be well served by increasing electricity and gas sales, there has been a gradual shift towards the revenue cap approach for the energy utilities, providing a fixed amount of income, independent of sales (OFFER, 1994; OFGAS, 1994).

The utility will, however, be mindful of the consequences of reducing costs for the next period. Provided that the approach to the periodic review is always forward looking, then lower than anticipated costs will result in lower prices in the next period, but gains in this period can be kept. Then cost minimization is the optimal strategy. However, if profits are clawed back at periodic reviews, then the incentives are blunted. The regime approximates *ex post* rate-of-return regulation, and utilities become equivalent to bonds in as far as the return is set, and cannot be exceeded.[22]

The current position in Britain lies between the two: it is neither pure price cap nor pure rate of return. The

---

[18] On the cost of capital there is now a substantive literature. See OFWAT (1991), Scott (1992), and Jenkinson (1993).

[19] A further strong distinction is that the DG of OFWAT has set the asset valuation on a long-term basis, but allowed an excess rate of return to be gradually phased out, whereas the DG of OFFER has immediately cut the rate of return to the assumed cost of capital, but allowed an asset valuation which is more generous.

[20] It is also to be expected that substitution effects from utility prices out of equilibrium to other closer-to-equilibrium prices in the general economy will create further welfare losses.

[21] Pressure for intervention to limit the increases in water prices before the 1992 general election provides an example (see Helm and Rajah, 1994).

[22] Formally, if the asset value is rolled forward and actual rather than expected CAPEX at the last periodic review is included, with only the cost of capital allowed, then the systems are close to identical. The remaining issue is unanticipated super-normal OPEX efficiency gains.

fixed periods run their course only to the extent that the regulator *chooses* to forgo opportunities for intervention. The temptation has, however, proved too great for most regulators. The types of intervention are several, but their effect is typically to claw back returns within periods. The most notable are:

- *Interim price reductions.* The DG of OFWAT has carried out two rounds of price reductions in the first period. The first was 'voluntary', under the threat of the MMC; the second was through the so-called interim determination mechanism, which is designed to provide within-period flexibility (see Helm and Rajah, 1994).
- *Quality of service enhancements, without compensating price increases.* Pressure from consumers to increase quality has led a number of regulators to increase standards, again by both 'voluntary' and compulsory means, thereby increasing the costs to utilities within a given price cap. This can also be government-induced, as in the Competition and Service (Utilities) Act 1992.
- *Increased investment, without compensating price increases.* In utilities with significant investment programmes, the required level of spending can be increased without compensating price increases within a period, usually through 'voluntary' pressure. The water industry is again an example. In the transition to competitive supply markets in electricity and gas, it is likely that the transmission and distribution businesses of the RECs and British Gas will be required to absorb cost shocks from metering and information technology to meet the requirements of competition. (This is formalized in the 1994–7 British Gas transportation and storage price cap, which is, in effect, conditional on the delivery of appropriate systems to ensure the operation of a competitive market in gas supply (OFGAS, 1994).) A variant of this category is energy-efficiency investments to meet environmental policy objectives.
- *Market-share reduction.* Where regulators exercise a duty to promote competition, this can result in interventions which reduce market share and, hence, revenue, where the price cap is linked to volume. The main examples here are gas and telecommunications.

The above cases of inter-period interventions are examples of *regulatory chiselling*; that is, the reduction in the value of the initial contract given by the price cap. In principle, the regulator can intervene to lower prices or increase costs to keep the actual rate of return at or around the normal level—to mop up excess returns. The power to intervene is typically exercised through informal pressure. Utilities, confronted with requests and proposals from the regulator, can in principle reject voluntary compliance, but this may then lead to a formal proposal to amend their licences, thereby compelling compliance. Utilities have the option of rejecting licence amendments, but then the matter is referred to the MMC which usually, but not always, reports back to the regulator who then decides, taking account of the MMC view. The utility is thus under the threat of the MMC in negotiations with its regulator. (A revision of the price cap at a periodic review is, technically, a licence amendment, and again rejection implies an MMC inquiry.)

The role of the MMC in encouraging compliance to regulators is therefore crucial. It is the lynch-pin of the system. If utilities face uncertainty about the outcome of an MMC inquiry, together with its costs, then the powers of the regulator to exercise discretion are increased. The major test case has been British Gas, and the consequences have not been encouraging to other utilities (see section V below). Indeed, to the extent that returns are above normal levels, the MMC may well find against the utility unless it can prove that these returns are the result of unanticipated efficiency gains, owing to managerial effort. Most utilities appear to have concluded that the MMC is more likely to be predisposed towards the regulator, and as a result have shied away from an MMC appeal. In the gas case the MMC was careful to avoid upsetting the regulatory regime. This is reinforced by the close relationship between the regulators and MMC Commissioners. Of the 12 RECs and 31 water and water and sewerage companies in England and Wales, only two—South West Water and Portsmouth—have appealed against the regulator in the major review of price caps in 1994. As regards South West Water, however, this is very much a special case driven by the environmental capital expenditure problems of Devon and Cornwall.[23] In addition, one Scottish company, Hydro-Electric, has also appealed, on the basis, it appears, of its outlying regional costs.

Initiating intervention between periods is, however, *a matter of choice* for regulators. Each has pursued his or her own preferred approach. Whereas the DG of OFWAT has repeatedly intervened in the first period, the DG of OFFER has consciously refrained from doing so, preferring to claw back (some) excess returns at the end of the period through a one-off price cut.[24] In gas, intervention on quality of service, market share,

---

[23] BAA is different from other utilities in as yet having no specific economic regulatory office. It is covered by the CAA, but an MMC referral is required for periodic reviews.

[24] See Helm (1994, pp. 101–3) and reply by Littlechild (1994, pp. 112–13).

and now the network code has become almost a continuous process.

2. Independent regulators

The second core principle of the new system—the rejection of direct government control—was initially thought to be largely achievable through privatization. Like the Labour government in 1945–51, which nationalized the utilities, the Conservative government placed great emphasis on the benefits of ownership, without due regard for the regulatory consequences.[25]

In contemplating regulation, the architects of the new system attempted to distance government—both politicians and civil servants—from the process. This was achieved in two ways: the granting of licences which formalized obligations on utilities, as we have seen above; and the establishment of Directors General with statutory duties and powers, appointed for periods of times. They are custodians of the licences, in the sense that they play the critical role in enforcing and revising the conditions. Offices were then created to support the Directors General, staffed, in the main, by civil servants on secondment.

Directors General are constrained in exercising their discretion by their general duties. These vary from industry to industry, mainly (but not exclusively) owing to the political circumstances which prevailed at privatization. They include, most importantly, a primary duty to promote competition (except in the case of the water industry) and to ensure that the utility can finance its functions (most explicit in the case of water). Additional duties relate to the need to protect customers, to promote efficiency, and to prevent discrimination. As is immediately apparent, these duties overlap, and are defined so generally that virtually any action by the regulator can be deemed to fall within them. For example, competition issues inevitably arise in almost all aspects of utilities. It is left to the regulators to determine what their particular interpretation is. It is hardly surprising that no substantial case of judicial review has consequently been successful.

3. The promotion of competition

The third core principle of the new system was the promotion of competition. From the outset, the promoters of privatization regarded regulation as distinctly second-best and a necessary but temporary expedient.

Competition would, in due course, largely replace a withering regulatory system. Thus the duty to promote competition in electricity, gas, and telecoms was given a central place in the system. Regulators were to manage the transition to the competitive market after privatization had taken place.

The introduction of competition into utilities has, however, proved much more complex than originally envisaged. Competition has not arisen spontaneously where there are core networks providing the connection between producers and customers. The policy of deregulation, in particular, has been ineffective. A process of *managed competition* has resulted, necessitating significant regulatory intervention. In most utilities this has extended to the deliberate reduction in the market share of incumbents, as well as the determination by regulators of transmission prices, grid and network codes, inset agreements, and divestment undertakings.[26]

In some cases, the transitionary process was formally prescribed in legislation, and therefore became part of the privatization prospectuses of the utilities. For example, in telecommunications, the duopoly of BT and Mercury was to last for an initial period of 7 years, with deregulation thereafter generally assumed. In electricity, an 8-year transition was set out from privatization in 1990, with the phased reduction of the supply franchise in 1994 and 1998, the Fossil-fuel Levy to support the nuclear industry expiring in 1998, and initial contracts for coal expiring in 1993.[27] In other cases, most notably in the gas industry, transitionary arrangements have been put in place after privatization.

The timing of the introduction of pro-competition measures has raised a debate about the treatment of shareholders and the status of prospectuses. To some, notably Veljanovski (1993a), the initial prospectus has a special status, representing an element of a permanent settlement of property rights. This *strong* contractual view has been supported by arguments advanced by financial institutions. However, as a matter of fact, the promotion of competition was a known feature at the time of privatization. Though the disturbance of property rights may have some efficiency effects in raising the cost of capital, it is primarily a distributional issue.

The more complex issues raised by the promotion of competition relate to uncertainty about how

---

[25] For an early government statement of the benefits of ownership transfer, see Moore (1983). See, for a critical assessment, Yarrow (1989).

[26] On transmission pricing, see OFFER (1993); on inset agreements, see Competition and Service (Utilities) Act 1992; on divestment, see MMC (1993) and the undertakings given to OFFER by PowerGen and National Power. A similar process has been evolving in the US, termed *contrived competition* by Viethof (1994).

[27] These are described in Helm (1993c, 1994).

competition will be interpreted by individual regulators, and the extent to which they will take steps artificially to protect entrants and to handicap incumbents. The two main examples in the area are the prohibition placed upon BT in developing new markets, such as entertainment, and the artificial support for gas power station entrants through long-term contracts with the RECs.[28] In engaging in *regulatory handicapping* by distorting competition between entrants and incumbents, regulators have used their discretion to promote competition, even where this may significantly distort resource allocation. In consequence, entrants have concentrated on gaining regulatory advantage by lobbying —an activity which might be described as *competitor capture*, in contrast to the traditional regulatory capture described in section II. In the case of gas power stations, the DG of OFFER has declared that the supporting contracts meet the licence requirement on the RECs to purchase economically, while intervening in the pricing of incumbent generators by fixing the Pool price at significantly below the entrants' prices.[29]

Regulatory handicapping also arises in the context of social obligations. Many of the utilities were regarded as providing merit goods in the public sector (see Dilnot and Helm, 1989). Under monopoly franchises, uniform pricing was encouraged, creating cross-subsidies between richer and poorer and between urban and rural customers. A degree of social cohesion was encouraged, and access to customers in peripheral areas facilitated.

Competition, however, undermines cross-subsidies. The relatively over-priced customers can be cherry-picked by entrants, unless the incumbent utility rebalances its tariffs. Governments are, however, understandably reluctant to face the resultant political reaction, especially in areas with marginal constituencies, such as the south-west. Therefore, there is a tendency to leave social obligations on dominant incumbents in place, with the effect that competition is artificially promoted. In the gas case, the social obligation was enshrined in the 1986 Gas Act. A similar requirement is likely to be placed upon the Post Office if it is privatized.

IV. Five arguments for reform

Having set out the general problems of regulatory failure in section II, and how the core features of the British system have, in practice, operated in section III, we now turn to the costs which result from the new system. These provide the case for reform and can be stylized under the following broad headings: arbitrage; capture; administrative costs; investment and capacity distortions; and political instability. In this section, each of these will be considered.

1. Regulatory arbitrage[30]

There are two main types of arbitrage or substitution effects which result from inconsistency between regulators in the various utilities. These lie in the capital and product markets.

Capital market effects

The potential and actual exercise of discretion over each of the main determinants of price caps (OPEX, CAPEX, asset valuation, and cost of capital), and over the promotion of competition, creates uncertainty about regulatory decision-making. This, in turn, has created a major activity among utilities, consultants, and financial analysts in modelling and attempting to predict how each individual DG will exercise his or her discretion. The uncertainty encourages speculation and, consequently, affects the pricing of utility shares in equity markets. The resultant volatility may raise the cost of capital. A process of regulatory capital market substitution takes place, as investors switch between utilities, betting on the conduct of the regulators.

There has been a variety of attempts to measure the costs of regulatory discretion. None has yet proved conclusive, since regulatory effects are hard to isolate and there has been dispute over whether regulatory risks are diversifiable. General methods of calculating the cost of capital do, however, highlight a significant premium for British utilities over those in the US and Germany.[31]

Share-price volatility around regulatory decisions also affects managerial behaviour. Reluctance to appeal to the MMC against regulatory decisions may be reinforced by negative share-price responses.[32]

---

[28] On the dash for gas, see Helm (1993*c*, 1994).

[29] A further issue is the extent to which the regulators have, by interfering in investments, usurped the role of government in setting energy policy. On this, see Souter (1994).

[30] The term 'regulatory arbitrage' was suggested to me by John Flemming.

[31] See OFGAS (1992) and OFWAT (1991, Vol. 2) for calculations of asset betas.

[32] The share-price reaction in August 1994 to South West Water's indication of its intention to appeal to the MMC is a recent example.

Product market distortions

In addition to capital market regulatory effects, similar problems arise in the product market. Each regulator, acting independently, exercises discretion over price levels and structure. They choose different approaches to the determination of allowed revenue for OPEX, CAPEX, and shareholders. Where these are inconsistent between utilities, this may lead to three forms of distortion: mispricing leading to under- or over-investment; differential pricing between networks leading to substitution between utilities; and location distortions.

Product-market regulatory arbitrage requires the existence of a degree of substitution. In the utilities, the ability to substitute is common between electricity and gas; postal services, telecommunications, and broadcasting; and road, rail, and air transportation. The closer the degree of substitutability, the greater the costs of inconsistency. It is, therefore, more important to maintain regulatory consistency within these sectors.

An example illustrates some of the issues involved. In the energy sector, gas and electricity industries are converging. They compete directly as fuels for heating and cooking in the domestic market, and, with oil, in industrial power supply. Gas is also the preferred fuel for new investment in electricity generation. Increasingly, the choice is between transporting gas or electricity to customers and whether to site generation plant near gas sources or final customers. Customers' fuel choice will be influenced by transmission prices, which are largely controlled by regulators. Suppliers' locational decisions will be sensitive to *relative* transmission prices. It follows that, if price/cost margins are markedly different between gas and electricity industries, if different costs of capital methodologies are applied, if assets are differentially valued, or if the price structures for transmission prices are regulated differently, then each will create an element of regulatory distortion. In a period of significant investment in gas power stations, the locational distortions have been important, with many major investments in the north and north-east, away from the demand centres in the south.

These opportunities for arbitrage have been exploited in both markets. In the next few years the Office of Gas Supply (OFGAS) and OFFER will reset price caps for British Gas's transportation and storage business and NGC's transmission services, respectively and separately. The price caps to be set for Railtrack will create arbitrage opportunities with road and air travel, and for the Post Office with telecommunications.

Figure 8.1. Shareholder returns in British privatized utilities (1 January 1990 = 100)

Source: Oxford Economic Research Associates and Datastream.

2. Capture

It has been forcefully argued that the British system has 'miraculously' avoided the pitfall of regulatory capture which has bedevilled the US system. Foster (1993), in particular, has advanced this claim. The major argument posited to support this claim is the *independence* of regulators.

While it is true that, were a benevolent regulator appointed determined to resist capture (presumably because the person's rent-seeking objectives were not concomitant with those of the utility as described in section II), then capture might for a time be avoided. Discretion could be exercised benignly. But it remains the case that the *scope* for capture increases with the degree of regulatory discretion: the more discretion the regulator has, the more scope to act in the utilities' interest. It is precisely because the regulator can choose to intervene that the prospect of capture arises.

An initial inspection of the evidence does not support the proposition that British regulators have been peculiarly immune to the interests of shareholders in utilities. Indeed, as Figure 8.1 shows, shareholders have done rather well in Britain.[33]

The returns to shareholders have greatly exceeded the cost of capital, and exceeded those in other countries' utility sectors. Shareholders have, in particular, done much better than under rate-of-return regulation.

That these gains were not incorporated in the share prices immediately after flotation is a matter of some debate. It has been argued that the gains from efficiency savings—above those anticipated at privatization—

[33] See, for further explanation, *Utility Finance*, February 1993 and September 1994.

have been exceptionally large. Although these have in some cases been considerable, they cannot, however, account for all (or even most of) the gains. It must be concluded that some part of these gains has arisen because rational investors assumed that high levels of profit would lead to intervention (Helm, 1994). They have, therefore, been *surprised* by the degree of regulatory laxity.[34]

In defence of the price-cap system, it has been argued that customers have also made extraordinary gains, with the result that a win–win outcome has occurred. There are, as yet, no comprehensive studies of price comparisons. However, Stern (1994) presents evidence on energy prices which suggests that fuel price falls have not been passed through in Britain to the extent that they have in other European countries. Furthermore, there is little *positive* evidence to suggest— outside the telecommunications sector—that British utility consumers have fared better than those in other comparator countries.

3. Administrative costs

The plethora of regulators and regulatory agencies is typically justified by the need for industry-specific knowledge. While it is obvious, for example, that technology and cost-drivers in rail differ from those in telecommunications and electricity supply, the degree of differences is often exaggerated.

As identified in section III above, the main information required for price-setting comprises the cost of capital, the asset valuation, OPEX, and CAPEX. There is a common set of generic tools for calculating these variables. Even for OPEX, cost trends and technical change can have some common elements, especially if geography is shared (as, for example, between RECs and water companies). The number of customers will be a cost-driver in most utilities, as will the length of the network and maximum demand. Indeed, it is possible to posit a general utility cost function, within which each is a special case. For the calculation of the cost of capital and asset valuation, the techniques do not vary by industry. Other activities of regulatory offices, such as handling complaints and monitoring quality of service, have common elements. In promoting competition, all regulators have to deal with terms of access and network pricing.

These common activities give rise to administrative economies of scale in regulation. Although they may

not be great compared to the cost of capital and product market effects identified above, a degree of merger between regulatory offices could lead to lower costs.[35] Furthermore, where economic, legal, and administrative skills in regulation are scarce, there may be a further reason for sharing resources.

The main costs of regulatory administration fall, however, on the utilities rather than the regulatory offices. Each utility has created its own regulatory administrative function to track the conduct of regulators, to attempt to predict how they will exercise their discretion, and to prepare for periodic reviews and anticipated interventions. These in aggregate probably swamp the costs of the offices, but cannot be publicly estimated. They nevertheless represent a largely dead-weight regulatory burden.

4. Investment, sunk costs, and regulatory hold-up

A major motivation for privatization of the utilities was a desire to avoid meeting their investment requirements within the public-sector borrowing requirement (PSBR). Targets had been set for the PSBR as part of the medium-term financial strategy (MTFS) from 1980 onwards. As the recession in the early 1980s led to increased unemployment, tax revenues fell while current expenditure rose. Capital expenditure, therefore, took the brunt of cuts. Although, in principle, investment in nationalized industries was controlled through the 1978 White Paper (HMSO, 1978) requiring a 5 per cent real return on projects overall (subsequently raised to 8 per cent), in reality, capital rationing was adopted.

BT was the first major utility to bring forward significant CAPEX (in its case to finance System X exchanges) under the MTFS regime. After experimenting with mixed ownership bonds (Busby bonds), privatization was adopted as a solution to the public expenditure constraint. Other industries posed similar problems—particularly water, airports, and, in the longer term, power generation. Privatization thus had a major rationale in relieving the artificial constraint on investment.

Regulation has replaced the role of public expenditure appraisal in controlling investment. Regulators now perform the functions once conducted by the Treasury and sponsoring departments. CAPEX is mainly reviewed at periodic reviews (although it can

---

[34] A further point in this respect is the extent to which the application of information technology to networks has provided the scope for significant reductions in labour.

[35] For actual costs, see the annual reports of the regulatory offices.

also be considered between reviews, as in the water industry). In resetting the price cap, regulators invite utilities to submit their estimate of expected CAPEX. This is usually overstated, since profits can be maximized by having a generous *ex ante* assumption of CAPEX incorporated in the price cap and then, in practice, delivering a lower *ex post* number. The informational monopoly problem is addressed through expert judgements (the process of certification) and crude percentage reductions.

The process itself leads to distortions in investment. However, for the utilities, the major problem is that investment is typically *long term* and *sunk*. This creates a regulatory difficulty: the time period of the investment is usually much longer than the 3–5-year regulatory periods. Private investors seek long-term contracts to match the life of the capital assets with commitment by customers to pay the sunk costs. Regulators, however, cannot fetter their discretion to review CAPEX at periodic reviews and, indeed, have powers to intervene more frequently. In consequence, capital is either rationed (i.e. long-term projects do not take place) or the cost of capital is increased. In effect, contracts struck *ex ante* to meet sunk costs can be *ex post* renegotiated or scrapped.

In the private sector, this problem has traditionally been solved through vertical integration. Industries with upstream sunk costs have integrated downstream to be assured of final markets. Oil companies have backed their refinery assets with petrol retailing outlets. Breweries have invested in pubs. In the utilities, franchises have been established by statute to assure a contracting base.

The abolition of franchises in electricity and gas, planned for 1998, and the opening up of telecommunications and postal services to competition, undermines this traditional contracting base. The market response is to replace vertical integration with long-term contracts. In electricity generation, 10–15-year contracts have emerged between independent power producers (IPPs) and RECs, encouraged by the regulator (Helm, 1994). In telecommunications, there has been a continuous search for strategic alliances.

The key question which emerges is whether the existing regulatory system can facilitate the emergence of long-term contracts with customers. The degree of discretion mitigates against regulatory commitment and, therefore, the answer is likely to be negative: the 5-year periods are time-limits on CAPEX contracts, and regulators are likely to prohibit utilities from signing up final customers for long periods of time, because this would limit entry. The result is a significant distortion of investment decision-making.

5. Political instability

The final argument for reform is political instability. Utilities will always remain under public scrutiny. They comprise a significant percentage of GDP and, hence, performance in the economy as a whole is affected by what happens in this sector. They provide basic social primary goods which, as discussed in section III.3 above, has resulted in widespread cross-subsidies. For the bottom 20 per cent of households, the average bills as a percentage of income for gas and electricity were 8 per cent and 8.5 per cent respectively in 1990. Together with water they comprise around 20 per cent of income. They account for much pollution, particularly in the electricity and transport industries. The performance of the water industry is critical to the state of rivers, estuaries, and bathing beaches.

Given that investment is long term and sunk, a degree of political stability is important in providing a basis for investment. The criticisms of government intervention have focused on short-termism—because elections are periodic (every 5 years or less), while investments in utilities typically straddle them—and on the exercise of political discretion over policy and investment decisions. However, the new regime displays both of these features, too. The distinctions are that regulators are not elected and that their own incentives may differ.

By changing the individuals who interpret the rules, the regulatory rules can themselves be altered. By replacing the current incumbent regulators,[36] the Labour Party could, for example, introduce very different interpretations of customer interests, the promotion of competition, and, in energy, the efficient use of energy. The price caps could themselves be reopened and set on a different basis. The role of the MMC and judicial reviews might, in such circumstances, be very limited.

As the next general election approaches, the prospect of a government of a different political complexion, which did not set up the current system or appoint the incumbent regulators, will create investor uncertainty, as it did in 1992.[37] This, in itself, will have consequences for the cost of capital and investment, even if the current government is then re-elected. Far from taking politics out of regulation (as, for example, Foster (1992) appears to claim), the current system has, if

---

[36] In theory, regulators are hard to replace during their appointed term of office. However, in practice, their position would rapidly be untenable faced with a hostile Secretary of State, backed up by a parliamentary majority, particularly if utilities figured as a substantive issue in an election campaign.

[37] See *Utility Finance*, April 1994, which shows the impact of the election on beta values.

anything, resulted in heightening the political sensitivity of the utilities. As the general election approaches, and the prospect appears of the system operating under a government which did not invent it, the scope for political intervention will become apparent. Analogous to the way in which the Conservatives' 1972 Industry Act provided the basis for Labour's industrial policies after 1974, the new regulatory system has granted the Labour Party considerable scope for intervention in the utilities.

In summary, the case for regulatory reform is grounded in the costs associated with the current regime, and the extent to which it meets the main regulatory failures set out in section II. It has been argued that the current system allows considerable discretion to regulators, enhancing their ability to engage in rent-seeking behaviour. This personalization gives rise to arbitrage opportunities created by the inconsistency between their decisions, and adds uncertainty, raising the costs of capital for investment. It is far from obvious that regulation has contributed significantly to minimizing prices to customers. On the contrary, the gains from privatization have been disproportionately retained by shareholders. The next section turns to possible reforms, and considers whether these are likely to increase or reduce regulatory failures.

V. Pragmatic reforms: options and evaluation

A wide range of reforms to the current system of regulation have been proposed. These include proposals for a utilities commission (Souter, 1994), for a move towards rate-of-return regulation (Waterson, 1994), for the establishment of a formal legal framework relying more heavily on established property rights and judicial review (Veljanovski, 1993a,b), through to defences of and apologies for the current regime (Foster, 1993). The purpose of this section is not to review all the proposals, but rather to advance a package of changes which meet two criteria: they are evolutionary, building on the current regime, and they reduce the overall burden of regulatory failure.[38]

The main proposals address the plethora of regulatory bodies, the rules for evaluation of the financial framework and cost comparisons, and the role of the MMC and judicial review.

1. Merging regulatory bodies

The scope for regulatory arbitrage arises largely because each industry is separately regulated, each with its own office and DG. A process of rationalization is an obvious first step to reduce the scope for inconsistency between regulators. The general rule to be employed in rationalization is that the closer the degree of substitution, the stronger the case for merger. Taking the current regulatory bodies, there is a strong case for merging OFFER and OFGAS into a single Office for Energy Regulation. This may include not only the function of the two existing offices, but also take on a number of regulatory functions for the coal and oil industries, currently residing at the Department of Trade and Industry (DTI). Oversight of the new Coal Authority might also fall within its ambit.

Transport and communications regulation would also benefit from a degree of rationalization. For the former, an Office of Transport Regulation, taking on the functions of the rail regulator, as well as responsibility for road pricing and the regulation of road investment and pricing schemes in the private and public sectors, would assist in reducing the artificial substitution by customers between alternative, inconsistently regulated, transport means. The addition of airports and the regulatory aspects of air traffic control might also be lodged with such a regulatory body, rather than the proposal to create a new OFAIR for air regulation. For communications, technical change is rapidly bringing about a convergence between telecommunications, postal services, and broadcasting. A single Office for Communications Regulation would have analogous advantages to those for energy and transport.

The main counter-arguments to the rationalization of regulatory bodies are that it would stifle initiative and innovation in regulation, and create over-powerful offices.[39] The former is often given a theoretical defence, through the concept of regulatory competition.[40] Just as firms compete in markets to deliver the best product and price combination, so regulators will compete to produce the best regulatory regime.

This model has obvious flaws: the market in regulation is far from the ideal of competition, and it would be hard to imagine a process of selection whereby bad regulation was driven out by the good. Indeed, given the regulators' objectives, it is possible to imagine a

---

[38] They were first outlined briefly in the *Financial Times* in 1993, at a time of regulatory crisis following the coal debate. These suggestions were explicitly rejected by Littlechild (1993) and Foster (1993).

[39] It is noticeable that Foster's critique of the author's views largely neglects this proposal of merger (Foster, 1993).

[40] The theory of regulatory competition has been developed by Siebert largely in the context of subsidiarity between member states of the EU and against harmonization. See Siebert and Koop (1993) and, for a comment, Helm (1993a).

process of *destructive competition*, in which each regulator tries to outbid the others in terms of toughness, each tightening the X factor at price cap reviews further than the last decision, and promoting competition more radically. Such a process could result in an unstable regulatory cycle, producing periods of under investment as prices are driven too low, leading to crisis and then step changes in the price levels.[41] Furthermore, regulatory competition has a clear cost which has been set out extensively in this paper: it creates uncertainty. Any gains in regulatory innovation would have to be greater than the losses from the higher cost of capital.

A more serious objection is that, by merging the regulatory bodies, the new offices would create powerful bureaucracies. The replies to this are that the total number of regulators and regulatory staff should fall by cutting out the duplication, and that the individual regulators would be less prone to regulatory capture. The monopoly of information would be weakened as each regulator dealt with several companies which could be formally compared in the same process.[42] A good example here is the extent to which the National Grid Company (the operator of the high-voltage electricity grid) and British Gas TransCo (operator of the gas transmission and distribution system) would have a reduced information monopoly if both fell within a joint periodic review. In theory, these comparisons could be made by each regulator separately, but in practice the powers to require information are separately located, and each regulator may be concerned, at different points of the regulatory cycle, with different elements making up the periodic review. Thus, a degree of rationalization may actually reduce the scale of bureaucracy.[43]

2. A common set of financial rules

Merged regulatory bodies would cut costs and reduce product market arbitrage. However, arbitrage in the capital market could be further diminished by the development of a consistent set of financial rules. It is far from obvious what gains there are from the employ-ment of different methods of valuing existing assets and estimating the cost of capital. Using different techniques does not alter the underlying costs and values—it simply leads to inconsistency. The relative returns are distorted, leading to substitution effects between utilities in addition to costs associated with regulatory mistakes over levels, as discussed in section IV.1 above.

The search for improvements is motivated by the evidence, set out in sections III.1, IV.2, and IV.4, of a considerable level of uncertainty created by the exercise of regulatory discretion, leading to capital market arbitrage and impacts on investment—two of the arguments for reform set out in the previous section. The obvious step is to create common financial rules across the utilities, requiring a common methodological approach—but, of course, not a common value.[44]

The establishment of rules could be more or less explicit. The practical options include a White Paper, guidelines, or a common statement by the regulators. The option of an MMC decision on methodology has been ducked in the gas case, and would now require a volte-face to provide the basis for future consistency.

The case for a White Paper is fourfold. First, it would have considerable force over regulatory decisions. Failure to adhere to it would provide strong grounds for an appeal by utilities to the MMC, and the MMC would be minded to take note. Second, by virtue of being a DTI/government paper, it would necessarily take a broad view across utilities, rather than concentrate on particular cases, thereby avoiding the risk of capture. Third, there is a precedent—the 1978 White Paper on nationalized industries (HMSO, 1978)—which has provided the basis for subsequent nationalized industry regulation. Fourth, it would, by virtue of being general, maintain an element of flexibility. (This has been a noticeable feature of the 1978 paper.)

The weaker form of guidelines also has a precedent. The so-called Tebbit rules have provided a basis for MMC investigations, in stressing the dominance of competition over other considerations in interpreting the 1973 Fair Trading Act. Similar guidance notes could be issued for utility regulators. However, the statutory powers of the responsible Secretary (or Secretaries) of State vary considerably, with the result that the force of such guidelines could be weak.

The final option considered here is for the regulators to seize the initiative and publish a joint paper. The problems here are several. First, they may not agree, and the evidence to date is they do not. Second, they

---

[41] Indeed, it is noticeable that virtually all regulators have tightened the price caps at successive periodic reviews. None has yet had seriously to address the problems of *relaxing* price constraints.

[42] An analogous argument can be mounted against industry versus general government departments. The agriculture, transport, and energy industries all managed significant capture of their sponsoring departments.

[43] Foster (1992), contrary to his desire to protect the current regime, makes the valid point that 'the more firms within an industry a regulator regulates, the less likely he is to be captured by any one of them' (p. 413).

[44] The vast economic literature on rules versus discretion, particularly in monetary policy, is relevant here.

will almost certainly want to maintain their discretion and consequently argue for a significant *judgmental* component. Although any of these options would improve on the current position, the White Paper approach is to be preferred.

3. A common basis for efficiency comparisons

A third, and complementary, set of reforms relates to the establishment of OPEX and CAPEX for utilities. As discussed above in sections III and IV, each regulator has been grappling with the problem of informational monopoly, and, in response, has attempted to use comparative information.

To date, these exercises have proved inconclusive and regulators have used the information as one input into their judgements about required cash to finance the business. However, such judgements affect the relative position of the companies, and are particularly important in ranking water companies and regional electricity companies (RECs). In the case of the RECs, the DG of OFFER has set common X factors for all companies, and therefore made adjustments to the price level (the P_0 or initial price) on the basis of cost differences and comparative efficiency. In the case of water, the DG of OFWAT is taking P_0 as given, and has set differential X (or rather, in water, K) factors.

It is probably not yet appropriate to set a common methodology for efficiency estimates, though it is fundamental as to whether these lead to common or differential X factors. Nevertheless, a degree of commonality would be helpful. Utilities are defined by their common cost characteristics and it is therefore to be expected that each industry can, in principle, be nested within a common cost function. At minimum, the establishment of a joint research programme would be of considerable value, facilitated by the rationalization of the regulatory bodies.

4. Reforming the MMC and judicial review

The discretion of the regulators is bounded by the rights of utilities to seek the judgement of the MMC in matters related to licence amendments, including changes to the price cap. Furthermore, utilities can seek judicial reviews. In theory, then, there is an inherent system for checking and balancing.

In practice, as we have seen in section III.2 above, the MMC has tended to have the opposite effect: it has reinforced the regulators' discretion rather than constrained it. The threat of an MMC reference has been used to extend the powers of regulators and to enlarge their domain. Judicial review has proved virtually impossible in practice.

There have been two clear examples of the MMC bolstering the position of the regulators—the gas case and the power generators. In the gas case, relationships between the DG of Gas Supply, Sir James McKinnon, and the Chairman of British Gas, Bob Evans, had broken down in the period running up to the MMC references. The reference to the MMC represented an attempt by the utility to seek redress for its grievances, in particular by establishing a price cap less stringent than that proposed by the DG and an adjudication on the development of competition. The MMC broadly supported the price cap recommended by the DG, but also proposed the break-up of British Gas into separate supply and distribution businesses. The price cap was to be slightly relaxed to take account of the restructuring costs. On the wider issue of the operation of the regulatory system, the MMC concluded that, 'the regulatory system established by the Gas Act is, in our view, fundamentally sound and the difficulties in the regulatory exchanges over the last two years are probably exceptional' (MMC, 1993, Vol. 2, p. 172).

The most explicit use of the threat of an MMC reference by a regulator arose in the case of National Power and PowerGen. Following the coal recontracting in 1993, the House of Commons Select Committee on Trade and Industry suggested that the DG should investigate the costs and margins in the contracts between the generators and the RECs which were passing these coal costs through. The study by OFFER took almost a year, but was never published. However, to avoid a reference, the generators were persuaded to 'voluntarily' enter into undertakings to use reasonable endeavours to dispose of 6,000 MW of plant and to cap Pool prices. In effect, the regulator used the threat of an MMC inquiry into *costs and margins* to bargain for a *structural change in the industry* and *an extension of price regulation into the electricity Pool*, in exchange for leaving the contracts alone. Thus, without MMC scrutiny or public debate, behind the scenes, the DG *extended* the domain of regulation into the previously unregulated Pool pricing and forced a structural change. Neither would obviously have been recommended by the MMC: but the contracts would also not necessarily have been left intact.

In both cases, regardless of the merits of the particular case, the MMC check to the system has proved less than adequate. However, at least in the gas case, the general reference led to a report back to the Secretary of State. In many licence amendment cases, the MMC reports not to the Secretary of State but to the DG, who must in turn take note of the MMC findings, but is not bound by them. In such circumstances, it is not remarkable that few have opted for this route of appeal. To an extraordinary degree, the DG is judge, jury, and executioner.

To argue that the MMC is ineffective is relatively straightforward. To suggest reforms is more difficult. There are some minor amendments, such as requiring major licence changes to be automatically referred, rather than leaving the matter to choice, and to require reports to be made to the Secretary of State rather than the DG for decision. More sweeping changes require the adjustment of competition law and the Fair Trading Act. There are numerous proposals for such reform, which are beyond the scope of this paper.

In addition to automatic referral and reporting to the Secretary of State, further pragmatic steps towards accountability might be taken in terms of the publication of reasons by regulators and judicial reviews.[45] The publications of reasons for decisions exposes regulators to challenge, both in terms of the consistency of the reasons given relative to their duties and powers, and in terms of their rationality. Both open up the prospect of judicial review. This is a less radical proposal than reversing the burden of proof which some have advocated. Nevertheless, such a requirement (rather than simply a matter of the exercise of discretion) would allow an element of redress. For example, in the case of the undertakings on Pool price cappings, new entrants and Nuclear Electric have both been significantly and adversely affected. Neither has had a right even to have its objections heard. Similarly, disappointed customers, witnessing the exceptional shareholder gains following the RECs distribution price reviews, have no right to challenge the leniency of the regulator.

The changes proposed here to the role of the MMC and its reporting, and for the production of reasons, would increase the accountability of regulators. Further steps in providing parliamentary scrutiny, via Select Committee investigations, may augment this.

VI. Conclusions

Regulation of monopoly poses generic problems common to all the main types of control, and in particular

to rate-of-return and price-cap regulation. These fall under three broad headings—the incentives of the regulator, the informational monopoly, and the incentives of regulatees. They give rise to regulatory failures, which are endemic. The choice between regulatory regime depends on the degree of failure.

The British RPI–X regulatory system was designed to improve upon the perceived failures of the US system. Over time, however, the two have increasingly converged. They require similar information and judgements—on OPEX, CAPEX, the cost of capital, and asset valuation. The key difference lies with the British fixed periods, and the associated cost-minimization incentives. However, in practice, these periods are open to regulatory chiselling and intervention. Furthermore, the fixed periods are not without their own difficulties: where price judgements by regulators are badly made (as appears to be the case in the recent resetting of the RECs' distribution formula), the costs of waiting for 5 years to correct errors may be very great. In practice, gross errors will lead to intervention, whether by regulators or politicians.

The price caps are supplemented in the British system by two further interventions: the creation of 'independent' regulators and the emphasis on promoting competition. The former has given regulators great discretion, and as a result has increased the scope for capture. The latter has led to complex intervention and created considerable regulatory uncertainty.

The British system has many attractive features. However, its performance has not been particularly successful: it has created significant regulatory arbitrage in capital and product markets, it has tended to benefit shareholders to an excessive degree and, in terms of outcome, has produced results consistent with capture; its administrative costs are excessive, it has raised the cost of capital, and it has not led to political consensus. There is, therefore, a strong *prima facie* case for reform.

The central problem of the British system is excessive discretion, and reforms should focus on creating greater stability by encouraging consistency between regulators and the adherence to common principles in addressing the core network utility issues. Reforms should aim to increase predictability. Practical steps advocated here include merging some of the regulatory bodies, the setting out of financial principles through a White Paper or similar approach, introducing a degree of commonality in adjudicating on cost estimates, and addressing the role of the MMC and judicial reviews.

These steps do not entail the rejection of the entire existing system: on the contrary, they are deliberately

---

[45] Many regulators would claim that they already meet this requirement. However, in stressing subjectivity and judgement, it is usually impossible to replicate the outcomes.

evolutionary. Nor do they involve going back to the past model under nationalization. In particular, these proposals do not accord with the more corporatist suggestions of regulatory commissions comprising all the 'stakeholders', as for example Souter (1994) suggests. Nevertheless, this paper has argued against the complacency demonstrated by some defenders of the current system, most notably Foster (1992, 1993). The claimed virtues of the current system—independence and discretion—are in large measure actually detrimental. They encourage capture and, in permitting different political parties simply to choose their own regulators to exercise discretion in their political direction, these features add to political instability and may, in the long run, actually make short-term government intervention worse.

The miracle which Foster and others have seen in the new regulatory system is more apparent than real. Though it has many merits on which reform should be built, it is not the best edifice. Indeed, far from matching up to Dr Pangloss's proof that the Baron's castle was the most magnificent of all castles, and the Baron's lady was the best of all baronesses, the current regulatory system is not a particularly stable edifice and has not produced the promised results. Nor should we rely on the best individuals automatically being selected. As Candide discovered, complacency is a dangerous philosophy.

References

Buchanan, J. M. (1972), *Theory of Public Choice*, University of Michigan Press.

Corry, D., Souter, D., and Waterson, M. (1994), *Regulating our Utilities*, London, Institute for Public Policy Research.

Dilnot, A., and Helm, D. R. (1987), 'Energy Policy, Merit Goods, and Social Security', *Fiscal Studies*, **8**(3).

Foster, C. D. (1992), *Privatization, Public Ownership and the Regulation of Monopoly*, Oxford, Basil Blackwell.

—— (1993), *Natural Monopoly Regulation—Is Change Required?*, London, Centre for the Study of Regulated Industries.

Hayek, F. (1948), *Individualism and Economic Order*, Indiana, Gateway.

Helm, D. R. (1986), 'The Assessment: The Economic Borders of the State', *Oxford Review of Economic Policy*, **2**(2), i–xxiv, reprinted in D. R. Helm (ed.) (1989), *The Economic Borders of the State*, Oxford, Oxford University Press.

—— (1993a), 'The Assessment: The European Internal Market: The Next Steps', *Oxford Review of Economic Policy*, **9**(1), 1–14.

—— (1993b), 'Rewrite the Rules for Regulation, *Financial Times*, 7 April.

—— (1993c), 'Energy Policy and Market Doctrine', *Political Quarterly*, **64**(4), 410–19.

—— (1994), 'Regulating the Transition to the Competitive Market', in M. E. Beesley (ed.), *Regulating Utilities: The Way Forward*, IEA Readings 41, Institute of Economic Affairs in association with the London Business School.

—— Rajah, N. (1994), 'Water Regulation: The Periodic Review', *Fiscal Studies*, **15**(2), 74–94.

HMSO (1978), *The Nationalised Industries*, CMND 7131, London, HMSO.

Jenkinson, T. (1993), 'The Cost of Equity Finance: Conventional Wisdom Reconsidered', *Stock Exchange Quarterly with Quality of Markets Review*, Autumn, 23–7.

Kahn, A. E. (1971), *The Economics of Regulation: Principles and Institutions*, Vols I and II, New York, Wiley.

Littlechild, S. C. (1985), *Regulation of BT's Profitability*, London, HMSO, para. 1.5 (b).

—— (1988), 'Economic Regulation of Privatised Water Authorities and Some Further Reflections', *Oxford Review of Economic Policy*, **4**(2), 40–67.

—— (1993), 'Regulatory Debate Should be Better Informed', *Energy Utilities*, **3**, May, 24–5.

—— (1994), 'Chairman's Comments' (reply to Helm, 1994), in M. E. Beesley (ed.), *Regulating Utilities: The Way Forward*, IEA Readings 41, Institute of Economic Affairs in association with the London Business School.

Mayer, C. P. (1994), 'The Regulation of the Water Industry: An Interim Assessment', in M. Beesley (ed.), *Regulating Utilities: The Way Forward*, IEA Readings 41, Institute of Economic Affairs in association with the London Business School, 112–13.

MMC (1993), *Gas and British Gas plc*, Monopolies and Mergers Commission Report, CM 2317, London, HMSO.

Moore, J. (1983), 'Why Privatise?', speech reprinted in J. Kay *et al.* (eds.) (1986), *Privatisation and Regulation in the UK Experience*, Oxford, Oxford University Press.

OFFER (1993), 'Consultation Paper on Transmission Services', Birmingham, Office of Electricity Regulation.

—— (1994), *The Distribution Price Control: Proposals*, Birmingham, Office of Electricity Regulation.

OFGAS (1992), *Estimating the Rate of Return for Gas Transportation*, London, Office of Gas Supply.

—— (1994), *Price Controls on Gas Transportation and Storage*, London, Office of Gas Supply.

OFWAT (1991), *The Cost of Capital: A Consultation Paper*, Vols 1 and 2, Birmingham, Office of Water Services.

—— (1992), *Assessing Capital Values at the Periodic Review*, Birmingham, Office of Water Services.

—— (1994a), *Setting the Price Limits for Water and Sewerage Services*, Birmingham, Office of Water Services.

—— (1994b), *Modelling Sewage Treatment Costs 1992–93*, prepared for OFWAT by M. Stewart, Birmingham, Office of Water Services

—— (1994c), *Future Charges for Water and Sewerage Services: The Outcome of the Periodic Review*, Birmingham, Office of Water Services.

Rees, R. (1989), 'Modelling Public Enterprise Performance', in D. R. Helm *et al.* (eds.), *The Market for Energy*, Oxford, Oxford University Press.

Sappington, D., and Stiglitz, J. (1986), 'Information and Regulation', in E. Bailey (ed.), *Public Regulation*, Cambridge, MA, MIT Press.

Scott, M. FG. (1992), 'The Cost of Equity Capital and the Risk Premium on Equities', *Applied Financial Economics*, **2**, 21–32.

Sherman, R. (1989), *The Regulation of Monopoly*, Cambridge, Cambridge University Press.

Shleifer (1985), 'A Theory of Yardstick Regulation', *Rand Journal of Economics*, **16**, 319–27.

Siebert, H., and Koop, M. J. (1993), 'Institutional Competition versus Centralization: *Quo Vadis* Europe', *Oxford Review of Economic Policy*, **9**(1), 15–30.

Souter, D. (1994), 'A Stakeholder Approach to Regulation', in D. Corry *et al.* (eds.) (1994), *Regulating our Utilities*, London, Institute for Public Policy Research.

Stern, J. P. (1994), 'The Government's Public Policy Towards Gas', in D. R. Helm (ed.), *British Energy Policy in the 1990s: The Transition to the Competitive Market*, Oxford, The OXERA Press.

Stigler, G. J. (1971), 'The Theory of Economic Regulation' *Bell Journal of Economics and Management Science*, **2**(1), 3–21.

—— Friedland, C. (1962), 'What Can Regulators Regulate? The Case of Electricity', *Journal of Law and Economics*, **5**, 1–16.

Utility Finance (various issues), published monthly, Oxford, Oxford Economic Research Associates.

Veljanovski, C. (1993a), *The Future of Industry Regulation in the UK*, London, European Policy Forum.

—— (1993b), *The Need for a Regulatory Charter*, London, European Policy Forum.

Vickers, J., and Yarrow, G. K. (1988), *Privatisation: An Economic Analysis*, Cambridge, MA, MIT Press.

Viethof, R. H. (1994), *Contrived Competition: Regulation and Deregulation in America*, Cambridge, MA, Belknap, Harvard University Press.

Waterson, M. (1994), 'The Future of Utility Regulation: Economic Aspects', in D. Corry *et al.* (eds.) (1994), *Regulating our Utilities*, London, Institute for Public Policy Research.

Yarrow, G. K. (1989), 'Does Ownership Matter?', in C. Veljanovski (ed.), *Privatisation and Competition: A Market Prospectus*, IEA.

PART IV

EXTERNALITIES AND THE ENVIRONMENT

9

The problem of global environmental protection

SCOTT BARRETT

London Business School

Suppose that land is communally owned. Every person has the right to hunt, till, or mine the land. This form of ownership fails to concentrate the cost associated with any person's exercise of his communal right on that person. If a person seeks to maximize the value of his communal rights, he will tend to overhunt and overwork the land because some of the costs of his doing so are borne by others. The stock of game and the richness of the soil will be diminished too quickly. It is conceivable that those who own these rights, i.e. every member of the community, can agree to curtail the rate at which they work the lands if negotiating and policing costs are zero . . . [However,] negotiating costs will be large because it is difficult for many persons to reach a mutually satisfactory agreement, especially when each hold-out has the right to work the land as fast as he pleases. [Furthermore,] even if an agreement among all can be reached, we must yet take account of the costs of policing the agreement, and these may be large, also.

Demsetz (1967, pp. 354–5)

I. Introduction

Demsetz's influential paper on the development of private property rights makes depressing reading for anyone concerned about global common property resources such as the oceans and atmosphere. Demsetz's view—and it is one that is shared by many others—is that users of a communally owned resource will fail to come to an agreement on managing the resource even though it is in the interest of all users to co-operate and reduce their rates of use of the resource. The reason is

First published in *Oxford Review of Economic Policy*, vol. 6, no. 1 (1990). This version has been up dated and revised to incorporate recent developments.

that if this improved situation is attained, every user will earn even higher returns by free-riding on the virtuous behaviour of the remaining co-operators. As a consequence, united action on the part of users can be expected to be unstable; co-operative agreements, even if they are reached, will not persist. The only way out of the common property dilemma, as Demsetz makes clear, is intervention by '*the* state, *the* courts, or the leaders of *the* community' (emphasis added). In Demsetz's example, the intervention manifests itself in the development of private property rights to the resource, but the intervention could just as easily involve regulation.

The reason this view is disquieting is that for global common property resources there is no World Government empowered to intervene for the good of all. To be sure, there do exist international institutions—most notably the United Nations Environment Programme—which have been given the mandate to co-ordinate international environmental protection efforts. But none of these institutions can dictate what is to be done; that requires agreement by the parties concerned. The problem is perhaps best exemplified by the International Whaling Commission (IWC), which was established to conserve whale stocks, but whose best efforts in this regard have been repeatedly foiled. IWC membership is open to any country, and this leaves open the possibility that the whales could be protected for the global good. But any member can object to a majority decision, and hence render that decision meaningless. For example, a 1954 proposal to prohibit the taking of blue whales in the North Pacific was rejected by the only members who hunted blue whales in this ocean—Canada, Japan, the US, and the USSR—and hence did nothing to protect this species. In 1981 the IWC sought to ban the use of the non-explosive harpoon for killing minke whales. The ban was objected to by Brazil, Iceland, Japan, Norway, and the USSR. Since these were the only countries that hunted minke whales, the ban had no effect.[1]

Because national sovereignty must be respected, the problem of conserving global common property resources is no different from that described by Demsetz. The only way out of the global common property dilemma is agreement. Yet, just as in the situation Demsetz describes, there are strong incentives for governments not to co-operate, or to defect from an agreement should one be reached. This is the crux of the problem of managing global common property, and what distinguishes this problem from the long studied one of common property management under the jurisdictional control of a central authority.

Attempts to correct global, unidirectional externalities will encounter similar difficulties. Consider the problem where certain activities by one country harm all others. A good example is deforestation of Amazonia by Brazil. The rain forests play a crucial role in the protection of biological diversity and in the functioning of the carbon cycle. When standing, the rain forests serve as habitat to about a half of all wildlife species and absorb carbon dioxide, one of the so-called greenhouse gases. When the forests are burned, masses of species can become extinct and substantial quantities of greenhouse gases are emitted. If the rights to generate these externalities are vested in the one country, as indeed they are in the case of Brazilian deforestation, then the others will have to pay this nation to cease its destructive activities. If the externality affected only one other country, then bargaining might be possible; the externalities might be internalized without outside intervention.[2] But in the case of global externalities, all countries except the generator suffer. All sufferers might be willing to bribe the generator to cease its harmful activities. But a contribution by any one country would confer benefits on all others and not just the one making the compensating payment. The others could therefore do better by free-riding. But then so too could the one that contemplated making the payment. Co-operation would again be foiled.[3] Mechanisms exist

that can lead countries to reveal their preferences for global public goods truthfully (see, e.g. Groves and Ledyard, 1977), and hence for correcting global externalities. But in the absence of a World Government these mechanisms cannot be employed without the consent of the sovereign nations themselves. Every country would be better off if it agreed to participate in the revelation exercise. But each would do even better if others participated and it did not. All will therefore choose not to participate. The crux of the problem of correcting global externalities, like that of managing global common property, is that global optimality demands global co-operation, and yet the incentives facing individual countries work in the opposite direction.

The theoretical arguments for supposing that co-operation will not develop are compelling. But they can hardly be complete. Co-operation *does* take place and is often codified in international agreements. Some of these are woefully ineffective—a famous example being the International Convention for the Regulation of Whaling (1946) which established the IWC. Others do appear to have achieved a great deal. Of these last, the Montreal Protocol on Substances that Deplete the Ozone Layer (1987) seems the most impressive, because it demands that its many signatories undertake substantial reductions in their emissions of ozone-depleting chlorofluorocarbons (CFCs) and halons. Though agreements dealing with unidirectional externalities are rare and almost invariably toothless, there is one—the World Heritage Convention—that at least holds some promise. This agreement places responsibility for safeguarding natural environments like the Serengeti and the Galapagos Islands on a community of nations, and could be invoked to protect the remaining tropical rain forests. There is clearly a need to explore why international co-operation might develop, and what the significance of particular forms of co-operation might be.

To make any progress we will need a basis from which to assess whether co-operation can in fact be expected to achieve much. Contrary to Hardin's (1968) famous allegory of the commons, the absence of co-operation need not lead to tragedy. Section II discusses some of the parameters that are important in determining the potential gains to co-operation. Having drawn the boundaries, we then consider how we might move closer to the full co-operative solution, the global optimum. Non-co-operation may sometimes wear the disguise of co-operation, and section III shows that an outcome better than the purely nationalistic one can

---

[1]   See Lyster (1985).
[2]   See Coase (1960). Bargaining has in fact taken place at the bilateral level. A famous example is the Trail Smelter case. The Canadian smelter emitted pollutants that crossed the US border. The case was arbitrated by an international tribunal comprised of an American, a Canadian, and a Belgian. The tribunal found that Canada was liable for damages, and also established emission regulations for the plant. The judicial decisions on this case make fascinating reading. See Trail Smelter Arbitral Tribunal (1939, 1941).
[3]   Demsetz (1967, p. 357) argues that in the large numbers case, 'it may be too costly to internalize effects through the market-place'. Elsewhere, Demsetz (1964) argues that it might in fact be optimal for the externality not to be internalized since the costs of internalization should include

the costs of transacting the agreement. But even then the free-rider problem would prevail; intervention, were it possible, might still be desired.

emerge even where binding agreements are absent. Effective management of global environmental resources does however seem to rely on the more formal institution of international law. Section IV discusses the rudiments of a model that explains why countries would co-operate when the free-rider problem must surely bite, and what international agreements mean for global social welfare and the welfare of citizens of individual countries. Just as failure to co-operate may not lead to tragedy, so co-operation may not buy us very much. Indeed, combining the analysis of the potential gains to co-operation with this model of formal agreements, it can be shown that co-operation is sometimes hardest to obtain when it is most needed.

II. The potential gains to co-operation

Where a global externality is unidirectional, the country causing the externality will, in the absence of a negotiated settlement, ignore the damages its activities impose on other countries. This is the full *non-co-operative* outcome. The full *co-operative* outcome is found by internalizing the externality. In this case the country inflicting the externality chooses its actions so as to maximize the net benefits of all countries, including itself. Global net benefits will of course be higher in this case. The difference between the global net benefits for the co-operative and non-co-operative outcomes defines the potential gains to co-operation.

Where the externalities of concern are reciprocal in nature, every country has some incentive to take unilateral action even in the absence of a binding agreement. Furthermore, the strength of this incentive will depend on the actions taken by all other countries. An example of a reciprocal externality is the emission of a global pollutant. If one country reduces its emissions, it will benefit from the improved environmental quality, provided other countries do not increase their emissions so as to fully offset the one country's action. The other countries will benefit partly by being able to increase their emissions somewhat and partly by enjoying a cleaner environment (again, provided their increase in emissions does not entirely offset the one country's extra abatement). The extent of the benefit enjoyed by the conserving country will clearly depend on the actions taken by the other countries, and of course all countries are subject to a similar calculus. It is this interdependence which makes calculation of the potential gains to co-operative management of global

common property more difficult. It is better, then, that we work with a specific model.

To fix ideas, reconsider the problem of global pollution. Suppose that the relevant number of countries is N. One might think that N would include all the world's countries, but that need not be so, a point we return to later. Let us however suppose for simplicity that N does include all countries and that each is identical. Each, therefore, emits the same quantity of a pollutant *ex ante*—that is, before the game is played—and each faces the same abatement cost and benefit functions. The problem is then perfectly symmetric. To simplify the analysis further, assume that the *marginal* abatement cost and benefit functions are linear. Clearly, the marginal abatement cost schedule for each country must depend on its own abatement level, while each country's marginal abatement benefit function must depend on *world-wide* abatement.

In the absence of any co-operation, each country will maximize its own net benefits of abatement and in so doing will choose a level of abatement at which its own marginal abatement cost equals its own marginal abatement benefit.[4] This is the non-co-operative (Nash equilibrium) solution to this game, and it is shown as abatement level Q^* in Figure 9.1. Were countries to co-operate fully, they would seek to maximize the global net benefits of abatement. Since we have assumed that all countries are identical, the global net benefits of abatement can be defined as the sum of every country's net benefits of abatement. In maximizing the global net benefits of abatement, each country will choose a level of abatement at which its own marginal costs of abatement equal the global marginal benefits of abatement, or the sum of the marginal abatement benefits enjoyed by all countries.[5] The full co-operative solution to this game is shown as abatement level Q^{**} in Figure 9.1.

One sees immediately that the full co-operative solution demands greater abatement but, equally, gives to every country a greater net benefit. For a given size of N, the difference between Q^* and Q^{**} can be shown to depend on the slopes of the marginal abatement

[4] I am assuming here that every country believes that its choice of an abatement level will not alter the choices of the other countries; that is, I am assuming zero conjectural variations. One can impose positive or negative conjectures, but these assumptions would be *ad hoc*. Alternatively, we could determine a consistent conjectures equilibrium—that is, one in whose neighbourhood every country's conjectures are confirmed by the responses of the other countries. Cornes and Sandler (1983) find that consistent conjectures can lead to even greater overuse of the resource compared with the Nash equilibrium.

[5] This is of course nothing but a restatement of Samuelson's (1954) rule for the optimal provision of public goods. For an alternative presentation of these principles, see Dasgupta's (1982) model of a global fishery.

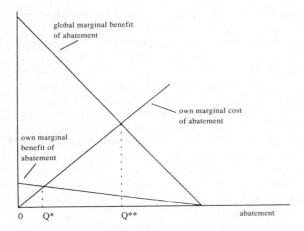

Figure 9.1. The potential gains to co-operation

benefit and cost curves. Denote the (absolute value of the) slope of each country's marginal abatement benefit curve by the letter b, and the slope of each country's marginal abatement cost curve by the letter c. Then it can be shown that the discrepancy will tend to be small whenever c/b is either 'large' or 'small' (see Barrett, 1994). The approximate implication of this result is that fairly innocuous pollutants (that is, pollutants for which b is small) that are very costly to control (that is, that have a large c) do not cause too great a problem. Nor do extremely hazardous pollutants (that is, pollutants associated with a large b) that are cheap to control (that is, pollutants that have a small c). In the former case, even collective action will not call for large abatement levels. In the latter, countries will want to abate substantial quantities of emissions unilaterally. The real problem is with pollutants whose marginal abatement benefit and cost curves are both either steep or flat—that is, hazardous pollutants that are costly to control, and mildly offensive pollutants that can be controlled at little cost. Of these, the former type naturally causes the greatest concern, for the cost of failing to co-operate in this case is very, very high.

Unidirectional and reciprocal externalities are plainly different in their effects. A country has no incentive to abate its emissions if the externality is unidirectional (provided side payments are ruled out), unless negotiations on this one issue are linked to another issue in which, in some sense, the tables are turned. Not so if the externality is reciprocal in nature. For then the emitting country will have private incentives to control its emissions.

III. Non-co-operative environmental protection

The politics of global environmental protection are not as sterile as the above models would imply. Once we permit alternative strategies to be chosen, widen the choice sets themselves, and allow motivations other than self-interest (narrowly defined) to guide decision-making, global environmental protection can be enhanced.

1. Supergames

In the above games, strategies are chosen once, and the games are never repeated. But in the common property game countries are unavoidably locked in a continuing relationship, and this leaves open the possibility that they may retaliate and hence that co-operative strategies may be countenanced. Suppose then that all countries choose one of two strategies: they either choose the full co-operative abatement level Q^{**} initially, and continue to choose Q^{**} in every future period provided all other countries chose Q^{**} in every previous period; or they choose not to co-operate in any period.[6] Then the co-operative trigger strategy will constitute an equilibrium to this supergame provided the rate of discount is sufficiently low (for then the gains to choosing the non-co-operative strategy will be low, too; see Friedman, 1986). Although this supergame equilibrium entails co-operation, the co-operation is tacit and is enforced by means of a non-co-operative mechanism, retaliation; there is no explicit agreement, no open negotiation.[7]

One variant of this game involves countries adopting a convention that says that a subset of countries should co-operate in the face of free-riding by the others (see Sugden, 1986). It may, for example, be believed that the industrialized countries should co-operate to reduce emissions of CFCs or greenhouse gases (because it was their emissions that caused the environmental reservoirs to be filled in the first place), and that the poor countries should be allowed to free ride. In this game, each of the members of the subset could adopt the trigger strategy with respect to the subset, and each

---

[6] If countries choose not to co-operate in the initial period, they need not choose Q^* in this period. The reason for this is that the optimal non-co-operative abatement level is contingent on the abatement levels chosen by the other countries.
[7] Axelrod's (1984) tournaments of the repeated prisoners' dilemma game suggest that behaviour in the disguise of co-operation may well emerge. Whether his findings carry over to the common property game with many players, however, is as yet unknown.

of the others could simply choose their optimal non-co-operative responses. This latter possibility may be fragile, because different countries may have different views about which should co-operate and which should not. This ambiguity may help explain why unilateral action to reduce CFC emissions was limited (US Environmental Protection Agency, 1988, p. 30576):

In 1978 the United States restricted the use of CFCs in aerosols. While several nations adopted similar restrictions (e.g. Sweden, Canada, Norway) and others partially cut back their use (European nations, Japan), there was no widespread movement to follow the United States' lead. Concerns existed then that other nations had failed to act because the United States and a few other nations were making the reductions thought necessary to protect the ozone layer. Similar concerns exist today that unilateral action could result in 'free riding' by some other nations.

It is not obvious how sufferers of a unidirectional externality could punish the offending nation. But so long as the countries are engaged in some form of exchange, potent weapons may be at the sufferers' disposal. The Packwood–Magnuson Amendment to the US Fishery Conservation and Management Act (1976) requires the US government to retaliate whenever foreign nationals compromise the effectiveness of the IWC. An offending nation automatically loses half its allocation of fish products taken from US waters, and if the country refuses to improve its behaviour within a year, its right to fish in US waters is revoked.

2. Matching

In the one-shot common property game, each country chooses an abatement level and nothing else. There is no reason why a country's choices need be limited in this way. We could, for example, allow countries to choose a 'base' abatement level—that is, a level of abatement which is not explicitly contingent on the abatement levels chosen by other countries—and a 'matching rate'—in our example, a fraction of the sum of all countries' base abatement levels. In effect, countries would then voluntarily subsidize each other's abatement levels. In the original game, one unit of abatement by country i buys country i one unit less of global emission (assuming that the emissions of all other countries are held fixed). In the matching game, one unit of abatement by country i may yield a much greater reduction in global emission. Matching might improve matters—Guttman (1978) shows that under certain conditions matching can sustain the full co-operative solution. But in the management of global common property, matching is rarely invoked. Recently, Norway announced that it would allocate one-tenth of one per cent of its GDP each year to a fund on climate change if other industrial countries matched its contribution (on a GDP percentage basis). The offer has yet to be taken up. Environmental groups in the United States have argued that the US should unilaterally surpass the reductions specified in the Montreal Protocol and at the same time impose restrictions on imports of products containing or made with CFCs from countries that fail to agree to make the same reductions. Their plea was rejected by the authorities (US Environmental Protection Agency, 1988, p. 30574).

3. Morality

In the models discussed thus far, the welfare of every country is assumed to depend solely on its *own* net benefits. An alternative way of looking at the problem is to assume that countries act according to some moral principle which requires that they take stock of the effect their actions have on the welfare of other countries. For example, suppose every country but one reduces its emissions of some global pollutant by at least x tonnes. Let us further suppose that the recalcitrant nation would like all others to reduce their emissions by y tonnes each. Then the leaders of the recalcitrant nation might feel compelled to obey the rule: if $y > x$ then we are morally obligated to reduce our emissions by at least x tonnes. If countries obey this rule, then the free-rider problem can be mitigated (see Sugden, 1984). That moral principles may guide non-co-operative abatement is suggested by the following remarks made by the House of Commons Environment Committee (1984, p. lxxi) in its report recommending that the UK join the Thirty Per Cent Club:[8]

As our inquiry has progressed the stance of the United Kingdom has become increasingly isolated by its refusal to legislate to reduce SO_2 and NO_x emissions. Since our work began three West European countries have joined those already in the 30 per cent club, and several Eastern European countries have committed themselves to reduce transfrontier emissions by 30 per cent. SO_2 emissions in the United Kingdom have indeed fallen by 37 per cent since 1970, but the levels of high-stack emissions which affect remote areas have not fallen. In 1970, when the 37 per cent fall began, we were the largest

[8] The Thirty Per Cent Club consists of the countries that have signed the Protocol to the 1979 Convention on Long-Range Transboundary Air Pollution on the Reduction of Sulphur Emissions or their Transboundary Fluxes by at least 30 Per Cent (1985). The UK has not joined this 'club' but it has committed itself to substantial reductions in sulphur dioxide and nitrogen oxides emissions by agreeing to comply with the European Community Large Combustion Plant Directive.

emitter in Western Europe. In 1984, we are still the largest emitter. NO_x emissions have not fallen. In Western Europe only West Germany deposits more SO_2 in other countries than does the United Kingdom, and further significant reductions cannot be achieved by either without controls.

The Committee's concern in this passage lies less with the net benefits to the UK of reducing emissions than with how UK abatement has lagged behind the rest of Europe. Indeed, the Committee's evaluation did not even consider whether the other European countries were abating more simply because it was in their own self interest to do so. The argument seems to be: 'The other European nations are reducing their emissions, so we should, too.' Compared with the supergame problem, co-operation in this case is not instrumentally important—the Environment Committee did not seek to reduce UK emissions so that others would reduce theirs even further—but intrinsically important. Concerns about fairness have been shown to militate against the free-rider problem in experimental tests (Marwell and Ames, 1981). However, in the next section we shall see that in a bargaining situation, obeying moral principles may serve only to undermine the cause of environmental protection.

IV. Co-operative environmental protection

In the absence of co-operation, outcomes better than the full non-co-operative one can sometimes develop, at least in principle. But such instances seem to be rare. Even two close neighbours with strong trading ties can fail to arrive at a preferred solution, as the disagreement between the United States and Canada over the exploitation of the North Pacific fur seal illustrates. Following an initial conflict between the two nations over the pelagic seal hunt, a Tribunal Arbitration was convened at the request of the two parties (with Great Britain acting for Canada). In late 1893 the Tribunal decided that the United States did not have territorial jurisdiction over the Bering Sea, and hence could not keep Canadian sealing vessels out of these waters. This effectively sanctioned open-access harvesting of the species, and co-operation proved impossible to secure (Paterson and Wilen, 1977, p. 94):

Following the decision of the Tribunal, the diplomatic efforts of both Great Britain and the United States had been directed to convincing the other to reduce its sealing in order to allow the herd to recover from earlier depradations. No agreement could be reached and in 1897 the United States unilaterally forbade its citizens to engage in pelagic sealing in the North Pacific. At the same time quota adjustments were made as the herd diminished in size. So strong was the reaction to the declining herd size and the continued Canadian pelagic hunt that a bill reached the [United States] Senate which called for the complete destruction of the herd. It did not pass . . .

Better management of the population had to await the signing of the North Pacific Fur Seal Treaty by Great Britain, the United States, Japan, and Russia in 1911— a remarkable agreement that remains in force today.[9] Effective management of global environmental resources seems to demand that countries co-operate openly and put their signatures on international agreements, treaties, and conventions. Explanations for why co-operation of this kind might emerge are offered below.

1. International environmental agreements

Consider the following modification to the common property game described earlier. Suppose a subset of the N identical countries 'collude' by signing an international environmental agreement and that the remaining countries continue to act non-co-operatively. Suppose further that the signatories to the agreement choose their collective abatement level while taking as given the abatement decision functions of the non-signatories, while the latter countries continue to behave atomistically and choose their abatement levels on the assumption that the abatement levels of all other countries are fixed. That is, the signatories act as 'abatement leaders', and the non-signatories as 'abatement followers'. Quite clearly, we would like the number of signatories, the terms of the agreement, and the abatement levels of all non-signatories to be determined jointly. We also require that the agreement itself is stable. A stable agreement is one where non-signatories do not wish to sign the agreement and signatories do not wish to renege on their commitment. Then it can be shown that for identical countries with linear marginal abatement benefit and cost functions a stable international environmental agreement always exists (Barrett, 1994).

The solution to this problem exhibits many of the features of actual agreements. The net benefits realized by both signatories and non-signatories are higher than in the earlier problem where negotiation was ruled out. What is more, the signatories would like the non-co-operators to sign the agreement. However, non-signatories do better by free-riding.

[9] For legal background on this treaty and its successors, see Lyster (1985).

It is important to emphasize that the agreement is *self-enforcing*. Any signatory that renounces its commitment can reduce its abatement level and hence its costs. However, in pulling out of the agreement, the number of co-operators is reduced and the agreement itself is weakened; the remaining co-operators reduce their abatement levels, too. A signatory will want to pull out of an agreement only if the saving in abatement costs exceeds the resulting loss in benefits. Similarly, a country that joins an agreement will have to abate more and hence incur higher costs. But the very act of joining will strengthen the agreement; the other co-operators will also increase their abatement levels. Joining appears attractive if the resulting increase in benefits realized by the new signatory exceeds the increase in costs that this country must incur in committing itself to the terms of the agreement.

Real treaties are not rewritten with every defection or accession, but mechanisms are at work that have a similar effect. It is common for treaties to come into force only after being ratified by a minimum number of signatories. The Montreal Protocol did not come into force until it had been ratified by at least eleven countries representing at least two-thirds of global consumption of the controlled substances. It is also common for treaties to be reviewed and altered when necessary and often at regular intervals. Over the last few years the Montreal Protocol has been amended three times. On each occasion the requirements of the agreement were significantly strengthened. That this agreement is self-enforcing is suggested by a comment made by the US Environmental Protection Agency (EPA) (1988, p. 30573):

EPA judged that the obvious need for broad international adherence to the Protocol counseled against the United States' deviating from the Protocol, because any significant deviation could lessen other countries' motivation to participate.

Self-enforcement is essential in any model of international environmental agreements because nation states cannot be forced to perform their legal obligations. A country can be taken to the International Court of Justice for failing to comply with the terms of a treaty, but only with the defendant's permission. Even then, the disputing countries cannot be forced to comply with the Court's decision.[10]

What are the gains to having international environmental agreements? The answer depends partly on the number of relevant and potential signatories. When N is large, international environmental agreements can achieve very little no matter the number of signatories.

The reason, quite simply, is that when N is large, defection or accession by any country has only a negligible effect on the abatement of the other co-operators.

Determination of N is not always a trivial matter. Some treaties do not restrict participation, but in these cases many of the signatories may have no effective say in environmental protection. Over 100 countries have signed the 1963 Partial Nuclear Test Ban Treaty, but only a few signatories possess nuclear weapons technology. The 1967 United Nations Treaty on Principles Governing the Activities of States in the Exploration and Use of Outer Space including the Moon and Other Celestial Bodies has been ratified by scores of countries but not by the two with space technology capabilities—the US and USSR. Other treaties explicitly restrict participation. The Agreement on the Conservation of Polar Bears can only be signed by five circumpolar countries (Canada, Denmark (including Greenland), Norway, the US, and the USSR). To become a signatory to the Antarctic Treaty of 1959 a country must maintain a scientific research station in the Antarctic and be unanimously accepted by existing parties to the agreement. In these cases non-signatories may quite clearly be affected by how the signatories manage the resource. Signatories to the Antarctic treaty voted recently to allow mineral exploration, despite appeals by non-signatories to designate Antarctica a nature reserve.

In the above model, N was assumed to represent both the number of countries that emit a (uniformly mixed) pollutant into the environment and the number harmed as a consequence. However, for some problems the number of emitters may be less than the number of sufferers (for global pollutants, all countries). When the number of emitters is small, an international environmental agreement signed by a subset of emitters may well have a significant effect on the welfare of these countries. However, the effect on global welfare may still be small because the emitters have no incentive to take into account the welfare losses suffered by non-emitting nations. The appropriate way to account for countries that do not emit the pollutant but nevertheless suffer the consequences of others' emissions is to admit side payments—payments which induce emitting nations to undertake greater abatement but which leave all parties no worse off compared to the situation where side payments are forbidden. We return to the side payments issue later.

The gains to international co-operation can also be shown to depend on c, the slope of each country's marginal abatement cost curve; and b, the (absolute value of the) slope of each country's marginal abatement benefit curve. For a given size of N, the number of signatories to a treaty increases as c/b falls. This suggests

---

[10] See Lyster (1985) for a discussion of other compliance mechanisms.

Table 9.1. Estimates of the reduction in percentage ozone depletion effected by the Montreal Protocol

Case	2000	2025	2050	2075
No controls	1.0	4.6	15.7	50.0
Montreal Protocol	0.8	1.5	1.9	1.9

Source: US EPA (1988), Table 3, p. 30575.

that we should expect to observe a large number of signatories (in absolute terms) when N is 'large', the marginal abatement cost curve is flat, and the marginal abatement benefit curve steep. However, we already know that when c/b is 'small' the benefit of having an agreement is diminished. It is commonly asserted that treaties signed by a large number of countries accomplish little of substance: 'The greater the number of participants in the formulation of a treaty, the weaker or more ambiguous its provisions are likely to be since they have to reflect compromises making them acceptable to every State involved' (Lyster, 1985, p. 4). This analysis suggests that the reason treaties signed by a large number of countries appear to effect little additional abatement is not that the signatories are heterogeneous—although that may be a contributing factor. Nor is the reason solely that in these cases N is also large. A major insight of the model is that a large subset of N will sign an agreement only when the non-co-operative and full co-operative outcomes are already close.

This latter observation may not seem consistent with all the evidence. The Montreal Protocol, for example, demands of its signatories significant reductions in the production and consumption of the hard CFCs and halons, and about 150 countries have already signed the agreement—a fairly large number by any standard. As Table 9.1 shows, the effect of the agreement on ozone depletion is estimated to be very significant. Percentage ozone depletion is estimated to be reduced from 50 to 2 per cent in 2075 as a result of the agreement. But of course each country has some incentive to take unilateral action in reducing emissions; in doing so all other countries will benefit, but so too will the country taking the action. Furthermore, non-signatories to the agreement may well face an incentive to abate less than they would otherwise for the simple reason that greater abatement on the part of signatories improves the environment for non-signatories as well. Hence it is by no means clear that the agreement necessarily means that the environment and global welfare will be significantly better off, contrary to what the figures in Table 9.1 imply. What the model does suggest is that so many countries would

not have committed themselves to the agreement in the first place unless they already intended to take substantial unilateral action. In other words, although the agreement itself may effect only little additional abatement, the very fact that so many countries have signed the agreement suggests that the potential gains to co-operation were in this instance not very great.

What does the model predict about the prospects of an agreement being reached on global warming? N will again be large, and this will militate against significant united action. However, in this case c will be large, too; the marginal costs of abating carbon dioxide emissions will rise very steeply as fossil fuels must be substituted for and energy is conserved. This suggests that the number of signatories to an agreement would be small, and that little additional abatement could be effected by co-operation. Whether or not this should be of concern depends on whether b is large or small. If b is small, as Nordhaus (1994) suggests, then the potential gains to co-operation will be small, too. If, however, b, is large, as Cline (1992) believes, then the potential gains to co-operation would be large. Failure to co-operate would, indeed, be a tragedy in this case.

2. Leadership

It is sometimes asserted that countries should, on their own, do more than the non-co-operative solution demands of them. US environmental groups, for example, have argued that the US should have taken greater unilateral action before the Montreal Protocol was drafted, that it should now comply with the terms of the Protocol in advance of the deadlines, and that it should exceed the agreed emission reductions and phase out production and consumption of these chemicals entirely. The House of Commons Energy Committee (1989, p. xvii), in its investigation on the greenhouse effect, recommended '. . . that the UK should . . . consider setting an example to the world by seriously tackling its own emission problems in advance of international action, especially where it is economically prudent to do so'.

We have already seen that such 'unselfish' unilateral actions need not be matched by other countries. The United States, Canada, Sweden, and Norway banned the use of CFCs in non-essential aerosols in the late 1970s, and yet other countries did not reciprocate.[11] Unilateral restrictions on pelagic sealing in the North

---

[11] Reciprocity was certainly not full. The European Community, for example, passed two decisions limiting production capacity of the so-called hard CFCs (CFC-11 and -12) and reducing their use in aerosols by 30 per cent.

Pacific by the US were not duplicated by Canada. We have also seen that countries may wish to give in to their moral beliefs and embrace a less insular view of their responsibilities. An important question is whether 'unselfish' unilateral action can be expected to have a positive influence on international negotiations. If one country (or group of countries) abates more than the Nash non-co-operative solution demands, and all others choose the abatement levels that are optimal for them in a non-co-operative setting, will the environment be any better protected when international treaties are later negotiated?

In a two-country analysis, Hoel (1991) shows that the answer depends on whether the unilateral action is taken before agreement is reached and is not contingent on that agreement or whether the action is a commitment to abate more than the negotiated agreement requires. Hoel shows that in the former case, 'unselfish' unilateral action may compromise negotiations and lead, ultimately, to *greater* emissions than would have occurred had both countries behaved 'selfishly'. In the latter case, however, the country's announced commitment to overfulfil its negotiated abatement level can be expected to reduce total emissions.

There is an obvious incentive compatability problem with this tactic, for the 'unselfish' country could do better by reneging on its commitment (the agreement is therefore *not* self-enforcing). Nevertheless, the analysis shows that the desire by environmentalists and others to reduce total emissions may not be well served by their calls for 'unselfish' unilateral action, a point that the EPA stressed in defending its ozone depletion policy (1988, p. 30574): 'Unilateral action by the United States would not significantly add to efforts to protect the ozone layer and could even be counter productive by undermining other nations' incentive to participate in the Protocol.'

It is important to note that the US and the European Community announced their intentions to phase out production and consumption of the ozone-depleting chemicals by the end of the century *after* the Montreal Protocol came into force but before renegotiation talks had started. It would be wrong, however, to ascribe these developments simply to 'unselfish' behaviour. After all, the world's largest manufacturer of CFCs, US-based Du Pont, announced its intention to phase out production of CFCs by the end of the century *before* the phase-out decisions were taken by the US and EC. Three days after the EC decided to phase out CFCs, the chairman of the leading European producer of CFCs, ICI, declared that production of CFCs should cease 'as soon after 1998 as is practicable'. Much more is at work here.

3. Efficient co-operation

Signatories to an international environmental agreement are assumed to maximize the net benefits accruing to the *group*. This means, among other things, that the marginal abatement costs of every signatory must be equal; the abatement undertaken by the group must be achieved at minimum total cost.

How realistic is this assumption? In the case of the Montreal Protocol, the assumption is not very wide of the mark. The Protocol imposes on every industrial country signatory an obligation to reduce its production and consumption of CFCs by an equal percentage. This requirement on its own is inefficient because at the margin the costs of complying with the Protocol will surely vary. For example, the UK can apparently meet its obligations by simply prohibiting the use of CFCs in aerosols—an action that is nearly costless. The US banned the use of CFCs in aerosols many years ago, and hence can meet the terms of the Protocol only by instituting more costly measures. However, the Protocol allows limited international *trading* in emission reductions. For any signatory, CFC production through mid-1998 can be 10 per cent, and from mid-1998 onwards 15 per cent, higher than it would have been without trading provided the increase in production by this signatory is offset by a decrease in production by another signatory. Furthermore, trades of consumption (but, strangely, not production) quotas are permitted by the Protocol within the European Community. These provisions will help increase the efficiency of attaining the total emission reduction implicit in the agreement, although they almost certainly do not go far enough.

4. Side payments

The equilibrium in the model of international environmental agreements is determined by a concept of stability that prohibits side payments. An important question is whether side payments might effect a Pareto improvement. To investigate this issue, reconsider the concept of stability employed in the model. In equilibrium, non-signatories do better than signatories, but no country can do better by changing its status. Signatories want non-co-operators to sign the agreement, because their net benefits would then increase. But non-signatories do worse by signing. Hence, without compensating payments, non-signatories will not want to sign the agreement. It is in this sense that the agreement is stable.

However, the very fact that signatories do better if

non-co-operators sign the agreement suggests that trade might be possible. In particular, it might be possible for signatories to make side payments to a subset of non-co-operators to encourage them to sign the agreement. All might be made better off. It is in fact very easy to show that this can happen, that an international environmental agreement that specifies abatement levels *and* side payments can manage the global common property resource better than one that prohibits side payments.

An important feature of the World Heritage Convention is that it does admit side payments. The Convention established a World Heritage Fund that is used to help protect natural environments of 'outstanding universal value'. Each party to the Convention (there are over 90 signatories) is required to provide the Fund every two years with at least one per cent of its contribution to the regular budget of UNESCO.[12] In practice this means that the Fund is almost entirely financed by the industrial countries. Clearly, both the industrial and poor countries benefit from the Convention—otherwise they would not have signed it—but the poor countries may not have signed the Convention were it not for the Fund. Though the Fund is small, the mechanism could prove instrumental in protecting many of the world's remaining natural environments, including the tropical rain forests.

The World Heritage Convention is not unique among international environmental agreements for incorporating side payments. The success of the Montreal Protocol, for example, ultimately hinged on the accession of poor countries, such as China and India. This was effected by amendments to the Protocol negotiated in London in 1990. These amendments created a fund, the purpose of which was to compensate poor countries for the 'incremental costs' of complying with the agreement. It was this 'carrot', coupled with the 'stick' of threatened trade sanctions, which has sustained nearly full participation in this agreement. The question this example raises is whether this apparent success can be replicated for other global environmental problems. The analysis presented here does not provide a ready answer to this important question. It does, however, provide a basis for formulating an answer.

References

Axelrod, R. (1984), *The Evolution of Cooperation*, New York, Basic Books.

Barrett, S. (1994), 'Self-enforcing International Environmental Agreements', *Oxford Economic Papers*, **46**, 878–94.

Cline, W. R. (1992), *The Economics of Global Warming*, Washington, DC, Institute for International Economics.

Coase, R. H. (1960), 'The Problem of Social Cost', *Journal of Law and Economics*, **3**, 1–44.

Cornes, R., and Sandler, T. (1983), 'On Commons and Tragedies', *American Economic Review*, **73**, 787–92.

Dasgupta, P. (1982), *The Control of Resources*, Cambridge, MA, Harvard University.

Demsetz, H. (1964), 'The Exchange and Enforcement of Property Rights', *Journal of Law and Economics*, **7**, 11–26.

—— (1967), 'Toward a Theory of Property Rights', *American Economic Review*, **57**, 347–59.

Friedman, J. W. (1986), *Game Theory with Applications to Economics*, Oxford, Oxford University Press.

Groves, T., and Ledyard, J. (1977), 'Optimal Allocation of Public Goods: A Solution to the "Free Rider" Problem', *Econometrica*, **45**, 783–809.

Guttman, J. M. (1978), 'Understanding Collective Action: Matching Behavior', *American Economic Review Papers and Proceedings*, **68**, 251–5.

Hardin, G. (1968), 'The Tragedy of the Commons', *Science*, **162**, 1243–8.

Hoel, M. (1991), 'Global Environmental Problems: The Effects of Unilateral Actions Taken by One Country', *Journal of Environmental Economics and Management*, **20**, 55–70.

House of Commons Energy Committee (1989), *Energy Policy Implications of the Greenhouse Effect*, vol. 1, London, HMSO.

House of Commons Environment Committee (1984), *Acid Rain*, vol. 1, London, HMSO.

Lyster, S. (1985), *International Wildlife Law*, Cambridge, Grotius.

Marwell, G. E., and Ames, R. E. (1981), 'Economists Free Ride, Does Anyone Else?', *Journal of Public Economics*, **15**, 295–310.

Nordhaus, W. D. (1994), *Managing the Global Commons*, Cambridge, MA, MIT Press.

Paterson, D. G., and Wilen, J. (1977), 'Depletion and Diplomacy: The North Pacific Seal Hunt, 1886–1910', *Research in Economic History*, **2**, 81–139.

Samuelson, P. (1954), 'The Pure Theory of Public Expenditure', *Review of Economics and Statistics*, 36, 387–9.

Sugden, R. (1984), 'Reciprocity: The Supply of Public Goods through Voluntary Contributions', *Economic Journal*, **94**, 772–87.

—— (1986), *The Economics of Rights, Co-operation and Welfare*, Oxford, Basil Blackwell.

Trail Smelter Arbitral Tribunal (1939), 'Decision', *American Journal of International Law*, **33**, 182–212.

—— (1941), 'Decision', *American Journal of International Law*, **35**, 684–736.

US Environmental Protection Agency (1988), 'Protection of Stratospheric Ozone; Final Rule', *Federal Register*, **53**, 30566–602.

---

[12] The United States and the UK continued to contribute to the Fund even after withdrawing their funding from UNESCO.

10

Pricing and congestion: economic principles relevant to pricing roads

DAVID M. NEWBERY

Department of Applied Economics, University of Cambridge

I. Introduction

The road network is a costly and increasingly scarce resource. For the UK the Department of Transport (1994a) calculates that total road expenditures (capital and current) or 'road costs' averaged £7.07 billion per year at 1995/6 prices for the period 1992/3–1994/5. Public expenditure on roads increased sharply from 1988/9 to 1992/3 but has since fallen, and over the decade from 1984/5 has risen by just 15 per cent, less than the increase in private car ownership (of 28 per cent), or vehicle km travelled (39 per cent). Capital expenditure on roads doubled between 1988/9 and 1992/3 and increased by 56 per cent over the whole decade. (Department of Transport, 1995, Tables 1.17, 1.20, 1.22, 3.2, 4.7.) From the 26.1 million vehicles registered, road taxes of £19.0 billion were collected, or 2.9 times the Department's figures for 'road costs'. In 1993 15.6 per cent of consumers' expenditure was on transport and vehicles, and 13 per cent was on motor vehicles alone. Clearly, road transport is of major economic significance. Car ownership per 1,000 population in the UK appears to be catching up on the rates in the larger European countries and is now about 83 per cent of French and Italian levels, 73 per cent of West German levels. Over the decade 1984–94 the number of private cars increased from 16.1 to 20.5 million, or by 28 per cent. From 1978 to 1988, the total vehicle-km driven rose from 303 to 422 billion or by 39 per cent. As the length of the road network increased by only 5 per cent, the average daily traffic on each km of road rose by 34 per cent over the same decade on all roads and by 62 per cent on motorways. Traffic on major roads in built-

up areas (i.e. those with a speed limit of 40 mph or less) increased by 25 per cent. (Department of Transport, 1995, Tables 3.17, 4.10.)

As road space is a valuable and scarce resource, it is natural that economists should argue that it should be rationed by price—road-users should pay the marginal social cost of using the road network if they are to be induced to make the right decisions about whether (and by which means) to take a particular journey, and, more generally, to ensure that they make the correct allocative decisions between transport and other activities. If road-users paid the true social cost of transport, perhaps urban geography, commuting patterns, and even the sizes of towns would be radically different from the present. The modest aim here is to identify these social costs, provide rough estimates of their magnitude for Britain, and hence identify the major policy issues.

One way to focus the discussion is to ask how to design a system of charges for road use. The problem of designing road charges can be broken down into various sub-problems. First, what is the marginal social cost (that is, the extra cost to society) of allowing a particular vehicle to make a particular trip? Part will be the direct cost of using the vehicle (fuel, wear and tear, driver's time, and so forth) and will be paid for by the owner. This is the private cost of road use. Other costs are social: some will be borne by other road-users (delays, for example); some by the highway authority (extra road maintenance); and some by the society at large (pollution and risk of accidents). These are called the *road-use costs*—the social costs (excluding the private costs) arising from vehicles using roads. It seems logical to attempt to charge vehicles for these road-use costs, in order to discourage them from making journeys where the benefits are less than the total social costs

First published in *Oxford Review of Economic Policy*, vol. 6, no. 2 (1990). This version has been updated and revised to incorporate recent developments.

(private costs plus road-use costs). The first task, therefore, is to measure these road-use costs.

The second question is whether road-users should pay additional taxes above these road-use costs. One argument is that road-users should pay the whole cost of the highway system, not just the extra cost of road use, either to be 'fair' in an absolute sense or to achieve parity or equity with, say, rail-users (in those rare countries where the railway is required to cover its total costs without subsidy). Another argument is that the government needs to raise revenues and some part of this revenue should be collected from road-users, since to exempt them would be to give them an unreasonable advantage over the rest of the population. Both arguments appeal either to the desire for equity or fairness, or to the need for efficiency in the allocation of resources (road versus rail), or both.

1. Relevant principles of taxation

The modern theory of public finance provides a powerful organizing principle for taxing and pricing. Under certain assumptions policies should be designed to achieve production efficiency, with all distortionary taxes falling on final consumers. Broadly, the conditions for this result, set out formally in Diamond and Mirrlees (1971), are (a) that production efficiency is feasible, and (b) that any resulting private profits are either negligible or can be taxed away. The feasibility condition would be satisfied if the economy were competitive and externalities could be corrected or internalized.

The theory has immediate implications for road charges and taxes. Road-users can be divided into two groups: those who transport freight, which is an intermediate service used in production, and those who drive their own cars or transport passengers, who enjoy final consumption. Freight transport, which is roughly and conveniently synonymous with diesel-using vehicles, should pay the road-use costs to correct externalities and to pay for the marginal costs of maintenance. Additional taxes (comprising the *pure tax element*) on (largely gasoline-using) passenger transport can be set, using the same principles that guide the design of other indirect taxes. We shall show below that one would expect a close relationship between road-use costs and total road expenditures. There is no logical reason to attribute the taxation of passenger transport to the highway budget, since it is a component of general tax revenue. But if all road taxes and charges are taken together, there are good reasons to expect that they will exceed total highway expenditure. In short, in a well-run country no conflict need arise between the goals of designing an equitable and efficient system of road-use charges and taxes and the desire to cover the highway system's costs.

The theory provides a useful framework for the study of road-user charges. The first step is to identify the road-use costs. The second is to see what methods are available for levying charges and how finely they can be adjusted to match these costs. The third step is to examine how far these methods have repercussions outside the transport sector and, where these occur, how to take them into account. These three steps will suffice for freight transport. For passenger transport, one other step is needed: to determine the appropriate level of (and method of levying) the pure tax element.

II. Quantifying the social costs of road use

Vehicles impose four main costs on the rest of society—accident externalities, environmental pollution, road damage, and congestion. Accident externalities arise whenever extra vehicles on the road increase the probability that other road-users will be involved in an accident. To the extent that accidents depend on distance driven and other traffic these accident costs can be treated rather like congestion costs. Newbery (1988a) argued that accident externalities could be as large as all other externality costs taken together, and are thus possibly of first order importance. There are two reasons for this high estimate, both disputed. The first is that the figure critically depends on the value of a life saved or the cost of a life lost. If one bases this on apparent willingness to pay to reduce risks, then the cost per life saved might be between £650,000 and £2 million at 1989 prices, based on the survey results of Jones-Lee (1990). The lower figure is over double that originally used by the Department of Transport, who based their earlier estimates on the expected loss of future earnings of a representative victim. Apparently the Department of Transport has been persuaded of the logic behind the willingness-to-pay approach, and now uses a figure of £500,000 (Jones-Lee, 1990).

The second reason is that in the absence of convincing evidence, the estimate assumed that the number of accidents increased with the traffic flow as the 1.25 power of that flow. (That is, if the traffic is twice as heavy, the risk of an accident happening to each car is increased by 19 per cent. Compare this with the number of pairwise encounters between vehicles, which rises as the square of the flow.) This in turn means that a quarter of the cost of mutually caused accidents is an uncharged externality, even if each driver pays the full cost of the accident to him. (To the extent that society pays through the NHS, these individual costs are borne by society and attributable as part of 'road costs'. The Department of Transport includes direct costs. It might argue that their earlier valuation of life was based on the loss of earnings which might have to be made good through the social security system to survivors.) Note that it is important to relate the accident rate to traffic levels in order to identify the size of the externality. Indeed, one might argue from the fact that the accident rate has fallen as traffic has increased that this 1.25 power law is invalid, and that at best there is no relationship between traffic and the accident rate. If so, then there would be no externality between motor vehicles (other than that already counted in the cost falling on the NHS). This would be the case if one took seriously the explanation of 'risk compensation', according to which road-users choose a desired level of perceived risk with which they are comfortable—too little risk is boring, too much is frightening. Improvements in road safety then induce compensating increases in risk taking, while deteriorating road conditions (ice, snow, heavier traffic) induce more caution. Of course, one should be wary of using time series information about accident rates as road improvements are continuously undertaken to improve road safety. The relationship between accident rate and traffic should be derived from a properly estimated cross-section analysis.

Jones-Lee (1990) does indeed assume that the accident *rate* (i.e. the risk of an accident per km driven) is independent of the traffic flow, from which it follows that there is no externality between motor vehicles (except those caused by the system of social and health insurance). He also assumes that the probability of any vehicle having an accident involving a pedestrian or cyclist is constant per km driven, in which case it follows that the accident rate experienced by cyclists and pedestrians is proportional to the number of vehicle km driven. If this is the case, then motor vehicles do impose an externality on non-motorized road-users (though not on other motorists), which Jones-Lee calculates to be quite large—perhaps 10–20 per cent of total road costs. Of course, we remain relatively uncertain about the relationship between accidents to other road-users and traffic. It has been remarked that not so long ago children were allowed to play in the street, and cycle or walk unaccompanied to school. The number of accidents to such children was quite high. Now it is so obviously insane to allow such activities that the number of accidents may have fallen with the increase in traffic. Of course, that accident externality is still there, though hidden in the form of the extra costs of ferrying children to school, and not allowing them to play or cycle unsupervised.

The main problem therefore lies in identifying the relationship between traffic and accidents—in the words of the US Federal Highway Cost Allocation Study 'Quantitative estimation of accident cost and vehicle volume relationships, however, has not yet proved satisfactory . . .' (US Federal Highway Authority, 1982). Given the huge costs involved and the potential gains from lowering accident rates, identifying such relationships should have overwhelming research priority.

Similarly, pollution costs share many of the same features as congestion costs (and tend to occur in the same places). Where they have been quantified (for the US) they appear to contribute less than 10 per cent of total road costs. They are normally dealt with by mandating emission standards, and by differential taxes on the more polluting fuels (for example, by having higher taxes on leaded petrol). A new European Directive on vehicle emissions, known as the Luxembourg Agreement, will be implemented in the UK. This mandates NO_x levels of half the current limit, and reductions in hydrocarbon releases of three-quarters, at an estimated cost to the motorist of £800 million or about 4 per cent of motoring costs (Department of the Environment, 1989). Provided the pollution costs are reflected in fuel taxes, and the requirement to meet emissions standards, these costs will have been satisfactorily internalized. One should, however, be rather cautious about mandating stringent emissions standards without a careful cost–benefit analysis. Crandall *et al.* (1986, pp. 114–15) estimate that the programme costs for the US of the more stringent 1984 emissions standards might be about $20 billion per year with a replacement rate of 10.5 million cars, which is several times greater than rather optimistic estimates of the potential benefits of reducing pollution. (Safety regulations in contrast, though expensive, seem to have been justified on cost–benefit criteria.) Some of these issues are discussed further in Newbery (1990).

1. Road damage costs

These are the costs borne by the highway authority of repairing roads damaged by the passage of vehicles, and the extra vehicle operating costs caused by this road damage. The damage a vehicle does to the road pavement increases as the fourth power of the axle load, which means that almost all damage is done by heavy vehicles such as trucks. Increasing the number of axles

Table 10.1. Road costs in 1993/4 prices (£ million)

Cost category	Annual average	
	5% TDR	8% TDR
Interest on capital	4500	7200
(Capital expenditure)	(3060)	
Maintenance *less* costs attrib		
to pedestrians	3252	3252
Policing and traffic wardens	408	408
Total road costs	8160	10860
of which attributable to		
road damage costs	446	446
Gross vehicle mass	683	683
VKT	479	479
Balance attributable to PCU	6552	9252
PCU km (billion)	456 billion km	
Cost per PCUkm pence/km	(1.33p/km)	(1.92p/km)
Cost per PCUkm incl.		
VKT costs pence/km	(1.44p/km)	(2.03p/km)

Source: Department of Transport (1994 *a*, *b*).
Notes: Figures are annual averages for the years 1991/2 to 1993/4 at 1993/4 prices TDR: Test Discount Rate; VKT: vehicle km travelled. Costs attributable to Gross Vehicle Mass taken from Department of Transport (1994 *a*), entirely allocated. VKT costs from same source adjusted in the same proportion as in Newbery (1988, Table 2).

is a potent method of reducing the damaging effect of a vehicle—doubling the number of equally loaded axles reduces the damage to an eighth of its previous level. Consequently most highway authorities closely regulate the axle configuration and maximum legal axle loads. Increasing the road thickness dramatically increases the number of vehicles that can be carried before major repairs are required—doubling the thickness increases this number by 2 to the power 6.5 or so (Paterson, 1987). Consequently the most damaging and therefore costly combination is a heavy vehicle on a thin road.

The theory which allows these costs to be quantified is set out in Newbery (1988*a*, *b*). The road-damage costs of a vehicle will be proportional to its damaging power (and will be measured in terms of Equivalent Standard Axles, or ESAs). Britain, in common with most advanced countries, follows a condition-responsive maintenance strategy in which the road is repaired when its condition reaches a predetermined state. In such cases, the road-damage costs will be equal to the average annual costs of maintaining the road network in a stable state, multiplied by the fraction of the road deterioration caused by vehicles, as opposed to weather, allocated in proportion to ESA-miles driven. The fraction of total costs allocated to vehicles will depend on the climate, the strength of the road, and the interval between major repairs, and the formula is given

in Newbery (1988*a*,*b*). In hot, dry climates it will be between 60 and 80 per cent, while in freezing temperate climates the proportion will be between 20 and 60 per cent, the lower figures corresponding to more stringent maintenance criteria or lower traffic volumes. For Britain, Newbery (1988*a*) argued that the appropriate fraction was 40 per cent. If maintenance is condition-responsive then it is not necessary to charge vehicles for the damage they do indirectly to subsequent vehicles which experience increased operating costs on the damaged pavement—on average the condition of the pavement will remain unchanged.

It is simple to update the road-damage costs given in Newbery (1988*a*) using the latest estimates of road-track costs provided in Department of Transport (1994*a*, Table 2.5). The total cost identified is £1,114 million, or 12.07 pence/ESAkm. The allocable fraction is 0.4, giving £446 million or 4.83 pence/ESAkm. As such, road-damage costs are a small fraction of total road costs. To provide a quick estimate of how large a fraction, Table 10.1 above updates the results from 1986 to 1993 from Newbery (1988*a*, Table 2). There the value of the road network was estimated at £50 billion excluding land. Updating to 1993 (Newbery, 1995) and adding the cost of land brings it to £90 billion. In Newbery (1988*a*) the rate of interest on this capital value was taken to be the then Test Discount Rate of 5 per cent real, and if this figure is again used, then interest on the value of the road network would be £4,500 million, compared to the actual capital expenditure of £3,060 million. Recently, the Test Discount Rate has been revised upward to 8 per cent real (presumably reflecting the perceived higher real rate of return in the rest of the economy), and at this rate the interest costs would rise to £7,200 million.

There is little logic in combining current and capital expenditures as the Department of Transport does in estimating 'road costs', and Table 10.1 only includes imputed interest at the two different rates of 5 per cent and 8 per cent. It will be seen that allocable road-damage costs amount to 4–5.3 per cent of total road costs, and are thus essentially negligible (which is not to deny that it is important to charge them appropriately to heavy goods vehicles).

This estimate is quite close to that for 1986 of 3.5 per cent given in Newbery (1988*a*). Even if repair costs currently allocated by the UK Department of Transport in proportion to gross vehicle weight are included (and the theoretical justification for so doing is rather unclear) the figure only rises to 10–14 per cent (depending on the choice of the TDR). Small *et al.* (1988) estimate that pavement costs, including construction and periodic resurfacing, are less than 16 per cent of road costs in their simulations of an optimized US road system, and road-damage charges would only account for 2 per cent of total charges. Far and away the largest element (again ignoring accident costs, which might also be very large) are the congestion costs.

2. Congestion costs

These arise because additional vehicles reduce the speed of other vehicles, and hence increase their journey time. The standard way of calculating the short-run marginal congestion cost (MCC) of an extra vehicle in the traffic stream starts by postulating a relationship between speed (v kph) and flow (q vehicles or PCU/h) where PCU are passenger car units, a measure of the congestive effect of different vehicles in different circumstances (e.g. higher for heavy lorries on steep hills than on the level). If the travel cost per km of a representative vehicle is

$$c = a + b/v, \qquad (1)$$

where b is the cost per vehicle hour, including the opportunity cost of the driver and occupants, then the total cost of a flow of q vehicles per hour is $C = cq$. If an additional vehicle is added to the flow, the total social cost is increased by

$$dC/dq = c + q.dc/dq. \qquad (2)$$

The first term is the private cost borne by the vehicle and the second is the marginal externality cost borne by other road-users.

The next step is to establish the speed–flow relationship, $v = v(q)$ and here one must be careful to pose the right question. Engineers designing particular sections of the road network are concerned with flow at each point, and most of the relationships estimated are of this form. They show that traffic flow is heavily influenced by junctions, where additional traffic enters or disrupts the smooth flow, and it is possible for the speed–flow relationship to be backward bending, as in Figure 10.1.

The curve is to be interpreted as follows. As traffic increases above q the speed is given by points such as A, B. As traffic nears the capacity of the link, k, at the point C, the flow changes to a condition of stop-start, and traffic flow through the bottleneck drops, to a point such as D, associated with a lower speed. This is an unstable situation, and as flow falls, so the traffic leaving the bottleneck will accelerate, and eventually clear the blockage. At that time, the speed will jump back up to point A. (Further details are given in Newbery, 1987, and Hall et al., 1986.)

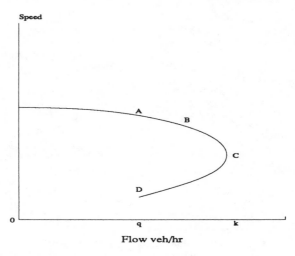

Figure 10.1. Speed flow relationship for a link

Useful though this relation is for road design, it is not what is wanted for estimating the cost of congestion, where we need a measure of the total extra time taken by the remaining traffic to complete their planned journeys, not their speed at a particular point on the road network. The Department of Transport, when planning roads to alleviate congestion, uses formulas estimated by the Transport and Road Research Laboratory, and reported in Department of Transport (1987). These are based on 'floating car' methods, in which the observing vehicle remains in the traffic stream for a period of time, and hence give a better estimate of the average relationship between speed and flow. They find a reasonably stable linear relationship of the form

$$v = \alpha - \beta q, \qquad (3)$$

where q is measured in PCU/lane/hr. The estimated value of β for urban traffic is 0.035. This agrees closely with a careful study of traffic flows within zones of Hong Kong, reported in Harrison et al. (1986), itself commissioned as part of Hong Kong's road-pricing experiment.

This linear relationship can be used to quantify the average and marginal costs of traffic and hence to determine the MCC. Figure 10.2 below gives this relationship for suburban roads at 1990 prices, based on the estimated COBA 9 formula. The left-hand scale gives the speed associated with the traffic flow, and on such roads average speeds rarely fall below 25 kph, so the relevant part of the diagram is to the left of that speed level. Another, quite useful way of representing this limitation is to suppose that the demand for using

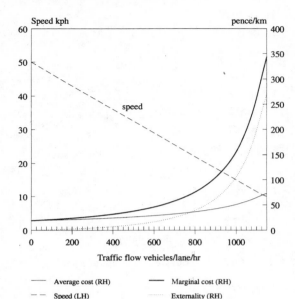

Speed kph / pence/km

— Average cost (RH) — Marginal cost (RH)
-- Speed (LH) ···· Externality (RH)

Urban non-central roads, 1990 prices

Figure 10.2. Average and marginal cost of trips

suburban roads becomes highly elastic at this level, an idea pursued further below.

In some ways a better measure of the congestion relationship is given by the marginal time cost (MTC) in vehicle-hours per vehicle-km, which can then be multiplied by the current value of the time use of the vehicle, b in (1). From (3), the MTC is just $\beta q/v^2$. Given data for q and v, the MTC can be estimated.

Newbery (1988a, Table 1) estimated these costs for Britain for the year 1985. Rather than repeat the rather time-consuming calculations reported there, the following short-cut has been adopted. If m is the MCC as a function of q, and if Δq is the increase in traffic over some period, then the revised estimate of the MCC is $m + dm/dq.\Delta q$. The factor by which to scale up the original estimates of MCC can be found from the above equations and is

$$\{1 + (2\beta q/v)\}(\Delta q/q). \qquad (4)$$

The results of this updating procedure are given in Table 10.2. If anything, the estimate will be on the low side, as the relationship is very non-linear. If some roads have an above-average increase in traffic while others have a below-average increase, then taking the average increase q/q will underestimate the average of the costs on each road.

Table 10.2 shows in a vivid way the great variation in marginal congestion costs by time of day and location. Urban central areas at the peak have an *average* congestion cost of 10 times the average over all roads, and more than 100 times that the average motorway or rural road.

The table shows that the average congestion cost is 4.2 pence/PCUkm, and, given the 456 billion PCUkm driven from Table 10.1, if road-users were to be charged for congestion, the revenue collected would have been £19,000 million. If we add to this sum the road-damage costs (£446 m), the amounts allocated according to gross vehicle mass (£683 m), and VKT (£479 m), all taken from Table 10.1, then the appropriate level of road charges should yield £20,700 million. Total road taxes were £19,000 million, or 92 per cent of the

Table 10.2. Marginal time costs of congestion in Great Britain, 1993

	MTC (veh h/ 100 PCUkm)	VKT per cent	MCC p/PCUkm	Congest cost share %	Index of MCC
Motorway	0.05	17	0.32	1	8
Urban central peak	5.41	1	44.74	13	1071
Urban central off-peak	4.35	3	35.95	27	861
Non-central peak	2.36	4	19.51	17	467
Non-central off-peak	1.30	10	10.75	26	257
Small town peak	1.03	3	8.47	6	203
Small town off-peak	0.63	7	5.17	9	124
Other urban	0.01	14	0.08	0	2
Rural dual carriageway	0.01	12	0.06	0	1
Other trunk and principal	0.04	18	0.23	1	6
Other rural	0.01	12	0.06	0	1
Weighted average			4.18		100

Source: Updated from Newbery (1990, Table 2)

required level. Congestion charges would amount to 92 per cent of the total appropriate road charge.

It is interesting to compare these estimates with those given in Newbery (1988a). The estimated congestion charges for Britain for 1986 were £6,203 million out of the total appropriate charge (excluding accident costs) of £7,033 million, or 88 per cent. The figures are high as the amount of time wasted is so high, though the costs are frequently ignored by highway authorities, as they are entirely borne by highway-users. The Confederation of British Industries has calculated that traffic congestion costs the nation £15 billion a year in 1989 prices, or £10 a week on each household's shopping bill (*The Times*, 19 May 1989). Uprating the CBI figure by the increase in family expenditure gives a 1993 value of nearly £19 billion, comparable to the £19 billion for the appropriate congestion charge calculated above, though the question of how best to measure the true social cost of congestion is discussed more fully below.

Small *et al.* (1988) cite evidence that suggests congestion costs are also high in the US. Thus average peak-hour delays in crossing the Hudson River to Manhattan have roughly doubled in the past ten years, while congestion delays in the San Francisco Bay Area grew by more than 50 per cent in just two years. In 1987, 63 per cent of vehicle-miles were driven on Interstate Highways at volume to capacity ratios exceeding 0.8, and 42 per cent on other arterials. Although their study does not quantify the congestion costs they suggest figures of some tens of billions of dollars annually— a figure which squares with the evidence in the next paragraph.

The correct charge to levy on vehicles is equal to the congestion costs they cause (in addition to other social costs like damage costs). If roads experience constant returns to scale, in that doubling the capital expenditure on the road creates a road able to carry twice the number of vehicles at the same speed, and if roads are optimally designed and adjusted to the traffic, then it can be shown that the optimal congestion charge would recover all of the non-damage road costs. (Newbery, 1989). These include interest on the original capital stock, as well as the weather-induced road-damage costs not directly attributable to vehicles, and other maintenance expenditures, collectively identified as 'road costs attributable to PCU' in Table 10.1. The available evidence supports constant returns to scale or possibly rather mildly increasing returns, of the order of 1.03–1.19. (This always surprises highway engineers, who *know* that it does not cost twice as much to double the capacity of a highway, as many costs— embankments, etc.—are fixed, and the capacity of a two-lane divided highway is considerably greater than of a one-lane divided highway. But most capacity increases are needed in congested urban areas where the costs of land acquisition can be extremely high. The econometric estimates pick this factor up. See Keeler and Small, 1977, and Kraus, 1981.) If we take the estimates as supporting constant returns, then the result is directly applicable, and provides a useful benchmark against which to judge the estimated congestion charges. If we assume increasing returns to scale, then road charges would not cover road costs of an optimal road network.

In 1986 the estimated average congestion charge was 1.42 times as high as the road costs attributable to PCU, suggesting either that the road network was inadequate for the level of traffic, or that the correct rate of interest to charge was higher than 5 per cent real. (At 8 per cent the ratio was only 1.0.) The corresponding ratio for 1993 is 2.90 (or 2.06 at 8 per cent interest). In short, if roads were undersupplied in 1986, they are becoming critically scarce as traffic volumes increase faster than road space is supplied. Notice that assuming that there are increasing returns to capacity, expansion strengthens the conclusion that roads are undersupplied.

III. Charging for road use

Ideally, vehicles should be charged for the road-use cost of each trip, so that only cost-justified trips are undertaken. In practice it is not too difficult to charge for road damage, which is largely a function of the type of vehicle and the extent to which it is loaded. Ton-mile taxes as charged by some of the states of the US can approximate the damage charge quite closely, provided they are made specific to the type of vehicle. Vehicle-specific distance taxes would be almost as good, provided axle loading restrictions were enforced. Fuel taxes are moderately good in that they charge trucks in proportion to ton-miles. As they charge different types of vehicles at (almost) the same ton-mile rate, they must be supplemented by vehicle-specific purchase taxes or licence fees and combined with careful regulation of allowable axle configurations and loadings (Newbery *et al.*, 1988; Newbery 1988c).

The more difficult task is to charge for congestion, which varies enormously depending on the level of traffic, which in turn varies across roads and with the time of day, as Table 10.2 shows dramatically. The most direct way is to charge an amount specific to the road and time of day, using an 'electronic number plate' which signals to the recording computer the presence of the vehicle. The computer then acts like a telephone exchange billing system, recording the user, the time and place, and hence the appropriate charge, and issuing monthly bills. The cost per number plate is of the order of $100, or perhaps a quarter of the cost of catalytic converters which are now mandatory for pollution control in many countries. Such systems have been successfully tested in Hong Kong (Dawson and Catling, 1986) but there was initially some pessimism at the political likelihood that they would ever be introduced (Borins, 1988). The stated objection was that the electronic detectors could monitor the location of vehicles and hence would violate the right to privacy. This objection may be valid in a society suspicious of (and not represented by) its government, though evidence suggests that this is not likely to be much of a problem in Europe (ECMT, 1989). The objection could be levied against telephone subscribers once itemized bills are introduced, and the objection can be overcome in much the same way by the use of 'smart cards', rather like magnetic telephone cards. The electronic licence plate would be loaded with the smart card and would debit payments until exhausted. Only thereafter would the central computer monitor and bill for road use.

A more plausible explanation for the lack of success in Hong Kong may have been that it was not clear to car owners that the new charges (which were quite high, of the order of $2–3 per day) would replace the existing and very high annual licence fee. Faced with a doubling of the cost of road use, commuters understandably objected. But the whole point of charging for road use by electronic licence plates is to replace less well-designed road charging schemes, such as fuel taxes and licence fees. The proposition that needs to be put to the public is that in exchange for the entire system of current road taxes (fuel taxes in excess of the rate of VAT, the special car purchase tax, and the licence fee), road-users will be charged according to their use of congested road space, at a rate which for the average road-user will be roughly the same. (For the UK this is still just about feasible on the figures given above, at least if the pure tax element on private motorists is allowed to fall to zero.) As more than half the road-using population drives less than the average number of miles in congested areas, this should command majority support.

An alternative method of selling the use of electronic licence plates might be to offer rebates for tax on fuel used (at the estimated rate per km, or on production of receipts) and to waive the licence fee for those installing the licence plates. This might be necessary as an interim measure when their use is confined to major urban centres, notably London. It is noticeable that despite the claim by Channon as Minister of Transport that the Government had no plans to introduce road pricing because of the perceived public hostility, that hostility seems to be diminishing, at least in London. An opinion survey conducted by the Metropolitan Transport Research Unit showed 87 per cent in favour of some form of traffic restraint, and 53 per cent in favour of a fixed charge to drive into Central London. Charging per mile was widely supported, and 48 per cent said they would use public transport if such charges were introduced (*Independent*, 26 January 1990).

Until road pricing is introduced, alternative and less satisfactory methods of charging are necessary. One such is selling area licences which grant access to congested zones such as city centres during rush hours. This solution has been used in Singapore for over a decade, with considerable success. Heavy parking charges and restricted access may also be effective to varying degrees (World Bank, 1986). At the moment, however, the only way to charge vehicles for the congestion they cause is in proportion to the distance they drive, by fuel taxes and/or vehicle purchase taxes (which approximate reasonably well to distance charges for heavily used vehicles, but less well for automobiles). Such taxes, combined with access charges (area licences, or even annual licences) achieve the desired effect of charging road-users on average for congestion, but do little to encourage them to drive on less congested roads or at less busy times of the day (or, indeed, to take public transport instead). In Britain, the estimates above suggest that road taxes might usefully be increased somewhat. It is worth remarking that there are clear advantages in raising such corrective taxes to their efficient level, as they allow other distortionary taxes, which incur deadweight losses, to be reduced.

IV. Measuring the costs of congestion

So far we have avoided discussing the actual cost of congestion in Britain, and instead calculated the revenue that would be generated if vehicles were to be charged for the congestion they caused. Figure 10.3 shows how the equilibrium demand for trips is established in the absence of such charges. If road-users pay only the private costs of the trip, their costs are given by the average cost schedule, which meets the demand schedule at point C. At that point the willingness to pay by the marginal road-user is equal to the cost of the trip. The efficient congestion charge would be an

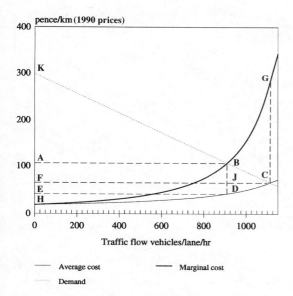

pence/km (1990 prices)

Figure 10.3. Costs of congestion: urban non-central roads

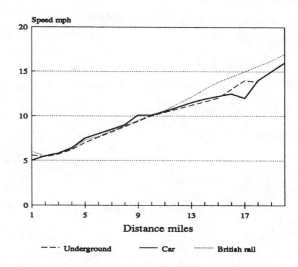

Speed mph

Figure 10.4. Equilibrium trip speed: average door-to-door speed, Central London

amount *BD*, which, if levied, would cause demand to fall to the level associated with point *B*. The revenue then raised would be *ABDE*, and this is the amount referred to above as the revenue attributable to the congestion charge. In the figure it would amount to £600 per lane-hour. But is this the correct measure of the congestion cost? Consider various alternative measures. One measure frequently cited in newspaper accounts of the cost of congestion is the extra costs involved in travelling on congested rather than uncongested roads. This might be measured by *FC* times *FH*, the excess of the average actual cost over the cost on a road with zero traffic. On the figure this would amount to £530 (per lane-hour). But this is an unrealistic comparison, as it would be uneconomic to build roads to be totally uncongested. Instead one might compare the extra costs of the excessive congestion at point *C* above that which would be efficient, at point *D*. These extra costs might be measured as *CF* times *EF*, or £270. This is not satisfactory either, as fewer trips would be taken at the efficient level of charges. A better alternative is the loss in social surplus associated with excessive road use. The efficient total social surplus associated with point *B* is the consumer surplus triangle *KBA*, plus the tax revenue *ABDE*. The social surplus associated with point *C* is just the triangle *KCF*, and the difference is the rectangle *FJDE less* the triangle *BCJ*, or £198. This is also equal to the area of the standard deadweight loss triangle *BCG*. In this case the deadweight loss is equal to one third of the revenue measure.

There is one important case in which the revenue measure accurately measures the deadweight loss, and that is where the demand for trips becomes perfectly elastic beyond its intersection with the marginal social cost schedule at point *B*. In this case there is no gain in consumer surplus in moving from the efficient level of traffic to the equilibrium level, and hence the loss is just equal to the forgone tax revenue. Put another way, by not charging the efficient toll in this perfectly elastic case, the government forgoes revenue but the consumer makes no gain. In crowded urban areas this is a plausible situation. The equilibrium level of traffic is found where the marginal road-user is indifferent between using a car or some alternative—public transport or walking. Thus traffic speeds in London are about the same as they were in the nineteenth century, and the time taken to get to work (or, more properly, the total perceived cost) for many commuters is no better by road than alternatives. Figure 10.4, which is taken from a graph in *The Times*, 5 December 1988, itself based on work by Martin Mogridge, illustrates this graphically for central London. The average door-to-door time taken between points in central London is remarkably similar for all three modes of transport, so car speeds in equilibrium are determined by the speeds of alternative public transport.

In such circumstances, the social costs of congestion may even be understated by the revenue measure. Consider the situation portrayed in Figure 10.5. Initially demand is *GC* and equilibrium is established at *C* with commuting costs of 0*F*. But if road-users were charged an amount *BD* = *CE* (the equilibrium efficient toll, less

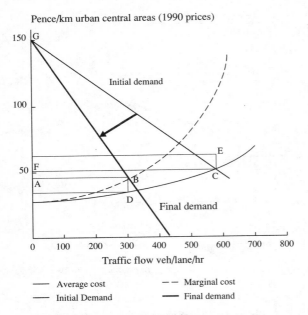

Figure 10.5. Congestion with public transport

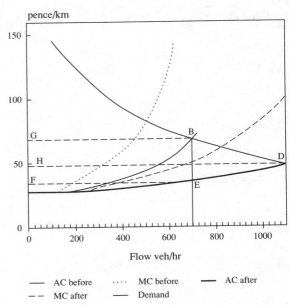

Figure 10.6. Cost–benefit of road improvements

the short run external cost), then some road-users would switch to public transport, reducing demand for private road use. This increased demand for public transport would, after appropriate investment and expansion, lead to an improved frequency of service, while the reduced traffic would lead to a faster public transport service, lowering the costs of travel. Given this lower public transport cost, the demand for private transport would fall from *GC* to *GD*, and the willingness to pay for private commuting would fall, from the level 0*F* to 0*A* for the marginal commuter. In this case charging the congestion tax would yield tax revenue (a social gain) while reducing the cost of commuting (an additional consumer gain). The tax forgone thus understates the cost of the congestion.

V. Cost–benefit analysis of road improvements

The average road tax paid by vehicles per km is roughly the same as the average efficient level. On roads of below average congestion, vehicles may be overcharged, but in urban areas they are certainly undercharged, in many cases by a large margin. Faced with growing congestion, one natural response is to increase road capacity. Figure 10.6 illustrates the pitfalls in simple-minded cost–benefit analysis. If the road capacity is doubled,

then the average and marginal cost schedules will move from 'before' to 'after'. The initial equilibrium will be at *B*, where demand is equal to the initial average cost (*AC*), and traffic will be *BG*. If the *AC* is lowered to *E*, then the apparent cost-saving is *GBEF*, to be compared with the cost of the improvement. But the lower *AC* will induce increased traffic and the new equilibrium will be at point *D*, not *E*. The benefit will be *GBDH*, which may be significantly lower.

Figure 10.7 shows that where traffic increases come from previous users of public transport the effect of the road 'improvement' may be to increase traffic volumes but to raise average costs, making everyone worse off, and adding negative value. It is hard to escape the conclusion that as journey speeds in London are now below their level at the turn of the century, before the introduction of the car, much of the road investment has been self-defeating.

The situation is radically changed when road-users pay the efficient congestion charge. Consider Figure 10.8, in which the demand for trips is perfectly elastic along *AC*, and congestion charges at the rate *AB* (marginal cost *less* average cost) are levied by means of an electronic number plate. If road capacity is expanded, but the charge maintained, then the social gain is the increase in the revenue collected, *ACDB*, which can be compared with the cost. If there are constant returns to capacity expansion and the road improvement is self-financing, it is justified. This is another applica-

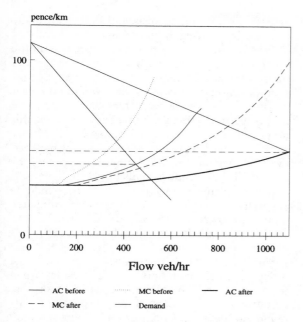

Figure 10.7. Perverse road improvement

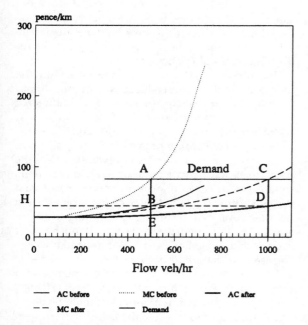

Figure 10.8. Road improvements with charges

tion of the proposition that with constant returns to road expansion, congestion charges will recover the costs of the road investment. If there are increasing returns to expansion, then expansion may still be jus-

tified even if it is not self-financing—one should compare the marginal expansion costs with the marginal benefit measured by the increased revenue.

The implications of this are clear—without road pricing, road improvements may yield low or even negative returns, but with efficient pricing, not only are improvements easy to evaluate, they should also be self-financing, at least if there are constant or diminishing returns to expansion, as is likely in congested areas.

VI. Pricing public transport

If private road-users are significantly undercharged for using the road in urban areas, then commuters face the wrong relative prices when choosing between public and private transport. If it is hard to raise the price of private driving, why not lower the price of public transport to improve the relative price ratios? There are a number of problems with this proposal. First, it is hard to compute the second-best public transport subsidies given the great variation of congestion costs by time of day and location. Second, the subsidies have to be financed by taxes which have distortionary costs elsewhere. (Note that congestion charges would reduce the distortionary costs of the tax system.) Third, subsidies to public transport appear to be rather cost-ineffective. Few motorists are attracted off the road into private transport, with much of the increase in public transport use coming from those previously not using either mode.

There are also political economic problems with operating public bus companies at a loss—there is a temptation to ration them and lower the quality, thus defeating the purpose of making them more attractive to commuters. It becomes more difficult to gain the benefits of deregulation and privatization. It may just lead to rent-dissipation by the supplier of public transport—as seems to have happened to some extent when the London Underground was heavily subsidized. The same applies to subsidizing rail travel—it becomes unattractive to expand capacity if this just increases the size of the loss.

A more promising approach is to make private transport relatively less attractive and public transport more attractive, by improving the quality of the latter, possibly at the expense of the former. Bus lanes which reduce road space to other road-users have this effect, as would electronic signalling to give priority to public transport at traffic lights. Banning private cars from congested streets during the working day has a similar effect. Arguably the greatest obstacle to overcome is that of making private road-users aware of the true social costs of their road use. Table 10.2 reveals that *average* congestion charges of 44 pence/km would be appropriate in urban centres at the peak, and 36 pence/km during the off-peak, with higher charges appropriate on roads with higher volume and/or lower speeds. Figure 10.2, which is plotted for 1990 costs for suburban areas, shows that when traffic speeds have fallen to 20 kph, then congestion charges of 50 pence/km are in order. It is hard to make public transport 50 pence/km cheaper than its unsubsidized level, and thus it is more productive to think of ways of raising the cost of private transport at congested periods, or directly reducing its level.

It was argued above that road pricing gives rise to sensible cost–benefit rules for road improvements. The same is also true for other transport investments, especially in public transport and that most capital intensive form, rail transport. If road-users paid the full social cost of road use, then there would be every reason to charge users of public transport the full social marginal cost, including congestion. It is unlikely that there are economies of scale in peak-period road or rail use in London, or in peak-period bus use in other cities, and this would lead to fares that would cover the full operating costs, including interest on capital. It would therefore again be easier to apply commercial criteria to investment in public transport, and, indeed, there would no longer be a strong case for keeping these services in the public sector.

VII. Conclusion

Road pricing is the best method of dealing with congestion, and would have far-reaching implications for the viability and quality of public transport, for the finance of urban infrastructure, and ultimately for the quality of life. The average road charges might not need to increase above current levels, for if roads were correctly priced, demand for the use of the most congested streets would fall, and with it the efficient charge to levy. Current road taxes are heavy and yield revenue substantially greater than the average cost of the current road system. In equilibrium, with efficient road pricing and an adequate road network, one would expect road charges to be roughly equal to road costs, so either road charges would fall below current tax levels, or substantial road investment would be justified, and possibly both.

A shift to road pricing would cause a fall in the cost of driving in non-urban areas, and an increase in the cost of urban driving. In the medium run the quality of urban public transport would improve, and the average cost of urban travel by both public and private transport might fall below current levels. Energy consumption would increase, as there would no longer be any reason to have heavy fuel taxes (other than those needed to reflect the costs of pollution, and this problem is arguably better addressed by mandatory emissions standards). A shift to road pricing matched by offsetting adjustments to other taxes to raise the same total tax revenue is unlikely to be inflationary, both because the average road tax/charge would be almost unchanged, and because any increase in charge leading to higher travel costs could be matched by lower taxes on other goods, leading to a fall in those elements of consumer expenditure.

Similarly, the impact on the distribution of income is likely to be slight and probably favourable. Urban private travel costs would rise, at least in the short run, and urban public transport quality-adjusted costs might fall (depending on how rapidly any subsidies were phased out, and how quickly the increased demand for public transport were translated into more supply at higher average quality). Rural transport costs would fall. As urban car-owners are richer than average, and users of public transport are poorer, the redistribution should be favourable.

The subject of road pricing and, more generally, the management of transport policy has moved firmly into the policy arena. The British government is attracted to a more commercial approach to the provision of transport infrastructure, and has restructured the railways with the intention of privatizing the rail track, which would charge train operating companies for the use of the track. Parity would suggest that road users should also be charged for using specific roads, and the Government has indicated that charges should not only cover maintenance and operating costs, but also the capital value of the road network and the wider costs such as noise and other environmental costs—consistent with the approach set out in this reprinted article. The Department of Transport published a Green Paper, *Paying for Better Motorways* (HMSO, 1993), suggesting that road pricing should be introduced for motorways, while the British government is keen to introduce private-sector finance into road building. The idea of commercializing the road network is discussed in Newbery (1994), where the particular suggestions of motorway charges and private toll roads are criticized. The House of Commons Transport Committee studied the government proposals on *Charging for the Use of Motorways* (House of Commons, 1994), and subsequently investigated *Urban Road Pricing* (House of Commons, 1995).

The environmental impact of road transport was examined by the Royal Commission on Environmental Pollution (1994), and various estimates of the social costs are provided in Newbery (1995).

Cambridge County Council has been experimenting with a simple form of congestion meter, which is activated when a vehicle enters the city, and which can then charge the vehicle (deducting from a prepaid magnetic card similar to a phone card). It may be programmed to charge for distance travelled, time elapsed, or speed (or any combination of these). The original idea was to charge for time spent travelling below a pre-determined speed (reasoning that this would be because of congestion), but there were considerable doubts about the safety implications and unpredictability of this otherwise attractively decentralized system. What emerges clearly to any participant in the experiments is that the simple speed-flow models described above deal poorly with delays to traffic waiting at junctions and traffic lights. The best design for a system of charging for urban congestion remains unclear, though the Department of Transport has now published the results of its extensive study of road pricing in London based on traffic simulation models that attempt to deal with the longer-run impacts on the location of commuters and business.

References

Borins, Sandford F. (1988), 'Electronic Road Pricing: An Idea whose Time may Never Come', *Transportation Research*, **22A**(1): 37–44.

Crandall, R. W., Gruenspecht, H. K., Keeler, T. E., and Lave, L. B. (1986), *Regulating the Automobile*, Brookings, Washington DC.

Dawson, J. A. L., and Catling, I. (1986), 'Electronic Road Pricing in Hong Kong', *Transportation Research*, **20A** (March): 129–34.

Department of the Environment (1989), *Environment in Trust: Air Quality*.

Department of Transport (1987), *COBA 9*, Department of Transport, London.

—— (1989a), *The Allocation of Road Track Costs 1989/90*, Department of Transport, London.

—— (1989b), *Transport Statistic Great Britain 1978–88*, Department of Transport, London.

—— (1994a), *The Allocation of Road Track Costs 1994/95*, Department of Transport, London.

—— (1994b), *Transport Statistics Great Britain 1994*, Department of Transport, London.

—— (1995), *Transport Statistics Great Britain 1995*, Department of Transport, London.

Diamond, P. A., and Mirrlees, J. A. (1971), 'Optimal Taxation and Public Production, I: Productive Efficiency', *American Economic Review*, **61**: 8–27.

ECMT (1989), European Conference of Ministers of Transport Round Table 80, *Systems of Infrastructure Cost Coverage*, Economic Research Centre, OECD, Paris.

Hall, F. L., Allen, B. L., and Gunter, M. A. (1986), 'Empirical Analysis of Freeway Flow-Density Relationships', *Transportation Research*, **20A**: 197–210.

Harrison, W.J., Pell, C., Jones, P. M., and Ashton, H. (1986), 'Some Advances in Model Design Developed for the Practical Assessment of Road Pricing in Hong Kong', *Transportation Research*, **20A**: 135–44.

HMSO (1993), *Paying for Better Motorways*, CM 2200, London, HMSO.

House of Commons (1994), *Charging for the Use of Motorways*, Fifth Report of the Transport Committee, Session 1993–94, Cm 376, London, HMSO.

—— (1995), *Urban Road Pricing*, Third Report of the Transport Committee, Session 1994–95, Cm 104–1, London, HMSO.

Jones-Lee, M. W. (1990), 'The Value of Transport Safety', *Oxford Review of Economic Policy*, **6**(2).

Keeler, T. E., and Small, K. (1977), 'Optimal Peak-Load Pricing, Investment and Service Levels on Urban Expressways', *Journal of Political Economy*, **85**(1): 1–25.

Kraus, Marvin (1981), 'Scale Economies Analysis for Urban Highway Networks', *Journal of Urban Economics*, **9**(1): 1–22.

Newbery, D. M. G. (1987), 'Road User Charges and the Taxation of Road Transport', *IMF Working Paper WP/87/5*, International Monetary Fund, Washington DC.

—— (1988a), 'Road User Charges in Britain', *The Economic Journal*, **98** (Conference 1988): 161–76.

—— (1988b), 'Road Damage Externalities and Road User Charges', *Econometrica*, **56**(2): 295–316.

—— (1988c), 'Charging for Roads', *Research Observer*, **3**(2): 119–38.

—— (1989), 'Cost Recovery from Optimally Designed Roads', *Economica*, **56**: 165–85.

—— (1990), 'Acid Rain', *Economic Policy*, **11**, October.

—— (1994), 'The Case for a Public Road Authority', *Journal of Transport Economics and Policy*, **28**(3), 325–54; also in *Minutes of Evidence*, Transport Committee Fifth Report, *Charging for the Use of Motorways*, Vol. II, 74–87 HC 376-(II).

—— (1995), 'Royal Commission *Report on Transport and the Environment*—Economic Effects of Recommendations', *The Economic Journal*, **105**, 1258–72.

—— Hughes, G. A., Paterson, W. D. O., and Bennathan, E. (1988), *Road Transport Taxation in Developing Countries: The Design of User Charges and Taxes for Tunisia*, World Bank Discussion Papers, 26, Washington, DC.

Paterson, W. D. O. (1987), *Road Deterioration and Maintenance Effects: Models for Planning and Management*, Johns Hopkins University Press for World Bank, Baltimore.

Royal Commission on Environmental Pollution (1994), *Transport and the Environment*, 18th Report, Cm 2674, London, HMSO.

Small, K. A., Winston C., and Evans, C. A. (1988), *Road Work: A New Highway Policy*, Brookings, Washington DC (In Press).

US Federal Highway Authority (1982), *Final Report to the Federal Highway Cost Allocation Study*, US Government Printing Office, Washington, DC.

World Bank (1986), *Urban Transport*, Washington DC.

11

Economic policy towards the environment

DIETER HELM

New College, Oxford

DAVID PEARCE

University College, London[1]

I. Introduction

When Mrs Thatcher declared that the challenge of the 1990s will be to preserve the environment for the next generation she was highlighting a perceptual change in the nature of environmental problems. What had hitherto been viewed as a local and, at best, national issue, became in the 1980s an international and global one. The fate of natural environments was suddenly everyone's concern. The globalization of environmental degradation had been anticipated in the 1970s with warnings about ocean pollution, ozone layer damage, and climate change. But the popular focus was misdirected: resources were running out; the world was getting colder, not warmer; and the ozone layer was under threat from supersonic air transport. A mixture of poor and incomplete science combined with alarmism to produce *Limits to Growth* (Meadows *et al.*, 1972) and *Blueprint for Survival* (Goldsmith *et al.*, 1972).

Global concerns remain subject to scientific uncertainty: rates of loss of biological diversity are not known, the greenhouse effect is not yet a scientific fact, and the precise functioning of global and regional ecosystems is ill-understood. But the scientific base is clearer and, above all, the manifestations of environmental neglect are now conspicuous.

While scientific evidence is essential to identify the extent of the problem, the policy questions are largely ones for social science. The problem can only be addressed through changing human behaviour—altering the demand for environmental services and changing and controlling their supply. Indeed, a major feature of the modern environmental debate is the widespread acceptance of the role which economics must play in analysing the causal processes of environmental decay and in formulating policy. In the 1970s the economic voice was heard, often in critical response to alarmist environmentalism, in defence of economic growth and in favour of the use of economic policy instruments.[2] But it seems fair to say that, with exceptions, economists then were transfixed by a presumption that environmental issues were localized examples of externalities, fairly minor deviations from the reasonably efficient workings of market and quasi-market economies. Transboundary pollution (acid rain, ocean pollution) and mutual destruction of the global commons (ozone layer holes over the Antarctic and Arctic, tropical deforestation, biodiversity loss) soon ended the misconception, backed by demonstrations of the theoretical foundations of the pervasiveness of the environment in economic life.[3]

In order to construct a viable environmental policy, it is necessary to start with a proper analysis of environmental problems. It is a task to which economic theory is well suited. To an extent, the relevant literature already exists. Environmental effects are externalities —effects of which the costs and benefits are not fully

First published in *Oxford Review of Economic Policy*, vol. 6, no. 1. (1990).

[1] The authors are grateful for detailed comments on early drafts from Christopher Allsopp, Patrick Lane, Derek Morris, and Mark Pearson. The usual disclaimers apply.

[2] See for example, Beckerman (1974).
[3] See, notably, Ayres and Kneese (1969).

reflected in potential or actual market exchanges. They represent incomplete or missing markets. A huge literature exists on the nature of these market failures and on theoretical solutions.[4] In part, the objective of this paper is to highlight the relevance of some of the major results to current policy problems.

However, much of the existing literature focuses on externalities as special cases in otherwise perfect markets. In practice, market failures rarely arise in neatly segmented boxes. Externalities arise in oligopolistic and monopoly markets, where there is risk and uncertainty, in conjunction with public goods, and in areas where the state is already involved. Indeed, a distinctive feature of global externalities is the requirement for international co-operative solutions. The conventional economic approach to externalities is therefore unlikely to prove sufficient to define the policy options. The institutional context and the associated market structure matter.

Complexity also arises from the fact that most environmental assets are not marketed. There is no explicit market in clear air, in unpolluted bathing beaches, in forest views, and in the carbon-fixing properties of tropical rain-forests. Though many regard these assets as priceless, such an approach is devoid of policy implications unless it is to leave the existing structure of environments untouched. Practical policy responses require trade-offs, and these in turn necessitate that values are placed on non-market goods in order to construct the appropriate policy interventions.

The task of environmental economics is therefore to adapt theoretical tools to provide an integrated framework of analysis and to develop existing tools to place valuations on environmental assets and consequences and, thereby, to develop appropriate policies. No doubt this task will take decades to perfect. However, since the lags are long and the effects may be irreversible, there is a substantial expected pay-off to early imperfect policy initiatives. The global nature of many environmental problems exacerbates the scale of the pay-offs. Investing in sea defences, inland water supplies, drainage, and flood control schemes now yields potentially very large benefits in the future in the form of avoided risks of massive sea-water inundation in, say, Bangladesh or Guyana. Moreover, the first steps in a cost-effective ladder of investments to combat global warming would, in any event, yield other benefits. Energy conservation reduces acid rain and saves foreign

exchange costs in resource-impoverished economies. Many of the policies will, no doubt, of necessity be crude, but they must be evaluated against the do-nothing option, not against an idealized solution. The purpose of this paper is to provide an overview of progress to date in constructing an analytical framework, and to suggest a number of policy conclusions which follow.

The structure of the paper is as follows. Following the Introduction, section II provides a classification of environmental externalities differentiated by their institutional contexts. Section III considers the conventional economic theory approaches, based upon relatively strong informational assumptions. Section IV then introduces the informational problems and indicates why co-operative solutions to global externalities may prove particularly hard to achieve. Section V concentrates on valuation of the future, and indicates a number of issues that arise with conventional discounting procedures. Section VI looks at the potential role of the market in environment policy and in particular the consequences of privatization, taxes, and marketable permits. Finally section VII sets out some tentative suggestions for the way forward.

II. The context of externalities

Recognizing environmental problems as externalities is essential in framing economic policy. It is however important to note that there are many different contexts within which they arise. These may be classified according to the number of parties respectively causing and suffering the consequences of pollution, the jurisdictions, and the economic systems within which the externalities arise.

1. The number of generators and affected parties

The numbers involved in producing and receiving an externality have an important effect on the ability of different institutions to deal with the consequences. The classic textbook examples of externalities which arise between two identified parties are in fact special cases. Though these one-to-one cases are easiest to model and hence are the ones on which the literature concentrates most heavily, nearly all pollution problems are more general. Indeed the distinctive feature

---

[4] See for recent surveys Cornes and Sandler (1986) and Baumol and Oates (1988). Other definitions, based on different conceptual approaches are provided by Buchanan and Stubblebine (1962), Arrow (1970), and Heller and Starrett (1976).

of the current environmental agenda is its global nature. Results which hold in the bilateral case do not necessarily carry over to the global one.

In these simple one-to-one cases, the parties are easily identified, and the costs of pollution can typically be evaluated. These cases can often be tackled either through taxes and subsidies or through negotiation and bargaining. For example, neighbours can often resolve problems of smoke, waste disposal, and noise through direct discussions and complaints, use of police, and through the legal process, whilst the Pollution Inspectorate can relatively straightforwardly regulate and if necessary prosecute individuals and firms.

Greater complexity is introduced when a large number of individuals and firms are affected. Many standard pollution problems fall into this one-to-many category: chemical spillages into water systems and oil tanker disasters, for example. In this case it remains relatively easy to identify the source of the pollution, but the affected parties are usually each too small to warrant the expense of solving the problem as in the one-to-one case above. The major new features introduced are the complexity of measuring environmental damage and the problems of establishing co-operative action amongst the affected parties where the costs to each are small relative to the costs of taking effective action against the polluter. The free-riding incentives for some affected parties on others are typically strong given the costs of enforcement. Class actions and the use of the political and regulatory process are typically required, introducing their own transactions costs and the burden of associated government failures.

The most persuasive externalities combine many generators with many recipients. These many-to-many cases include a number of new problems which have arisen in the 1980s, most noticeably the increasing concentration of greenhouse gases (carbon dioxide, methane, nitrous oxide), ozone depletion, and biodiversity losses. They can be called global mutual externalities. They also include the range of household and industrial wastes, including sewage, paper, and plastics. Measurement problems are much more pressing with multiple pollution generators. Their identification can itself pose difficulties and detailed emissions data is typically costly to collect. Greater reliance on the polluters to provide information is necessitated, increasing the chances of regulatory bias and even capture. Distributional considerations can also arise in this category. Many of the associated products, especially energy and transport, are inelastic in demand, and have strong income effects.

2. Jurisdictions

Since, as we shall see in section III.2 below, property rights play an important role in the defining and solving of externalities, the legal system matters greatly in framing economic policies towards the environment. In cases where externalities are within nations, the legal base is co-extensive with the externality, and existing taxation and regulatory systems can typically be adapted for environmental policy. Environmental consequences do not, however, always respect national boundaries. Hence the domain of the externality and judicial boundaries do not always coincide. National law and national regulation provide weak methods of control, while general international law is usually too weak to provide adequate remedies. For example, the UN Convention on the International Law of the Sea in 1982 has yet to be signed by the US and the UK, and the UN International Whaling Convention has not yet been signed by the major whaling countries. In these circumstances, the benefits to the polluters from the polluting activity frequently exceed the costs of resisting international pressure from the affected parties, or indeed, in some cases, of breaking signed agreements.

3. Economic systems

All these problems are common to different types of economic regime, from free market through to planned. Nevertheless the type of economic system is likely to affect the extent of externalities and the efficiency of environmental policy. Planned economies reduce the likelihood of bargaining between the polluters and pollutees to internalize externalities, and the emphasis on production rather than consumption in many planned systems is likely to result in less weight being placed on the consequences of environmental degradation. Where planning is associated with single party dominance of the political process, the growth of regulation via the political process is also likely to be hindered. It is widely agreed that pollution problems in Eastern Europe and the USSR are more severe than in the West European market-based economies.

The policy options are also constrained by the type of economic system. The creation of marketable pollution permits does assume a market system, as does the wider use of property rights. The impact of taxes rather than direct controls also presumes a price system.

The emergence in the last decade of regulatory activity and privatization in the developed and developing world has further highlighted the relationship between environmental concerns and free market activity. The shift of emphasis towards markets in Eastern Europe and in the Soviet Union can only increase this focus.

Whatever the economic system, the distribution and incidence of pollution, and the burden of environmental policy is unlikely to be even. The developing world faces particular concerns over environmental quality owing to its much greater direct reliance on natural resources—e.g. wood for fuel, direct abstraction of water, and the use of marginal lands for subsistence crops—and its extensive sensitivity to ecosystem shocks and stresses (droughts, wars, and floods). Hence the emergence of an environmental economics applied to the Third World.

III. Conventional economic approaches

Having established the salient institutional characteristics, the range of possible economic instruments can then be considered. The conventional economic approaches to externalities provide the framework of environmental policy. The models are simplistic, and deliberately so, to illustrate the fundamental theoretical characteristics which pervade both simple and complex practical examples. We examine first the early ideas for using taxes and subsidies to modify imperfect markets—to alter costs and incentives. These pragmatic tax/subsidy interventions are then contrasted with the more full-blooded free market approaches, associated with Coase and the Chicago school. Together they provide a number of quite general results and a framework for assessing the extent to which markets, regulation, and planning are appropriate policy regimes. More complex global problems require the addition of co-operative models, and therefore can be analysed through models of collusion and games.[5]

1. Pragmatic solutions to market failures: Pigouvian taxes and subsidies

The standard economic approach to externalities is typically ascribed to Pigou (Pigou, 1920). While regarding externalities as a minor problem (compared, for

example, to monopoly), Pigou devised a system of taxes and subsidies to correct for the social costs which were not incorporated in private decision-making. Crudely, a tax is placed on the polluter to bring his cost function into line with what it would have been had he faced the true social costs of production. The polluter pays, and therefore reduces his output to the socially optimal level. Conversely, a subsidy can be paid to the pollutee, to compensate for the damage done.[6]

The government provides the mechanism to force the polluter to pay the full costs of his activities. The tax may or may not be exactly offset by the subsidy, depending on whether the tax revenue is transferred to the victim or not, and on demand and supply elasticities. Clearly, if, for example, the revenue from an energy tax were spent on energy conservation, as opposed to reducing income tax, the impact on energy demand and supply would be much more marked.

This problem corresponds to the simple one-to-one case identified in the previous section. The model provides a number of insights into the policy problems besetting governments. Indeed it is this Pigouvian model which remains the basis of the taxation proposals currently being actively discussed. It provides a simple benchmark, and its shortcomings have provided much of the research agenda in the literature.

The following points are particularly important. First, there is no suggestion that any level of pollution is *per se* bad. It is, after all, the by-product of an activity which is economically valuable. Rather, its full cost needs to be reflected in decision-making. The problem of the market is not the creation of pollution, but rather the wrong amount of it. The optimal level of pollution is only zero in the extreme case that the externality costs require a tax so great that the firm stops production altogether.

Second, it is assumed that, after the tax, firms face the true marginal costs of production. There is therefore no distortion of competition between polluting firms. Thus it is assumed in this simple analysis that an externality arises in a context in which there are no other market failures. In particular, there is no oligopoly or monopoly, no uncertainty, no co-ordination problems, or other public goods. However, since externalities in practice always arise in markets riddled with other failures, models with joint-failures are of great importance. The design of more complex optimal Pigouvian taxes must therefore take these into account.

Third, it is assumed that the costs of the polluting firm and the damage function of the polluted firm or

[5] Accessible texts surveying the literature include Mäler (1974), Tietenberg (1988), Baumol and Oates (1988), and Pearce and Turner (1990). See also Greuenspecht and Lave (1989).

[6] The payment of subsidy does not however reduce the level of pollution in this case. It is purely compensatory.

consumer are known. In particular, there is no private information unavailable to the regulator, no strategic revelation of information by the affected parties, and there is no uncertainty about the pollution impacts. Thus, this approach is informationally very demanding.

Finally, there are no regulatory failures associated with the incentives of authorities. Regulators are concerned only with maximizing economic efficiency. Other social objectives—such as distribution and rights—are ignored. There is no regulatory capture.

These assumptions provide a menu of issues which the policy-maker needs to evaluate empirically in designing optimal interventions. The presence of monopoly or of substantial distributional consequences will modify the optimal form of intervention. Only if all the assumptions of the model are met will simple tax/subsidy solutions be the obvious first-best solution. Nevertheless, the Pigouvian model does carry a number of policy presumptions. The most important basic insight is that environmental damage has a cost, and that this should be reflected in economic decisions by facing the participants with a price. Furthermore, to the extent that taxes rather than subsidies are utilized, there is a presumption in favour of the *polluter pays principle*. There is certainly no role for the *victim pays principle*. Furthermore, since social costs are uniquely defined for each case of pollution, the Pigouvian model points inevitably towards pragmatism in the uses of taxes and subsidies to regulate markets, and provides the basis for the piecemeal case-by-case approach which is the hallmark of UK environmental policy.[7]

2. Laissez-faire approaches: Coase and property rights

The pragmatic approach to externalities has been directly challenged by the more full-blooded market theorists. This challenge is associated most closely with Coase's seminal article (1960).

The free-market approach identifies the problem of externalities as the absence of markets and the associated property rights. An economy in which every asset is owned would internalize all externalities. On this view, over-grazing of pastures and pollution of the oceans and atmosphere result from the fact that common land, seas, and air are not owned. If they were,

then the resolution of damage levels and payments would be organized through the valuation and enforcement of the relevant property rights. These are determined either through the market or through the legal system. Crudely, if a chemical firm pollutes a river, the river owner, if he owns the right to clean water, will demand compensation, or sue. Alternatively, if he does not own the right to clean water, it will be in his interest to bribe the chemical firm to reduce pollution.

In Coase's original model, the externality problem is one-to-one.[8] The parties bargain with each other, with the result that the equilibrium is determined irrespective of the allocation of the property rights between polluter and polluted. Thus, whether the polluter pays compensation for the damage done, or the affected party bribes the polluter to reduce emissions is irrelevant to the efficiency of the outcome, being only of distributional concern.

If correct, Coase's bargaining model would have quite radical implications for policy. First, emphasis on the polluter pays principle would be invalid, or, at least, an equity judgement with no foundation in economic efficiency. It would be equally appropriate for the injured party or the government itself to bribe polluters with subsidies.[9] Second, the assignment of property rights to 'free' assets—such as air and water—would solve externalities. Finally, the fact that most environmental assets are not owned by identified individuals creates a very strong presumption against 'do nothing' policies.

The simple Coasean model inevitably suffers many deficiencies. First, Coase tends to assume that markets exist. In practice, the major global environmental problems arise in circumstances where property rights are impossible to define. The essential feature—excludability—is not present. Second, like the Pigouvian tax solution, it, too, assumes well-functioning markets. Yet, if there is monopolistic competition, the bargain becomes more complex, involving polluter, polluted, and consumer (Buchanan, 1969). Third, when there are many parties involved, there may be significant free-ride incentives and transactions costs reducing the efficiency of the bargaining process. Finally, in the intergenerational context, bargains take on a new meaning because it is not clear who is bargaining on behalf of the next generation. (We return to this aspect in section V.)

---

[7] See Vogel (1986) for a contrast between US and UK policy approaches. It should be noted that European Community regulation typically pursues a rule-based approach in contrast to that of the UK.

[8] See Farrell (1987) for an exposition and critique.
[9] There are other reasons why the polluter pays principle might be sub-optimal. Affected parties may have little incentive to minimize their exposure to pollution—there may be moral hazard. See on this Olson and Zeckhauser (1970).

Yet, despite the unreality of the examples frequently cited in support of the Coasean argument, the idea that the optimality of the outcome is unaffected by whether the polluter or pollutee pays is much exploited in international problems. The notion that the victim should pay the polluter is a stark reality in the context of international environmental policy. This is the import of Mäler's (1990) exposition of the underlying principles of international environmental negotiations. The reality of global or regional environmental problems is that they are a game in which those who gain by co-operation must devise incentives to make those who lose play the game. Game theory predicts that this requires side payments—inducements to participate to those who stand to gain little by co-operation, but whose co-operation is essential to the objective. Inducements are all the more essential when the polluter is poor and therefore lacks the economic resources to tackle control.

3. Comparing the Pigouvian and Coasean approaches

A fundamental difference between the two approaches lies in the mechanisms proposed for resolving externalities. The Pigouvian approach creates a presumption in favour of pragmatism with civil servants and government agencies evaluating each case on its individual merits. The official identifies the parties and then attempts to estimate the marginal costs and benefits to each. Information is gathered from the parties, and demand and cost functions are estimated. The 'optimal' tax is then imposed.

The Coasean approach, by contrast, relies on the market itself to facilitate bargaining between the affected parties. If they cannot agree, the dispute is viewed as one about the definition of their respective property rights. The appropriate forum is then the courts, with the legal process providing for the resolution of the differences between the parties. Lawyers and judges calculate the costs and benefits to the parties of the externality, and in practice conduct a similar enquiry to that of the Pigouvian civil servant. In deciding the rival claims, and in assigning compensation, the legal process requires the same information as government regulation. The differences therefore lie less in the specification of the problem than in the costs of each method of resolution—the relative transaction costs of legal and government failure. It is by no means obvious that the legal approach is the more cost-effective. We turn now to the common problem—information.

IV. Imperfect information, strategic behaviour, and global co-operation

Both the Pigouvian and Coasean approaches assume that markets function well. The associated assumptions, as we saw above, rule out precisely those aspects of environmental problems which are so endemic in practical examples. The analysis of cases where these assumptions have been relaxed has provided the subsequent research agenda. We shall concentrate on two related aspects—imperfect information and the problems of global co-operation.

1. Imperfect information and the assessment of environmental risks

In contrast to the case of the simple full-information models, we typically lack precise information on the nature of externalities and the costs and benefits of alternative methods of dealing with them.[10] Uncertainty is a pervasive characteristic of environmental problems.

The first question to be addressed is that of the appropriate method of scientifically modelling uncertainty. Second, there is the incentive problem of individuals, firms, and countries revealing private information, and negotiating co-operative agreements. Many of the major environmental externalities are uncertain in their effect. For example, it will be at least a decade before we can be certain whether global warming is really occurring, or whether it is merely a climatic cycle caused by non-greenhouse-gas phenomena. Although the increases in carbon can be measured and predicted relatively accurately, the process of climatic change is very poorly understood. Furthermore, the impact of carbon is complex. Its effects are not limited to simply increasing *pro rata* the total greenhouse ability to absorb and retain solar energy; carbon has effects on other gas impacts, on cloud cover, and water vapour content.[11]

Our degree of uncertainty can be reduced by further research. The question is: should we take action now on the basis of very imperfect information, given that if we do not and the problem turns out to be serious, it may be very much worse to start later? Alternatively, should we engage in research now in the hope of

---

[10] See Johansson (1990) for a survey of the major measurement problems.
[11] See House of Commons Select Committee on Energy (1989) for a survey of the evidence.

better-designed policies later and indeed better technologies for tackling the problem? The answer must be pragmatic: the expected costs and benefits must be evaluated and a balanced decision taken.

Cost–benefit analysis, however, requires a method for measuring uncertainty. Conventional economic approaches assume that we at least know the subjective expected utility loss to individuals of the environmental damage, their risk preference, and the marginal costs of pollution control to firms. These assumptions are always questionable. They are increasingly so where the environmental problems are global, requiring the aggregation of individuals' preferences, and where uncertainty about costs and consequences is great. In these circumstances, it is often appropriate to consider a series of scenarios: what would happen if the probabilities were some assumed set? Crudely, a worst and best case scenario maps the range of possible outcomes. This kind of approach has the added advantage of helping to specify the bounds within which particular problems are nested, and may be extremely useful in providing a framework for considering the gains from co-operative solutions, to which we now turn.

2. Global co-operation

Mang modern environmental problems are instances of the 'tragedy of the commons' (see Hardin, 1968). Essentially, the atmosphere, the oceans outside exclusive economic zones, and the stratosphere are open-access resources, *res nullius*—owned by no one. Biological models predict a steady-state equilibrium for open-access resources, but one that may be perilously close to the carrying capacity of the habitat (see Pearce and Turner, 1990). Put another way, the risk of extinction of the resource—the tragedy—is potentially high under open-access. Common property—*res communes*—on the other hand, relates to resources held in common by a reasonably well-defined group of owners who, typically, establish rules of use. The distinction helps to characterize modern international environmental agreements as attempts to modify property rights away from open-access towards common property rights.

But even common property agreements risk breakdown because of the essential internal contradiction between the maximization of individual gains and the maximization of the collective good. This is the essence of the 'Prisoners' Dilemma' characterization of the common property problem.[12] Each player in the game

stands to gain by not co-operating with other players, but all players would be better off if they did co-operate. Non-co-operative equilibria are inefficient and co-operative solutions require binding agreements. Any agreement that is not wholly binding risks individual defection by free-riders.

Are environmental agreements in the global sphere subject to the Prisoners' Dilemma? Many would argue that they are and that binding agreements require incentive systems in the form of side payments, cash or technology or in-kind transfers, to potential defectors. As Mäler (1990) notes, such side payments can easily turn the morality of the polluter pays principle upside down, so that victims pay polluters not to pollute—the victim pays principle. Examples of the victim pays principle are already evident, as with Sweden's technical assistance to reduce acid emissions from Poland, and the currently negotiated technology transfers to China and India with respect to chlorofluorocarbons (CFCs) emission reductions. The issue of 'side payments' dominated the 1992 United Nations Environment Conference in Brazil.

Global environmental negotiation and agreement need not be as bleak a prospect as the Prisoners' Dilemma suggests. In game theory pay-offs tend to be characterized by single-dimensions—time spent in jail or monetary fines in the original Prisoners' Dilemma example, profits or utility in the generalized case. In the real world, however, multiple objectives characterize the game. Countries may be prepared to act counter-preferentially for a greater good, out of obligation, fairness, or out of environmental stewardship motives. A second feature of real-world games, familiar in game theory as well, is that they are repeated. If one player defects in the first game, he may face a coalition to his disadvantage in a second game, and so on. *Sequential games* may not face the Prisoners' Dilemma syndrome, particularly if the time period over which games are played is a long one.[13]

The weapons at the disposal of co-operative coalitions are familiar, including international disapprobation, as Britain has learned from its unco-operative stance on European Community environmental legislation.

Game theory models suggest that the incentives to co-operate depend critically on the analysis of the counterfactual—what happens if the parties do not agree? In particular, if the two parties are differentially affected so that, for example, one country experiences large-scale destruction before others, or if the parties

---

[12] On the Prisoners' Dilemma, see Taylor (1976).

[13] See for example Axelrod (1984) for an exposition of tit-for-tar rules. For a formal treatment of sequential games, see Kreps and Wilson (1982).

take different views of the probability of significant damage, they may have differential incentives to pay the pollution costs. Bankruptcy—in the sense of inability to pay—may also be highly significant. Many developing countries simply cannot meet the costs of environmental degradation.

In environmental problems, the end-game can at least be sketched in outline. If increasing concentrations of greenhouse gases lead to rising temperatures, and if these raise sea level, then those countries with low-lying, densely populated areas will face major population displacement and increased sea defence and drainage costs. Furthermore, agricultural areas sensitive to temperature change would experience depopulation. Large scale population movements, adverse food production trends, and higher population levels are likely to create instability in international relations and ultimately these may become security issues.[14]

Although such an analysis is, of course, conjectural, it indicates which countries face the greatest costs if repeated games fail to produce a co-operative outcome and which countries are likely to gain little by co-operation. Bangladesh would face very high costs but lacks the resources to build appropriate sea defences. The UK, by contrast, might even benefit from an improved climate, and the costs of sea defences might be manageable.

A further important consideration in appraising the prospects for international co-operation is noted in Barrett's article in this volume. Global environmental agreements are not homogeneous in nature. An agreement on CFCs was feasible, first because of the small number of players in the game (the CFC producers of USA, Europe, and the Eastern bloc) and the small number of potentially interested parties (industrializing developing countries). Second, the costs of substituting for CFCs in several major uses are small. No such conditions apply to greenhouse gases. All the world becomes the set of players and the costs of carbon cutbacks are formidable for some of the players. Offsetting this is the potential for some major emitters to co-operate in the initial stages and use demonstrated reductions in carbon dioxide as a bargaining instrument.

International environmental issues represent very fruitful ground for economic analysis in terms of game theory. For example, Mäler (1990) and Barrett in this volume, reveal some of the potential and some of the insights.

V. Valuing the future

Most of the major consequences of global externalities will fall on the next generation and beyond. Almost all environmental externalities have an intertemporal dimension. Nuclear waste generated now imposes a cost on future generations in terms of disposal costs and hazards; greenhouse gas emissions now may commit the future to irreversible global warming; a species lost now imposes a user cost on future generations in terms of foregone benefits from that species.

Intertemporal resource allocations are incorporated into economic analysis by discounting the future. The value of £100 now is greater than £100 in a year's time because of the return between now and a year's time if the money is invested, or because consumption now is certain, whereas consumption in one year's time depends on being alive to consume it.[15] Discounting allows for the lower weight that individuals place on the future—their myopia—compared to the present. But discounting in the environmental context is contentious precisely because it justifies the forward shifting of environmental costs to future generations. Although it may be rational for individuals to value the future consumption at a discount to present consumption, it is by no means obvious that society should make the same trade-off.[16] Although technical progress may enhance the consumption possibilities of future generations over the present, environmental damage may have the opposite effect.

The first-best solution to this intertemporal bias is the downwards adjustment of discount rates, perhaps to zero to reflect indifference about the temporal incidence of costs and benefits.[17] Indeed, if society is risk averse concerning the environment, and wishes to hand on to future generations environmental assets at least as good as it inherited, it may even be negative.

In practice, however, the optimal policy towards future generations is not so straightforward. Again, the treatment of one aspect of the environmental problem—valuing the future—cannot be considered in isolation from other market failures. There are, in consequence, a number of additional factors which should be borne in mind. First, by altering the normative balance between aggregate investment and consumption, lowering discount rates across the board

---

[14] See Grubb (1989) for an extensive discussion of the role of international negotiations in framing agreements on greenhouse gas emissions.

[15] Respectively, we consider the cost to society of waiting as the social opportunity cost, and the demand valuation as the social time preference rate. Only in competitive equilibrium will the two approaches yield the same answer.

[16] See Parfit (1984, Annex F).

[17] For a survey of environmental concerns about discount rates see Markandya and Pearce (1988).

could accelerate environmental degradation if invest-ment is more materials/energy intensive.[18] This effect is of particular importance in considering the impact of privatization. As we argue below, privatization typi-cally raises the discount rate and may consequently have the environmentally beneficial effect of provid-ing a premium to small, less capital-intensive produc-tion techniques. Second, the impact of lowering the discount rate may be affected by the size of the errors in calculating the costs and benefits of projects. If, for example, the benefits of a project are overstated and the environmental consequences undervalued, a lower discount rate may exacerbate the total effect. It is there-fore important to incorporate externality costs fully before applying a discount rate.

It is therefore not surprising that the discount rate debate remains unresolved. One suggestion is that discounting is permissible only within an ecological constraint which sets limits on the degradation that would be permitted and which would protect future generations' capability to enjoy an undegraded environment.[19]

VI. Market-orientated solutions

It is currently fashionable to advocate the use of mar-kets to solve environmental problems. This approach draws upon the basic Pigouvian insight, noted above in section III, that individuals and firms should be ex-plicitly faced with the costs of environmental damage resulting from their activities. It also fits neatly with the trend towards expanding the role of markets in tradi-tional production areas and in the provision of wel-fare services. The collapse of state planning in Eastern Europe has given powerful impetus to this trend, while the continuing world debt crisis has encouraged de-veloping countries to sell assets.

Environmentalists have, however, typically argued for greater state intervention. It has often been assumed that, since environmental problems result from mar-ket failures, state intervention is necessitated. This sim-plistic approach is not, however, supported by evidence from the planned economies of Eastern Europe. It ig-nores the costs of intervention: market failure only jus-tifies intervention if the costs of that failure are greater than the resultant costs of government failure conse-quent upon the intervention. The latter are often at least as important as the former.

Furthermore, there are typically a number of differ-ent responses to market failure: the options are, broadly, to replace the market; to make it work better by altering the incentives and costs; or to extend the market by the application of property rights.[20] These strategies are exemplified by a number of practical policy suggestions which are currently the focus of de-bate: introducing private ownership; utilizing the taxa-tion system; and creating a market in pollution permits.

1. Privatization

Privatization in the narrow sense involves the transfer of assets from one set of owners (the government) to another (private shareholders). It does not introduce new property rights (à la Coase). Rather it changes the nature of existing property rights. Its impact thus de-pends upon the incentives and constraints faced by the two sets of owners. Despite almost a decade of privat-ization, the efficiency consequence of changing in-centives and the replacement of government control by shareholders remains poorly understood. Never-theless, since the sectors which have been privatized are frequently those which are most environmentally sensitive—water, energy, and transport—the conse-quences of this policy are important.

Government objectives in operating firms reflect wider considerations than profit maximization. Recent models have focused on the maximization of output (Rees, 1984, 1989) rather than profit, leading to over- rather than under-provision. In the public sector in the UK, electricity witnessed substantial over-capacity, and coal output was maintained beyond profit maximiza-tion. This trend towards output rather than profit was reinforced by the lower cost of capital to government compared with private ownership. In this sense, if out-put and pollution are correlated, public ownership may result in higher pollution.

Privatization can, in these models, be assumed to re-duce output and investment at the margin, given the profit objective and a higher cost of capital. A higher discount rate induces shorter-term investment hori-zons and therefore the assignment of lower valuations to the future. In the case of electricity investments, for example, Sizewell B nuclear power station passed the critical 5 per cent real rate of return requirement laid down in the 1978 White Paper. In the private sector, Hinkley B would face at least 11 per cent, and there-fore not be viable (Dimson, 1989). Choice of technique

---

[18] Markandya and Pearce (1988).
[19] See, for example, Page (1977).

[20] See Helm (1986) for an overview of these strategies and Helm (ed.) (1989) for applications to a range of economic activites.

for long-term utility industries will, therefore, on this argument, be profoundly affected by privatization. Paradoxically, this change in discount rates may actually be environmentally beneficial in the electricity case. It will raise the price of electricity, reducing consumption at the margin. It will also place a premium on small generating units, and especially favour combined heat and power plants.[21]

Some commentators have argued that the efficiency of the resources controlled in the private sector will be greater, thereby economizing on environmental damage. These effects fall into three categories: that more output will be produced from given inputs (thereby reducing the demands on natural resources); that the ratio of capital to labour will be closer to the optimum (correcting for labour bias in the public sector) and hence reduce costs of production of environmental improvements; and finally that prices and hence outputs will be more closely related to costs, thereby eliminating over-production.[22]

Since the magnitude of these factors will vary on a case-by-case basis, the dynamic effects on investment will need to be compared with static efficiency gains. The more substantial the environmental impact of longer-term investments—as for example in the electricity and water industries—the greater the impact of privatization. When investment is environmentally benign—as in the water industry—privatization may only be beneficial if the static efficiency gains are large. When investment is environmentally damaging, the balance goes the other way.

Private firms do not, however, operate in a vacuum. In developed countries virtually all firms are subject to environmental regulation. The final and perhaps most important aspect of privatization is its impact on regulation. Is regulation likely to be tougher and easier to impose and monitor in the private or the public sector? The intuitive and conventional answer that greater control is engendered through ownership is highly misleading. It may be much better not to own the regulatee. The problem can be modelled through 'principal–agent' analysis.[23] The incentives of government regulators need first to be assessed. If they also own the polluter, they are likely to be susceptible to its financial performance. In the public sector, a politician is answerable for the performance of the firm, and will inevitably want to defend its record. In the UK water industry, Government Ministers frequently acted as *de facto* apologists for the low standards of water quality.

Now that the industry is privatized, Ministers are still answerable for water quality, but have no financial responsibility to the shareholders of the water companies. There is an incentive gain through privatization.

On the other hand, access to the relevant information to monitor performance is much reduced and there may be an offsetting cost created by the strategic behaviour of regulatees. This provides another opportunity for regulatory capture.[24] On balance, UK evidence suggests that privatization has significantly improved regulation. The establishment of the National Rivers Authority and the Office of Water Supply have provided an opportunity to create a programme of sustained environmental improvement.

2. Taxes

As we noted in section III above, the Pigouvian approach to externalities suggests that the tax system may provide a mechanism by which the incentives of polluters can be brought closer to a position reflecting the costs of environmental damage. Its attractions to government are considerable. Environmental taxes raise revenue, they elicit widespread acceptance and therefore compliance, and they leave the market to sort out the most efficient methods of pollution production and control. Once the desired level of pollution is set, the need for further complex regulatory oversight is minimal.

As we saw in section III.1 above, the ideal tax from an efficiency point of view is one which exactly reflects the costs of pollution at the margin. However it is often impractical to tax the pollution precisely, and therefore a number of proxy solutions are often adopted. The options can be illustrated by considering the example of carbon emissions from power stations.

The first option is to tax carbon-producing fuels, on the basis of their approximate carbon pollution potential. This alters the polluting input price and encourages substitution towards fuels with lower pollution potential (gas for coal, for example) and towards non-fossil fuels, like nuclear, water (barrages), and wind (windmills). The disadvantage of this method is that it treats all coal plants alike, and therefore penalizes coal plants with higher efficiency levels and hence fails to match actual pollution. A second option is to tax power station emissions, on a plant-by-plant basis. On this approach, each station is regarded as a unit converting inputs into two outputs, e.g. electricity and pollution.

---

[21] In the case of water, the effects may go the other way.
[22] See Bishop and Kay (1988) for some early efficiency estimates.
[23] See Rees (1985) for a survey of the principal–agent literature.

[24] See Helm, this volume, for a summary of the major problems in regulating utilities.

The tax exactly penalizes plants according to pollution emission.[25]

The third option is to tax the output of electricity: to tax final consumers. This could be achieved through the imposition of VAT. This would, however, be a crude measure, creating no incentive to substitute cleaner technology at the margin because it taxes all inputs equally, with no account being taken of their different carbon contents. It is also unlikely to achieve the desired effect of significant reductions in emissions since the price elasticity of demand is very low.[26] Very substantial price increases would be required, illustrating the point that careful case-by-case empirical studies are required if policy is not to be misdirected.

Thus far, taxes have been considered in terms of their substitution effects. Income effects are also likely to be important. Income effects from taxes may at least partially offset the substitution effect. Many goods produced by polluting technologies are merit goods. Electricity, transport, and water are obvious examples and the resulting demand behaviour from taxes may conflict with distributional objectives. Indeed, in the case of a tax on electricity, the substitution effect is very small, while the income effect is very large.[27] On an international scale, environmental taxes would require a compensating redistribution to developing countries. Taxes may also be non-neutral at the national level, adversely affecting aggregate demand, and thus requiring compensatory expenditure or reductions in other taxes.

The latter point raises the question of the use to which additional revenues are put. For example, the low electricity price effect discussed above would not be so much of a problem if the resulting revenues were spent on energy conservation measures—i.e. if the tax funded a subsidy. This would create a double effect, and have the attractive feature of avoiding an extra call on the exchequer. Similarly, an environmental tax on rich countries (perhaps on energy consumption) may provide a politically more acceptable method of funding a transfer to developing countries to provide sidepayments for reducing their pollution.

Taxes on a national scale may therefore provide an attractive policy option to reduce national pollution and to fund subsidies. In isolation, however, the impact may induce perverse substitution effects between countries. A unilateral tax on energy users in the UK would disadvantage the competitiveness of some UK traded goods. The competitors without the tax would gain market share, and hence increase total pollution. This is another example of the Prisoners' Dilemma, discussed above in section IV.2. The policy implication is clear: tax based solutions of international externalities are best dealt with consistently at the international level. Unilateral action may have a considerable demonstration effect, but it may be counterproductive.[28]

3. Marketing pollution rights

Pollution taxes seek to regulate waste, effluent, and ambient emissions through prices. But economists have long debated the merits of price incentives compared to quantity incentives. The idea of regulating the environment through emission quotas which are then traded, was first espoused in the 1960s.[29] The environmental quality objective can be translated into an emissions target. Suppose the target is 100 units of pollution. Permits allowing the emission of 100 units can be issued to polluters. The initial allocation rule is important. Typically, the historical pattern of emissions will form the basis of the allocation: polluters will each receive permits according to their emissions at some agreed baseline date—'grandfathering'. Polluters are then free to trade the permits which then command a market price. For some polluters with low abatement costs, the market price (P) will exceed the abatement cost (A). As long as $P > A$, such polluters have an incentive to sell permits, thus surrendering the right to pollute, and to abate pollution. High cost polluters will face a context in which $P < A$, giving them an incentive to acquire permits in the market. The attraction of tradable permits is that the concentration of abatement in low cost polluters will minimize the compliance costs.

Tietenberg (1990) shows how this result can be achieved in addition to environmental quality being improved. Any polluter able to emit pollutants below the initial allocation will secure certified emission reduction credits. It is these credits that become the currency of the emissions trading programme. A new source of pollution can be allowed only if it acquires adequate credits, thus offsetting the initial gain in quality. By allowing trade only if credits exceed debits, the regulating authority can actually improve environmental quality. Some debate exists as to whether emissions

---

[25] The optimal ranking of the electricity merit order is then, given the inputs, a function of the two efficiency parameters (electricity and pollution) considered jointly.

[26] See Department of Energy (1989).

[27] See Baker et al. (1990) for micro disaggregated consumption patterns for electricity, and Pearson and Smith (1990) for estimates of the impact of electricity taxes on different consumer groups. See also Dilnot and Helm (1987) on energy as a merit good.

[28] In this context, it is interesting to note that UK discussion of the possibility of carbon taxes has stressed the international discussion. See Ridley (1989).

[29] See Dales (1968).

trading under the US Clean Air Act has achieved improvements in air quality. Certainly it appears not to have deteriorated, so that trading has fared no worse than the alternative of command and control and has certainly achieved cost compliance benefits of several billion dollars (see Hahn and Hester, 1987, 1989).

The potential for using the tradable permit as an incentive system is enormous. It does, however, require imaginative administration. Most of the cost-savings under the US legislation have come from within-plant (internal) trading (see again Hahn and Hester, 1987, 1989). The greatest potential almost certainly lies with inter-firm trading. Moreover, trading offers a means of handling international environmental agreements. A carbon convention, for example, will have to function via emission targets allocated to individual countries. Grandfathering with some initial discount—e.g. carbon dioxide emissions in 1990 less, say, 20 per cent—is the most likely initial allocation. Emissions trading options are then twofold. At the very least, within-country trading can occur, just as the US proposes for compliance with the Montreal Protocol on the protection of the ozone layer.

More imaginatively, permits could be traded between nations. A country that is able to secure carbon dioxide reductions of more than the initial discount can secure credits which can be traded with other countries. The obvious problem with this solution lies with the grandfathering clause, since developing countries will acquire a fairly low initial allocation if rights are allocated on the basis of base year emissions, and will be unable to afford traded permits. One solution is to bias the initial allocation to developing countries according, say, to population. Trade will then be from developing countries to the richer world, with a consequent significant transfer of funds to the Third World.

Such a prospect opens up imaginative possibilities. Permit trading could be subject to its own form of conditionality. For example, sales might be contingent upon agreed proportions of permit revenues being used for energy conservation expenditure in the Third World. Offsets would also be permitted in the form of carbon-fixing investments such as afforestation. New additions to carbon dioxide emitting capacity would be allowed if the potential permit holder agreed to fund tree-planting, anywhere in the world. Tietenberg's enthusiasm for permits is therefore warranted at least in terms of the potential for tradable permit solutions to major environmental problems. Moreover, the quantity solution avoids a major pitfall of tax policy—the political difficulty of getting new taxes accepted. This difficulty might be significantly reduced by aligning green taxes with reductions in taxes on labour and capital. The advantage here is that the incentive effects of green taxes are preserved in a revenue-neutral budget, and the excess burden of the supply-side disincentive taxes is reduced. Nonetheless, the psychology of tax burdens is likely to remain an obstacle to pricing solutions. Tradable permits thus have considerable attractions.

VII. Conclusions

The prospect for the 1990s will be one of movements towards green economies. Both planned and free markets have failed lamentably to provide adequate environmental protection. Moreover, green market phenomena, in the form of green consumerism and, potentially more important, the green investor, cannot be relied upon to solve environmental problems. Major new policy initiatives will be required.

Environmental economics offers a number of important insights into the appropriate economic policies. The Pigouvian framework provides a strong presumption in favour of market-based approaches which utilize the price mechanism to confront individuals and firms with the real costs of environmental damage. The Coasean approach suggests that policy should be pragmatic between the polluter and the victim paying. Much, however, depends on the number of parties involved, and the institutional and legal framework.

The presumption in favour of market-based policies does not, however, imply the unfettered operation of market forces. Rather, the market should be harnessed to generate the most efficient method of achieving desired pollution reductions. The role of the state is to regulate through command and control procedures, in setting maximum pollution levels. The role of the market is to find the best method of achieving them. Although it may be possible in some cases to create property rights, the scope is limited. None of the current major environmental concerns falls into the pure Coase category.

The type of intervention will vary on a case-by-case basis. There is no general first-best solution. The pursuit of single instrument solutions is naïve and possibly even dangerous. The universal pursuit of taxes or command-and-control regulations is suboptimal and sometimes perverse. There is no escape from pragmatism: the application of empirically based cost–benefit analysis to the evaluation of alternative policies.

Market and government failures vary on a case-by-case basis, and so inevitably must the solutions.

The balance of the argument will, however, generally favour the exploitation of the market's mechanisms for revealing information, as compared with the excess costs and bureaucracy associated with total reliance on the command-and-control approach. Governments will be forced to search out cost-minimizing procedures to lower the projected costs of future environmental policy. The way forward lies with market-based incentives—taxes, charges, deposit-refund systems, tradable permits, and off-set policies.

References

Axelrod, R. (1984), *The Evolution of Cooperation*, New York, Basic Books.

Arrow, K. (1970), 'The Organisation of Economic Activity', in R. Haverman and J. Margolis (eds.), *Public Expenditures and Policy Analysis*, Chicago.

Ayres, R. V., and Kneese, A. (1969), 'Production, Consumption and Externality', *American Economic Review*.

Baker, P., Blundell, R. McKay, S., Symons, E., and Walker, I. (1990), 'A Simulation Programme of Consumer Expenditure', Institute for Fiscal Studies Working Paper.

Baumol, W., and Oates, W. (1988), *The Theory of Environmental Policy*, 2nd edn., Cambridge, Cambridge University Press.

Beckerman, W. (1974), *In Defence of Economic Growth*, Jonathan Cape, London.

Bishop, M., and Kay, J. A. (1988), *Does Privatisation Work? Lessons from the UK*, London Business School, Centre for Business Strategy.

Buchanan, J. M. (1969), 'External Diseconomies, Corrective Taxes and Market Structure', *American Economic Review*, March.

—— Stubblebine, W. C. (1962), 'Externality', *Economica*, **29**: 371–84.

Coase, R. H. (1960), 'The Problem of Social Cost', *Journal of Law and Economics*, **3**: 1–44.

Cornes, R., and Sandler, T. (1986), *The Theory of Externalities, Public Goods, and Club Goods*, Cambridge, Cambridge University Press.

Dales, J. H. (1968), *Pollution, Property and Prices*, Toronto, University of Toronto Press.

Department of Energy (1989), 'The Demand for Energy', in D. R. Helm, J. A. Kay, and D. Thompson (eds.), *The Market for Energy*, Oxford, Oxford University Press.

Dilnot, A., and Helm, D. R. (1987), 'Energy Policy, Merit Goods and Social Security', *Fiscal Studies*, (reprinted in Helm *et al.*, 1989).

Dimson, E. (1989), 'The Discount Rate for a Power Station', *Energy Economics*, 11.

Farrell, J. (1987), 'Information and the Coase Theorem', *Journal of Economic Perspectives*.

Goldsmith, E. *et al.* (1972), *Blueprint for Survival*, Penguin Books, London.

Grubb, M. (1989), *The Greenhouse Effect: Negotiating Targets*, London, Royal Institute of International Affairs.

Gruenspecht, H. K., and Lave, L. B. (1989), 'The Economics of Health, Safety and Environmental Regulation', in R. Schmalensee and R. D. Willig (eds.) (1989), *Handbook of Industrial Organisation*, Amsterdam, North-Holland, Vol. 2, 1507–50.

Hahn, R., and Hester, G. (1987), 'The Market for Bads', *Regulation*, 3–4.

—— (1989) 'Where did all the Markets Go? An Analysis of EPA's Emissions Trading Program', *Yale Journal of Regulation*, **6**(1): 109–53.

Hardin, G. (1968), 'The Tragedy of the Commons', *Science*, **162**: 1243–8.

Heller, W. P., and Starrett, D. A. (1976), 'On the Nature of Externalities', in S. A. Lin (ed.), *Theory and Measurement of Economic Externalities*, New York, Academic Press.

Helm, D. R. (1986), 'The Economic Borders of the State', *Oxford Review of Economic Policy*, **2**(2).

—— (ed.) (1989), *The Economic Borders of the State*, Oxford, Oxford University Press.

—— Yarrow, G. (1988), 'The Regulation of Utilities', *Oxford Review of Economic Policy*, **4**(2).

Helm, D. R., Kay, J. A., and Thompson, D. (eds.) (1989), *The Market for Energy*, Oxford, Oxford University Press.

House of Commons Select Committee on Energy (1989), 6th Report, *Implications of the Greenhouse Effect*, HMSO.

Kreps, D., and Wilson, R. (1982), 'Reputation and Imperfect Information', *Journal of Economic Theory*, **27**: 253–79.

Mäler, K.-G. (1974), *Environmental Economics: a Theoretical Inquiry*, Baltimore, Johns Hopkins University Press.

—— (1990), 'International Environmental Problems', *Oxford Review of Economic Policy*, **6**(1), 80–108.

Markandya, A., and Pearce, D. W. (1988), 'Environmental Considerations and the Choice of the Discount Rates in Developing Countries', Environment Department, World Bank Working Paper No. 3, Washington D.C.

Meadows, D. H., Meadows, D. L., Randers, J., and Behrens, W. (1972), *Limits to Growth*, New York, Earth Island.

Olson, M., and Zeckhauser, R. (1970), 'The Efficient Production of External Economies', *American Economic Review*, LX: 512–17.

Page, T. (1977), *Conservation and Efficiency*, Baltimore, Johns Hopkins University Press.

Parfit, D. (1984), *Reasons and Persons*, Oxford, Oxford University Press.

Pearce, D. W., and Turner, R. K. (1990), *The Economics of Natural Resources and the Environment*, London, Harvester-Wheatsheaf.

Pearson, M., and Smith, S. (1990), 'Taxation and Environmental Policy: Some Initial Evidence', IFS Commentary, No. 19, Institute for Fiscal Studies.

Pigou, A. (1920), *The Economics of Welfare*, London, Macmillan.

Rees, R. (1984), 'A Positive Theory of Public Enterprise', in M. Marchand, D. Pestieau, and H. Tulkens (eds.), *The Performance of Public Enterprises*, Amsterdam, North-Holland.

—— (1985), 'The Theory of Principal and Agent, Parts 1 and 2', *Bulletin of Economic Research*.

—— (1989), 'Modelling Public Enterprise Performance', in Helm *et al.*, 1989 (op. cit.).

Ridley, N. (1989), *Policies Against Pollution*, London, Centre for Policy Studies.

Taylor, M. (1976), *Anarchy and Cooperation*, Chichester, John Wiley.

Tietenberg, T. (1988), *Environmental and Natural Resource Economics*, 2nd edn., Glenville, Illinois, Scott Foresman.

—— (1990), 'Economic Instruments for Environmental Regulation', *Oxford Review of Economic Policy*, **6**(1), 17–33.

Vogel, D. (1986), *National Styles of Regulation: Environmental Policy in Great Britain and the United States*, Ithaca and London, Cornell University Press.

PART V

INTERNATIONAL TRADE

12

Recent advances in international trade theory: a selective survey

HENRYK KIERZKOWSKI[1]

Graduate Institute of International Studies, Geneva

I. Introduction

International trade theorists have lived for many decades in a blissful state of accepting a common set of assumptions on which to construct the edifice of their theory. While macro-economists drew fine distinctions between Keynesians and neo-Keynesians; monetarists Mark I and monetarists Mark II, the fundamentals of the trade theory were rock hard. The outcome of this consensus was a very solid theory which has come to be known as the Heckscher-Ohlin-Samuelson model.

Research progress in the field of international trade tended to add continuously to the stock of knowledge and build on previous achievements. It is interesting to note that this research consensus and continuity could be observed in, among other things, the reference lists of articles and books. Even today it is not unusual to find citations of trade literature from the 1950s, 1940s or even 1930s, in sharp contrast with macroeconomics and international finance, where occasionally one gets the impression that only articles written during the last six months seem to count.

But all was not well with the theory of international trade. While trade theorists looked with a great deal of pride on the results of their intellectual efforts, policy makers, businessmen and the public at large regarded the policy conclusions of the Heckscher-Ohlin-Samuelson model with considerable scepticism, if not disbelief. When, some thirty years ago, Max Corden (1965) surveyed the field of international trade, he made the following observation: 'It must be confessed,

in conclusion, that the pure theory of international trade has suffered from bad public relations. Some of its main conclusions are often misunderstood, and, even when understood, very often disagreed with. There are two reasons for this. Firstly, the models of the pure theory usually make a large number of assumptions, some of which when stated explicitly sound so unrealistic as to discredit the whole model from the start, while others tend to be forgotten. . . . The second reason for the poor image in some countries of trade theory is the commitment to free-trade liberalism of many of the leading theorists.'

Indeed the assumptions of the Heckscher-Ohlin model are rather stringent. The theory assumes in particular that:

1. There are only two countries and two goods.
2. Production functions involve only two factors of production (usually called labour and capital) and are homogeneous of degree one.
3. Countries have access to the same production functions which are however different for each good.
4. Perfect competition prevails in commodity as well as in factor markets.
5. Tastes are identical within and between countries.
6. Factors of production are perfectly mobile between industries in each country but not mobile at all between countries.
7. No transportation costs or other impediments to trade exist.

The above assumptions practically eliminate all differences between countries except with regard to factor endowments. Thus relative factor endowments become the sole explanation of trade patterns in the Heckscher-Ohlin model. The country relatively well-endowed with capital, exports the relatively capital-

First published in *Oxford Review of Economic Policy*, vol. 3, no. 1 (1987). This version has been updated and revised to incorporate recent developments.

[1] I wish to thank Ronald Jones, Andre Sapir and Ethan Weisman for helpful comments.

intensive good and imports the labour-intensive commodity. A set of very restrictive assumptions leads to a very powerful prediction. The three other basic theorems of the Heckscher-Ohlin-Samuelson model are: (1) the factor-price equalisation theorem, demonstrating that under non-specialisation free trade evens factor rewards between countries; (2) the Stolper-Samuelson theorem, showing how a factor intensively used in the import-competing sector gains from protection; (3) the Rybczynski theorem, explaining that with constant commodity prices factor accumulation results in an expansion of the sector employing this factor intensively and a contraction of the other sector.

The critics of the Heckscher-Ohlin model have focused on the realism of the above assumptions as the basis of their discontent. Although I am in sympathy with the general logic of the argument, I find this criticism somewhat misplaced when applied only (and the word only needs to be stressed) to trade theory. For better or worse, the economics profession has accepted the 'as if' methodology of Milton Friedman expressed in his Essays in Positive Economics. The proper test of a theory should be, it was claimed, the accuracy of its predictions rather than the realism of its simplifying assumptions. Given this methodology, the appropriate evaluation of the Heckscher-Ohlin theory should be done in the light of its empirical test. Alas, here is where the real problem started.

The most famous test of the Heckscher-Ohlin model was carried out by W. Leontief as early as 1953. The outcome of this test was that the United States was found to be a net exporter of labour-intensive goods and a net importer of capital-intensive commodities and was taken to contradict the Heckscher-Ohlin theory. Interestingly enough, the result has come to be known as the Leontief paradox, where it should, more correctly, be called the Leontief falsification, if it was a correct test of the theory. If Newton, in an attempt to verify his theory, threw an apple into the air and it went higher and higher instead of falling to the ground, he would not have called the result a paradox. The christening of the Leontief test revealed that not only the minds but also the hearts of trade theorists were with the Heckscher-Ohlin model.

Reversing the Leontief paradox became, for almost three decades, a growth industry in international economics. Many ingenious and painstaking empirical studies have been done which greatly enriched the field. Possibly, or even probably, the biggest contribution has been made by Leamer (1980, 1984) who pointed out that the data used by Leontief revealed the United States to be both a net exporter of capital services and a net exporter of labour. This could happen in a situation of unbalanced trade. Leamer then went on to demonstrate that, with unbalanced trade the relationship between the capital/labour ratio used in exports and imports, and the overall relative factor endowment breaks down. Under unbalanced trade it is quite consistent with the Heckscher-Ohlin theory for a capital-rich country to have a higher capital/labour ratio in imports than in exports. The valid test is a comparison of the capital/labour ratio in production against the capital/labour ratio embodied in consumption. Applying the relevant test, Leamer found that indeed the capital/labour ratio embodied in US production exceeds that contained in consumption. Leamer (1984) could thus conclude that '. . . the paradox rests on a simple conceptual misunderstanding . . . If the correct calculations are done, the United States is revealed by trade to be relatively abundant in capital compared with labour . . . The impropriety of the Leontief inference is a consequence of the fact that the inference is made without benefit of a fully articulated theory.'

Nevertheless, the controversy surrounding the Leontief paradox turned out to be a stimulating influence in the field of international trade. It helped to articulate the basic paradigm and improve the quality of empirical work. For example, more factors, and in particular natural resources and human capital, have been brought into the standard model. Trade patterns in a multi-country and multi-commodity world have been investigated. Transportation costs and other barriers to trade have been formally introduced into analysis. This list could go on and on.

In fact, it would be accurate to described theoretical research in international trade over the past 20 years as systematic attempts to relax the basic assumptions of the Heckscher-Ohlin model and test its robustness. Of course, not all of this was done because of the existence of the Leontief paradox. Other stylised facts and empirical regularities, in addition to sheer intellectual curiosity, have played a role in this process. In particular, the existence of multinationals and intra-industry trade led trade theorists to expand the framework of their analysis.

This paper reviews some of these developments. Naturally, one must be very selective in a field as vast as international trade theory. I focus, in Section II, on some extensions of the basic trade model. In Section III models of monopolistic competition are discussed. Finally, in Section IV, I take up some issues related to modelling of trade in services. Although the survey deals with positive analysis, some basic welfare questions cannot be escaped when discussing monopolistic competition in international trade.

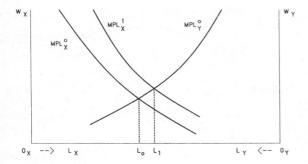

Figure 12.1. Equilibrium in the specific-factor model

II. Extensions of the basic model

I propose to review in this section some of the work and issues which go beyond the 2 × 2 × 2 (two goods, two factors, two countries) format. Some of the models which will be discussed here have a very specific and tight structure, while others are very general. However, they all share the basic feature of altering the 'twoness' of the standard model in one way or another.

1. The specific-factor model

The first major departure in this direction was the so-called specific-factor model. The model has been developed by Jones (1971), Mayer (1974), Mussa (1974) and Neary (1978) among others. The basic structure is rather simple: there are only two goods, (X and Y), and three factors of production (labour and two types of capital). Labour moves freely and costlessly between the industries in response to the wage rate differential, while capital is specific to each sector (immobile between industries).

The specific-factor model has a number of interesting properties which are worth flushing out. This can be accomplished with the help of Figure 12.1. The total amount of labour available in the economy is given by the distance $O_X O_Y$. The wage rates are measured along the two vertical axes. The curves MPL_X and MPL_Y denote the value of the marginal product of labour in the two industries and are drawn with reference to O_X and O_Y respectively. The position of these curves depends on the commodity prices and the amount of the specific capital in each industry. Assume that initially the value of the marginal product of labour curves are located at MPL_X^0 and MPL_Y^0. The equilibrium allocation of labour must be given by the point directly

below the intersection of the two curves. Any other sectoral distribution of employment would imply that wages would not be equalised between the industries. Perfect labour mobility assures, however, that this cannot happen.

Figure 12.1 also shows that equalisation of commodity prices through free trade will in general not lead to equalisation of factor rewards. If there were two identical countries, except that one had more capital specific to the X industry than the other, the value of the marginal product of labour curve would be situated above the MPL_X curve in the capital rich country. As a result, the wage rate would be higher and the two rental rates lower in the latter country. In the model containing three factors but only two goods, commodity prices do not suffice to determine factor prices, and factor endowments exert an independent role. This result lends itself to an immediate generalisation (discussed below).

The second attractive feature of the specific-factor model shows the response of factor rewards to changes in commodity prices to be markedly different from the Stolper-Samuelson theorem. As is well known, this theorem states that an increase in the price of X, say, through the imposition of a tariff, will benefit the factor intensively used in the production of X and lower the return of the other factor. The effects of a tariff in the specific-factor model can be analysed in terms of Figure 12.1 by noting that a tariff of 20 per cent will shift the MPL_X curve upwards by an equiproportionate distance to, say, MPL_X^1. The new equilibrium shows more labour ($O_X L_1$ instead of $O_X L_0$) employed in the industry being protected and hence a greater output of X. In order to induce reallocation of labour, the wage rate must increase. Note, however, that as long as the MPL_Y curve is not vertical, the wage rate increases by less than the rise in the domestic price of the protected sector. Since the wage rate increased by less than the price of X, it follows that the rental on capital specific to the protected industry, r_x, must increase proportionally more than P_X. Furthermore, with P_Y remaining constant, r_y must necessarily decline.

It is useful to contrast the patterns of responses of factor prices to changes in commodity prices in the Heckscher-Ohlin-Samuelson and the specific-factor models. These patterns are respectively given by inequalities (1) and (2):

$$\hat{w} > \hat{P}_X > \hat{P}_Y > \hat{r} \quad \text{or} \quad \hat{r} > \hat{P}_X > \hat{P}_Y > \hat{w} \tag{1}$$

$$\hat{r}_X > \hat{P}_X > \hat{w} > \hat{P}_Y > \hat{r}_Y \tag{2}$$

While the Stolper-Samuelson result depends crucially on the relative factor intensity assumption, inequality

(2) holds regardless of this presupposition. One appeal-ing element of the specific-factor model is that it can possibly explain why, in so many countries, both labour and capital employed in the same industries demand tariff protection.

In spite of the fact that the Heckscher-Ohlin-Samuelson and specific-factor models give different comparative static results, they need not contradict each other. The latter is a better description of short-run behaviour, whereas the former may be seen as focusing on long-run responses. Even though capital specificity is clearly observed in reality, the existence of rental rate differentials should encourage investment in some industries, and lead to capital depletion in others. This process is likely to be slow and costly but it should be expected to occur. As the degree of capital mobility increases, the specific-factor model produces responses which become increasingly similar, and in the limit identical, to the predictions of the Heckscher-Ohlin-Samuelson model.

Generalisation of the specific-factor model to allow for n industries, n specific factors and one perfectly mobile factor that can be employed in any sector presents no special problem. Jones (1975) has shown that in such a model an increase in the price of com-modity i, P_i, will reduce rewards to $n-1$ specific factors outside the favoured industry. The reward to the mo-bile factor and to one specific factor goes up as a result of the price increase. The specific factor gains propor-tionally more and the mobile factor proportionally less than the price rise. An implication of this generalisa-tion is that an expansion of one sector provoked by a slight price increase must be accompanied by a con-traction of $n-1$ sectors.

The assumption that certain factors are trapped in certain industries may go too far, even as a description of short-run reality. It could be plausibly argued that there is always some degree of factor mobility in the economy. On the other hand, it may also be plausible to postulate that no factor is perfectly mobile across industries. A Ph.D. in physics can easily transfer from employment in a personal computer company in the Silicon Valley, California to the Space Research Cen-tre in Houston, Texas or to the Research Laboratory of Boeing in Seattle, Washington, but he cannot easily become a heart surgeon or even a hospital nurse.

Limited factor specificity is the focus of attention in the model of neighbourhood production structures developed by Jones and Kierzkowski (1986). The model is quite general in that it allows for any number of goods and factors: however, the number of commodities is assumed to be equal to the number of factors. Pro-

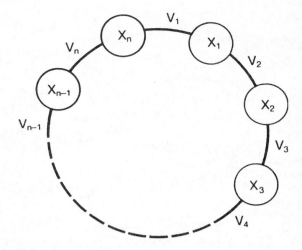

Figure 12.2. Neighbourhood production structure

duction of any good requires only two factors of production and each and every factor has two alterna-tive sectors where it can be employed. For the ease of presentation one can arrange the industries (and the factors) along a circle. Thus each sector (and factor) has two neighbours, as shown in Figure 12.2.

Factor V_i ($i = 1, \ldots n$) can be employed in the neigh-bour sectors, X_{i-1} or X_i. Every pair of neighbours shares one factor and this feature of the model makes the whole economy interdependent. A disturbance such as a price increase or factor endowment expansion spreads through the whole system.

Consider, for instance, an increase in price in the last sector, P_n, and assume that n is an even number. The two factors employed in this sector are V_1 and V_n, with corresponding rates of return w_1 and w_n. Suppose that it is w_1 which increases as the result of the disturbance. Since all the other prices remain constant, w_2 must de-cline to assure that the zero profit condition continues to hold in the sector producing X_1. The decline in w_2, however, allows w_3 to go up and so on until the 'ripple' effect has come back full circle to X_n. Since w_1 was as-sumed to increase, w_n must decline. Of course, in the case of an initial decline of w_1, w_n would rise. Which of these two outcomes actually occurs depends on rela-tive factor intensities. However, the relevent measure of factor intensity becomes a multilateral concept in this model; every single sector of the economy will have a share in it.

As long as n is an even number, the rewards to any pair of factors employed in the same industry move in

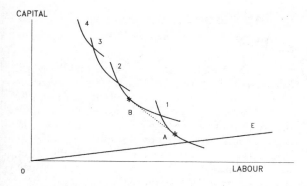

Figure 12.3. Unit-value isoquants

Figure 12.3 is useful in describing the trade patterns of a small country in static as well as dynamic contexts.

A labour-rich country can have a factor-endowment ray such as OE which cuts the unit-value isoquant to the right and below point A. The wage-rental ratio in this country is uniquely determined by its factor endowment. As capital accumulation takes place, the factor-endowment ray rotates counter-clockwise. Capital accumulation leads to a continuous rise in the relative wage rate until point A is reached. When the relative factor endowment ray falls between A and B, commodities 1 and 2 are being produced. For a small country with exogenously given commodity prices, factor prices become locked, within the AB chord, and independent of factor endowment. Under non-specialisation it is commodity prices and not factor endowment that determine factor rewards.

As factor accumulation continues, this process repeats itself. The country traverses the commodity space moving to more and more capital-intensive products and, in the process, abandons the production of labour-intensive goods. The relative wage rate rises but not in a strictly monotonic fashion.

Figure 12.3 also brings out the point that a country in a multi-commodity world is likely to produce only a small subset of goods. It also shows that free trade should not be expected to equalise wages and rentals across the world. Even countries at a similar stage of economic development may have different factor prices. For example, two similarly endowed countries with overlapping production structures may employ different techniques in the production of the same good. This can be seen in the case where one country produces only good 1 but another country with slightly more capital, produces commodity 2 in addition to 1. The latter country will use labour more sparingly in the production of good 1 than the former.

Anne Krueger (1977), who developed a model quite similar to Jones (1974), pointed out that the Heckscher-Ohlin explanation of trade will manifest itself, in a multi-commodity world, in the pattern of production and specialisation rather than relative factor intensities of exports and imports. 'Countries in the middle of the factor-endowment ranking will tend to specialise in producing commodities in the middle of factor-intensity ranking. They will import labour-intensive commodities from more labour-abundant countries and capital-intensive commodities from countries with relatively higher capital-labour endowments. The implications of these propositions for empirical testing of the factor-proportions explanation of trade are immediate.'

the opposite directions. 'Even' models produce 'non-cooperative' results. The simplest case of an even model with 'non-cooperative' outcomes is the Heckscher-Ohlin-Samuleson model.

It can be readily established that when the number of sectors, and factors, is an odd number, both factors employed in an industry favoured by a price rise will gain at least in nominal terms. Thus the 'odd' model produces 'cooperative' outcomes. Of course, the specific-factor model is just a simple version of an 'odd' model, but with the number of factors greater than the number of goods.

2. Specialised production models

The usual assumption, in the context of the Heckscher-Ohlin model, is that specialisation in production does not occur, which means that relative factor endowments of the trading countries are not too dissimilar. In the $3 \times 2 \times 2$ specific-factor model specialisation cannot occur, and therefore each country produces both goods. I now wish to turn to models which are specifically designed to allow only a small subset of goods to be produced by an individual country. The first of these models, due to Jones (1974), looks at a small country in a world of many commodities. Figure 12.3 shows unit-value isoquants for four different commodities in the Lerner diagram.

The position and the shape of each unit-value isoquant is determined by technology and the world price of the commodity in question. The isoquants show combinations of labour and capital required to produce one dollar's worth of output under zero profit conditions. Goods 4 and 1 can be seen to be the most capital-intensive and labour-intensive, respectively.

It was also noted by Krueger (1977) that distortions in commodity and factor markets have an important bearing on the pattern of specialisation and the composition of trade. In the $2 \times 2 \times 2$ model, market distortions divulge themselves through departures of factor rentals from their free-trade values. In the framework under discussion, on the other hand, a tariff on a previously unproduced good can make production of this good justifiable from the perspective of private interests, and at the same time lead to the elimination of production of a good that was produced under an efficient allocation of resources. Other policy measures can also result in a distorted production mix. Of course, that may be exactly what policy measures are sometimes designed to accomplish. It may be recalled that, several years ago, Singapore's authorities embarked on a policy of rapid wage increases which, until the late 1970s, had not been allowed to exceed the pace of inflation. One of the main justifications for engineering this wage explosion was to force domestic and foreign firms to move up the ladder of comparative advantage and undertake production of more sophisticated goods while abandoning labour-intensive commodities. This particular episode clearly shows that higher dimensions of the trade model are of keen interest not only to trade theorists but also to policy makers.

3. Other higher-dimensional findings

So far I have discussed specific departures from the Heckscher-Ohlin model. I wish to conclude this section by briefly mentioning several important studies and, in particular, Deardorff (1980, 1982) and Dixit and Norman (1980). The essence of their contribution is that, in higher dimensions, correlation between autarkic commodity price differences and import volumes, and between autarkic factor-price differentials and the factor content of imports, holds only on average. For example, a capital-rich country only tends to import labour-intensive goods; it could happen that its imports also contain some capital-intensive goods. Stated in other words, this means that a country may import some goods in which it actually has a comparative advantage.

Another important generalisation is due to Ethier (1974), who demonstrated that if the price of one produced good goes up, the real return to some factor must rise. If this factor is also employed in another industry, the real return on some other factor must fall. This result is very general and it holds for any number of goods and any number of factors. To identify the loser(s) and the winner(s) requires imposing some restrictive assumptions on the productive structure of the economy.

III. International trade under imperfect competition

It has been recognised for a long time that the world economy does not consist of small and powerless countries nor is any single economy a collection of atomistic firms. A substantial literature on the optimal tariff in the presence of monopoly power and numerous writings on tariff wars testify to the willingness of trade theorists to depart from the competitive paradigm. Yet, it is only during the last few years that monopolistic competition has become one of the central subjects of trade theory.

The most immediate reason for this increased interest in non-competitive market structures can be attributed to the alleged failure of the Heckscher-Ohlin model to explain the existence of intra-industry trade. Reality has not borne out the prediction of the standard model that trade flows should be most intensive between countries with substantial differences in factor endowments. As Grubel and Lloyd (1975) demonstrated in their pioneering study, the bulk of international trade occurs between countries with similar factor endowments and particularly among the highly developed economies. Furthermore, this trade is not inter- but intra-industry. Thus the UK, for instance, exports cars to France, Germany, Italy, Sweden and the United States and at the same time imports motor vehicles from the same destinations. The same is true for just about any industrial product. Intra-industry trade consists of flows in similar but not identical goods. Jaguar, BMW, Mercedes, Volvo and Cadillac, to pick only one segment of the car industry, are sold to customers with similar incomes, yet they have their distinctive characteristics. This fact is often underlined by the producers.

1. Trade in one good

I intend to give a short exposition of several models which aim to explain intra-industry trade and then discuss some general issues related to monopolistic competition in international trade. Let me start off with the simplest model comprising two countries and a single good. The model has been developed by Brander (1981), Brander and Spencer (1984) and Brander and Krugman (1983) and it establishes that market structure alone (independent of technology, taste and endowment differences), suffices to generate international trade. In this one-good model all trade has, of course, an intra-industry character.

Assume that under autarky the domestic market in each country is supplied by a monopolist. The familiar condition equating the marginal cost with marginal revenue establishes equilibrium prices and quantities. For the time being suppose that the marginal cost, c, is constant. Now, what happens when free trade is allowed between the two countries? It would seem that there is no apparent reason for trade because there is just one good. To make trade even more difficult introduce international transportation costs, *à la* Samuelson. As the good is shipped abroad a fraction, g (where $O < g < 1$) of it melts on its way, like an iceberg. In spite of these difficulties, the Brander model does generate trade, as will be seen shortly.

In order to complete the specification, the demand conditions have to be spelled out. This is done in equations (3) and (4)

$$P_1 = a - b(X_{11} + X_{21}) \qquad (3)$$
$$P_2 = a - b(X_{12} + X_{22}) \qquad (4)$$

The demand functions are taken to be linear and are written in an inverted form. X_{ij} denotes the quantity of the good sold by the producer located in country i and selling in market j (i,j = 1,2). The expressions in the parentheses of equations (3) and (4) denote the aggregate quantity of the good made available in each market.

Given the above equations, the profit functions for each of the duopolists can be written as:

$$\pi_1 = P_1 X_{11} + P_2 X_{12} - c(X_{11} + 1/g \, X_{12}) - F \qquad (5)$$
$$\pi_2 = P_1 X_{21} + P_2 X_{22} - c(X_{22} + 1/g \, X_{21}) - F \qquad (6)$$

The profit functions also contain fixed costs, F, in addition to variable costs.

Now enter the crucial assumption of the Brander model: the producers are said to play a Cournot strategy. Each producer decides how much to supply to each market believing that his competitor's behaviour will not alter as a result of his actions. Differentiating equations (5) and (6) with respect to X_{11}, X_{12}, X_{21}, and X_{22} gives four reaction functions (two for each market) which determine the equilibria of the system. The assumption of constant marginal costs permits a look at each market separately.

Figure 12.4 illustrates the results of the model for country 1. The reaction function of the domestic product is represented by $R_1 R_1$ and that of the foreign producer by $R_2 R_2$. (The picture for the market of country 2 is symmetric). Equilibrium is established at E and it is stable given the slopes of the two reaction functions. It can be readily seen that the market is split between the two duopolists, with the domestic firm enjoying a

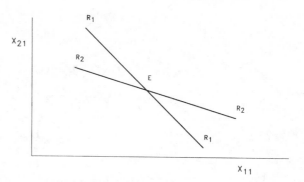

Figure 12.4. The Brander model

bigger share of sales. (A 50–50 split would occur if transportation costs were zero).

The driving force behind this model is the desire of each producer to invade the foreign market. Trade increases the degree of competition, indeed there are now two competing duopolists rather than two separate monopolistic systems. As a result, prices tend to fall and consumers in both countries are better off. Gains from competition may more than compensate social losses involved in sending the same good back and forth across the border.

One possible and very interesting extension of this model is to assume decreasing rather than constant marginal costs. As a firm produces more, it does so more cheaply. Krugman (1984) showed that under these circumstances protection of the domestic market allows the local producer to become more efficient and, hence, more competitive abroad. Tariffs can thus serve as a double-edged instrument for protection of the domestic market and for export promotion.

2. Characteristic approach to differentiated products

As I pointed out earlier, intra-industry trade seems to involve similar but not identical products and, therefore, considerable efforts have been made to develop an appropriate model. Lancaster (1979) developed the so-called characteristics approach to demand for variety. Helpman (1981) and Lancaster (1980) have shown how the interaction of demand for variety with increasing-returns-to-scale technology results in intra-industry trade. Their models are cast in terms of general equilibrium.

Assume that there are two industries: one producing a standard good and another producing differentiated products. Both sectors use labour and capital as the

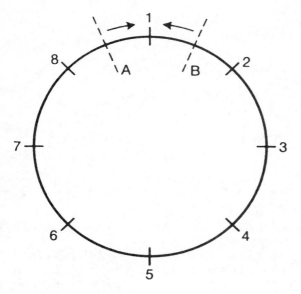

Figure 12.5. Equilibrium in the Helpman model

factors of production. The production function for the homogenous good is characterised by constant returns, while in the differentiated goods sector production of each model offers economies of scale. Models can be distinguished by a characteristic defined for simplicity along a unit circle, such as Figure 12.5.

With regard to the demand side, each consumer is assumed to have a preferred model of the differentiated good. Imagine now that in a closed economy the consumers are uniformly distributed along the unit circle. Each point on it represents the desired model for some individuals. The individual utility function favours consumption of the desired model, however the consumer can do with a less-than-ideal specification if that's what is available. In fact, a sufficiently lower price of an alternative model would make him give up the desired model.

If an infinite number of models of the differentiated good are demanded, why not produce them? The existence of increasing returns to scale prevents this outcome happening. Only a limited number of models will be produced. The exact number depends on the demand functions, production technology and the size of the market. Every model will be produced by only one firm. In Figure 12.5, the equilibrium in the closed economy is shown with eight different specifications. As cost functions are assumed identical and the consumers are uniformly distributed along the circumference of the circle, the prices of these models will be the same. Furthermore, the producers will be spaced equidistant between themselves, each capturing the same fraction of the total market. Thus producer of model 1, for instance, will attract all consumers in the AB segment of the market. Points A and B are located exactly half-distance in between 1 and 8 and 1 and 2, respectively. The marginal consumers at A and B are indifferent between neighbouring models. Of course, the consumers whose preferred specification is given by point 1 are better off, in the absence of price discrimination, than those whose preferences are located some distance from it.

The consequence of opening to foreign trade can now be analysed readily. When the market expands, more models can be produced. So the new equilibrium must involve greater variety. Each model can be produced by only one firm, either domestic or foreign. The expansion of the market also allows producers to increase output of each variety. Hence, the gains to the consumers in this model involve greater choice and lower prices. Of course, distributional effects are likely to be present as well, but this model has too much symmetry built into it to pin down the actual location of firms either in the closed or open economy equilibrium.

A powerful feature of the Helpman-Lancaster model is that it allows countries to trade differentiated and homogeneous goods and hence inter- and intra-industry trade can co-exist. If the differentiated products are relatively capital-intensive, the capital rich country can be shown to export more of them than it imports. The country well-endowed with labour runs a deficit in differentiated products which it covers by exporting the standard good. This shows that factor endowments do matter but other things matter as well. It is clear, however, that to explain the co-existence of inter- and intra-industry trade one needs two independent reasons for trade. The combination of Heckscher-Ohlin and monopolistic competition is only one alternative.

3. Love of variety approach to differentiated products

Dixit and Stiglitz (1977) developed a different approach to modelling demand for differentiated products. The approach was applied to international trade by Krugman (1979, 1981, 1982) and Dixit and Norman (1980). In their formulation, every individual loves variety and would like to consume as many types of differentiated products as possible. Assume for simplicity, that there is no outside good and that the individual utility function is of the following form:

$$U = \sum v(C_i) \qquad v' > 0, \quad v'' > 0 \qquad (7)$$

where C_i denotes consumption of the ith good by the representative consumer. An important property of this function is that if n goods were available, all of them would be demanded by every individual. Furthermore, if an individual consumer were offered additional goods, *ceteris paribus*, he would gladly buy them and his welfare would increase. In contrast with the Helpman-Lancaster approach, demand for variety already exists at the micro-level.

In modelling the supply side, assume that labour is the only factor of production and write the production functions in inverted form:

$$L_i = \alpha + \beta x_i \qquad (8)$$

where L_i stands for the amount of labour required to produce the ith commodity. Equation (8) reveals the existence of increasing returns to scale. For a large fixed labour cost, α, one would expect only a small number of goods to be produced.

In determining the equilibrium number of products in the closed economy one needs to invoke the condition equating marginal cost and marginal revenue in every sub-market:

$$P_i(x_i)(1 - 1/e_i) = \beta w \qquad (9)$$

where e_i is the elasticity of demand facing the ith producer. The elasticity depends on the specification of the utility function of the representative consumer. In the Chamberlinian world of monopolistic competition, each producer attempts to create pure profits, yet free entry leads to the equality of the total revenue with the total cost of production of the good.

$$P_i x_i = (\alpha + \beta x_i) w \qquad (10)$$

Equations (9) and (10) suffice to determine the level of output of each firm as well as the real wage rate. The full employment condition for labour then gives the number of firms in the closed economy.

Introduction of trade implies that more products can be produced in the integrated market than in either of the two countries in isolation. Once again, gains from trade may involve not only greater variety but also lower prices as economies of scale are realised when every firm increases output.

The model can be modified to analyse North-South trade issues. Dixit (1984) focused on the question of North-South terms of trade. Production of differentiated products requires an intermediate good which is produced in developing countries under constant-returns-to-scale technology. Developed coutries produce differentiated goods and enjoy monopoly power. Growth in the North increases demand for intermediate goods and improves the South's terms of trade. Labour expansion in developing countries has the opposite effect, but even then, welfare losses stemming from adverse price changes can be more than compensated by increased variety.

Dynamic effects are pursued in Krugman (1979). New products can be introduced in the market, not instantaneously, as in the basic model, but only over time. Product innovation takes place in the North. However, the South eventually learns how to produce new goods and can do it more cheaply. A technological gap gives the North certain monopoly power and is responsible for trade. Developing countries export 'old' products and developed countries specialise in 'new' products, with the division between the old and the new shifting continuously. Product innovation can also explain why per capita incomes differ between countries. However, in order to maintain an income differential the North has to keep innovating.

Product innovation, technological competition and dynamic economies of scale are becoming a central issue in the new trade literature. In particular, the concept of the so-called learning curve developed by Spence (1981) has found application in several trade models. It is assumed that in certain industries large current output can help to reduce production costs in the future. If this is indeed the case, then protection of the domestic market (or export subsidies) today can make the home industry more competitive later on in foreign markets. The mechanism is really quite similar to that evoked in the Brander model with decreasing marginal costs, except that the effects are spread over time.

4. New trade models and commercial policy

I have attempted to convey the flavour of the new trade literature by singling out several important contributions. Should these new models give rise to new thinking about commercial policy? While in the traditional framework free trade tended to be the best solution, the recent wave of research produced numerous examples where government intervention can dominate laissez-faire policy. This should not after all be a surprising finding. Non-competitive market situations usually call for some policy intervention. However, this need not imply that the case for free trade is buried. As a general methodological issue, it is not enough to demonstrate that a commercial policy measure can improve welfare. One has to show that trade interference is the best form of intervention. So far, I have not seen this accomplished frequently in a convincing way.

A case for intervention can be made where monopoly profits can be shared between the home and the foreign country as in the Brander model. However, one has to remember that this model is based on the Cournot strategy. It is hard to find an example of a monopolistic industry where firms decide on quantities and not on prices. Once firms are allowed to compete in prices, the case for intervention goes by the board. Equally disconcerting is the assumption that firms totally lack anticipation of some response from competitors when they made their strategic decisions. Alternative assumptions regarding firms' conjectural variations produce vastly different outcomes with vastly different optimal policies. But even within the rules of the game of the Cournot model, Dixit (1984) demonstrated that the justification for an export subsidy loses its power when the number of firms is even moderately increased.

In the Helpman-Lancaster and Dixit-Krugman models, profits are driven to zero so the argument for intervention needs to be based on the ability to affect the terms of trade. But this is, of course, an old argument and product differentiation does not bring in new elements. I should add, however, that this strand of literature has greatly enriched welfare analysis by identifying a new and, possibly, a very important source of gains from trade. There is, of course, a larger issue of socially optimal product diversity.

It would seem that the strongest case for trade policy intervention arises in the context of technological spillovers generated by some sectors for the rest of the economy. Those 'strategic' sectors, if they indeed exist, could clearly have special value for the economy. But as Krugman (1986) put it 'Are there "strategic" activities in the economy, where labour and capital either directly receive a higher return than they could elsewhere or generate special benefits for the rest of the economy? This is the question on which old and new thinking about trade differs.'

The identification of 'strategic' sectors becomes a formidable task. Unfortunately, they are not listed in the Yellow Pages, nor can they be readily spotted based on available market information. Furthermore, it is not really 'strategic' industries that the policy makers would wish to single out for a special treatment but individual firms, small or large, with great market potential. I, for one, would be willing to accept that policy makers in Washington, DC could have had enough wisdom to realise at an early stage that the personal-computer industry was such a strategic activity. But even this is not certain. I am much less certain that a small firm run out of a garage—it will be realised that I am making a reference to the Apple company—could have been identified as a future market leader. New industrial (rather than commercial) policy towards 'strategic' industries would involve many policy misses, just like betting on horses. Furthermore, helping some firms or sectors bids up the rental of factors jointly shared with other producers and this constitutes a form of reverse protection.

In entertaining new commercial strategies, one should not forget a valuable lesson from an area of international trade theory which I do not have enough space to discuss here, namely the political economy of protection. Prospects of government hand-outs are likely to encourage firms to invest resources in seeking them. This process would create unproductive activities and further cloud the economic landscape from which to pick winners.

Having said all this, I wish to counter the view that questions the research value of new trade theories. It would be a pity if trade economists refrained from exploring alternative models because their work can be misused by policy makers and others. What needs to be stressed is the very tentative nature of these models, the fragility of their results and the difficulties of formulating and implementing new policies.

IV. A new challenge: trade in services

Let me now turn to a topic which is, in my view, on the point of attracting a great deal of attention from trade theorists, i.e., international trade in services. The issue of trade in services has been very much in the minds of international trade negotiators as they strive to launch a new round of negotiations. But deregulation of certain industries, most notably banking and insurance, also has important international aspects which have not escaped the attention of policy makers.

It may be useful to start off with a brief classification of the effects of human economic activities and their status with regard to international transactions. This is done in the figure below.

We use resources to produce goods or services which can be either consumed domestically or traded internationally. Perhaps quite naturally, international trade

	Traded	Non-traded
Goods	1	2
Services	3	4

Figure 12.6. Trade classification

theorists put most of their research efforts into square one. (The pun is not intended). Yet, at one stage, it was also important to bring non-traded goods into the analysis and see how their existence affected the basic trade theorems. Curiously enough there was a basic consensus that most services are in square four. Perhaps for this reason the field of services became a *chasse gardee* of development economists. The main themes of their investigations have been the role of services in the development process, the relative share of tertiary production in national income, and productivity in service sectors.

There have been some notable exceptions to the general neglect of services by trade theorists. Bhagwati (1984), for instance, provided an explanation for the well-established fact that the relative price of services is higher in the developed than in the developing countries. The explanation can be related to the models of Jones (1974) and Krueger (1977) discussed earlier. The basic argument is that factor endowments differ substantially between countries and hence the factor-price equalisation theorem does not hold. If service industries employ labour intensively, production costs should be higher in the countries well endowed with capital.

What determines the line of demarcation between traded and non-traded goods, and services? And, why is it that the latter seem to be produced to a greater extent for the domestic market? In both cases the key may lie in obstacles to trade, such as high transportation costs, tariffs and quotas which prevent international exchange from materialising. In addition, certain physical characteristics of goods and services may render them non-tradable. To elaborate on the last point, it will be useful to refer to the classification of service transactions suggested by Bhagwati (1985) and Sampson and Snape (1985). They distinguish various groups of transactions according to the physical proximity of the suppliers and the receivers of services:

1. Transactions which can be executed at arms length, i.e. suppliers and receivers of services can be geographically separated. An individual living in New York can obtain an insurance policy from Lloyd's of London without having to be in London or without the insurance company being present in New York.
2. Transactions which require the receiver to move, at least temporarily, to the country where a particular service is provided. International tourism is a case in point.
3. Transactions involving movement of factors of production to the country where a service is provided. Development of a coal mine in Brazil requires a foreign constructor to be on the site.
4. Transactions occuring in a third country where neither the supplier not the receiver reside. An American bank established in London can undertake financial operations for, say, an Australian customer.

I find this classification illuminating because it shows that many so-called trade transactions actually involve no trade but international movements of factors of production. Only the first category of service transactions is comparable with trade in goods. The obstacles to the exchange of services between countries, thus consist not only of trade measures but also of limits to foreign investment, rights of establishment, visa requirements and so on. It is quite clear that complete liberalisation of the international exchange of services would also, or even primarily, involve removal of obstacles to factor movements. Bhagwati (1984) pointed out that technological progress allows more and more services to be traded, just like goods, by relaxing the requirement of physical proximity. Advances in telecommunications and information sectors rendered many banking and insurance services tradeable at long distances. But in other sectors, the natural barriers will continue to limit direct trade in services for a long time to come.

Explanation of trade in services calls for application of the theoretical apparatus of international trade theory. The question can be asked whether the existing models are suitable for the problem at hand. Hindley and Smith (1984) argued forcefully that the theory of comparative advantage is equally applicable to goods and services. The fact that services differ from goods does not imply a need to construct new theoretical models. Indeed some researchers used the standard Heckscher-Ohlin model to provide an explanation for the existing trade patterns in services. In particular, Sapir and Lutz (1981) attempted to explain net service trade flows in freight, insurance and passenger services of developed and developing countries by using variables related to factor endowments. Their results suggest that the Heckscher-Ohlin model has some explanatory power but quite a lot of trade remains unexplained.

One of the challenges facing trade economists is to fully incorporate services into Heckscher-Ohlin and other models. The task is not as trivial as it may seem because it demands careful articulation of the characteristics of the service and its market conditions. To explain this point more fully let me turn to the model developed by Findlay and Kierzkowski (1983).

The Findlay-Kierzkowski model investigates the formation of human capital through educational services. Its structure is relatively simple; it involves two goods-producing industries, and an educational sector. The goods, X and Y, are produced with neo-classical functions, each using two factors of production—skilled and unskilled labour. No physical capital is required in the X and Y industries but this simplifying assumption is of no great importance and it could be relaxed. The total population is stationary, however, N individuals are born every period and N die. All individuals are alike and they all live T periods.

Each individual has a choice of either entering the labour force immediately and working as an unskilled worker with the wage rate w_u, or acquiring education to be employed later as skilled labour at the wage rate of w_s. It takes n periods to pass through the educational system.

Turning to the educational system, assume that it is located in Oxford and consists of a large number of colleges. The colleges with their fellows, rich libraries and beautiful buildings constitute a specific factor of production, K, which cannot be used elsewhere in the economy. The total amount of human capital produced in Oxford is governed by the neo-classical production function: $Q = F(K,E)$ where E is the number of students enrolled in the educational system. This production function has the normal properties. With K historically given, an increase in E causes Q to rise. However, as the number of students expands, the system gets overcrowded so the amount of human capital generated per student, Q/E, is reduced.

Let us assume that each college behaves like a perfectly competitive firm charging the students a tuition fee. No entry restrictions exist, so as many individuals as wish to can acquire education. The three important questions to ask at this stage are: How many students will want to come to Oxford every year? What is the total stock of skilled labour in the economy? Finally, how high are the tuition fees? The tuition fees charged by a competitive college should be equal to the contribution of K to the future earning power of an individual, that is:

$$\int_n^T w_s F_K(K,E) \, (K/E) e^{-rt} dt \qquad (11)$$

where r is the discount rate. Tuition fees are only one element of total individual costs of acquiring education, the other being lost income during the period when a person is in Oxford and also foregone future income as an unskilled worker. The benefit of having obtained education is the discounted stream of w_s to be earned during the period from n to T. An individual will decide to invest in education if the benefits at least cover the costs. However, given the fact that the colleges in Oxford are assumed to be competitive and there are no enrolment limits, the equilibrium requires that property discounted costs and benefits are equal for each and every individual. This can be shown to happen when:

$$w_u/w_s = F_K \, (e^{-rn} - e^{-rT})/(1 - e^{-rT}) \qquad (12)$$

Now the system can be closed by noting that w_u and w_s are known, once the prices of X and Y are given. Consequently the above condition determines the number of new entrants into the colleges. The total number of educated people must be equal to nE.

It becomes a rather simple matter to demonstrate that, *ceteris paribus*, a country with a larger stock of educational capital or a lower discount rate, will end up having more skilled labour. Consequently, when trade in goods is allowed this country will specialise in exporting the skill-intensive commodity X and importing Y. The relative factor endowment has been endogenised in this model. The pattern of trade is based on the Heckscher-Ohlin mechanism.

Returning to the proximity classification of international transactions in services discussed earlier, it is clear that the first type of exchange cannot occur in the industry under discussion. However, any of the remaining types of transactions are, in principle, possible. Educational services cannot be traded (at least not yet), so liberalisation of educational services would have to involve eliminating restrictions on international movement of the educational capital, K, or the international movement of students. The important question to ask is whether such a liberalisation would be welfare increasing. Note first of all that even with free trade in goods, factor prices will not be equalised between countries because the world stock of K is unequally distributed. The return on K in England should be lower than in the countries poorly endowed with this factor. Free movement of K would thus increase world welfare by improving the allocation of resources.

It is, of course, true that although Oxford fellows may be internationally mobile, the Bodleian Library cannot be displaced. Under these circumstances, international mobility of students would be a perfect substitute for movement of the educational composite factor.

One way or another, England would be earning income from foreign countries by exporting educational services. One implication of this analysis is that the UK would have a deficit in goods trade. Another would be that the average amount of human capital per British citizen would be lowered. It is interesting to note that some general implications of this model are similar to the predictions of the consequences of Big Bang.

A conclusion to be drawn at this point is that services can be incorporated into the traditional trade framework by articulation of the Heckscher-Ohlin model. But as I stated before this requires some care in specifying the nature of a particular service and of demand and supply conditions. Furthermore, given the nature of some services transactions, the standard trade model has to be combined with the theory of foreign investment. Similar attempts could be made with regard to such services as banking and insurance. Quite clearly, however, risk would have to be introduced into the analysis.

There are, however, alternative ways of modelling services well worth pursuing. Many service sectors are non-competitive and therefore the insight of the 'new' trade models discussed in Section III can prove very valuable in this context. Telecommunications, shipping and computer services are clear examples of oligopolistic market structures. Furthermore, it seems that the nature of certain services requires a variant of the Lancasterian characteristic specification of demand and not the traditional approach. All this remains to be done.

V. Conclusion

In conclusion, let me cite again from Corden's (1965) critical review of the international trade theory. 'The pure-theory models usually assume "perfect competition"; in fact this could be restated as an assumption of equal degrees of monopoly, and when restated in this way is a reasonable first approximation which then requires modification for particular circumstances. Other assumptions—such as two factors, two products, two countries, internal factor mobility and international immobility—are not always necessary to sustain the main conclusions, though they are often necessary to provide simple but rigorous proofs'. If nothing else, international trade economists have demonstrated in the course of the last three decades their willingness to explore alternative assumptions. In doing so they have provided a greater variety of models

and—in a curious way—strengthened the basic framework which they had been so reluctant to abandon.

The emergence of a large number of international trade models means different predictions and policy conclusions. As a result, the international trade economist of today, and most likely tomorrow, would be well advised to be cautious in giving policy advice or analysing consequences of an economic change. Perhaps paradoxically, I see this development as stengthening rather than weakening the position of the theorist vis-a-vis the policy maker.

Finally, the rapid expansion of the field of international trade and the emergence of alternative theories call for an intensification of empirical research. Alternative models need to be tested to help further development of the theory and to provide guidance in making policy recommendations.

Postscript

The above essay, originally written in the fall of 1986, showed the field of international trade theory as it was entering a new stage of its development. It was an exciting time to do research, exploring new theoretical possibilities and looking for surprising results. The 'new' trade theory has now come of age and is more complete in that its original focus on imperfect competition, product differentiation and intra-industry trade has been considerably widened. I can only briefly indicate the main directions of research and cite important writings. For a very thorough and masterly overview of recent developments and their integration with the traditional trade theory the reader can do no better than consult Ronald Findlay (1995).

The new growth theory and the new trade theory have come to prominence at about the same time and it was only natural for the latter to incorporate insights of the former. We knew and appreciated the importance of technological progress as a source of economic growth at least since the late 1950s when Denison, Kendrick and Solow begun their search for explanation of the so-called growth residual. However, bringing in imperfect competition and increasing returns to scale has given the modern growth theory a completely new dimension. And trade theorists were quick to incorporate an endogenous process of technological change and product innovation into their models. The work of Grossman and Helpman, 1992) focused on economic determinants of technical progress and showed how comparative advantage can evolve over time. While the trade theorists borrowed from others they also gave others something back in return, namely an analysis which is general equilibrium in its scope.

It is interesting to note that the growth theorists went on to explore the question of economic convergence in time and space while the trade theorists (re)discovered the importance of geography in explaining the location of production in different regions and inter-regional flows of goods. Paul Krugman has, once again, led the way and 'new economic geography' has come into being. (See Krugman, 1991.) The basic result of geography/trade models is that economic divergence may often occur under sufficiently strong increasing returns to scale and low transportation costs. Certain regions emerge as industrial hubs and, once in that position, they tend to dominate industrial production for a long time to come. Do we observe economic divergence or convergence in the real world? Think of possible scenarios for ex-East Germany or reforming countries of Eastern Europe. Surely, this question is of utmost importance and it calls for solid empirical work to be carried out.

Unfortunately, I cannot report outstanding empirical results obtained as a result of new theoretical work of the last ten years or so. Perhaps this is so because it is no longer possible to make as powerful predictions as within the Heckscher-Ohlin or Ricardian models.

References

Bhagwati, J. (1985), 'International Trade in Services and its relevance for Economic Development', Xth Annual Lecture of the Geneva Association held at the London School of Economics, November, London.

—— (1984), 'Why are Services Cheaper in the Poor Countries', *Economic Journal*, June, 279–286.

Brander, J. (1981), 'Intra-industry Trade in Identical Commodities', *Journal of International Economics*, Vol. 11, 1–14.

—— and P. Krugman (1983), 'A Reciprocal Dumping Model of International Trade', *Journal of International Economics*.

—— and B. Spencer (1984), 'Tariff Protection and Imperfect Competition', in H. Kierzkowski, ed., *Monopolistic Competition and International Trade*, Oxford University Press, Oxford, 313–321.

Corden, W. M. (1965), *Recent Developments in the Theory of International Trade*, Special Papers in International Economics, Princeton University.

Deardorff, A. (1980), 'The General Validity of the Law of Comparative Advantage', *Journal of Political Economy*, Vol. 80, October, 941–957.

—— (1982), 'The General Validity of the Beckscher-Ohlin Theorem', *American Economic Review*, Vol. 72, 683–694.

Dixit, A., and J. Stiglitz (1977), 'Monopolistic Competition and Optimum Product Variety', *American Economic Review*, Vol. 67, 297–308.

—— and V. Norman (1980), *Theory of International Trade*, Cambridge University Press, Cambridge.

—— (1984), 'International Trade Policy for Oligopolistic Industries', *Economic Journal*, Supplement, 1–15.

—— (1984), 'Growth and Terms of Trade under Imperfect Competition', in H. Kierzkowski, ed., *Monopolistic Competition and International Trade*, Oxford University Press, Oxford.

Ethier, H. (1974), 'Some of the Theorems of International Trade with many Goods and Factors', *Journal of International Economics*, Vol. 4, May, 199–206.

Findlay, R. (1995), *Factor Proportions, Trade and Growth*, MIT Press.

—— and H. Kierzkowski (1983), 'International Trade and Human Capital: A Simple General Equilibrium Model', *Journal of Political Economy*, Vol. 91, December, 957–978.

Grossman, G., and Helpman, E. (1992), *Innovation and Growth in the Global Economy*, MIT Press.

Grubel, H., and P. Lloyd (1975), *Intra-industry Trade: The Theory and Measurement of International Trade in Differentiated Products*, Macmillan, London.

Helpman, E. (1981), 'International Trade in the Presence of Product Differentiation, Economies of Scale, and Monopolistic Competition', *Journal of International Economics*, Vol. 11, 305–340.

Hindley, B., and A. Smith (1984), 'Comparative Advantage and Trade in Services', *The World Economy*, Vol. 7, December, 369–389.

Jones, R. W. (1971), 'A Three-Factor Model in Theory, Trade and History', in J. Bhagwati *et al.*, eds., *Trade, Balance of Payments, and Growth: Essays in Honor of Charles P. Kindleberger*, North-Holland, Amsterdam.

—— (1974), 'The Small Country in a Multi-Commodity World', *Australian Economic Papers*, Vol. 13, December, 225–236.

—— (1975), 'Income Distribution and Effective Protection in a Multi-Commodity Trade Model', *Journal of Economic Theory*, Vol. 11, 1–15.

—— and H. Kierzkowski (1986), 'Neighbourhood Production Structures, with an Application to the Theory of International Trade', *Oxford Economic Papers*, Vol. 38, 59–76.

Krueger, A. (1977), *Growth, Distortions and Patterns of Trade Among Many Countries*, Princeton Studies in International Finance, No. 40, Princeton University.

Krugman, P. (1979), 'A Model of Innovation, Technology Transfer and the World Distribution of Income', *Journal of Political Economy*, Vol. 87, 253–266.

—— (1984), 'Import Protection as Export Promotion: International Competition in the Presence of Oligopoly and Economies of Scale', in H. Kierzkowski, ed., *Monopolistic Competition and International Trade*, Oxford University Press, Oxford.

—— (1986), 'Introduction: New Thinking about Trade Policy', in P. Krugman, ed., *Strategic Trade Policy and*

New International Economics, MIT Press, Cambridge, Massachusetts.

—— (1991), *Geography and Trade*, MIT Press.

Lancaster, K. (1979), *Variety, Equity and Efficiency*, Blackwell, Oxford.

—— (1980), 'Intra-industry Trade under Monopolistic Competition', *Journal of International Economics*, Vol. 10, 151–175.

Leamer, E. (1980), 'The Leontief Paradox Reconsidered', *Journal of Political Economy*, June, 495–503.

—— (1984), *Sources of International Comparative Advantage*, MIT Press, Cambridge, Massachusetts.

Leontief, H. (1953), 'Domestic Production and Foreign Trade: The American Capital Position Re-examined', *Proceedings of the American Philosophical Society*, September, 322–349.

Mayer, W. (1974), 'Short-run and Long-run Equilibrium for a Small Open Economy', *Journal of Political Economy*, Vol. 82, 955–967.

Mussa, M. (1974), 'Tariffs and the Distribution of Income: The Importance of Factor Specificity; Substitutability, and Intensity in the Short and Long Run', *Journal of Political Economy*, Vol. 82, 1191–1204.

Neary, J. P. (1978), 'Short-run Capital Specificity and the Pure Theory of International Trade', *Economic Journal*, Vol. 88, 488–510.

Sampson, G., and R. Snape (1985), 'Identifying the Issues in Trade in Services', *The World Economy*, Vol. 8, June, 171–182.

Sapir, A., and E. Lutz (1981), 'Trade in Services: Economic Determinants and Development-related Issues', World Bank Staff Working Paper, World Bank, Washington.

Spence, M. (1981), 'The Learning Curve and Competition', *Bell Journal of Economics*, Vol. 12, 49–70.

13

The new trade theory and economic policy

CHRISTOPHER BLISS[1]

Nuffield College, Oxford

I. Trade theory and experience

In recent years trade theory has enjoyed a great revival. Ten years ago I would tell a student who enquired what to read on trade theory to look at Bhagwati and Corden, certainly, and best of all, if he could manage it, Chipman.[2] Even at that time these works were many years old, but they still contained excellent expositions of most of the pure trade theory that a student needed to know. In 1980 there appeared a book which insisted on its inclusion in my core reading list. Dixit & Norman (1980) provided a fresh approach to trade theory, treated several topics at a higher level of generality than had been usual previously, and did more than any other work to establish the duality approach. However, much of what Dixit & Norman offered was already present, although differently exposited, in those older sources.

These works catalogued a trade theory and brought its presentation to a point of high perfection. However, a trade theorist who fell asleep in 1960 and woke up in 1980 would have found himself, once he had decoded some new terminology and mastered new approaches, in a rather familiar world. The same would not have been the case for a similarly comatose balance-of-payments theorist, still less for a macro-economic theorist, who would have awoken to find their fields transformed.

Historians of thought, including economic thought, tend to explain periods of relative intellectual stagna-tion in terms of a lack of the stimulus provided by new problems and new questions. Thus one could argue that almost any economic theory, and particularly a beautiful one, will command acceptance provided that it is neither in clear conflict with current observations nor wholly unable to address questions to which people would like answers.[3] The theory may well develop and enrich itself under its own momentum, but it usually takes new observations or anomalous findings to generate exciting new departures.

The pure trade theory which had matured by the 1960s really had two branches between which it is important to distinguish. To put it crudely, there was a high-brow version and a low-brow version. In the high-brow version there were many different goods and factors and a more general mathematical specification. The low-brow version always had smooth production functions and just two factors (called labour, and capital or land). The high-brow version was superior in terms of generality and elegance, but the low-brow version nearly always came out on top because it could obtain definite results where the high-brow version often lead to ambiguity.[4] We shall refer to these two versions of the theory as respectively the general model and the standard model.

Broadly speaking, events of the 1960s and 1970s did not pose great difficulties for received trade theory. Trade was increasing at an unprecedented rate in a

---

First published in *Oxford Review of Economic Policy*, vol. 3, no. 1 (1987).

[1] Before completing this article I was fortunate to have access to Henryk Kierzkowski's paper (also included in this volume). He therefore deserves both a genuine acknowledgment for help received and a total acquittal from blame for any errors in my own piece.

[2] The references are to: Bhagwtai (1969), Corden (1965) and Chipman (1965–66).

[3] Thomas Kuhn (1962) has described the origin of a paradigm change in science as being partly the inability of existing science to explain current observations.

[4] There was a deep mathematical reason for this. Some of the underlying concepts of the standard model did not generalise beyond the two by two case. With two goods and two factors, for example, each good must use a particular factor intensively relative to the other good. With three goods and three factors this pairing of goods and factors may not occur.

fairly liberal environment. Most trading nations seemed to gain from trade. The successful development of the European Common Market (ECM) gave pause for thought, as it plainly involved a great deal of trade diversion, but as the standard model could be extended to treat customs unions and to illustrate trade diversion, this development did not seem particularly threatening to received theory. Above all, economic theorists and policy makers took more or less the same view: that trade was beneficial and protection harmful, and that some customs unions could be a good thing.

It is true that difficulties associated with trade seemed to increase during the period. Certain countries, among them Britain, suffered from chronic balance of payments difficulties, the Bretton Woods system collapsed under the strains caused by inflation and profligate expenditure by the United States, and trade did not involve the less developed countries in a manner which was always felt to be beneficial and successful. However, none of these problems seemed to arise from sources which had to be identified as shortcomings of the pure trade model. The difficulties with the Bretton Woods system surely arose from the system itself, or from the inflationary policies adopted by governments. If the *raison d'etre* of the ECM was not factor-endowment based comparative advantage, the ECM was at least consistent with other kinds of comparative advantage. Moreover economies of scale were widely felt to be important and were used to justify Britain's entry to the ECM. True they were not included in the pure trade model in either its general or its standard versions, but they seemed intuitively to reinforce the case for specialisation. Finally, the experience of the less developed countries could be seen as providing an object lesson in the benefits of comparative advantage and of the costs of ignoring it as recklessly as many developing countries did.

It is instructive to contrast the way in which developments in trade left mainstream theory more or less untouched with what happened to macro-economics. There, as with trade theory, the 1960s was a period of consensus and what can now only be seen as complacency. The majority of economists in the Anglo-Saxon world adhered to some form of the Keynesian model, and a number of relationships seemed to be established and solid, among them the consumption function, the demand for money function and, most important for our present concerns, the Phillips curve. At the time of course the agreement did not always appear to be impressive. A great deal of controversy was generated by Milton Friedman, who promulgated a version of the Keynesian model which he claimed to be fundamentally different from the orthodox version, and which

went under the name of monetarism. These differences were not unimportant and in them lay the roots of later and far more fundamental changes in the views of macro-economic theorists. However, they disguised a very considerable amount of consensus. Certainly policy makers in the Anglo-Saxon countries were broadly in agreement with the Keynesian model and believed themselves to be regulating their economies by means of Keynesian demand management. It was a happy time for economic theorists and, as with trade theory, the same material was taught to students year after year, and old references were still relevant, indeed sometimes the best references were years old.

Then came the 1970s[5] and within the space of a few years the whole structure collapsed. The Phillips curve broke down, double-digit inflation arrived in the company of the highest levels of unemployment since the end of the Second World War, a new and ugly word was coined, 'stagflation', and macro-economic theory was pitched into the most radical revision of its assumptions and arguments since Keynes' *General Theory*. In revising their views theorists and econometricians were only doing the same as the policy makers, who likewise radically revised their understanding of how the economy functions. These changes were the inevitable result of new observations which did not fit the old theory.

Nothing similar happened to pure trade theory. The problems for trade, which were considerable, did not, as I have argued, seem to come from that direction. Also trade theory had developed much less than macro-economics in the direction of well-established econometric relations. Trade theory had no Phillips curve for experience to demolish. There had been attempts to test the theory empirically, most notably by Leontief in his study of the effect on the factor requirements of the US economy that would follow from displacing some international exchange.[6] This study seemed to show that US exports were more labour intensive than US imports, which was in contradiction to what the standard version of the trade model would lead one to expect. This result came to be known as the Leontief paradox, in recognition of the fact that it represented an anomaly in terms of the standard theory. However, pure trade theory had several lines of defence available, the most interesting of which was Leontief's own suggestion that when allowance was made for the greater efficiency of US labour, the United States was really a

---

[5] I am dividing the period into decades which provides a convenient short-hand for various time-spans. In fact stagflation began in the late 1960s. However, the response of theory and policy to this new phenomenon belongs largely to the 1970s.

[6] See Leontief (1954).

labour-abundant capital-scarce economy.[7] As there was no alternative theory that did explain the Leontief paradox, most people were more or less satisfied. This is typical. It takes theory to beat theory and a model never falls before its own negation.

Another observation that appeared to be damaging to received trade theory was provided by the European Common Market and the rapid growth in trade that followed upon its establishment. If trade was based on comparative advantage and comparative advantage was due to differences in factor endowments, as the standard model at least maintained, then what was the source of so much exchange between countries that seemed to have somewhat similar factor endowments? The consideration of this question did generate new theory, the product cycle model,[8] in which countries were allowed to have different technical possibilities in the short- or medium-term, due to the recent development in one or another country of a new product, although in the long-run no country could enjoy a technical advantage over any other in the production of a good.

Other developments in the new theory can also be attributed to experience. There was for example the observation that a large proportion of international trade came to be accounted for by large multinational companies. Regardless of the explanation for this fact, and an obvious one was the existence of economies of scale, it plainly carried the implication that the assumption of perfect competition which had been a feature of nearly all pure trade theory had to be dispensed with.

Another example of observation moving theory was provided by the study of the commodity composition of the high volume of trade between industrial countries. This revealed that even when detailed categories of goods were used, a great deal of two-way exchange was revealed. By two-way exchange is meant here that one country exported to another goods in a category from which it also imported from the same country. An obvious example was provided by passenger cars which were exported from most producing countries into all the same countries. Was this simply evidence that even after detailed classification of goods important differences remain, and if so what were the implications of that for a trade model?

It is not my intention to argue that all the recent advances in trade theory are due to observations that have called for a theoretical explanation. The relation between theory and observation is more subtle than that account would suggest, and theory sometimes moves forward 'under its own steam'. Trade theory has in part been the passive beneficiary of developments in other areas of economic theory, in industrial economics and game theory for example. However it probably is the case that the need for models to deal with new problems is what has enlivened trade theory and brought into it a new generation of theorists. It is the implication of their work for economic policy that will be considered in the following sections.

II. Theory and policy

No one can doubt that the old trade theory was elegant or that it absorbed the minds of a large number of outstanding economists. However most of its practitioners saw it, not as a game, but as a tool to use in understanding the world, and particularly as a means to making policy recommendations. What were the policy implications of the old theory? It is useful to divide these policy recommendations into those that were implied by nearly every version of the theory, and which were therefore implications of the general model, and those which were specific to the standard model.

The general policy implications of the trade model follow from the fact that the trade model is an instance of the allocation of economic resources, and as such is subject to the welfare economic principles which apply to all examples of resource allocation. The most powerful principle concerned goes under the name of *the fundamental theorem of welfare economics.*[9] This result states that any efficient allocation of resources may be supported by a price system. That means that all goods and factors will have prices, producers will maximise profit at those prices, and consumers will maximise (choose the best available consumption) given those prices and their incomes. The incomes of consumers will need to be adjusted to suit the particular allocation, so that each consumer can just afford the welfare level that the allocation assigns to him. As the income level assigned to a particular consumer may not correspond to the value of his resources and labour at the prices which support the allocation, this process may be interpreted as including lump-sum transfers of income between consumers.[10]

---

[7]   Another suggestion, that the role of natural resources, including climate, would explain the paradox was really an implicit criticism of the two goods and factors model. One reason why Leontief's findings had a relatively mild impact is that what had been tested was a particular version of a more general theory.

[8]   See Vernon (1966).

[9]   See Koopmans (1957).

[10]   The transfers are lump-sum because they cannot be related to many economic variables, such as income or labour supplied, without changing the optimising decision of the household.

We shall return to the implications of not allowing lump-sum transfers. However it is appropriate to postpone the consideration of that important issue because to a remarkable extent the policy implications of the pure trade model were developed under assumptions which amounted to the same thing as admitting lump-sum transfers. The most usual way in which the equivalent of lump-sum transfers gained admittance to the analysis was by the use of community indifference curves.[11] A community indifference curve has the same affect as reducing the preferences of the community to preferences exactly like those of a single maximising individual. As the preferences of the community, which are manifested in its final demand for goods, depend upon how income is distributed between its members, assuming community indifference curves clearly sets aside issues of income distribution between consumers. In general this cannot be justified[12] and results derived from that assumption are always limited in their application.

What follows for trade policy from the fundamental theorem? We note some leading results and then show how the fundamental theorem implies them. Important implications include:

(i) trade is gainful. In particular, free trade is superior to autarky (no trade);

(ii) for a small country, tariffs are inefficient. They impose a burden in the sense that they are a more costly way of redistributing income than are lump-sum transfers;

(iii) when a tariff is imposed on a good this can improve the welfare of a group only if it worsens the welfare level of another group.

To see how these results follow from the fundamental theorem, consider them in turn. First consider trade and whether it constitutes an improvement on no trade. We suppose an allocation without trade and ask whether it can be supported by some price system. If it cannot, we know that it is inefficient,[13] as every efficient allocation can be supported by a price system. If trade were permitted feasible allocations would include exchanges through international trade and normally

some of these would allow a welfare improvement. Certainly allowing the use of international exchange can only make things better, never worse. Hence no trade can be inefficient and optimal trade can never make things worse. Hence trade is gainful, strictly not pernicious. This result is rather trivial once one understands what it claims. Notice that it says that trade normally permits a better allocation. For that allocation to be a price equilibrium we shall usually need lump-sum transfers of income.

To see the potential[14] inefficiency of tariffs for a small country, notice that an allocation with tariffs is supported by prices which do not constitute a price system as the term is intended by the fundamental theorem. This is because a price system implies that all agents face the same prices and producers maximise at those prices. However with tariffs prices for goods in the home market differ from world prices, so that the notional agents responsible for importing and exporting would not be maximising. Such an agent could transfer 1 unit of steel into 100 units of wheat, say, in international exchange, but a domestic producer might make a loss from the same transformation. Hence normally a tariff-bound allocation cannot be supported by any price system and so is inefficient. Another allocation would improve and could be supported by a price system.[15]

The statement of this last result has had to be somewhat complicated because of the possibility that an efficient allocation might be an equilibrium with tariffs, because the tariffs might make no difference to resource allocation. A Simpler result to state is the following. Every efficient allocation can be supported by a price system, hence can be an equilibrium without tariffs.

The last result provides a simple opportunity to illustrate the difference between the general and the standard model. In the standard model it is a theorem that a tariff always makes one group, specifically the owners of one factor, better off.[16] For the general model

[11] Community indifference curves are meant to show the preferences of the community over the total of resources allocated to consumption in the same way that ordinary indifference curves show the preferences of a consumer over various consumption bundles.

[12] The single exception is when income may be distributed between consumers without affecting the final demand of the collectivity. This requires linear parallel Engle curves, which may be interpreted as the poor having the demands of the rich scaled down to their smaller incomes. As this excludes any interesting income effects it only underlines how special are community indifference curves.

[13] An allocation is efficient if no alternative feasible allocation would make one consumer better off and no consumer worse off.

[14] The inefficiency is potential because it could happen that a tariff made no difference whatsoever to resource allocation in which case it would of course be benign.

[15] The assumption that this is a small country plays an essential role in the argument, as transformation possibilities in trade are assumed fixed and constant. If the terms of trade vary with the extent of trade, as in the optimum tariff model, an efficient allocation may be supported by a price system in which marginal transformation rates at home and in trade are equalised and all agents maximise at prices different from average exchange rates in trade. The allocation is efficient, and is supported by a price system, but prices are not the terms of international trade.

[16] This result depends upon how the tariff revenue is distributed between the factors. If we assume that it provides a uniform subsidy on all expenditure then it is the case that a tariff must help the owners of one factor. This is the Stopler-Samuelson result.

we suppose the imposition of a tariff and a distribution of its revenue which makes some group better off. As the initial position is without tariffs it is supported by a price system, from which it follows that it is efficient. This is the converse of the fundamental theorem and is also true. But if the reallocation corresponding to the imposition of the tariff has made one group better off, and if no group has been made worse off, the original allocation was not efficient, which contradicts the fact that it was supported by a price system.

Notice that all the results that have just been rehearsed are implications of the general trade model. They do not depend upon two-good, two-factor or two-country assumptions. Stronger results are available from the standard model, mainly because of its assumption of a smooth technology and continuous substitution. In this case, for example, one can be more definite concerning the effects of a tariff. The movement of prices away from world prices always introduces a production distortion, as even a small price change causes substitution in domestic production towards goods that have risen in price; and this production distortion always entails inefficiency. There is an additional distortion on the consumption side. All this is equally true of the general model when its functions are smooth and responses to price changes non-zero.

How useful are these results for a policy maker? At first sight it appears that they are not useful at all. The trade model, whether in its general or in its standard formulation, and the results derived from it, depend on assumptions that in the eyes of most policy makers would disqualify it from serious consideration. In particular:

(i) perfect markets are assumed, so that prices change to ensure that resources are fully employed, and agents act competitively taking the prices that they face as fixed;
(ii) there are no externalities or increasing returns to scale; and
(iii) lump-sum transfers of income are available to adjust the distribution of income, or to compensate those who have lost from a reform.

It is true that these restrictions underline the need for a broader analysis and we shall shortly consider such an analysis, but the theory should not be dismissed simply because it makes a number of strong assumptions.

First, by laying out its assumptions, the argument puts the onus on someone who wants to claim that trade is not gainful, or to argue that a tariff might be good for everyone, to say which of the assumptions he would like to change. We shall see that the argument is not vulnerable to every change in its assumptions, but even where it is vulnerable, conducting the argument against the background of a strong result will only help to advance understanding.

Secondly, the assumption of lump-sum transfers appears to be particularly unsatisfactory, as no real system of taxation or subsidy corresponds to a lump-sum transfer. We shall shortly see that we do not need such an implausible form of taxation to show that tariffs lead to distortion. But leaving that point aside for the moment, compensation systems that are not strictly lump-sum transfers may nevertheless do the trick. Suppose, for example, that a tariff on the import of wheat is distorting the British economy.[17] However, if the tariff is removed landlords or farmers will lose. Suppose we compensate the losers from general taxation. The results already stated show that if these transfers could be achieved by the lump-sum method, everyone, farmers included, could be made better off.

The problem seems to be that the revenue to pay the compensation cannot be collected without itself causing further distortions. An income tax for example may discourage effort. However the distortion caused by an income tax might be small compared with the distortion caused by the tariff. Economists like to be able to *demonstrate* that an improvement will follow from a certain policy and this is difficult to do if offsetting effects are involved. However to assume that the result of offsetting effects always nets out as unfavourable to reform is an unduly pessimistic approach.

Transfers in the form of compensation are not always infeasible. For example, so large is the distortion caused by the protection of domestic sugar production in temperate countries, that it is probable that farmers growing sugar (that is sugar beet) in the EEC, could be paid enough to set aside the land presently growing sugar without income loss, and the consumers still gain.[18]

As an example of the analysis of policy conducted without the assumption of lump-sum transfers, we consider a result due to Diamond and Mirrlees as it applies to international trade.[19] We show this result for the standard two-good model, as this allows a simple diagrammatic representation of the result. However the same result applies in the general model, provided

---

[17] This hypothetical assumption was satisfied in the early Nineteenth Century, when Ricardo attacked the Corn Laws, and is satisfied again today, when the Common Agricultural Policy of the European Community raises the domestic wheat price above the world price.
[18] This is not the usual type of resource reallocation following the removal of protection, as in that case resources released are assumed to migrate to their next best alternative use. With land set-aside the land released is unused.
[19] See Diamond & Mirrlees (1971) and Dasgupta & Stiglitz (1974).

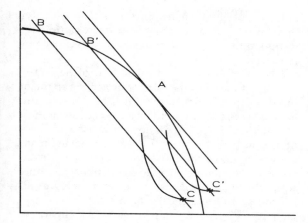

Figure 13.1. The effects of tariffs and taxes on trade

that there are constant returns to scale in production,[20] and the method of proof is the same.

The theorem states that if the value of production at world prices is not being maximised, say because a tariff has been imposed, then an improvement is possible which will make all consumers better off. This improvement does not require lump-sum transfers but may be implemented by means of consumption, production and factor-use subsidies.

In Figure 13.1 the curved frontier is the production possibility curve. World prices are given by the slope of the line that is tangential to the frontier at A, so that A is the value maximising production. However, due to a tariff, production is at B, and domestic goods prices are the slope of the tangent to the production possibility frontier at B. Factor prices are not illustrated, but we should bear in mind that they have been determined by the goods prices at B and are thus determining individual incomes. Consumption is at C which has the same value at world prices as B so the movement from B to C is attainable by international exchange at world prices.

The idea is to proceed as follows. We move along the production possibility frontier to a point such as B' which has a higher value at world prices. To do this we change producer prices, for goods and factors, so that the new production becomes profit maximising. However we keep the prices, for goods and factors again, that consumers pay and receive constant. To maintain the separation of producer prices from

consumer prices we employ indirect taxes and/or subsidies.

As consumer prices and incomes are unchanged, consumers continue to consume at C. The indifference curve through C is illustrated. Now however the value of production at world prices is higher. We may therefore cut all goods prices to consumers somewhat, relative to the factor prices that consumers receive, hence relatively to their incomes. Aggregate consumption moves to C'. This makes every consumer better off. So we have achieved an unambiguous improvement without recourse to lump-sum transfers.

The Diamond-Mirrlees result shows that the assumption of lump-sum transfers in the orthodox argument for efficient allocation in trade is not really required. However this particular line of argument cannot settle the case for and against protection. For that purpose we need to consider alterations to the standard model, particularly the effect of distortions of various kinds, and their implications for optimal economic policy. This will be the task of the next section.

III. Policy rankings and the second-best

We have seen in the previous section that trade theory can have strong implications for economic policy. However so far these implications seem to be compromised by the extremely restrictive assumptions on which they depend. The particular assumption which we shall examine in this section is the requirement that, apart from some distortion, such as a tariff, which is being examined, everything else in the economy is ideal. To put it another way, we have been considering policy for an undistorted economy, or 'first-best'[21] theory as it is sometimes called. However most real cases of intervention, it will be argued, concern, or are perceived to concern, the 'second-best'. To take a tariff as an example, most justifications for tariffs really depend upon the assertion of a distortion which the tariff is meant to correct. To understand the arguments concerning policy which will eventually settle the issue, we need to look at distortions and the second-best.

It goes without saying that a distortion is a good reason for intervention, we would hardly call it a distortion otherwise. The question is, what will be the consequences of various interventions, and can some

---

[20] The reason why constant returns to scale is required is that it ensures that no productive activity will make a surplus of revenue over costs of inputs, with the consequence that changes in producer prices do not change the pure profits associated with the ownership of firms. If these profits can be taxed away, constant returns to scale is not required. See Dasgupta & Stiglitz (1974).

[21] This illogical terminology gained currency after the term 'second-best' was used to describe an allocation in which not all the welfare conditions for a full optimum could be satisfied. The so-called 'first-best' is simply the best, the optimum. See Lipsey & Lancaster (1956).

be shown to be better than others. This line of enquiry has given rise to a large field of trade theory from which some definite conclusions emerge.[22] These conclusions may be summarised as follows:

(i) a distortion calls for an intervention of some kind, in the sense that policy interventions in the form of taxes, subsidies, tariffs, etc. can improve on the laissez-faire outcome;

(ii) not all interventions have equally good results, and typically a policy ranking emerges from the comparison of different types of intervention in which the best of one type of intervention may be shown to dominate the best of another type;

(iii) the best intervention in the policy ranking is usually directed closely at the source of the misallocation, where inferior interventions are indirect and affect changes not relevant to the original distortion.

These rather vague and sweeping statements may be illustrated by means of an example. We consider one of the oldest arguments for intervention in the form of tariff or quota protection, the infant industry,[23] which was considered by Adam Smith and the classical economists, and which frequently reappears in contemporary discussions, not always bearing the title used here. The infant industry is supposed to be an industry presently uncompetitive in the face of foreign competition, but which will become competitive in due course if provided with a period of protection during which its costs will fall until it eventually can compete. The idea of the classic argument is to give this industry protection until it can compete without it.[24]

To make sense of the infant industry argument one needs more than the story of an industry presently uncompetitive that will later become competitive. First, there has to be some reason why the industry should not wait its time until it is competitive. The reason will usually be that only by operating now and gaining experience, or economies of learning by doing, can the industry prove competitive later. Even that alone is not enough. It has to be explained why private investors cannot foresee that present operation at a loss will be rewarded by profits later and why, if they do, they do not arrive at socially efficient decisions, as they presumably do in other cases in which present costs are offset by future benefits. Why are the losses of an infant

industry not simply an investment cost, like any other investment cost, and if they are, where is the presumption that private decisions will be improved by intervention?

It is important to understand the force of these questions and to see how the case for protecting an infant industry depends on the answers to them. However this is not to say that answers cannot be provided. The most plausible and important case arises when the efficiency of an industry improves with operation, not in a manner which producers cannot foresee but policy makers can, an assumption hard to credit, but in a manner which the producers cannot capture and keep outsiders from sharing the benefit. Suppose, for example, that an industry will enjoy an international comparative advantage once local labour has been trained in the operation of its processes. However this labour is footloose, it cannot be tied by contract to a particular employer. Hence if investors borrow money to train labour and take operating losses during this period, they will reap no benefit. The labour can be attracted away by late-arriving employers who have not bothered to suffer the investment costs of training labour. This seems to provide a genuine case for infant protection.

This is the case that we shall examine in more detail. It needs a little more filling out of the example just to describe the situation. Since workers benefit from the training, one way of supporting the optimum in this case would be to have the workers finance their training, say by working unpaid and using borrowed money to see them through the training period. So we have to tell a story according to which this solution is impossible. However we shall not go into too much detail but simply suppose that that method is infeasible. We may call it an imperfection of the capital market that workers cannot borrow against future earnings.[25] We have now provided an example of the infant industry argument in which the case can be spelt out in detail and withstand obvious objections.

We now consider some policies which will achieve the end of allowing the infant industry to operate during its period of growing-up and we then derive a policy ranking. Policies which would allow the infant industry to operate include:

(a) a limited period of tariff protection;[26]
(b) a limited period of investment subsidy;

---

[22] For more thorough treatments, see Bhagwati (1971), Corden (1974) and (1984), and Michaely (1977).

[23] See Johnson (1970).

[24] In the past the argument was largely theoretical, a counterexample to what was seen as a general case for free trade. However in modern times policies based in part on the infant industry case have been influential in practice, particularly in developing countries.

[25] Such an imperfection may be quite explicable. As collateral, earnings have the property that they are difficult to attack if repayment of the loan is not forthcoming. Mortgaged property for example provides better collateral.

[26] Or another kind of protection such as a quota on imports. We ignore differences between different kinds of protection in the present argument.

(c) a limited period of production subsidy;

(d) a state-sponsored loan scheme to enable workers to finance their own training.

There may well be further interventions which would enable the infant industry to get going but the above will serve our need for an example of a policy ranking. Notice that in regard to directness or indirectness, the policies are ranked above in order of increasing directness. Thus a tariff is furthest from the source of the problem, which is the mobility of labour and the employer's difficulty in attaching the benefits of his training. An investment subsidy is closer in that the employer is compensated for the fact that his investment shows a return below the social return. A production subsidy is closer still in that the employer is rewarded for doing the action which provides an external social benefit, namely producing and training labour. A training loan scheme goes directly to the heart of the problem. In fact it overcomes the imperfection of the capital market and supports the best outcome.

The same ordering above is in order of increasing efficiency. Thus any policy high on the list may be dominated by a policy lower on the list. As usual, this requires lump-sum transfers. The reason why this should be so is that each of policies (a), (b) and (c) correct the distortion caused by the imperfection of the capital market only at the cost of introducing another distortion which is not introduced by a policy lower on the list.

Consider the tariff for example. This allows the infant industry to operate but does this by raising the price in the domestic market. It thus distorts the level of production, which is lower than in the optimum solution, so that the infant takes longer to grow up than it should, and it distorts consumption in that consumers pay more than the true social opportunity cost of the product and end up consuming less of it. An investment subsidy overcomes the problem that the scale of operation of the industry is too small but at the cost of introducing another distortion. It is investment which is encouraged and hence production, but this leads to production which is too capital intensive. A production subsidy partly avoids that difficulty, and also the contraction of the industry which would be caused by a tariff. However to the employer labour is still more expensive than it really is from the social point of view, and so production is still too capital intensive (but not as capital intensive as it would be with an investment subsidy). Finally, with the labour training loan scheme we remove all distortions and attain the 'first-best'.

In the case of the infant industry example protection came high in the list of policies, that is low in terms of desirability. How typical is this? A little thought will reveal what conditions have to be satisfied for protection to rank high in terms of desirability. We need only to apply the principle that direct intervention, that is intervention targeted at the source of any misallocation, is superior to indirect intervention. From this it follows that protection will be an optimal intervention when protection is similarly targeted. But what would that mean?

Protection is targeted at trade as such and it therefore follows that it will be the optimal intervention only when trade is itself the source of the misallocation. Two examples illustrate this point. First, we know that a tariff is optimal, not surprisingly, in the case of an optimal tariff. But this is precisely a case in which trade is the source of misallocation. From the point of view of the home country, for an individual agent to engage a little more in trade, whether as exporter or importer, is an action to which an external diseconomy attaches. The diseconomy arises because the terms of trade vary slightly with a small change in the quantity traded, and this affects the intra-marginal trades, an effect which the agent does not take into account. The optimal tariff simply faces the individual agent with the true social shadow price that attaches to his action. It is a direct intervention and it is therefore not surprising that it supports the optimum.

Secondly, consider the case in which national self-sufficiency is itself an objective. This may be for good reasons, a prudent need to survive a possible crisis, or bad, simple xenophobia. In either case trade as such enters into the national objective function with a negative weight. This will mean, of course, that an individual agent deciding on an action which leads to more trade generates an external economy from the point of view of the national objective function. With tariffs the same agent may be faced with the exact correct shadow prices. Once again a tariff is the direct targeted intervention and once again the 'first-best' may be supported with a tariff.[27]

It should now be clear why, in the received theory of policy design and policy rankings, protection is seldom an optimal intervention. On the whole, instances in which protection is the correctly targeted intervention are unusual. This is not the same as saying that they are unimportant. However it is significant that the advocates of protection are usually not content to rely on

[27] It is worth noting how this is consistent with the fundamental theorem of welfare economics. The 'first-best' is clearly an efficient allocation. However the example includes an externality where these are not included in the framework within which the fundamental theorem is valid.

variable terms of trade or xenophobia, although both of these are encountered. However without relying on these arguments the advocate of protection always runs up against the difficulty that his policy proposal can be trumped by a more direct intervention.

It is important to bear in mind that while the theory of policy design is an impressive apparatus, it has relied more than it ought to on lump-sum transfers or community indifference curves. This is unfortunate because those assumptions are often not required to make the point. We saw in section II above that a tariff-bound equilibrium could be improved using only indirect taxes and subsidies. However in other cases an analysis which employs lump-sum transfers leads to too complacent a view of non-intervention.

Anand & Joshi (1979) consider an example in which the distortion is inequality of incomes between the same factor according to where it is employed. The correction of this situation by means of taxes and subsidies is supposed to be impossible.[28] What happens is that under free trade the industrial sector of the economy expands too much. In a sense the expansion is excessive because there is an external diseconomy from the advanced sector, rather like pollution, but in this case the pollutant is mal-distribution of income. Intervention is required in this case, however a tariff is not optimal, as it plainly is not targeted and may distort consumption.

Another example which illustrates the difficulties that may arise when we cannot make use of lump-sum transfers follows from a subtle feature of the Diamond-Mirrlees result. We presented that result above as showing that commodity and factor taxes or subsidies could improve on a tariff. It was pointed out that the argument assumed either constant returns to scale or that pure profits were taxed away. Neither of these conditions is satisfied in the example which follows. The example is fanciful, but it illustrates a serious point.

We imagine a man who owns some land which he can devote to rearing sheep, and his own labour, which is of poor quality, so that if he sells it on the market he will earn very little. However valued at world prices his output is more in industry than on his farm. Presumably his country has no comparative advantage in rearing sheep. How can policy help this man? Nothing that is done to consumer prices, by subsidy for example, will help, because he earns so little.[29] Producer prices are meant to reflect comparative advantage, and lump-sum transfers are not permitted. However if a large tariff is placed on the import of mutton or wool, their prices will rise in the home market, and our hypothetical man may make a much better living following his comparative disadvantage as a sheep farmer. As in the Anand-Joshi example, so in this case, a distorting policy intervention is the only way to produce a favourable redistribution of income.

We have covered enough ground to see what kind of results the theory of optimal policy and policy rankings can establish. The argument has been conducted so far in terms of the long-established general and standard models of trade. What difference does it make when we come to consider the recent advances in trade theory? That is the question that will be addressed in the next two sections.

IV. What does the new theory imply for policy?

The new theory is reviewed in the paper in this volume by Henryk Kierzkowski in a contribution which he explicitly calls a selective survey. Despite its modest designation that paper covers most of the new theoretical departures that we shall need to consider in order to see what new theory has done to policy. However before embarking on the consideration of the models included in the Kierzkowski paper, it is worth mentioning a contribution which has profoundly affected the way that economists think about protection and allied topics: the theory of rent seeking.[30]

To understand the importance of rent seeking one needs to consider the quantitative importance of distortions. So far our assessment of distortions and non-optimal interventions has been qualitative—subsidies are better than tariffs, etc. However economists obviously tried to assess the quantitative importance of tariffs and, at least for modest tariffs, they tended to find that the costs were small, the equivalent of some tiny fraction of national income. This was not surprising when one considers that the analysis was based on the implicit assumption that lump-sum taxes could redistribute income as necessary. Only the efficiency cost, or excess burden, of tariffs was being measured. So it was perhaps not surprising that the costs turned out to be small.

The idea behind rent seeking is that the redistributive consequences of protection and other intervention are not neutral, because real resources are diverted into

---

[28] That would be the case if workers in the industrial sector can press for and maintain higher wages because of their greater political 'muscle'.

[29] As he supplies little effective labour, subsidising sales of labour will not work.

[30] See Bhagwati & Srinivasan (1980), Buchanan, Tollison and Tullock (1980), Collander (1984) and Krueger (1974).

trying to steer these rents in the direction of particular agents. Businessmen, for example, will spend time and money to lobby politicians to obtain tariff protection for their industry.[31] Hence the transfers of income consequent upon tariff protection are not neutral transfers that may be costlessly reversed by opposing transfers. They use real resources.[32]

The development of the theory of rent seeking has coincided with a world wide movement away from interventionist theories and policies, and the growth in influence of the idea that trade promoting 'open' economic policies are superior to the 'closed', import substituting, policies that characterised the developing countries in the 1950s and 1960s. It is too soon now to say whether this represents a permanent shift of opinion, or whether there will be a reaction in due course back towards interventionism.

We turn now to the new theories included in the Kierzkowski survey and their consequences for policy. We consider here extensions that are such by virtue of going beyond the standard model, which are not necessarily extensions of the general model. Included are the specific factors model in its various versions, specialised production models, other higher dimension models, and trade in services. We postpone until the next section the consideration of increasing returns and imperfect competition.

Consider first the specific factors model. This has a number of important theoretical implications but they are not particularly relevant to policy design. Thus with the specific factors model there is no factor price equalisation result. This is hardly surprising, as the model has essentially more factors than goods. However the factor price equalisation result is not required, and is not used, in developing the theory of economic policy. The model implies a different response of factor prices to commodity prices and this should have implications for the design of policy, although they will be of a particular nature rather than general points. Perhaps the most important conclusion for the policy maker is that he cannot expect to divide and rule along factor divisions when trade liberalisation proposals are concerned. In the Heckscher-Ohlin-Samuelson (HOS) model the Stopler-Samuelson result applies. One factor gains and one factor looses from a tariff cut unaccompanied by income transfers. Empirically this always

looked dubious, as typically labour and capital from a particular industry line up together to oppose a cut in the protection of that industry. The specific factors model explains that fact but does not unseat the fundamental result that with a tariff reduction and transfers all parties could gain, and that an all round gain could also be achieved with optimal commodity and factor taxes and subsidies.

What is true for the basic two-sector specific factors model is equally applicable to its elegant n-dimensional extensions. It would be easy to dismiss the importance of the specific factors model where policy is concerned, but this would be a mistake. The model points to an important policy issue which, as is often the case, is of a quantitative and not a qualitative nature.

We have seen that the theory of optimal economic policy is importantly dependent on the use of compensation and transfer mechanisms. This provides a reference point for the assessment of real-life policy decisions in which the transfers to a great extent will not be made and the implied consequences for income distribution will simply have to be suffered by the parties concerned. The old theory made it appear that these unfortunate consequences of reform were perhaps not very serious. A change in the relative earning and income levels of different factor groups would follow from trade liberalisation. However this would be dispersed throughout the economy and should not perhaps be of catastrophic importance when compared, for example, with the consequences for factor incomes of a few years' technical progress.

The specific factors approach paints a much less rosy picture. The impact of a cut in protection will be concentrated in a few sharp reductions in income or, if their prices are inflexible, unemployment. What emerges then is sharp redistributions of income. From the theoretical point of view this is somewhat reassuring, because it has always been something of a problem for the received theory with its lump-sum transfers to explain the strength of pressures for protection that one observes, and which now become much more understandable.

We next consider specialised production models. The assumption that equilibrium does not result in a country producing only one good was always a feature of the HOS model, and it was long ago pointed out by Chipman (1965–66) that this assumption is not independent of the differences in factor endowments between countries, nor of the form of the production functions, nor even of the factor intensity reversal condition itself. Specialisation seems to be an important feature of reality, although reality might be held to include less specialisation than theory predicts, and for

---

[31] Bhagwati noted that because the allocation of rationed inputs in India was related to capacity, producers tended to overinvest in capacity so as to gain favourable allocations.

[32] Under the assumption that rent seeking is a constant returns to scale activity, costs will equal revenue, in which case the resource cost of rent seeking will be equal to total tariff revenue. This contrasts with the much smaller triangles of lump-sum burden theory.

this reason the existence of specialised solutions in the trade model should be welcomed.

What difference does specialisation make to policy? Once again the basic results are unaffected but some quantitative conclusions are affected. With non-specialisation a small tariff will typically not be large enough to lead to specialisation. True a change in factor prices is induced, and this leads to an alteration in factor input proportions and hence to a change in the quantities of the outputs produced. However the menu of goods produced is unaffected. In the Jones-Krueger model[33] a small tariff frequently induces a change in the pattern of specialisation but this difference is of less moment than may at first appear. The shifts in specialisation only involve local movements along the spectrum of many goods that a country may produce. Hence the welfare costs of a misallocation that results in the precise goods produced being slightly wrong will not be very large. This point is an example of a more general point. Closeness is a relative concept, it depends on the metric at issue. Thus it may happen that a large change in production may be a small change in welfare level or conversely.

Other higher dimension models bring few new policy implications with them. This is largely because the policy framework never required most of the specific properties of the HOS model. Of course the HOS model was so popular that its recitation became like a creed of trade theorists, and it was frequently employed to illustrate policy conclusions that did not in fact depend on it.

Finally we come to trade in services. It is probable that the most important single way in which services differ from goods is that the greater difficulty of standardising services makes the competitive case even less usual than it is where goods trade is concerned. That consideration belongs to the next section, so for the time being we assume competitive markets.

The problem, as Kierzkowski's discussion shows, is to isolate the characteristic differences between goods and services. It is intuitively obvious that the export of a car is very different from the export of an insurance service, but are the differences that strike us as obvious germane to trade theory? It is after all an implication of the HOS model that trade in goods, assumed possible, substitutes for trade in factors, assumed impossible. That is how factor price equalisation comes about. With many services the factors move to the customer, but this is not always so, indeed it is not always the case that the factors and the customer need meet. Thus tourism requires the customer to visit the factors.

However an insurance service may require no more than a telex message and an international money transfer. The factors and the customer both stay put.

From the point of view of the welfare economics that lies at the base of the theory of commercial policy the most important issue raised by services surely concerns information and assessment of quality. No doubt it is often the case that the producer of a good is in a particularly advantageous position compared with the buyer when it comes to assessing the quality of what he is selling. However these difficulties are greatly increased where services are concerned. Very often if the buyer could assess the quality of the service that he is receiving he would not need the service. This is plainly the case where the service is medicine or education. The student who can fully assess and evaluate the education that he receives is probably already educated. These ideas point to intervention to improve information and quality assessment. Unfortunately, this is one of the disguises that protection is quick to adopt.

We have remarked on the close relation between the consequences of trade and the consequence of factor mobility. In the special case of the HOS model the former is a perfect substitute for the latter, but more generally there is scope for gains from factor mobility even after trade has been fully exploited.[34] In the light of this observation it is surprising that economists, who have been vocal in support of free trade, have been rather hushed when it comes to advocating greater international mobility of labour. This contrasts with a firmer advocacy of the removal of restrictions on capital mobility.

V. Policy with variety, increasing returns and imperfect competition

In this section we come to probably the most interesting implications of the new trade theories for policy. Previously there was a certain sameness about our argument. We reviewed a model and concluded that, while it was not the HOS model, it was nevertheless more or less covered by existing commercial policy theory. Of course we could find some things to say about these models and policy, but even so the ground was more or less familiar once one viewed it in the right way. With the topics of this section we come to areas in which the theory of economic policy can require radical reconsideration and extension.

Let us begin with the love of variety. The appeal of

---

[33] See Jones (1974) and Krueger (1977).

[34] This would be the case in the Jones-Krueger model for example.

this concept in trade theory is the possibility that it might explain the intra-industry trade which is such a marked feature of contemporary trading patterns. Notice that love of variety by itself carries few interesting implications. In the formal general equilibrium model we treat goods as different goods if consumers distinguish between them and we allow as many goods as necessary. An international trade equilibrium might be a special case of that model and standard policy conclusions will apply.

Of course this model will fail to explain why goods with similar production conditions are produced in various countries but not in all countries. This is because the general equilibrium model cannot admit non-convexities of production sets and cannot therefore explain why a good of a particular detailed type will tend to be produced in one country only, with intra-industry trade resulting. This suggests the conclusion that the importance of love of variety arises from its natural association with non-convexities, that is increasing returns, and not from variety as such which only leads to many more goods than factors.[35]

Increasing returns is a more fundamental change in assumptions, particularly as it requires us to abandon the assumption of perfect competition, and the introduction of imperfect competition is itself of interest, as presumably one could imagine a monopolised industry with constant costs. We consider first in fact a simple model without increasing returns in production but with imperfect competition due to the fewness of the sellers. This is the model we shall refer to as the Brander model.[36]

The Brander model generates trade, in fact cross-hauling in one good, from market structure, that is imperfect competition. The interesting thing about this starting point is that, unlike the usual one, we begin from a situation which is plainly non-optimal, and in which it is sure that some kind of intervention can do good. This contrasts with standard trade theory, in which we start from an equilibrium in which it is far from obvious that intervention would help, the intervention concerned usually has a minimal direct effect on trade.[37]

What is the optimal intervention in the Brander model? To answer that question we need to specify both the model and the policy interventions available. We shall take the case of constant costs of production of the one tradeable good and consider decreasing costs later. We assume that lump-sum transfers of income may be used so that our conclusions will be comparable with the usual trade theory.

The optimal trade policy would be the policy adopted by a single agent acting in full knowledge of trading conditions including the Cournot behaviour of the foreign producer. Such a hypothetical agent would import the good only if its price was below home marginal cost and would export it as long as marginal revenue exceeded marginal cost. These marginal costs are the same as average cost, which is constant. As the foreign producer will not export at a price below domestic average cost, as this is the same as his own average cost, this implies that prices will stop the inflow of the good. However this does not require a prohibitive import tariff. If the domestic price is set at average cost of production there will be no imports, the transport costs guarantee that.

Hence the following prices support the optimum. The domestic price is equal to average cost and the export price maximises profit from exports. How can this price system function when the producer is a monopolist as keen to exploit the domestic market as he is keen to exploit the foreign market? The answer must be a subsidy of sales in the domestic market financed by a tax on the monopolist's profit. This is better than a tariff, as the domestic consumers get the good at a price equal to social opportunity cost. However a tariff is better than no intervention.

What happens when there are decreasing costs in domestic production? This is the case for which Krugman (1984) showed that a tariff, by protecting the domestic market and leading to a decline in domestic costs of production, promotes exports. We should again ask what is the optimal policy intervention, and this will once more give us prices that will support what a maximising and comprehending single agent would do. Consumers should again get the good at marginal cost, which is now variable. Exports should again maximise profit with output charged at marginal cost. The difference is that with decreasing costs these conditions may not automatically imply the optimum. They may not even exclude exports.

Suppose we start at a point at which our output is low, and let foreign output be high. The foreign producer has low costs and may export profitably into our market. His prices in his market may be below our own marginal cost, which is high, and so we do not export. However if the two countries are symmetrical, there must exist a similar equilibrium in which we are big

[35] Which is another example of a change which is important from the point of view of the standard model but not important from the point of view of the theory of policy.

[36] We refer to it as the Brander model for the sake of brevity although Spencer and Krugman are also associated with it. See Brander (1981), Krugman (1984) and further references in Kierzkowski above.

[37] For example lump-sum transfers may be the only optimal interventions and of course by redistributing income they affect trade flows. However they do not act directly on trade.

and our trading partner is small. The question is not what equilibria can be supported by locally reasonable price systems, but rather how we leap from one equilibrium to another better, from our point of view, equilibrium some distance away. Clearly a tariff will do the trick as it enables the domestic market to enlarge and this eventually allows exports.

Notice that the role of a tariff in this example is quite different from its usual role in the theory of economic policy. It is only needed temporarily and it functions by shifting the system from one equilibrium to another. The case is reminiscent of the infant industry, but his is an infant which grows due to a scale effect. To a certain extent it is misleading to regard this argument as an argument for protection. The tariff is basically a second-best intervention. Taxing the monopolist's profit and subsidising domestic sales is always better. However even with the best type of policy we may get stuck in the wrong equilibrium and need a jolt to move us to a better one. And a tariff will serve well in this regard.

If we look back at the earlier discussion of policy intervention we can see why this was likely to be the case. The new trade models introduce important new considerations but they do not demolish the principle of policy rankings, and they do not negate the very solid rule that interventions are best when targeted. If we look at the Brander model and ask where misallocations are arising we find them in the exploitation of domestic consumers by a monopolist. The wasteful imports are an incidental consequence of this exploitation. Hence the targeted intervention removes the monopolistic exploitation, by a subsidy of sales in this case. A tariff is inferior for a reason which is the same as would apply in the old theory—it is not targeted.

Lastly consider differentiated products. Once again the important new principles which these introduce come from their association with decreasing costs and imperfect competition. These as we have seen do introduce fundamentally new possibilities, particularly local optima that are not global optima. They do not however, and could not, upset the notion of a policy ranking and they do not introduce new arguments for tariffs, although a tariff might be used to jolt the system as with the Brander model.

VI. Concluding remarks

For a paper concerned with the implications of the new trade theories for policy this piece has devoted a remarkable amount of space to the old theories and the old trade policy. There are two reasons why this imbalance may be justified. First, it is important to put the new theories in a proper perspective. Of course this typically shows that the new theories are not all new. It is true that trade theory was never exclusively the HOS model, and that indeed higher dimension models have been around and have been discussed for the last 25 years. Yet they were always the preserve of a few specialists, mainly an untypically mathematical subset of trade theorists. The HOS model did used to dominate the subject, and it certainly dominates it less now as a result of the recent advances.

The second reason why the careful consideration of old commercial policy theory may be right is that the new theories have made much less of a dent in the normative theory than they have in the positive theory. This is partly because the old normative theory never used or needed all the assumptions that were commonly used in the positive theory. It is also because the basic ideas of the old normative theory, the notion of policy rankings, the idea of targeting interventions, really are particularly solid and robust ideas. They could not be easily displaced. However despite the difficulty of injecting new principles into the field of commercial policy theory, the new trade models have succeeded in doing just that. By drawing attention to the fact that, once we abandon the convexity assumption, an optimum may be only local, and noting that a discrete policy intervention might shift the system to a higher solution in such a case, the new theories have presented policy theorists with a challenging new idea. As trade theory develops further in the future it may be expected to produce further genuine novelties regarding economic policy design.

References

Anand, S., and Joshi, V. R. (1979), 'Domestic distortions, income distribution and the theory of optimum subsidy', *Economic Journal*.

Bhagwati, J. N. (1964), 'The pure theory of international trade: A survey', *Economic Journal*, **74**.

—— (1971), 'The generalised theory of distortions and welfare', in J. N. Bhagwati and others, eds., *Trade, balance of payments and growth* (North-Holland: Amsterdam).

—— (1982), 'Directly unproductive profit-seeking (DUP) activities: A welfare-theoretic synthesis and generalisation', *Journal of Political Economy*, **90**.

—— and Srinivasan, T. N. (1980), 'Revenue-seeking: A generalisation of the theory of tariffs', *Journal of Political Economy*, **88**.

Brander, J. (1981), 'Intra-industry trade in identical commodities', *Journal of International Economics*, **11**.

Buchanan, J. M., Tollison, R. D., and Tullock, G. (1980), *Towards a theory of the rent-seeking society* (Texas A&M University Press: College Station).

Chipman, J. S. (1965–66), 'A survey of the theory of international trade', *Econometrica*, **33, 34**.

Collander, D. (1984), *Neoclassical political economy: The analysis of rent-seeking and DUP activities* (Ballinger Publishing Company).

Corden, W. M. (1965), *Recent developments in the theory of international trade*. Special papers in international economics, Princeton University.

—— (1974), *Trade policy and economic welfare* (Clarendon Press: Oxford).

Dasgupta, P. S., and Stiglitz, J. E. (1974), 'Benefit-cost analysis and trade policies', *Journal of Political Economy*, **82**, 1–33.

Diamond, P. A., and Mirrlees, J. A. (1971), 'Optimal taxation and public production', *American Economic Review*, **61**, Mar. and June.

Dixit, A. K., and Norman, V. D. (1980), *Theory of International Trade* (Cambridge University Press: Cambridge).

Johnson, H. G. (1970), 'A new view of the infant-industry argument', in I. A. MacDougall and R. H. Snape, eds., *Studies in International Economics:* Monash Conference Papers (North-Holland: Amsterdam).

Jones, R. W. (1974), 'The small country in a multi-commodity world', *Australian Economic Papers*, **13**.

Koopmans, T. S. (1957), *Three essays in the state of economic science*, McGraw Hill.

Krueger, A. O. (1974), 'The political economy of the rent-seeking society', *American Economic Review*, **64**.

—— (1977), *Growth, distortions and patterns of trade among many countries*, Princeton Studies in International Finance 40.

Krugman, P. (1984), 'Import protection as export promotion', in H. Kierzkowski (ed.) *Monopolistic competition and international trade*, Oxford University Press.

Kuhn, T. S. (1962), *The structure of scientific revolutions*, Chicago.

Leontief, W. W. (1954), 'Domestic production and foreign trade: the American capital position re-examined', *Economica Internazionale*, **7**, Feb.

Lipsey. R. G., and Lancaster, K. (1956), 'The general theory of the second-best', *Review of Economic Studies*, **24**.

Michaely, M. (1977), *Theory of Commercial Policy*, Phillip Alan: Oxford.

Vernon, R. (1966), 'International investment and international trade in the product cycle', *Quarterly Journal of Economics*, **80**.

PART VI

EDUCATION AND TRAINING

14

The failure of training in Britain: analysis and prescription

DAVID FINEGOLD

Pembroke College, Oxford

DAVID SOSKICE[1]

Wissenschaftszentrum, Berlin

I. Introduction

In the last decade, education and training (ET) reform has become a major issue in many of the world's industrial powers. One theme which runs throughout these reform initiatives is the need to adapt ET systems to the changing economic environment. These changes include: the increasing integration of world markets, the shift in mass manufacturing towards newly developed nations and the rapid development of new technologies, most notably information technologies. Education and training are seen to play a crucial role in restoring or maintaining international competitiveness, both on the macro-level by easing the transition of the work force into new industries, and at the micro-level, where firms producing high quality, specialized goods and services require a well-qualified workforce capable of rapid adjustment in the work process and continual product innovation.

This paper will highlight the need for policy-makers and academics to take account of the two-way nature of the relationship between ET and the economy. We will argue that Britain's failure to educate and train its workforce to the same levels as its international competitors has been both a product and a

cause of the nation's poor relative economic performance: a product, because the ET system evolved to meet the needs of the world's first industrialized economy, whose large, mass-production manufacturing sector required only a small number of skilled workers and university graduates; and a cause, because the absence of a well educated and trained workforce has made it difficult for industry to respond to new economic conditions.

The best way to visualize this argument is to see Britain as trapped in a low-skills equilibrium, in which the majority of enterprises staffed by poorly trained managers and workers produce low-quality goods and services.[2] The term 'equilibrium' is used to connote a self-reinforcing network of societal and state institutions which interact to stifle the demand for improvements in skill levels. This set of political-economic institutions will be shown to include: the organization of industry, firms and the work process, the industrial relations system, financial markets, the state and political structure, as well as the operation of the ET system. A change in any one of these factors without corresponding shifts in the other institutional variables may result in only small long-term shifts in the equilibrium position. For example, a company which decides to recruit better-educated workers and then invest more funds in training them will not realize the full

First published in *Oxford Review of Economic Policy*, vol. 4, no. 3 (1988).

[1] The authors would like to thank Kay Andrews, Geoffrey Garrett, Ken Mayhew, Derek Morris, John Muellbauer and Len Schoppa for helpful comments; and to acknowledge intellectual indebtedness to Chris Hayes and Prof. S. Prais. Research on comparative aspects of training was financed in part by a grant to Soskice from the ESRC Corporatist and Accountability Research Programme.

[2] 'Equilibrium' is not meant to imply that all British firms produce low-quality products or services, or that all individuals are poorly educated and trained. A number of companies (often foreign-owned multi-nationals) have succeeded in recruiting the educational élite and offering good training programmes.

potential of that investment if it does not make parallel changes in style and quality of management, work design, promotion structures and the way it implements new technologies.[3] The same logic applies on a national scale to a state which invests in improving its ET system, while ignoring the surrounding industrial structure.

The argument is organized as follows: section two uses international statistical comparisons to show that Britain's ET system turns out less-qualified individuals than its major competitors and that this relative ET failure has contributed to Britain's poor economic record. Section three explores the historical reasons for Britain's ET problem and analyses the institutional constraints which have prevented the state from reforming ET. Section four argues that the economic crisis of the 1970s and early 1980s and the centralization of ET power undertaken by the Thatcher Administration increased the possibility of restructuring ET, but that the Conservative Government's ET reforms will not significantly improve Britain's relative ET and economic performance. The fifth section proposes an alternative set of ET and related policies which could help Britain to break out of the low-skill equilibrium.

II. International comparisons

1. Britain's failure to train

Comparative education and training statistics are even less reliable than cross-national studies in economics; there are few generally agreed statistical categories, wide variations in the quality of ET provision and qualifications and a notable lack of data on training within companies. Despite these caveats, there is a consensus in the growing body of comparative ET research that Britain provides significantly poorer ET for its workforce than its major international competitors. Our focus will be on differences in ET provision for the majority of the population, concentrating in particular on the normal ET routes for skilled and semi-skilled workers. This need not be technical courses, but may—as in Japan or the US—constitute a long course of general education followed by company-based training.

The baseline comparison for ET effectiveness begins with how students in different countries perform during compulsory schooling. Prais and Wagner (1983) compared mathematics test results of West German and English secondary schools and found that the level of attainment of the lower half of German pupils was higher than the average level of attainment in England, while Lynn (1988, p. 6) reviewed thirteen-year-olds' scores on international mathematics achievement tests from the early 1980s and found that 'approximately 79 per cent of Japanese children obtained a higher score than the average English child'. The results are equally disturbing in the sciences, where English fourteen year-olds scored lower than their peers in all seventeen countries in a recent study (Postlethwaite, 1988).

This education shortfall is compounded by the fact that England is the only one of the world's major industrial nations in which a majority of students leave full-time education or training at the age of sixteen. The contrast is particularly striking with the US, Canada, Sweden and Japan, where more than 85 per cent of sixteen year-olds remain in full-time education. In Germany, Austria and Switzerland, similar proportions are either in full-time education or in highly structured three or four-year apprenticeships. Britain has done little to improve its relative position. It was, for example, the only member of the OECD to experience a decline in the participation rate of the sixteen–nineteen age group in the latter half of the 1970s. (OECD, 1985, p. 17) Although staying-on rates have improved in the 1980s—due to falling rolls and falling job prospects—Britain's relative position in the OECD rankings has not.

The combination of poor performance during the compulsory schooling years and a high percentage of students leaving school at sixteen has meant that the average English worker enters employment with a relatively low level of qualifications.

Workers' lack of initial qualifications is not compensated for by increased employer-based training; on the contrary, British firms offer a lower quality and quantity of training than their counterparts on the Continent. A joint MSC/NEDO study (1984, p. 90) found that employers in Germany were spending approximately three times more on training than their British rivals, while Steedman's analysis (1986) of comparable construction firms in France and Britain revealed that French workers' training was more extensive and less firm-specific. Overall, British firms have been estimated to be devoting 0.15 per cent of turnover to training compared with 1–2 per cent in Japan, France and West Germany (Anderson, 1987, p. 69). And, as we will show in section IV, neither individuals nor the Government have compensated for employers' lack of investment in adult training.

---

[3] An excellent discussion of the differences in each of these dimensions between British and German companies is contained in Lane (1988).

2. Why train? The link between ET and economic performance

Britain's relative failure to educate and train its work-force has contributed to its poor economic growth record in the postwar period. While it is difficult to demonstrate this relationship empirically, given the numerous other factors which affect labour productivity, no one is likely to dispute the claim that ET provision can improve economic performance in extreme cases, i.e. a certified engineer will be more productive working with a complex piece of industrial machinery than an unskilled employee. Our concern, however, is whether marginal differences in the quality and quantity of ET are related to performance. We will divide the evidence on this relationship in two parts: first, that the short-term expansion of British industry has been hindered by the failure of the ET system to produce sufficient quantities of skilled labour; and second, that the ability of the British economy and individual firms to adapt to the longer-term shifts in international competition has been impeded by the dearth of qualified manpower.

A survey of the literature reveals that skill shortages in key sectors such as engineering and information technology have been a recurring problem for UK industry, even during times of high unemployment. The Donovan Commission (1968, p. 92) maintained that 'lack of skilled labour has constantly applied a brake to our economic expansion since the war', a decade later, a NEDO study (1978, p. 2) found that 68 per cent of mechanical engineering companies reported that output was restricted by an absence of qualified workers. The problem remains acute, as the MSC's first *Skills Monitoring Report* (May, 1986, p. 1) stated: 'Shortages of professional engineers have continued to grow and there are indications that such shortages will remain for some time, particulary of engineers with electronics and other IT skills.'

The shortages are not confined to manufacturing. Public sector professions, i.e. teaching, nursing and social work, which rely heavily on recruiting from the limited group of young people with at least five O-levels, are facing a skilled (wo)manpower crisis as the number of school-leavers declines by 25 per cent between 1985 and 1995. In the case of maths and science teachers, the shortages tend to be self-perpetuating, as the absence of qualified specialists makes it harder to attract the next generation of students into these fields (Gow, 1988, p. 4; Keep, 1987, p. 12).

The main argument of this paper, however, is that the evidence of skill shortages both understates and

oversimplifies the consequences Britain's ET failure has on its economic performance. Skill shortages reflect the unsatisfied demand for trained individuals within the limits of existing industrial organization, but they say nothing about the negative effect poor ET may have on how efficiently enterprises organize work or their ability to restructure. Indeed, there is a growing recognition among industry leaders and the major accounting firms that their traditional method of calculating firms' costs, particularly labour costs, fails to quantify the less tangible benefits of training, such as better product quality and increased customer satisfaction (*Business Week*, 1988, p. 49).

There are, however, a number of recent studies which show the strong positive correlation between industry productivity and skill levels. Daly (1984, pp. 41–2) compared several US and UK manufacturing industries and found that a shift of 1 per cent of the labour force from the unskilled to the skilled category raised productivity by about 2 per cent, concluding that British firms suffered because 'they lacked a large intermediate group with either educational or vocational qualifications'. The specific ways in which training can harm firm performance were spelled out in a comparison of West German and British manufacturing plants (Worswick, 1985, p. 91): 'Because of their relative deficiency in shop-floor skills, equivalent British plants had to carry more overhead labour in the form of quality controllers, production planners . . . the comparative shortage of maintenance skills in British plants might be associated with longer equipment downtime and hence lower capital productivity.'

Likewise, employee productivity levels in the French construction industry were found to be one-third higher than in Britain and the main explanation was the greater breadth and quality of French training provision (Steedman, 1986).

While these studies have all centred on relatively comparable companies producing similar goods and services, a high level of ET is also a crucial element in enabling firms to reorganize the work process in pursuit of new product markets, what Reich has called 'flexible-system' production strategies (Reich, 1983, pp. 135–6). 'Flexible-system' companies are geared to respond rapidly to change, with non-hierarchical management structures, few job demarcations and an emphasis on teamwork and maintaining product quality. They can be located in new industries, i.e. biotechnology, fibre optics, or market niches within old industries, such as speciality steels and custom machine tools.

A number of recent studies have highlighted the role of training in 'flexible-system' production: in Japanese firms, Shirai (1983, p. 46) found that employees in 'small, relatively independent work groups . . . grasped the total production process, thus making them more adaptable when jobs have to be redesigned'. Streeck (1985) took the analysis one step further in his study of the European car industry, arguing that the high-quality training programmes of German automakers have acted as a driving force behind product innovation, as firms have developed more sophisticated models to better utilize the talents of their employees. Even in relatively low-tech industries, such as kitchen manufacturing, German companies are, according to Steedman and Wagner (1987), able to offer their customers more customized, better-quality units than their British competitors because of the greater flexibility of their production process—a flexibility that is contingent on workers with a broad skill base.

III. Why has Britain failed to train?

Economists' normal diagnosis of the undersupply of training is that it is a public good or free ride problem: firms do not invest in sufficient training because it is cheaper for them to hire already skilled workers than to train their own and risk them being poached by other companies. While the public good explanation may account for the general tendency to underinvest in training, it does not explain the significant variations between countries' levels of training nor does it address the key public policy question: Given the market's inability to provide enough skilled workers, why hasn't the British Government taken corrective action? To answer this question we will look first at why political parties were long reluctant to intervene in the ET field, and then, at the two major obstacles which policymakers faced when they did push for ET change: a state apparatus ill-equipped for centrally-led reform and a complex web of institutional constraints which kept Britain in a low-skills equilibrium.

1. Political parties

Through most of the postwar period, the use of ET to improve economic performance failed to emerge on the political agenda, as a consensus formed among the two major parties on the merits of gradually expanding educational provision and leaving training to industry. Underlying this consensus was an economy producing full employment and sustained growth,

which covered any deficiencies in the ET system. The broad consensus, however, masked significant differences in the reasons for the parties' positions: For Labour, vocational and technical education were seen as incompatible with the drive for comprehensive schooling, while the Party's heavy dependence on trade unions for financial and electoral support prevented any attempts to infringe on union's control over training within industry (Hall, 1986, p. 85). In the case of the Conservatives, preserving the grammar school track was the main educational priority, while intervening in the training sphere would have violated their belief in the free market (Wiener, 1981, p. 110). An exception to the principle of non-intervention came during the war, when the Coalition Government responded to the manpower crisis by erecting makeshift centres that trained more than 500,000 people. When the war ended, however, these training centres were dismantled.

2. The state structure

One of the main factors which hindered politicians from taking a more active ET role was the weakness of the central bureaucracy in both the education and training fields. On the training side, it was not until the creation of the Manpower Services Commission (MSC) in 1973 (discussed in section four) that the state developed the capacity for implementing an active labour market policy. The staff of the primary economic policy-making body, the Treasury, 'had virtually no familiarity with, or direct concern for, the progress of British industry' (Hall, 1986, p. 62) and none of the other departments (Environment, Trade and Industry, Employment or Education and Science) assumed clear responsibility for overseeing training. There was, for example, a dearth of accurate labour market statistics, which made projections of future skill requirements a virtual impossibility (Reid, 1980, p. 30). Even if the state had come up with the bureaucratic capability to develop a coherent training policy, it lacked the capacity to implement it. Wilensky and Turner (1987, pp. 62–3) compared the state structure and corporatist bargaining arrangements of eight major industrialized nations and ranked the UK last in its ability to execute manpower policy.

While responsiblity over education policy in the central state was more clearly defined, resting with the Department of Education and Science (DES), the historical decentralization of power within the educational world made it impossible for the DES to exercise effective control (Howell, 1980; OECD, 1975). Those groups responsible for delivering education, local authorities (Jennings, 1974) and teachers (Dale, 1983), were able to block reforms they opposed, such as vocationalism. The lack of central control was particularly apparent in the further education sector, an area accorded low priority by the DES until the 1970s (Salter and Tapper, 1981).

The main obstacle to ET reform, however, was not the weakness of the central state, which could be remedied given the right external circumstances and sufficient political will, but the interlocking network of societal institutions which will be explored in the following sections, beginning with the structure, or lack of it, for technical and vocational education and entry-level training.

3. The ET system

Technical and work-related subjects have long suffered from a second-class status in relation to academic courses in the British education system (Wiener, 1981). The Norwood Report of 1943 recommended a tripartite system of secondary education, with technical schools to channel the second-quarter of the ability range into skilled jobs; but while the grammar schools and secondary moderns flourished, the technical track never accommodated more than 4 per cent of the student population. In the mid-1960s two programmes, the Schools Council's 'Project Technology' and the Association for Science Education's 'Applied Science and the Schools', attempted to build an 'alternative road' of engineering and practical courses to rival pure sciences in the secondary curriculum (McCulloch *et al.* 1985, pp. 139–55). These pilot experiments were short-lived due to: 1) conflicts between and within the relevant interest groups, 2) minimal co-ordination of the initiatives and 3) the absence of clearly defined objectives and strategies for implementing them (ibid., pp. 209–12).

The efforts to boost technical education were marginal to the main educational tranformations of the postwar period: the gradual shift from division at eleven-plus to comprehensives and the raising of the school-leaving age to fifteen, and eventually sixteen in 1972. The education establishment, however, was slow to come up with a relevant curriculum for the more than 85 per cent of each age cohort who were now staying longer in school, but could not qualify for a place in higher education. Success for the new comprehensives continued to be defined by students' performance in academic examinations (O- and A-levels), which

were designed for only the top 20 per cent of the ability range (Fenwick, 1976) and allowed many students to drop subjects, such as mathematics and science, at the age of fourteen. The academic/university bias of the secondary system was reinforced by the powerful influence of the public schools, which while catering for less than 6 per cent of students produced 73 per cent of the directors of industrial corporations (Giddens, 1979), as well as a majority of Oxbridge graduates, MPs and top education officials; thus, a large percentage of those charged with formulating ET policy, both for government and firms, had no personal experience of state education, much less technical or vocational courses.

The responsibility for vocational education and training (VET) fell by default to the further education (FE) sector. The 1944 Education Act attempted to provide a statutory basis for this provision, declaring that county colleges should be set up in each LEA to offer compulsory day-release schemes for fifteen–eighteen year-olds in employment. The money was never provided to build these colleges, however, with the result that 'a jungle' of different FE institutions, courses and qualifications developed (Locke and Bloomfield, 1982). There were three main paths through this 'jungle': the academic sixth form, the technical courses certified by independent bodies, such as City & Guilds, BTEC or the RSA, and 'the new sixth form' or 'young stayers on', who remain in full-time education without committing to an A-level or specific training course (MacFarlane Report, 1980). A host of factors curtailed the numbers pursuing the intermediate route: the relatively few careers requiring these qualifications, the lack of maintenance support for FE students and the high status of the academic sixth, which was reinforced by the almost total exclusion of technical students from higher education.

The majority of individuals left education for jobs which offered no formal training. Those who did receive training were almost exclusively in apprenticeships. The shortcomings of many of these old-style training programmes, which trained 240,000 school-leavers in 1964, were well known: age and gender barriers to entry, qualifications based on time-served (up to seven years) rather than a national standard of proficiency and no guarantee of off-the-job training (Page, 1967). The equation of apprenticeships with training also had the effect of stifling training for positions below skilled level and for older employees whose skills had become redundant or needed updating.

In the early 1960s the combination of declining industrial competitiveness, a dramatic expansion in the number of school-leavers and growing evidence of skill shortages and 'poaching' prompted the Government to attempt to reform apprenticeships and other forms of training (Perry, 1976). The route the state chose was one of corporatist compromise and minimal intervention, erecting a network of training boards (ITBs) in the major industries staffed by union, employer and government representatives (Industrial Training Act, 1964). The ITBs' main means of overcoming the free-rider problem was the levy/grant system, which placed a training tax on all the companies within an industry and then distributed the funds to those firms that were training to an acceptable standard, defined by each board (Page, 1970).

The boards created a fairer apportionment of training costs and raised awareness of skill shortages, but they failed to raise substantially the overall training level because they did not challenge the short-term perspective of most companies. The state contributed no new funds to training and each board assessed only its industry's training needs, taking as given the existing firm organization, industrial relations system and management practices and thus perpetuating the low-skill equilibrium. Despite the Engineering ITB's pioneering work in developing new, more flexible training courses, craft apprenticeships remained the main supply of skilled labour until Mrs Thatcher came to power in 1979.

4. Industrial/firm structure

Industry Type.   One of the main reasons that British industry has failed to update its training programmes is the concentration of the country's firms in those product markets which have the lowest skill requirements, goods manufactured with continuous, rather than batch or unit production processes (Reich, 1983). An analysis of international trade in the 1970s by NEDO found that the UK performed better than average in 'standardized, price-sensitive products' and below average in 'the skill and innovation-intensive products' (Greenhalgh, 1988, p. 15). New and Myers' 1986 study of two hundred and forty large export-oriented plants confirmed that only a minority of these firms had experimented with the most advanced technologies and that management's future plans were focused on traditional, mass-production market segments.

Training has also been adversely effected by the long-term shift in British employment from manufacturing to low-skill, low-quality services. Manufacturing now accounts for less than one-third of British employment and its share of the labour market has been declining.

The largest growth in employment is in the part-time service sector where jobs typically require and offer little or no training. The concentration of British service providers on the low-skill end of the labour market was highlighted in a recent study of the tourist industry (Gapper, 1988).

While the type of goods or services which a company produces sets limits on the skills required, it does not determine the necessary level of training. Recent international comparisons of firms in similar product markets (i.e. Maurice *et al.*, 1986; Streeck, 1985) have revealed significant variations in training provision depending on how a company is organized and the way in which this organizational structure shapes the implementation of new technologies. In the retail trade, for instance, 75 per cent of German employees have at least an apprenticeship qualification compared with just two percent in the UK. The brief sections which follow will outline how, in the British case, the many, integrally-related components of firms' organizational structures and practices have combined to discourage training.

Recruitment.   British firms have traditionally provided two routes of entry for young workers: the majority are hired at the end of compulsory schooling, either to begin an apprenticeship or to start a semi- or unskilled job, while a select few are recruited from higher education (HE) for management posts (Crowther Report, 1959). (Nursing is one of the rare careers which has sought students leaving further education (FE) at the age of 18.) As a result, there is little incentive for those unlikely to gain admittance to HE to stay on in school or FE. Indeed, Raffe (1984, Ch. 9) found that Scottish males who opted for post-compulsory education actually had a harder time finding work than their peers who left school at sixteen. Vocational education is perceived as a low status route because it provides little opportunity for career advancement and because managers, who themselves typically enter employment without practical experience or technical training, focus on academic examinations as the best means of assessing the potential of trainees.

Job design and scope.   After joining a company, employees' training will depend upon the array of tasks they are asked to perform. Tipton's study (1985, p. 33) of the British labour market found that 'the bulk of existing jobs are of a routine, undemanding variety' requiring little or no training. The failure to broaden individuals' jobs and skill base, i.e. through job rotation and work teams, has historically been linked to craft unions' insistence on rigid demarcations between jobs, but there is some evidence that these restrictive practices have diminished in the last decade. The decline in union resistance, however, has been counterbalanced by two negative trends for training: subcontracting out skilled maintenance work (Brady, 1984) and using new technologies to deskill work (Streeck, 1985). The latter practice is particularly well documented in the automobile industry, where British firms, unlike their Swedish, Japanese and German rivals, have structured new automated factories to minimize the skill content of production jobs, instead of utilizing the new technology to increase flexibility and expand job definitions (Scarbrough, 1986). Tipton concludes (p. 27): 'the key to improving the quality of training is the design of work and a much needed spur to the movement for the redesign of work . . . may lie in training policies and practice'.

Authority Structure. In the previous section we used job design to refer to the range of tasks within one level of a firm's job hierarchy (horizontal scope); how that hierarchy is structured—number of levels, location of decision-making power, forms of control—will also affect training provision (vertical scope). *A Challenge to Complacency* (Coopers and Lybrand, 1985, pp. 4–5) discovered that in a majority of the firms surveyed, line managers, rather than top executives, are generally responsible for training decisions, thereby hindering long-term manpower planning. British firms also lack structures, like German work councils, which enable employees to exercise control over their own training.

Career/Wage Structure. A company's reward system, how wages and promotion are determined, shapes employees' incentives to pursue training. While education levels are crucial in deciding where an employee enters a firm's job structure, these incentives are low after workers have taken a job because pay and career advancement are determined by seniority not skill levels (George and Shorey, 1985). This disincentive is particularly strong for the growing number of workers trapped in the periphery sector of the labour market (Mayhew, 1986), which features part-time or temporary work, low wages and little or no chance for promotion.

Management. Linking all of the preceding elements of firm organization is the role of management in determining training levels. The poor preparation of British managers, resulting from a dearth of technical HE or management schools and a focus on accounting rather than production, is often cited as a reason for the lack of priority attached to training in Britain. A recent survey of over 2,500 British firms found that less than half made any provision at all for management training (Anderson, 1987, p. 68). In those firms

which do train, managers tend to treat training as an operating expense to be pared during economic downturns and fail to incorporate manpower planning into the firm's overall competitive strategy. For managers interested in career advancement, the training department is generally seen as a low-status option (Coopers and Lybrand, 1985, pp. 4–5). And for poorly qualified line managers, training may be perceived as a threat to their authority rather than a means of improving productivity. It is important, however, to distinguish between bad managers, and able ones who are forced into decisions by the institutional structure in which they are operating. We will explore two of the major forces impacting on their decisions, industrial relations and financial markets, in the following sections.

5. Financial markets

The short-term perspective of most British managers is reinforced by the pressure to maximize immediate profits and shareholder value. The historical separation of financial and industrial capital (Hall, 1986, p. 59) has made it harder for British firms to invest in training, with its deferred benefits, than their West German or Japanese competitors, particularly since the City has neglected training in its analysis of companies' performance (Coopers and Lybrand, 1985). Without access to large industry-oriented investment banks, British firms have been forced to finance more investment from retained profits than companies in the other G5 nations (Mayer, 1987).

6. Industrial relations

Just as the operation of financial markets has discouraged training efforts, so too the structure, traditions, and common practices of British industrial relations have undermined attempts to improve the skills of the work force. The problem must be analysed at two levels: a) the inability of the central union and employer organizations to combine with government to form a co-ordinated national training policy; and b) the historical neglect of training in the collective bargaining process.

Employer Organizations. The strength of the CBI derives from its virtual monopoly status—its members employ a majority of Britain's workers and there is no competing national federation. But while this membership base has given the CBI a role in national training policy formulation, the CBI lacks the sanctions necessary to ensure that employers implement the agreements which it negotiates with the Government. The power lies not in the central federation, nor in industry-wide employers' associations, but in individual firms. The CBI's views on training reflect its lack of control, as Keep (1986, p. 8), a former member of the CBI's Education, Training and Technology Directorate, observes: 'The CBI's stance on training policy . . . was strongly anti-interventionist and centred on a voluntary, market-based approach. Legislation to compel changes in training policy . . . was perceived as constituting an intolerable financial burden on industry.'

This free-market approach, combined with the absence of strong local employer groups, like the West German Chambers of Commerce, has left British industry without an effective mechanism for overcoming the 'poaching' problem. Among the worst offenders are the small and medium-sized firms, poorly represented in the CBI, which lack the resources to provide broad-based training.

Trade Unions.   There are four key, closely connected variables which determine the effectiveness of a central union federation in the training field (Woodall, 1985, p. 26). They are: degree of centralization, financial membership and organization resources, degree of youth organisation and structure and practice of collective bargaining. Woodall compared the TUC with European central union federations and found it weak along all of these axes. Like the CBI, it could exert a limited influence on government policy, but it lacked the means to enforce centrally negotiated initiatives on its members.

The TUC has had to deal with 'the most complex trade union structure in the world', (Clegg, 1972, p. 57) while having little control over its affiliated unions. And whereas the German central union federation, the DGB, claims 12 per cent of its member unions' total receipts, the TUC has received less than 2 per cent and devotes only a small fraction of these resources to training. This inattention to education and training is reflected in unions' lack of involvement in the transition from school to work. Britain's major youth organizations, the National Unions of Students and Youthaid, grew outside the formal union structure and have often criticized the labour movement for failing to address the needs of the nation's school-leavers, particularly the unemployed. The unco-ordinated nature of British collective bargaining, with agreements varying from coverage of whole industries to small portions of a particular factory, and the lack of central input in the negotiations further hinder TUC efforts to improve training provision. The combination of these factors prompted Taylor (1980, p. 91) to observe that 'by the

standards of other Western industrialised nations, Britain provides the worst education services of any trade union movement.'

Although we have broken down this analysis into separate sections for conceptual clarity, it is essential to view each element as part of a historically evolved institutional structure which has limited British ET. In the next part we will examine how the economic crisis of the 1970s destabilized this structure, creating the opportunity for the Thatcher Government's ET reforms.

IV. Mrs Thatcher's education and training policies

During the 1970s a confluence of events brought an end to the reluctance of central government to take the lead in ET policy-making. The prolonged recession which followed the 1973 oil shock forced the Labour Government to cut public expenditure, necessitating a re-examination of educational priorities. This reassessment came at a time when the education system was drawing mounting criticism in the popular press and the far Right's 'Black Papers' for allegedly falling standards and unchecked teacher progressivism (CCCS, 1981). The response of the then Prime Minister, Callaghan, was to launch the 'Great Debate' on education in a now famous speech at Ruskin College, Oxford in October 1976, where he called on the ET sector to make a greater contribution towards the nation's economic performance (*TES* 22/10/76, p. 72).

The increase in bipartisan political support for vocational and technical education was matched by a strengthening of the central state's capacity to formulate ET policy. The Manpower Services Commission (MSC), a tripartite quango funded by the Department of Employment, was established in 1973 to provide the strong central organization needed to co-ordinate training across industrial sectors which was missing from the industrial training board structure. In practice, however, the ITBs were left to themselves, while the MSC concentrated on the immediate problem of growing youth unemployment. The Commission supervised the first substantial injection of government funds into training, beginning with TOPS (Training Opportunities Scheme) and later through YOP (Youth Opportunities Programme). The rapid increase in government spending—the MSC budget rose from £125 million in 1974–5 to £641 million in 1978–9—did little to improve skills, however, since the funds were concentrated on temporary employment, work experience

Table 14.1. Mrs Thatcher's education and training policies

Phase/Date	Characteristics	Programmes		
		Education	Youth Training	Adult Training
I. Preparation 1979–81	Market orientation Weaken resistance Lack overall strategy	Budget cuts	Apprenticeship collapse	Dismantle ITBs
II. NTI 1982–86	Focus on 14–18s Concern with youth unemployment Enterprise economy Increase central control	TVEI Pilot-National Programme in 4 yrs	YTS/ITeCs NCVQ YOP; 1 yr YTS; 2 yr YTS YTS apprentice route	TOPS/JTS/CP TOPS-new JTS Focus on adult unemployment
III. Expansion 1987–	Education-new priorities Adults–first attempt at coherence.	GERBIL/CTCs TVEI extension or extinction?	Weaken MSC Compulsory YTS NCVQ finish in 1991.	Weaken MSC Training for employment 600,000 places; no new money.

and short-course training measures and the demands for quick action precluded any long-term manpower planning.

Spurred on by its new rival, the MSC, the DES set up the Further Education Unit (FEU) in 1978, which produced a steady stream of reports that helped shift educational opinion in favour of the 'new vocationalism', (i.e. *A Basis for Choice*, 1979). The Department teamed up with the MSC for the first time in 1976 to launch the Unified Vocational Preparation (UVP) scheme for school-leavers entering jobs which previously offered no training. Although this initiative never advanced beyond the early pilot phase, it set a precedent for subsequent reform efforts.

The state structure was in place for the new Thatcher Government to transform the ET system. The first half of this section will outline three distinct phases in the Conservatives' ET reform efforts (see Table 14.1), examining how the Government has avoided many of the pitfalls which plagued past efforts at change, while the latter portion will argue that these reforms, while leading to significant shifts in control over ET, will not raise Britain's relative ET performance.

1. Phase 1: preparation

It is only in retrospect that the first few years of the Thatcher Administration can be seen as an effective continuation of the movement towards greater centralization of ET power. At the time, Government economic policy was dominated by the belief that controlling the money supply and public expenditure were the keys to reducing inflation and restoring competitiveness. Education and training accounted for approximately 15 per cent of the budget and thus needed

to be cut if spending was to be curtailed. The cuts included: across the board reductions in education funding, a drop in state subsidies for apprenticeships and the abolition of seventeen of the twenty-four training boards (one new one was created), despite the opposition of the MSC. The financial rationale for the cuts was underpinned by the then strongly held view of the Government that training decisions were better left to market forces.

The net effect of these cuts, coming at the start of a severe recession in which industry was already cutting back on training, was the collapse of the apprenticeship system. The number of engineering craft and technician trainees, for example, declined from 21,000 to 12,000 between 1979 and 1981, while construction apprentice recruitment fell by 53 per cent during the same period (from EITB and CITB in TUC Annual Report, 1981, pp. 434–5). The destruction of old-style apprenticeships, combined with the Government's attacks on trade unions' restrictive practices through industrial relations legislation, meant that when the state eventually chose to reform initial training within companies, there was only minimal resistance from organized labour and employers.

2. Phase II: 'the new training initiative'

By 1981 the deepening recession and the dramatic rise in youth unemployment which it caused compelled the Government to reassess its non-interventionist training stance. While the Conservative's neo-liberal economic philosophy offered no immediate cure for mass unemployment, it was politically essential to make some effort to combat a problem which the polls consistently showed to be the voters' primary concern

(Moon and Richardson, 1985, p. 61). This electoral need was highlighted in a Downing Street Policy Unit paper from early 1981:

We all know that there is no prospect of getting unemployment down to acceptable levels within the next few years. (Consequently) we must show that we have some political imagination, that we are willing to salvage something—albeit second-best—from the sheer waste involved. (Riddell, 1985, p. 50.)

What this 'political imagination' produced was the New Training Initiative (NTI) (1981), whose centerpiece, the Youth Training Scheme (YTS), was the first permanent national training programme for Britain's school-leavers. YTS replaced YOP, which had begun as a temporary scheme in 1978 to offer a year's work experience and training to the young unemployed. In just four years, however, YOP had swelled to more than 550,000 places, and as the numbers grew so did the criticism of the programme for its falling job-placement rates and poor quality training. YTS attempted to improve YOP's image by upgrading the training content, 'guaranteeing' a year's placement with at least thirteen weeks off-the-job training to every minimum age school-leaver and most unemployed seventeen year-olds and more than doubling the programme's annual budget, from £400 to £1,000 million.

Despite these improvements, the scheme got off to a difficult start, with a national surplus of close to 100,000 places, as school-leavers proved reluctant to enter the new programme. In response, the MSC implemented a constant stream of YTS reforms: the scheme was lengthened from one to two years, with off-the-job training extended to twenty weeks, all sixteen and seventeen year-olds, not just the unemployed, were made eligible, some form of qualification was to be made available to each trainee, and monitoring and evaluation were increased by requiring all training providors to attain Approved Training Organisation (ATO) status. While the majority of YTS places continue to offer trainees a broad sampling of basic skills ('foundation training') and socialization into a work environment, some industries, such as construction, engineering and hairdressing, have used the scheme to finance the first two years of modernized apprenticeships.

The other major ET reform originating in this period was the Technical and Vocational Education Initiative (TVEI), launched by the Prime Minister in November 1982. TVEI marked the Thatcher Administration's first attempt to increase the industrial relevance of what is taught in secondary schools, through the development of new forms of teacher training, curriculum organization and assessment for the fourteen–eighteen age group. Under the direction of MSC Chairman David (now Lord) Young, the Initiative grew extremely rapidly, from fourteen local authority pilot projects in 1983 to the start of a nationwide, £1 billion extension just four years later. Lord Young conceived TVEI as a means of fostering Britain's 'enterprise economy', by motivating the vast majority of students who were not progressing to higher education: 'The curriculum in English schools is too academic and leads towards the universities. What I am trying to show is that there is another line of development that is equally respectable and desirable which leads to vocational qualifications . . .' (Education, 19 Nov. 1982, p. 386).

This line of development was extended into the FE sector in 1985 with the introduction of the Certificate of Pre-Vocational Education (CPVE), a one-year programme of broad, work-related subjects for students who wished to stay on in full-time education, but were not prepared for A-levels or a specific career path. In 1985 the Government set up a working group to review Britain's increasingly diverse array of vocational qualifications. The De Ville Committee's Report (1986) led to the establishment of the National Council for Vocational Qualifications (NCVQ) which has the task of rationalizing all of the country's training qualifications into five levels, ranging from YTS to engineering professionals, with clear paths of progression between stages and national standards of proficiency. The Council, which is scheduled to complete its review in 1991, will be defining broad guidelines for training qualifications into which the courses of the independent certification bodies (i.e. RSA, BTEC, City and Guilds) can be slotted.

Taken together these initiatives represent a dramatic reversal in the Government's approach to ET. The scope and pace of reform was made possible by the centralization of power in the hands of the MSC, an institution which has proved adept at securing the co-operation required to implement these controversial changes. In the case of YTS, the MSC has thus far retained trade union support, despite protests from over one-third of the TUC's membership that the schemes lead to job substitution and poor-quality training (TUC Annual Reports, 1983–86), because the TUC leadership has refused to give up one of its last remaining channels for input into national policy-making.

The MSC has also become a major power in the educational world because it offered the Conservatives a means of bypassing the cumbersome DES bureaucracy (Dale, 1985, p. 50). The Commission was able to convince teachers and local authorities, who had in the past resisted central government's efforts to reform the curriculum, to go along with TVEI through the enticement of generous funding during a period of fiscal austerity and the use of techniques normally associated with the private sector, such as competitive bidding and contractual relationships (Harland, 1987). Its influence over education increased still further in 1985, when it was given control over 25 per cent of non-advanced further education (NAFE) funding, previously controlled by the LEAs. This change has, in effect, meant that the MSC has the power to review all NAFE provision.

3. Phase III: expanding the focus

The constantly changing nature of ET policy under Mrs Thatcher makes it hazardous to predict future developments, but early indications are that education and training reform will continue to accelerate in her third term. The combination of a successful economy (low inflation, high growth and falling unemployment) and a solid electoral majority has enabled the Conservatives to turn their focus toward fundamental social reform. As a result, the narrow concentration of ET policy on the fourteen–eighteen age group appears to be broadening to include both general education (The Great Education Reform Bill (GERBIL), 1987) and adult training (Training for Employment, 1988).

The 1987 Conservative Election Manifesto signalled the emergence of education reform as a major political issue. While GERBIL is primarily an attempt to raise standards by increasing competition and the accountability of the educational establishment, a number of its provisions will impact on the vocational education and training (VET) area: the National Curriculum, which will ensure that all students take mathematics and science until they reach sixteen; City Technical Colleges, which may signal the beginning of an alternative secondary school track, funded directly by the DES with substantial contributions from industry; the removal of the larger Colleges of Further Education (CFEs) and Polytechnics from LEA control, freeing them to compete for students and strengthening their ties with employers; and increased industry representation on the new governing body for universities, the UFC (University Funding Council).

At the same time, the Government has begun restructuring adult training provision. Over the previous eight years, the MSC concentrated on reducing youth unemployment, while financing a succession of short-duration training and work experience programmes for the long-term unemployed: TOPS (Training Opportunities Scheme—short courses normally based in CFEs), JTS, and new-JTS (Job Training Scheme—work placement with minimal off-the-job training for eighteen-to-twenty-fours), and the CP (Community Programme—state-funded public work projects). In February 1988 the Government's White Paper, *Training for Employment*, introduced a plan to combine all of these adult initatives into a new £1.5 billion programme that will provide 600,000 training places, with initial preference given to the eighteen-to-twenty-four age group. To attract the long-run unemployed into the scheme the Government is using both carrot and stick: a training allowance at least £10 above the benefit level, along with increases in claimant advisors and fraud investigators to ensure that all those receiving benefit are actively pursuing work.

The new scheme will be administered by the Training Commission, the heir to the MSC. The Employment Secretary surprised both critics and supporters when he announced that the Government's most effective quango would come to an end in 1988. The new Training Commission lacks the MSC's employment functions, which have been transfered to the DoE, and its governing board structure has been altered to give industry representatives, some now appointed directly rather than by the CBI, effective control. The changes seem to indicate that the Thatcher Government no longer feels the need to consult trade unions and wants to play down the role of the CBI in order to push forward its training reforms.

The Government has also started to devote a limited amount of resources to broadening access to ET for those already in employment. The DES is expanding its PICKUP (Professional, Industrial and Commercial Updating) Programme, which is now spending £12.5 million a year to help colleges, polytechnics and universities tailor their courses more closely to employers' needs. And in 1987, the MSC provided start-up money for the Open College, which along with Open Tech uses open-learning techniques to offer individuals and employers the chance to acquire new skills or update old ones.

4. Problems with Mrs Thatcher's ET policies

While Mrs. Thatcher brought about more radical and rapid changes in the ET system than any British leader in the postwar period, there are a number reasons to doubt whether her reforms will succeed in closing the skills gap which has grown between Britain and its major competitors. Rather than detail the short-comings of specific programmes, we will focus on two major flaws in the Government's ET policy: the lack of coherence and weakness in the many initiatives designed to change the transition from school to FE or employment (reforms for the fourteen–eighteen age group) and the absence of an adult training strategy and sufficient funding to facilitate industrial restructuring.

The Transition from School to Work.   Oxford's local education authority has coined a new term, 'GONOT'. GONOT is the name of a committee set up to coordinate GCSE, OES, NLI, OCEA and TVEI,[4] just some of the reforms introduced by the Government since 1981 for the fourteen–eighteen age group. The need to create abbreviations for abbreviations is symptomatic of the strains which the Conservatives' scatter-shot approach to ET policy has placed on those charged with implementing the reforms. The case of TVEI provides a clear illustration of the difficulties created by this incoherence.

When TVEI was first announced one of its primary objectives was to improve staying-on rates. This goal has since been de-emphasized, however, because TVEI's sixteen–eighteen phase comes into direct conflict with YTS. Students have a dual incentive to opt for the narrower training option: first, because YTS offers an allowance, while TVEI does not, and second, because access to skilled jobs is increasingly limited to YTS apprenticeships. The failure of the MSC to co-ordinate these programmes is evident at all organizational levels, from the national, where the headquarters are based in different cities, to the local, where the co-ordinators of the two initiatives rarely, if ever, come into contact.

The success of individual TVEI pilot schemes is also threatened by recent national developments. Local TVEI consortia, for example, have built closer ties between schools and the FE sector to rationalize provision at sixteen-plus, a crucial need during a period of falling student numbers. But these consortia are in jeopardy due to GERBIL's proposals for opting out, open enrollment and the removal of the larger Colleges of Further Education (CFEs) from LEA control, which would foster competition rather than co-operation among institutions. Likewise, TVEI's efforts to bridge traditional subject boundaries and the divide between

academic and vocational subjects are in danger of being undermined by the proposed national curriculum with its individual subject testing and the failure to include academic examinations (GCSE and A-level) in the National Review of Vocational Qualifications (DeVille Report, 1986, p. 4).

These contradictions stem from divisions within the Conservative Party itself. Dale (1983) identifies five separate factions, industrial trainers, populists, privatizers, old-style Tories and moral educationalists, all exercising an influence on Thatcher's ET policies. Do the Conservatives, for instance, want to spread technical and vocational subjects across the comprehensive curriculum (the TVEI strategy) or ressurrect the old tripartite system's technical school track (the City Technical College route)? Another conflict has emerged in the examination sphere, where modular forms of assessment pioneered under TVEI and GCSE, which are already improving student motivation and practical skills (HMI, 1988), have been stifled by Conservative traditionalists, such as the Minister of State at the DES Angela Rumbold, insisting on preserving the narrow, exclusively academic focus of A-levels and university admissions (Gow, 1988, p. 1). The splits within the Party were highlighted in a leaked letter from the Prime Minister's secretary to Kenneth Baker's secretary, indicating Mrs Thatcher's reservations concerning the forms of assessment proposed by the Black Committee to accompany the National Curriculum (Travis, 1988, p. 1).

Emerging from this unco-ordinated series of reforms appears to be a three-tiered, post-compulsory ET system (Ranson, 1985, p. 63) which will not significantly raise the qualifications of those entering the work force: At the top, higher education will continue to be confined to an academic élite, as the White Paper 'Higher Education—Meeting the Challenge' (1987) projects no additional funds for HE in the next decade, despite growing evidence of graduate shortages; the middle rung of technical and vocational courses in full-time FE seems equally unlikely to expand, given that the Government refuses to consider educational maintenance allowances (EMAs) and that the extension funding for TVEI appears inadequate to sustain its early successes (Dale, 1986); the basic training route, then, will remain YTS, a low-cost option which has not succeeded in solving the skills problem (Deakin and Pratten, 1987). As of May 1987, more than half of all YTS providers had failed to meet the quality standards laid down by the MSC (Leadbeater, 1987). And though the quality of training may since have improved, organizations are finding it increasingly difficult to attract school-leavers on to the scheme, as falling rolls

---

[4] These initials stand for: General Certificate of Secondary Education (GCSE), Oxford Examination Syndicate (OES), the New Learning Initiative (NLI)—part of the Low-Attaining Pupils Programme (LAP), Oxford Certificate of Educational Achievement (OCEA)—part of the Record of Achievement Initiative and, of course, TVEI.

lead to increased competition among employers for sixteen year-olds to fill low-skill jobs (Jackson, 1988).

Restructuring/Adult Training.   As we have shown (section II.2), the capacity for continuously updating the skills of the work force is a key factor in the process of industrial restructuring, either at firm or national level. But in the rush to develop new ET initiatives for the fourteen–eighteen sector, the Conservatives have neglected the largest potential pool of trainees: adults in employment. The Government has not secured sufficient extra resources from any of the three basic sources of funding for post-compulsory ET, the state, individuals or companies, to finance a major improvement in British ET performance.

The largest increase in expenditure has come in the state sector, but it is crucial to examine where the money was spent. Although the MSC's budget tripled (to £2.3 billion) during the Conservatives' first two terms, only just over 10 per cent of these funds were spent on adult training, the vast majority on the long-term unemployed. Those courses, like TOPS, which did offer high-quality training geared to the local labour market, have been phased out in favour of the much-criticized JTS and new-JTS, which offer less costly, lower-skill training (Payne, 1988). This emphasis on quantity over quality was continued in the new 'Training for Employment' package, which proposes to expand the number of training places still further without allocating any new resources. Mrs Thatcher's efforts to improve training within companies have been largely confined to a public relations exercise designed to increase 'national awareness' of training needs (*Training for Jobs*, 1984). Former MSC Chairman Bryan Nicholson made the Government's position clear: 'The state is responsible for education until an individual reaches sixteen. From sixteen to eighteen, education and training are the joint responsibility of industry and government. But from eighteen on, training should be up to the individual and his employer.' (Press Conference at People and Technology Conference, London, November, 1986.)

The Conservatives, however, have had little success in convincing the private sector to assume its share of responsibility for training. While the MSC has been gradually placing a greater portion of YTS funding on employers, the bulk of the cost is still met by the state. In fact, an NAHE study (1987) revealed that private training organizations were making a profit off the MSC's training grants. The Government may be regretting its decision to do away with the one legislative means of increasing employers' funding for training,

as this remark made by Nicholson indicates: 'Those industries who have made little effort to keep the grand promises they made when the majority of ITBs were abolished should not be allowed to shirk forever.' (Clement, 1986, p. 3)

Mrs Thatcher has made somewhat more progress in her attempts to shift the ET burden on to individuals, who can fund their own ET either through direct payments (course fees, living expenses) or by accepting a lower wage in exchange for training. The state has compelled more school-leavers to pay for training by removing sixteen and seventeen year-olds from eligibility for benefits and then setting the trainee allowance at a level well below the old apprenticeship wage. It has also forced individuals staying on in full-time education to make a greater financial contribution to their own maintenance costs through the reduction of student grants, a policy which seems certain to accelerate with the introduction of student loans.

These measures, however, are not matched by policies to encourage adults to invest their time and money towards intermediate or higher-level qualifications. This failure can be traced to three sources: lack of opportunity, capital and motivation. The state's assumption of the full costs of higher education (HE), among the most expensive per pupil in the world, has resulted in a strictly limited supply of places. Those individuals who wish to finance courses below HE level suffer both from limited access to capital and a tax system which, unlike most European countries, offers employees no deductions for training costs (DES, 1988). But the main reason for workers' reluctance to invest in their own training is that the Government has done nothing to alter the basic operation of British firms which, as we saw in section III, are not structured to reward improvements in skill levels.

This underinvestment in ET raises the question: If it is true that training is critical to economic restructuring and that Mrs Thatcher has failed to improve Britain's poor ET record, why has the UK grown faster than all the major industrial nations, except Japan, over the last eight years? Part of the answer lies in the Conservatives' success in creating more efficient low-cost production and services economy. A series of supply-side measures, weakening Wage Councils and employment security legislation, subsidizing the creation of low-wage jobs (the Young Workers Scheme) and attacking trade unions, have improved labour mobility and company profitability. Training programmes, like YTS, have played a pivotal role in this process, providing employers with a cheap means of screening large numbers of low-skilled, but well-socialized young workers (Chapman and Tooze, 1986). The liberalization of financial markets, with the resultant pressure on firms to maximize short-term profits, and the explosion of accountancy-based management consultancy (*Business Week*, June 1988) have further reinforced industry's cost-cutting approach. The irony is that while Britain is striving to compete more effectively with low-cost producers such as South Korea and Singapore, these nations are investing heavily in general education and training to enable their industries to move into flexible, high technology production.

V. Policies for the future

This section suggests in broad terms what policies could remedy the insufficiencies of our system of education and training. It covers both those in the sixteen to twenty age group and the (far larger) adult labour force. We take the quantitative goal to be the broad level which the Japanese, Germans, and Swedes have achieved, namely where about 90 per cent of young people are in full-time highly-structured education and training until nineteen or twenty. And, less precisely, that major improvements take place in the training of those already in the workforce, both by the employer and externally. Training of managers, in particular of supervisors, is treated in relation to these goals.

What type of education and training? There is broad agreement about the need to raise ET standards and levels, but less about its content. This reflects the failure of the (opposed) ET methodologies of the post-war decades: manpower planning, on the one hand, and human capital theory, on the other. Manpower planning has proved too inflexible in a world in which long-run predictions about occupational needs can seldom be made. And the rate of return calculations underlying human capital approaches to optimal training provision have foundered on the difference between social and market valuations. While both approaches have a role to play when used sensibly, few practitioners would see either as sufficient to determine the content of ET.

Reform of education and training is seen in this section as part of the process of 'managing change'. This context argues for three general criteria as determining the content of education and training.

First, the uncertainty of occupational needs in the future requires *adaptability*. Many people in the labour force will have to make significant career changes in their working lives, which will require retraining. There is some agreement that successful retraining depends on a high level of general education and also on previ-

ous vocational training. Moreover, as much training for new occupations covers skills already acquired in previous ET (e.g. computing skills), a modular approach to training is efficient.

Second, ET needs to equip workers with the skills required for *innovation in products and processes* and the *production of high quality goods and services*. One implication is that participation in higher education will have to steadily increase. And there is a more radical implication: effective innovation and quality production requires participation; that means that workers and managers should acquire not just technical competence, but also the social and managerial skills involved in working together. We may need increasingly to blur the distinction between management ET and worker ET. The implications are various: a high level of general education, sufficiently broad that young people are both technically competent and educated in the humanities and arts; strong emphasis on projects, working together and interdisciplinary work; vocational education and training which provides management skills as well as technical understanding. More generally, ET should be designed to reduce class barriers (not only as a good in itself, but also) because of the requirements of innovation and high-quality production.

Third, ET must be *recognizable* and *useful*, so that employers want to employ the graduates of the ET system and young people and adults want to undertake ET. There is a potential tension here with the previous paragraph. For the abilities stressed there are at present only demanded by a minority of companies. Vocational education is thus a compromise between the characteristics needed in the longer term and the skills and knowledge which companies can see as immediately useful to them. A second implication of the need for recognition and usefulness is that there be a widely agreed and understood system of certification, based on acceptable assessment.

Much policy discussion, sensibly, concerns potential improvements within the broad context of the existing framework of ET provision within the UK. As a result less thought has been given to the wider transformations which we believe the management of change and the move to a high skills equilibrium imply. The discussion of this section thus takes a longer-term perspective.

There are five interdependent parts to these recommendations for reform: reforming ET provision for the sixteen to twenty age group; training by companies; individual access to training; the external infrastructure of ET; and the macro-economic implications of a major ET expansion.

1. The education and training of sixteen to twenty year-olds

The focus of this section is on how incentives, attitudes, institutions and options can be changed so that young people will choose to remain in full-time education and training until the age of nineteen or twenty, rather than entering the labour market or YTS at age sixteen.

For two reasons the next decade offers a window for reform which was not previously open. First, the demographic decline in the sixteen-plus age cohort will mean a drop of nearly a third over the next ten years in the numbers of young people aged between sixteen and nineteen. It will therefore be an ideal period for bringing our system into line with that of other advanced countries. For the resource cost, although considerable, of a substantial increase in the ET participation ratio of sixteen to nineteen year-olds will be significantly less than in the past decade.

The second reason was spelt out in section IV. The institutional constraints against change are in two ways significantly weaker now than a decade or two decades ago. Unions at national level, far from seeking to frustrate change, would support it in this area; they would see it as a means of regaining membership, rather than a threat to the bargaining position of existing skilled workers. The education system (teachers, LEAs, educationalists, teachers unions) no longer sees itself as having the right to determine education policy alone; central government has far stronger control over it than in the past, and this will increase over the next decade as opting out develops; the larger CFEs will no longer be run by LEAs; teachers unions are moving away from the belief that they can successfully oppose government to the view that they need to cultivate wider alliances, including industry; and educationalists today are far more aware of the role which schools can play in helping children to get employment. In addition political parties are no longer constrained as they were (say) two decades ago in formulating policy in these areas.

What basic requirements are implied for a sixteen to twenty ET system by the discussion in the introduction above? Five should be stressed:

— good general education, covering both technical subjects and the humanities;
— this should be designed to encourage interaction (project etc.) and reduce social class differences;
— rising percentage over time going into HE, and ease of switching between more vocational and more academic routes;
— structured vocational training for those not going on to HE, with acquisition of broad skills, including communications and decision-making competences;
— modularization and certification.

Despite the 'window of opportunity' how feasible is the sort of major change envisaged? Aside from the question of financing, formidable problems will need to be resolved:

(a) Young people have the option at sixteen to remain in full-time education. About 65 per cent choose not to. Raising the legal minimum school leaving age to eighteen is politically not a possibility, and in any case it is desirable that young people should choose to stay on. How are incentives to be structured and attitudes changed to raise the staying-on rate to above 80 per cent?

(b) Relatively few businesses are currently capable of providing high-quality training. And, while employer organizations are becoming more committed to involvement in ET, effective action on their part will require a co-ordinating capacity which is beyond their present power or resources.

(c) In comparison to other countries with well-developed vocational training systems the UK lacks an effective administrative structure and a major research and development capacity.

Of these constraints the first must be overcome. It will be argued in this section that the involvement of employers and their organizations and a proper state infrastructure will be needed to achieve both this and the ET desiderata set out above. To see why this is the case, we look first at why sixteen year-olds choose to leave education and training, and with this in mind, examine the experience of sixteen–twenty ET in other countries.

Why do such a large proportion of young people choose to join the labour market or YTS at sixteen? There are two main reasons. The first is financial. On YTS or social security young people get a small income. If they remain in full-time education they receive nothing (their parents receiving child benefit). There are therefore strong inducements to leave full-time education at sixteen. The demographic shrinking of the sixteen-plus age group (while it will make reform easier) will, in the absence of reform, strengthen the incentive to leave; this is because employers are accustomed to recruiting from this age group, directly or nowadays through YTS, since it provides relatively cheap and pliable labour, so that relative earnings at sixteen-plus may be expected to rise.

In the second place, staying on in full-time ET has not been seen as a bridge to stable employment. The best route to employment for most sixteen year-olds today is via YTS, which is used by many employers as a screening device for the choice of permanent employees. YTS trainees who show themselves to be co-operative have a high probability of securing permanent employment; and that probability will rise as the demographic decline in the sixteen-plus age cohort sets in.

Foreign experience can give an idea of different possible systems of sixteen–twenty ET, as well as alerting to some of the problems.

— One country often cited as an exemplar is the US. About 75 per cent of the relevant age group graduates from high school by age eighteen after a broadly based course, more academically geared for those going on to HE, more vocational for those going directly into the labour market. Over 40 per cent go on to two year junior colleges or university, producing a remarkably educated population. But there are problems with the education and training of those who do not go on to HE. In many areas, lack of co-ordinated employer involvement has meant there is no clear bridge between education and employment. The 'Boston compact', under which a group of companies guaranteed training and employment for those with good high school performance, acknowledged this need. And lack of involvement by companies in sixteen to twenty ET has limited firms' provision of training for manual workers and low-level white collar workers.

— France has a more highly structured system of initial vocational training. Less able children can go to vocational schools from fourteen to eighteen, and end with craft-level qualifications. More emphasis in the future is being placed on the various higher-level vocational *baccalaureat* courses, from sixteen to nineteen, which turn out technician engineers with managerial skills. Compared with the UK, both routes are impressive, especially the second. But, as in the US, there is limited employer involvement. One consequence is staying-on rates at sixteen-plus well below the Northern European and Japanese, and a higher rate of youth unemployment. A second is limited training for manual workers in companies.

— In the Germanic (Germany, Austria, Switzerland) system, those going on to higher education spend two years from sixteen to eighteen in a high school before taking the *abitur*. Those working for vocational qualifications become appreticed at sixteen for three or four years and follow a highly structured, carefully monitored system of on-the-job and off-the-job training and education, with external exams on both practical and theoretical subjects.

— In the Scandanavian (Norway, Sweden) system, young people remain in the same college between sixteen and eighteen, specializing in vocational or academic areas; vocational education is then completed in vocational centres post-eighteen.

— Denmark has been actively experimenting with post-sixteen ET in the last two decades. The Danes have been moving towards a system in which all young people remain within the same educational institution between sixteen and eighteen, more or less a tertiary college. If they choose the vocational route, they move into a two year apprenticeship at eighteen, for which much work will have already been covered in the college.

Both the Germanic and Scandinavian systems succeed in attaining very high participation rates for the sixteen–eighteen age groups, and in delivering high-quality vocational training as well as good general education. There are, however, arguments against both Germanic and Scandinavian systems as the optimal model for the UK, despite the fact that both systems are greatly superior to our own. The main argument against applying the Scandinavian system to the British context is that Britain lacks the infrastructure to make it work: the close involvement of employer organizations with the public system of vocational education. Moreover, there is powerful union and state pressure on companies to maintain training standards.

The Germanic system also has disadvantages, in part because it would be based too strongly on employers if transplanted to the UK. There are four reasons why we should be wary of advocating a German-type division at sixteen between academic education and an employer-based three or four-year apprenticeship:

— The greater the employer involvement (unless restrained by powerful employer organizations and unions as in Germany), the more the apprenticeship will reflect the short-term needs of the employer. This is illustrated by the otherwise excellent EITB engineering apprenticeship scheme in the UK: broken into modules, employers select those modules most relevant to their own needs, rather than to the longer-term needs of the trainee.

— Few UK employers are in a position to run quality three or four year apprenticeships; but these would be needed across the board in public and private sectors, and in industry and services.

— If young people were to move into employer-based apprenticeships at sixteen, it would *de facto* close them off from higher education.

— Equally, by dividing the population at sixteen, the opportunity to reduce class distinctions would not be taken.

How, then, should sixteen–twenty ET evolve in the future? We believe a system very roughly along Danish lines is the most feasible model to aim for, given the current UK position.

(1) *A common educational institution from sixteen to eighteen.*   Apart from the Germanic countries, the US and Scandanavia, as well as Japan (more or less), have a common institution from sixteen to eighteen. France and Denmark have both been moving towards it as a matter of conscious choice. It is an obvious vehicle for encouraging a rising percentage of young people to go on to higher education at eighteen. Equally it has a necessary part to play in reducing class differences.

(2) *Accelerated apprenticeships post-eighteen: the bridge to employment.*   The Germanic and Scandinavian systems, and Japan and South Korea, provide at least four years of ET post-sixteen. This could be done in the UK by short, highly structured apprenticeships, which would at the same time build clear bridges to employment. If further training was carried out mainly in vocational schools post-eighteen, this bridging perception would be less clear; of course, vocational schools would be important post-eighteen, since UK companies would require considerable help if they were to provide high-quality training. The next section discusses how companies could develop high-quality training capacities: it is evident that if they can the benefits would go beyond sixteen–twenty ET; the need for companies in both public and private sectors to develop effective training capacities is central to the management of change.

(3) *Linking post-eighteen apprenticeships with pre-eighteen ET.*   In order for two-year apprenticeships to be of high quality, considerable preparatory work towards them will need to have been completed pre-eighteen. It is also important to make clear to students the link between what is expected from them in the sixteen–eighteen period and their subsequent training opportunities. Preparatory work covers both general and vocational education. The role of a good general education, covering technical subjects and the humanities, has already been stressed, as has the parallel need for vocational education to include the acquisition of broad skills including communications and decision-making competences, with emphasis on developing individual initiative and team-work through projects. Vocational education will also be focused in part on the chosen apprenticeship area. Thus, for those who choose it at sixteen, there will be a 'vocational' route, with specific and general requirements for particular apprenticeship areas.

(4) *Modules and certification.*   Vocational qualifications would be awarded and HE entrance requirements satisfied by successfully completed modules. In the case of HE the modules would all be taken in the common institution; it would be natural to think of AS levels as module-based (the original intention), and that the major part of the most common route to satisfying HE entrance requirements would consist in completing the modules needed to gain so many AS levels. To gain a vocational qualification, and to fulfil the condition for entry to an apprenticeship, a substantial proportion of the necessary modules could and should be completed pre-eighteen. A modular system in a single institution provides considerable flexibility. Most students would choose early on a vocational or an HE route; but if some proportion of AS modules were allowed for vocational qualification purposes and some proportion of vocational modules for entry into HE, those students who wished to do so could keep their options open for longer. Modules could also be used to broaden HE entry requirements, and to increase the general education component in vocational qualification. There might in addition be a case for a college graduation diploma, as in many countries, based on successful completion of modules.

(5) *Employer co-ordination and involvement.*   A high degree of employer co-ordination and involvement will be needed to make this system work. That is the positive lesson of Northern Europe. Local co-ordination is necessary to link 'training' employers with educational institutions and with students. At a regional and national level, employer involvement is needed to help develop curricula, monitoring of 'trainers', assessment procedures, and so on. This will require more powerful employer organizations, nationally, sectorally and locally than the UK has now. How this might be achieved is further discussed below.

(6) *Role of unions.*   Many 'training' employers, especially in the public sector, are unionized, so that union co-operation will be needed. Union involvement in curriculum development and the like will also be important in balancing the power of employer organizations. This again is a lesson from the experience of Sweden and Germany.

(7) *Local and national government.*   Government has played a key role in providing a coherent framework for the sixteen–twenty ET system at local, regional and national level in each of the countries discussed, with the exception of the US. The UK lacks institutional coherence in this area, and has only a limited research and policy-making capacity.

(8) *Education maintenance allowance and financial incentives.*   A central purpose of the reform strategy suggested above has been to construct a clear bridge

from education to employment so that young people stay within a well-structured ET system from the age of sixteen to nineteen or twenty. This is in line with the instrumental view of education taken by most young people who leave at sixteen (Brown, 1987). But to be successful in raising the sixteen-plus participation rate, it is also necessary to ensure that leaving at sixteen is less attractive than staying on. This will require, first, an educational maintenance allowance for those who stay on, at least equal to state payments for those who leave. More fundamentally, it raises the question of reducing employer incentives to hire sixteen year olds, and convincing them to stop seeing the sixteen-plus age group as its main recruiting ground for unskilled and semi-skilled labour (Ashton and Maguire, 1988). This is discussed in the next section.

2. Developing the training capacity of employers

International comparisons suggest that UK employers devote a smaller share of value added to training expenditures than any other major advanced country. For radical reform to be successful, the attitude of employers will have to change, as has been seen in the discussion in the last section of post-sixteen ET and restructuring: specifically, the development by employers of a training capacity is necessary for a system of accelerated apprenticeships. In addition to sixteen–twenty ET, a training capacity is needed for restructuring within organizations for training and retraining existing employees.

In looking at restructuring, it is useful to distinguish between retraining by the existing employer, which will be referred to as internal retraining, and retraining elsewhere, primarily in state/union/employer-organization or private vocational training centres. This will be referred to as external retraining and will be discussed below. Roughly the internal/external retraining distinction corresponds to that between internal (e.g. changing product composition within a company) and external (e.g. closures/running down an industry) restructuring.

With internal restructuring companies meet declining demand by product innovation. In countries where product innovation strategies are emphasized they are associated with reliable sources of long-term finance, and long-term relations with suppliers which the company does not wish to disrupt. More important, they are associated with internal training capacities in companies, a retrainable workforce with on-the-job flexibility and a high perceived cost to making workers

redundant (Streeck *et al.*, 1985; Sorge and Streeck, 1988; Hotz-Hart, 1988). The high perceived cost may arise from legal requirements, as in Germany, or collective bargaining power, as in Sweden, or from a basic communitarian view of the enterprise, as in Japan (Dore, 1987). Cost reduction strategies under these circumstances will tend to focus on reducing capital or material or financing costs, rather than labour saving changes. Again, retraining capacities are critical.

In the UK much more use has been made of external restructuring. This reflects the lack of the characteristics described in the last paragraph as associated with internal restructuring in countries such as Germany, Japan and Sweden. Instead the UK is characterized by:

(i)   The organization of production around relatively standardized goods and services, with low skill requirements and cost-cutting rather than technically competent management; aggravated by:

— the public goods problem; and
— the pressure of financial institutions and, in the public sector, cash limits against long-term investment activity.

(ii)   The lack of pressure from employees to maintain training; and the ease with which companies can make workers redundant without being required to consider product innovation and retraining as alternative ways of maintaining employment.

(iii)   The lack of an effective infrastucture. Few sectors of the economy have well developed training structures, with worked out systems of certification, training schools, and information and counselling for companies. Employers organizations are weak, and unions are seldom equipped to provide good training services to their members.

The difficulties involved in increasing company expenditure on training and ensuring it is of the right quality are thus substantial. In a longish-term perspective two general points may be made. First, the increase in the educational level of young people entering the labour force and a different attitude to adult education and training will make it easier for companies to move to a higher skills equilibrium. Second, policies to change company behaviour on training should be one part of a co-ordinated strategy to help companies focus on marketing, product innovation, new technology, high-quality production, and provision of long-term finance. Education and training policies should be closely linked to industrial and regional policies; but to trace out these links would be beyond the scope of this paper. Four main policy directions are set out here:

how they might be financed, where not implicit, is discussed below.

(1) *Financial incentives.*   There is little question that companies in both public and private sectors need financial incentives (positive or negative) if they are significantly to increase their training activities. This is because, for the foreseeable future, there will be a divergence between private and public returns because of the public good problem and the low-skills equilibrium. (The general strategy advocated in this paper is designed to reduce the divergence over time, but specific incentives will be necessary until then.)

The form of the incentives is critical. A minimum legal requirement is unlikely to be productive, at least by itself. It might take one of two forms: a requirement to spend a certain minimum percentage of value added or payroll on training; and/or a requirement to carry out certain types of training, e.g. to take so many apprentices, with a significant enough penalty to gain compliance. One problem with both approaches is that some companies may be better placed to carry out effective training than others. In addition, the minimum percentage approach (by itself) says nothing about who gets trained: in France this approach led to senior managers being sent to expensive hotels in the French Pacific to learn English. And the 'minimum number of apprentices' approach poses formidable quality problems.

A sensible approach, at least to start with, is to give financial incentives to companies (private and public) who are prepared to train and undergo the monitoring and other conditions necessary to ensure both quality and coverage (i.e. that training covers apprenticeships and semi-skilled workers as well as managers, etc.). The further conditions are discussed in the next paragraph. These incentives would not need to be uniform across industries, regions or types of training.

(2) *Meisters and certification.*   How are we to ensure that companies train to the right quality and over the desired coverage? In Japan, Germany and similar countries, the role of the supervisor in both industry and services is different to the UK supervisor, (see e.g. Prais and Wagner, 1988). In those countries supervisors (in German '*meister*') are technically skilled as well as playing a management role; moreover they have major responsibility for training. In the German system, they have themselves to pass a rigorous training after having gained a technician or craft-level qualification. The above suggests ideas along the following lines:

(a)   A distinction should be drawn between certified skills and non-certified skills. This would be similar to the distinction between marketable and firm-specific skills. In practical terms it would reflect those that the NCVQ included as certifiable.

(b)   Companies wishing to participate in the training of employees for certified skills would be required to employ certified 'training supervisers', i.e. similar to German *meisters.*

(c)   The Government could then negotiate with employer organizations tariffs for different certified skills, and use this as one means of influencing the size and distribution of training. Those companies would then get automatic payments for certified training, subject to periodic inspections and subject to satisfactory results of trainees in external assessment.

In summary, financial incentives should be used, not just to produce a desired amount of training, but also to ensure that companies acquire a training capacity and supervisory staff with a professional commitment to training.

(3)   *Changing the age structure of hiring.* Specific disincentives will be needed to dissuade businesses from hiring sixteen–eighteen year olds over the next decade.

(4)   *Employee representation.* Again, as in Northern Europe, it is sensible to give employees a role in decision-making on training within companies. They have an interest in the acquisition of certified skills. For this role to be effective, decisions on training would need to be codetermined between management and employees. In addition, continental experience suggests that employee representatives need union expertise if they are to challenge low-spending management with any chance of success.

In particular, it is important to enable employees to challenge management decisions on redundancies. In the German model, management is required to reach an agreement with the works council on how redundancies are to be dealt with. The cost to management of not reaching an agreement means that managers emphasize innovation and retraining in their long-term planning.

(5) *External infrastructure.*   Both (2) and (3) impose strong demands on an external infrastructure. Companies will in practice rely heavily on the advice of employer organizations, whom they can trust at least to give advice in the interest of the sector they represent, if not in the interest of the individual company. Employees need the advice of unions if they are to challenge company decisions on training and redundancies. Public or tripartite bodies will be required to provide R & D on training technology and labour market developments (e.g. skill shortages); to run a system

of certification; and to provide training where it is needed to complement company training. How this can be done is discussed in V.4.

3. A culture of lifetime education and training

There is an apparent lack of interest by adults in the UK in continuing education and training. In countries with good training systems, a strong belief by individuals in the benefits of ET reinforces the system: parents can see the value of education and training for their children; employees put pressure on laggardly employers to provide training; the public good problem which companies face is reduced by individuals paying for the acquisition of marketable skills. Yet in the UK little adult training takes place which is not paid for by the employer; this is in particular the case for unskilled and semi-skilled employees and for the unemployed. Why is human capital theory wrong in asserting that individuals will be prepared to pay for the acquisition of marketable skills? Why especially is this the case when vacancies for skilled jobs coexist with high unemployment and insecure semi-skilled employment?

In the first place, individuals seldom have access to financial resources sufficient to finance any extended period of vocational training:

(1)   Financial institutions are reticent about lending without security for training, except for a few cases where returns from the training are high. This is not particular to UK financial institutions. Banks in most countries will not lend for ET purposes to individuals, unless the loans are guaranteed or subsidized or unless the bank has close connections and knowledge of a community. This likely reflects both moral hazard and adverse selection problems.

(2)   There is limited access to state subsidy for most adult vocational training, particularly for maintenance, but also for tuition. Individual expenditure on training is in general not tax deductible. The unemployed likewise have limited access to funds: their retraining possibilities seldom relate to those areas in which there are vacancies.

(3)   Major reductions in income are seldom feasible for those who are employed; *a fortiori* for those who are unemployed.

Secondly, the individual return from much vocational training is not high. There are several reasons for this:

(1)   The low-skills equilibrium organization of work means that the marginal productivity of skills for individual workers is below what it would be in an economy where a large enough proportion of the workforce was skilled to permit a high-skills pattern of work organization.

(2)   For a large proportion of the workforce (manual and low-level white-collar) there reflects the organization of work discussed. Second, differentials for skilled workers were heavily compressed in the 1970s, and though they have widened since, they are still not high in comparison to high-skill countries. (Prais and Wagner, 1988.)

(3)   A large proportion of the workforce does not have the basic education required to proceed to craft-level vocational training; so a major prior investment is necessary.

(4)   The existing system of certification is unhelpful, as the NCVQ has emphasized. Aside from being confusing, it fails to give employers real guarantees in many areas as to the competences of the certified employee, because of the lack of proper assessment procedures. In addition, and more important, portability is limited. In the modern economy skills obsolesce. The acquisition of new skills should not involve returning to square one, as it frequently does today.

(5)   Finally, for those who are currently employed, and wish independently to take leave to pursue education or training, there is seldom a guarantee that they will be able to keep their job.

This means that major self-financed training or retraining is not seen as a realistic possibility, if it is considered at all, by most unskilled or semi-skilled workers or those who are unemployed. Moreover, with the exceptions of a few unions who provide good counselling services, little advice is available.

A comprehensive external training system

Those who seek, or might be persuaded to seek, external training fall into two categories with some overlapping: people with clear goals and courses in mind, adequate previous education and training, but held back by unavailability of finance or employment insecurity; and the unskilled, semi-skilled and unemployed with little belief in the possibility of effective retraining. For both groups adequate financing is necessary. There is a strong case for formalizing a system of education credits for adults. These credits would be intended for training not covered by companies. The general question of financing is considered below, but it should be noted here that if individuals had their own 'training accounts', into which education credits were put, these credits could be added to by saving, perhaps topped-up by public funding. For most people in the second group, additional financing will be necessary, since it will not be reasonable to expect them to save enough. It is of great importance that those threatened by redundancy or made redundant are given sufficient resources for long periods of ET. Along Swedish lines, a reasonable income might be conditioned on in effect a contract to train for a given range of skills in which there are vacancies or in which employment is likely.

For this group, much more is required than financing. Also needed are counselling, an information system covering vacancies and future areas of demand, structured basic education if necessary, training and retraining facilities (though they might be in the private sector and hired by the state), and a support system to facilitate mobility if needed. How an external retraining system might be set up is discussed in the next section.

Returns to skills

This is an important problem to which there are few easy solutions. We argued above for policies to encourage the development of a supervisory grade with technical qualifications: if successful, that would help the concept of a career ladder based on skills. It is harder for the government to intervene in the process of wage determination, and widen skill differentials even if there is case for doing so. In our view, the more sensible approach is to give incentives to employers to increase training, on the one hand, and to develop an external training policy to help redundant and potentially redundant workers, who have less need of incentives to acquire skills, on the other.

4. Institutional infrastructure

Radical reform of ET requires a more effective institutional infrastructure than presently exists. Our view is that radical reform is not a simple political option, but one requiring major institutional changes which will be difficult to bring about in the UK, at least if reform is to realize its full potential. This returns the argument to those economic historians that our basic economic problems lie in our institutions.

It was argued in section IV that the old constraining infrastructure has broken down; and that the Government has substituted increased centralized control via the MSC (as was) and the DES, combined with the use of contracts with training agencies. The centralization of policy-making has not been accompanied by a significant expansion of the very limited research and information-gathering capacities of the MSC and the

DES. A parallel can be drawn between this system and large conglomerates controlled by a small financially-oriented headquarters. The new system will become more pronounced as: (a) local education authorities have a diminished role in post-sixteen ET, with the removal of polytechnics and the larger CFEs from their control, with the decline in importance of TVEI, and with the possible opting out of secondary schools; (b) the wide variety of course-development, assessment and accreditation bodies are encouraged to behave more competitively; and (c) the NCVQ becomes more a body carrying out government instructions, especially in relation to certification of YTS trainees, than a forum in which different points of view, of the business community, of unions and of educationalists and trainers can be expressed.

The new system is hardly adequate for dealing with YTS and ATS; it has major drawbacks if it is to carry through radical reform. We will argue that a different system needs to be developed in which employers organizations, unions, educationalists and the regions should all ideally play a more important part; and in which the role of government should be more concerned with the provision of information, research and development, and coordination, than with unilateral policy-making.

The need for better information, R & D, and co-ordination

The reforms discussed in the preceding sub-sections involve major course developments: for sixteen–eighteen year olds; for accelerated apprenticeships; for those at work; for *meisters*; for those undertaking external retraining; together with development of assessment procedures, certification and accreditation of examining bodies. It will be necessary to co-ordinate academic examining boards with vocational training institutions such as BTEC; and to co-ordinate the activities of the vocational institutions themselves. Also, it is important to allow experimentation and thus course development by individual teachers or trainers, and a mechanism is needed to permit the diffusion of best-practice innovations. All this demands a much greater role of government in the R & D and co-ordination process. This might perhaps be on the lines of regional labour market and regional education boards in Sweden.

For two broad reasons, a more effective ET system also requires involvement by the social partners (employers' organizations and unions) as well as educational institutions and the Government. The first is to ensure that policy-making is conducted in a balanced way. The second is to bring about the participation of companies (3), and employees (4).

Multilateral participation in ET governance

Running a complex ET system is a principal-agent problem. However clear the ideas of the Government (the principal) and however effective its own research and development activities, the co-operation of teachers and trainers as agents is essential to efficient course development, assessment, etc. But educators will have their own interests. (Japan is a case in point, where educationalists dominate the development of sixteen–eighteen education, business has no influence, and where rote learning still plays a major role.) A tempting solution is for governments to use expert civil servants as additional agents; of course it is important that government experts should be involved, but there is a danger: if detailed policy-making is left to government experts and educationalists, the former may assimilate over time the goals of the latter, particularly if governments change.

A more effective solution is to balance the interests of educators against the interests of employers and those of employees. Hence the case for involving their representatives as additional agents, to bring about more balanced objectives. If this is to be successful, both employers' organizations and unions need expertise; here again Northern European experience, where the social partners have their own research institutions, in some cases financed by the state, is suggestive. Moreover, as employers' organizations and unions acquire expertise, so a common culture of understanding and agreement on a range of training issues gets built up by professionals on all sides. Thus the agents, with their different interests but shared culture, become players in a co-operative game over time in which compromise and flexibility are available to meet changing conditions. (For a broader use of this type of approach, see the insightful Lange, 1987.)

A similar case can be made for involving representatives of regions in addition to central government. For individual regions will have their own economic goals, and more political stability than central government. Again, effective involvement requires expertise. This reinforces the argument for regional labour market and regional education boards.

Employers' organizations and the participation of companies

Most companies see no gain in participating in training in marketable skills and associated activities to a socially optimal degree. This is both because of the standard prisoner's dilemma problem and the low skills equilibrium. As a partial solution to both problems we suggested the use of financial incentives to encourage the building up of a training capacity within companies. Important though that is by itself, its effectiveness can be greatly enhanced through employers' organizations. First, getting companies to train in the right way is difficult for government, because of an assymetry of information: the company knows much more about how good its training is than the Government. Companies are often loathe to be monitored by, or give detailed information to, government, because they distrust the use to which the information will be put. Employers' organizations are in a better position to engage the co-operation of companies, because they are seen to be on the side of companies as a whole. Secondly, powerful employers' organizations, as in Germany, can sanction free-riders more cheaply than the Government. This is the case where employers' organizations distribute a range of valued services to companies, not necessarily just in the training area; and have a degree of discretion over their distribution. One of these services may be training advice; others might be in, say, export marketing. This gives the organization potential sanctions, which might enable it, for instance, to organize local co-ordination of companies with respect to the bridge between education and employment; or to prod companies into increasing training activities.

Employees and unions

Unions have several important roles to play in an effective ET system, as mentioned above. Here we want to stress the role of unions in promoting employee involvement in training decision-making. Such involvement is a critical component of high-skill economies. If it is to be effective, employees must be properly backed up by union advice and expertise.

Much of the argument of this sub-section is influenced by the study of why the Scandinavian and Germanic ET systems have been successful. There is an important research agenda here for the UK. We do not want to suggest the type of powerful employers organizations or union confederations in those countries, or regional government as in Germany is transplantable, it is not. But there is a strong case for giving muscle to employers' organizations and unions, and to regions and perhaps metropolitan areas, in the training field. Unions are moving in the UK (some much faster than others) to consider training as a core area of their interests. Business organizations are moving less fast, but in the right direction. Radical reform of ET will need a push by government. One possibility, for a radical re-forming government, is to give the social partners the resources to develop major expertise in training. A second is to consider whether chambers of commerce can play a more significant role at local level, so as to enable them to develop local employer networks. Third, to consider the possibilities of regional labour market and regional education boards as quadripartite institutions, with educationalists and regional representatives as well as the social partners.

5. Macroeconomic and financing implications

The preceding four sub-sections have looked at the micro aspects of policies needed for transforming the post-sixteen education and training system. They have suggested how to change incentives facing individuals and organizations; how co-ordinating and providing institutions could be built up; and how training policies should be seen as part of a broader micro-economic strategy directed at changing ways in which companies operate. If successful these changes carry great benefits in terms of macro-economic performance. But to be successful they require a major injection of resources.

In a steady-state, the benefits can be assumed to outweigh the resource cost. But in the process of transforming the system, resource costs would be likely to precede the benefits of additional resources. There is not the space in this article to discuss in detail the financing of this gap. But we want to make some brief points to indicate why we believe that increased expenditures in this area can be more easily managed than in many others.

The increased resources devoted to ET can be met in one or more of three ways:

— an increase in GDP;
— a reduction in other expenditures;
— an increase in imports.

There are two reasons why some part of the resource cost can be met by reduction in other expenditures. First, specific forms of taxation or quasi-taxation can be exploited with minimal economic damage.

— A training levy on companies who do not undertake certified training. It will be difficult for these companies to pass on the levy in the form of higher prices if some competitors are undertaking certified training and hence not paying the levy. And since most of the non-training companies are likely to be in the sheltered sector of the economy, any reduction in their activity levels as a result of the levy will have the beneficial effect of transferring business to training competitors.

— Individual training accounts. If individuals choose to contribute to an individual training account, it will come from a voluntary reduction in consumers expenditure.

Second, other government expenditures will be reduced:

— Reduction in government expenditures on YTS and other MSC related activities which would be phased out as a new system of sixteen–twenty ET developed.

— Reduction in government expenditures on education and training post-sixteen as a result of demographic decline.

Thus some part of the necessary resources can be met from reduced expenditure elsewhere but without relying on an increase in general taxation. The damage caused by the latter is not only political, but also, via its inflationary potential, economic. But there are limits beyond which it may be unwise or impossible to push these reductions.

This means that the resources to finance a training programme will have to come in part from increased GDP and increased imports. The point to be made here is that the standard problems associated with an expansionary policy can be more easily handled within the context of a training programme than in other cases.

The first problem is that of inflation caused by the increased bargaining power of employees as employment rises. Appropriate increases in the skilled workforce can reduce inflationary pressures in two ways. Directly, it reduces skilled labour bottlenecks and the power of 'insiders' relative to outsiders. Indirectly, it facilitates wage restraint especially if unions are involved in the training institutions.

The second problem is financing the external deficit and the public sector deficit, at least without a fall in the exchange rate or a rise in the interest rate. Avoiding these consequences requires that inflation does not increase and that the increase in the PSBR and the external deficit are seen as eventually self-correcting. The last paragraph was concerned with inflation. A training programme can, more easily than most programmes involving increased government expenditure, be credibly seen as self-correcting in its effect on the PSBR and the external deficit.

VI. Concluding remarks

The UK has long suffered from a low-skills equilibrium in which the ET system has delivered badly educated and minimally trained sixteen year-old school-leavers to an economy which has been geared to operate—albeit today more efficiently—with a relatively unskilled labour force. Some companies have broken out of this equilibrium with the aid of strategic managers, to see training and innovation as core activities. Most have not.

Despite the much-vaunted reforms of the ET system of the last few years, major improvements are unlikely to be brought about:

— The majority of children will still leave school at sixteen, and will gain a low-level training in YTS; referring to the certification of YTS by the NCVQ, Jarvis and Prais argued that it would lead to 'a certificated semi-literate under-class—a section of the workforce inhibited in job-flexibility, and inhibited in the possibility of progression'. (*Financial Times*, 1/7/88, quoting Jarvis and Prais, 1988.)

— There are no substantive policies to remedy the vacuum in training in most companies.

— There are no measures to undertake the depth of education and training frequently needed in a rapidly restructuring world economy to enable those made redundant to acquire relevant skills.

We have argued the case in section V for: full-time education to eighteen, with 'accelerated' apprenticeships thereafter, for those not going on to higher education; building up training capacities within companies; and an external retraining system to deal with restructuring between companies and industries.

Instead of summarizing these proposals, we want to underline certain points which have not always been adequately brought out in discussions of reform:

— It is important to think in terms of the incentives which face individuals, rather than make the mistake of some educators of just talking about institutions or educational innovations. But equally the economist's mistake, of treating incentives as only financial, must be avoided. We lay stress on the idea of enabling individuals to see career progressions: thus importance is attached to the bridge from education to employment for sixteen to twenty year-olds.

— Companies should be seen not as profit-maximizing black boxes, but as coalitions of interests, particularly among managers. We argue that, rather than incentives being used to increase the amount of training as such, they can more effectively be used if they increase a company's training capacity, by giving companies an incentive to train or hire meisters, or training supervisors. This produces a stake in training as a company activity.

— Along similar lines, employees should be given a role in training decision-making within the company. Here, there are lessons to be learned from industrial democracy procedures in Germany and Sweden. This reinforces the idea of groups within the company with a stake in training.

— More generally, the problem of moving companies from a low-skill to a high-skill equilibrium involves much more than training and education. It requires changes in management style, R & D, financing, marketing, etc. so training policy should be seen as part of a wider industrial strategy.

— Countries with successful ET systems devote substantial resources to research on education and training and labour market developments. In the UK today policy-making has become highly centralized but based on limited information and research.

— Successful countries also place great reliance on employers' organizations and unions. In the UK their role in the governance of training has been progressively reduced. If radical reform is to be successful, it will be important to build up the expertise and involvement of the social partners.

To conclude, the UK is becoming isolated among advanced industrialized countries. They have either attained or are targeting a far higher level of generalized education and training than is being considered here. This should be worrying enough in itself. What makes it more so, is the progress made by other countries with substantially lower labour costs: South Korea has currently 85 per cent in full-time education to the age of seventeen or eighteen, and over 30 per cent in higher education. (*Financial Times*, 30/6/88.)

References

Anderson, A. (1987), 'Adult Training: Private Industry and the Nicholson Letter', in Education & Training UK 1987, Harrison, A., and Gretton, J. (eds.), *Policy Journals*, pp. 67–73.

Brady, T. (1984), *New Technology and Skills in British Industry*, Science Policy Research Unit. *Business Week* (1988), 'How the New Math of Productivity Adds Up', pp. 49–55, June 6.

Callaghan, J. (1976), Ruskin College Speech, *Times Educational Supplement*, 22 October, p. 72.

Centre for Contemporary Cultural Studies (1981), *Unpopular Education*, London, Hutchinson.

Chapman, P., and Tooze, M. (1987), *The Youth Training Scheme in the UK*, Aldershot, Avebury.

Clegg, H. (1972), *The System of Industrial Relations in Great Britain*, Oxford, Basil Blackwell.

Clement, B. (1986), 'Industry Threatened over Training Lapses', *Independent*, p. 3, 29 November.

Coopers and Lybrand Associates (1985), *A Challenge to Complacency: Changing Attitudes to Training*, MSC/NEDO, Moorfoot, Sheffield.

Crowther Commission (1959), *15 to 18*, Report to the DES, HMSO.

Dale, R. (1983), 'The Politics of Education in England 1970–1983: State, Capital and Civil Society', Open University, unpublished.

—— (1983), Thatcherism and Education, In Ahier, J., and Flude, M. (eds.), *Contemporary Education Policy*, London, Croom Helm.

—— (1985), The Background and Inception of TVEI, in Dale (ed.), *Education, Training and Employment*, Milton Keynes, Open University.

Daly, A. (1984), 'Education, Training and Productivity in the U.S. and Great Britain', NIESR no. 63, London.

Deakin, B. M., and Pratten, C. F. (1987), Economic Effects of YTS, *Department of Employment Gazette*, **95**, 491–7.

Department of Education and Science (1987), Education Reform Bill, 20 November.

—— (1988), *Tax Concessions for Training*, HMSO, May.

Department of Employment (1988), *Training for Employment*, HMSO no. 316, February.

Department of Education and Department of Education and Science, *Training for Jobs*, HMSO, Jan.

De Ville, H. G. *et al.* (1986), *Review of Vocational Qualifications in England and Wales*, Report to MSC and DES, April.

Donovan, Lord (1968), *Royal Commission on Trade Unions and Employers' Associations 1965–1968* Report, HMSO, London.

Dore, R. (1987), *Taking Japan Seriously*, Athlone Press, London.

Fenwick, I. G. K. (1976), *The Comprehensive School 1944–1970*, London, Methuen.

Gapper, J. (1987), '£500,000 scheme to boost training in tourist sector', *Financial Times*, 17 March.

George, K. D., and Shorey, J. (1985), 'Manual Workers, Good Jobs and Structured Internal Labour Markets', *British Journal of Industrial Relations*, 23:3, pp. 425–47, November.

Giddens, A. (1979), 'An Anatomy of the British Ruling Class', *New Society*, 4 October, pp. 8–10.

Gow, D. (1988), 'Fury at A-Level Rejection', *Guardian*, p. 1, 8 June.

—— (1988), 'Teaching Shortage Catastrophe Feared', *Guardian*, p. 4, 16 June.

—— and Travis, A. (1988), 'Leak Exposes Thatcher Rift with Baker', *Guardian*, p. 1, 10 March.

Greenhalgh, C. (1988), *Employment and Structural Change: Trends and Policy Options*, mimeo, Oxford.

Hall, P. (1986), *Governing the Economy*, Oxford, Polity Press.

Harland, J. (1987), 'The TVEI Experience', in Gleeson, D. (ed.) *TVEI and Secondary Education*, Milton Keynes, Open University.

Hotz-Hart, B. (1988), 'Comparative Research and New Technology: Modernisation in Three Industrial Relations Systems', in Hyman, R. and Streeck, W. (eds.) *New Technology and Industrial Relations*.

Howell, D. A. (1980), 'The Department of Education and Science: its critics and defenders', *Educational Administration*, 9, pp. 108–33.

Hyman, R., and Streeck, W. (eds.) (1988), *New Technology and Industrial Relations*, Oxford, Blackwells.

Independent (1986), 'Managers "a Decade Out of Date" ', 11 December.

Jackson, M. (1988), 'More leavers shun youth training scheme', *Times Educational Supplement*, 19 February, p. 13.

Jennings, R. E. (1977), *Education and Politics: Policy-Making in Local Education Authorities*, London, Batsford.

Keep, E. (1986), *Designing the Stable Door: A Study of how the Youth Training Scheme was Planned*, Warwick Papers in Industrial Relations No. 8, May.

—— (1987), *Britain's Attempts to Create a National Vocational Educational and Training System: A Review of Progress*, Warwick Papers in Industrial Relations no. 16, Coventry.

Lane, C. (1988), 'Industrial Change in Europe: the Pursuit of Flexible Specialisation', in *Work, Employment and Society*.

Lange, P. (1987), *The Institutionalisation of Concertation. International Political Economy*, WP no. 26, Duke University.

Leadbeater, C. (1987), 'MSC criticises standard of youth training', *Financial Times*, 13 May, p. 1.

Lynn, R. (1988), *Educational Achievement in Japan*, Basingstoke, MacMillan.

MSC (1981), *A New Training Initiative, a Consultative Document*, HMSO, May.

—— (1986), *Skills Monitoring Report*, MSC Evaluation and Research Unit, Sheffield.

Maurice, M., Sellier, F., and Silvestre, J. J. (1986), *The Social Foundations of Industrial Power: A Comparison of France and West Germany*, Cambridge, MIT Press.

Mayer, C. (1987), 'The Assessment: Financial Systems and Corporate Investment', *Oxford Review of Economic Policy*, Winter.

Mayhew, K. (1986), 'Reforming the Labour Market', *Oxford Review of Economic Policy*, Summer.

McArthur, A., and McGregor, A. (1986), 'Training and Economic Development: National versus Local Perspectives', *Political Quarterly*, 57, 3, July–September, pp. 246–55.

McCulloch, G. *et al.* (1985), *Technological Revolution? The Politics of School Science and Technology in England and Wales since 1945*, London, Falmer.

Macfarlane, N. (1980), Education for 16–19 Year Olds, report to the DES and Local Authority Associations, HMSO, December.

Moon, J., and Richardson, J. (1985), *Unemployment in the UK*, Aldershot, Gower.

Morton, K. (1980), *The Education Services of the TGWU*, Oxford University, Ruskin College Project Report.

National Economic Development Council (1984), *Competence and Competition: Training in the Federal Republic of*

Germany, the United States and Japan, London, NEDO/MSC.

—— (1978), *Engineering Craftsmen: Shortages and Related Problems*, London, NEDO.

New, C., and Myers, A. (1986), *Managing Manufacturing Operations in the UK, 1975–85*. Institute of Manpower Studies.

Nicholson, B. (1986), Press Conference at People and Technology Conference, London, November.

OECD (1975), *Educational Development Strategy in England and Wales*, Paris.

—— (1985), *Educational and Training After Basic Schooling*, Paris.

Page, G. (1967), *The Industrial Training Act and After*, London, Andre Deutsch.

Perry, P. J. C. (1976), *The Evolution of British Manpower Policy*, London, BACIE.

Postlethwaite, N. (1988), 'English Last in Science', *Guardian*, 1 March.

Prais, S. J., and Wagner, K. (1983), Schooling Standards in Britain and Germany, London, NIESR Discussion Paper no. 60.

Raffe, D. (1984), *Fourteen to Eighteen*, Aberdeen University Press.

Rajan, A., and Pearson, R. (eds.) (1986), *UK Occupational and Employment Trends*, IMS, London, Butterworths.

Ranson, S. (1985), 'Contradictions in the Government of Educational Change', *Political Studies*, 33, 1, pp. 56–72.

Reich, R. (1983), *The Next American Frontier*, Middlesex, Penguin.

Reid, G. L. (1980), 'The Reserch Needs of British Policy-Makers', in McIntosh, A., *Employment Policy in the UK and the US*, London, John Martin.

Riddell, P. (1983), *The Thatcher Government*, Oxford, Martin Robertson.

Salter, B., and Tapper, T. (1981), *Education, Politics and the State*, London, Grant McIntyre.

Scarbrough, H. (1986), 'The Politics of Technological Change at BL.', in Jacobi, O. *et al.* (eds.), *Technological Change, Rationalisation and Industrial Relations*.

Sorge, A., and Streeck, W. (1988), 'Industrial Relations and Technological Change', in Hyman and Streeck (1988).

Steedman, H. (1986), 'Vocational Training in France and Britain: the Construction Industry', *NI Economic Review*, May.

Steedman, H., and Wagner, K. (1987), 'A Second Look at Productivity, Machinery and Skills in Britain and Germany', *NI Economic Review*, November.

Streeck, W. (1985), 'Industrial Change and Industrial Relations in the Motor Industry: An International Overview', Lecture at University of Warwick, 23/10/85.

Streeck *et al.* (1985), 'Industrial Relations and Technical Change in the British, Italian and German Automobile Industry'. IIM discussion paper 85–5, Berlin.

Taylor, R. (1980), *The Fifth Estate*, London, Pan.

Tipton, B. (1982), 'The Quality of Training and the Design of Work', *Industrial Relations Journal*, pp. 27–42, Spring.

TUC Annual Reports, 1980–1986.

Wiener, M. (1981), *English Culture and the Decline of the Industrial Spirit*, Cambridge, Cambridge University Press.

Wilensky, H., and Turner, L. (1987), *Democratic Corporatism and Policy Linkages*, Berkeley, Instititute of International Studies.

Woodall, J. (1985), 'European Trade Unions and Youth Unemployment', unpublished Kingston Polytechnic Mimeograph, London.

Worswick, G. D. (1985), *Education and Economic Performance*, Gower, Aldershot.

15

Higher education: expansion and reform

MARTIN CAVE

Brunel University

MARTIN WEALE

Department of Applied Economics and Clare College, Cambridge

I. The development of mass higher education

Wide availability of higher education in the United Kingdom is a new phenomenon. As Figures 15.1 and 15.2 demonstrate, the fraction of the population educated at post-secondary level declines sharply with age. It is lower for women than for men in all age groups. The fraction of the population educated to degree level declines even more rapidly with increasing age, reflecting the fact that, for professions such as teaching, there has been a shift from sub-degree to degree-level qualification. There was a major increase in the availability of higher education beginning in the 1960s after the publication of the Robbins Report (HMSO, 1963a) in 1963. In response to the report, the government stated:

The basic assumption of the Report is that courses of higher education should be available for all those who are qualified by ability and attainment to pursue them, and who wish to do so. The Government accepts this assumption. (HMSO, 1963b)

A related expansion of the polytechnic sector was announced in 1966 (HMSO, 1966) and the whole system was made financially practical from the students' point of view by means of a system of student grants introduced following a report published in 1960 (HMSO, 1960).

First published in *Oxford Review of Economic Policy*, vol. 8, no. 2 (1992). This version has been updated and revised to incorporate recent developments.

Over the ten-year period from 1965 to 1975 the number of university students almost doubled, and the number of polytechnic students rose by over 50 per cent, raising the fraction of the female 25–9 age cohort with degrees in 1981 to 8.1 per cent from the level of 4.6 per cent ten years earlier and raising the male proportion from 10.1 per cent to 12.1 per cent.

Since 1975 there has been a further expansion which has been particularly rapid in the early 1990s following the conversion of the polytechnics into 'new' universities. In 1987 the government restated its commitment that higher education should be available to all suitable candidates who wish to take it up (HMSO, 1987). The White Paper noted that the demand for qualified manpower was unlikely to fall in line with the reduction in the size of the 18–19-year-old cohort, and that this in itself implies a further rise in participation rates. The traditional concern that there was a shortage of scientists and engineers was restated. It should, however, be noted that data on graduate salaries are more suggestive of a shortage of engineers than of other types of scientists. At this stage the government's plan was for a 5 per cent increase in student numbers between 1985 and 1990 with a reduction to 1985 levels in absolute numbers by the mid-1990s.

In fact student numbers increased by over 20 per cent between 1985 and 1990 and in 1991 the decision was taken to place the polytechnics on the same footing as the existing universities. At the same time financing methods were changed so that universities faced incentives to expand their student intake, particularly if they were relatively weak at research (HMSO, 1991). The

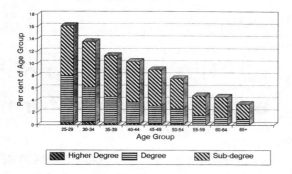

Figure 15.1. Tertiary education, women (United Kingdom: 1981 Census Data)

Source: HMSO (1984).

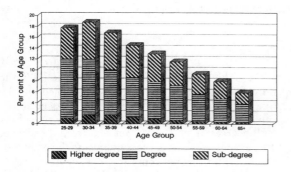

Figure 15.2. Tertiary education, men (United Kingdom: 1981 Census Data)

Source: HMSO (1984).

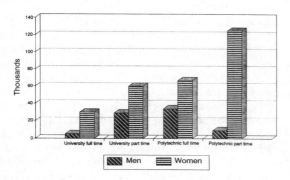

Figure 15.3. Change in student numbers (United Kingdom: 1980/1–1989/90)

Source: HMSO (1991).

result was a further sharp increase in student numbers which continued until 1993 when the government became alarmed at the costs of the expansion and decided to limit further growth.

The expansion of the 1980s, and of the first half of the 1990s, has been among groups which were traditionally under-represented in higher education. As Figure 15.3 shows, the number of full-time male students at 'old' universities has risen only slightly since 1980, with the expansion coming in the part-time sector, among women, and in the former polytechnics or 'new' universities. This made sense from the supply side because there is evidence (Weale, 1992) that the returns to education in the new universities were likely to be higher than they would have been for the same students in the old universities. Bennett, Glennerster, and Nevison (1992) point to an increase in the return to higher education as a possible factor behind increased participation.

At the same time as fostering an expansion of higher education, the government took the view that there should be better value for money from the public funds made available to higher education and this has led to wide-ranging reforms in the provision of student finance and in the manner in which higher education institutions are funded.

The system of student grants was changed radically from 1990. A system of loans was introduced to top up the grants to an amount believed necessary for student support. The loan was frozen in nominal terms so that, as inflation erodes its real value, the gap will be made up by increasing the size of the loan available. These changes were justified on the grounds that the grant system was regressive and also on the simple argument that increased participation meant simply that the government could not afford to be as generous as it had been in the past (HMSO, 1988).

In parallel with changing the system of student funding, the government is developing a market structure for higher education. This is being done with the aims of improving efficiency and providing incentives for the system to expand. We discuss this in section III of this survey.

International comparison of higher education provision and attainment is notoriously difficult, because different countries adopt different definitions of higher education, while course structures differ considerably. Many other European countries have traditionally had higher enrolment rates than the United Kingdom. These do not necessarily translate into higher graduation rates but, in assessing this, one should not fall into the trap of assuming that time spent on a course partially completed is time wasted. High participation rates quoted for the United States often include courses which would be labelled as further education in the United Kingdom.

Williams (1992) argued that participation rates in degree courses were still low in the UK in comparison with France, Germany, Japan, and the US; however, the UK has relatively more non-degree students in higher education. Public expenditure per student year is similar to that of other countries, but degree courses are shorter in the UK than elsewhere so that the cost per graduate (as a percentage of GNP) is lower than anywhere except France.

We can identify three main issues concerning higher education in the UK. First of all there is the question how much should there be and of what type. Second, should there be a further shift away from public provision toward charging the consumer? Third, can one identify any institutional structure which will lead to the most efficient provision of both teaching and research functions of higher education?

II. Costs and efficiency

1. Measuring performance

Until the last decade or so, decisions relating to resource allocation in higher education and the monitoring of outcomes were left largely to academics in individual higher education institutions. This was especially true of the universities, whose funding body, the University Grants Committee (UGC), allocated resources to institutions on the basis of opaque judgements concerning academic merit. The universities were then free to use these resources as broadly as they thought fit. As the UGC observed in 1984, the resulting system was one of deficiency grants. The grant was raised in cases of what were believed to be high-cost institutions, and lowered to take account of universities' other income. Polytechnics and colleges, then under the control of local authorities, were subject to a variety of monitoring and accounting procedures.

This system has changed considerably throughout the 1980s as part of the Conservative government's general attempts to introduce accountability and performance measurement within the public sector. Over this period, the higher education funding bodies increasingly sought to impose transparent resource-allocation mechanisms and uniform measurement procedures upon the institutions which they funded. In the case of the universities in particular, the new measures were resisted. But the government was able to use the threat of withdrawal of funding to enforce its will.

This process was most transparent in 1986, when the Secretary of State for Education and Science told the House of Commons that the Government's willingness to make further financial provision for the universities in 1987/88 and subsequently depended crucially on evidence of real progress on implementing and building upon the changes that are needed . The areas identified were selectivity in the distribution of resources, the rationalization and, where appropriate, the closure of small departments, better financial management, and improved standards of teaching (Cave *et al.*, 1991, pp. 9–10). As part of the agreement then struck, the university sector began to prepare and publish volumes of performance indicators.

Some of these are reviewed in Johnes (1992). If performance measures are to be effective, they must satisfy a number of criteria. First and most importantly, they must accurately capture whatever attribute of the activity of the unit in question is considered to be desirable. As a corollary of this, in order that the indicator can properly be interpreted, it is necessary to have a view of the desired level or rate of change of the variable in question. These characteristics may sound easy to satisfy, but experience teaches otherwise. As an example, cost per student is often proposed as a performance indicator for higher education institutions. One of the obvious difficulties with it is that, without further information about quality of outcomes and other matters, one cannot say whether an increase or a decrease in unit cost is preferable.

A further desirable characteristic of performance indicators is that they should not be manipulable by the organization whose performance is being measured. There are numerous examples of this, but one taken from the field of research may suffice. Research output is often measured in terms of the number of articles published by an individual or a department. Anecdotal evidence suggests that this leads to publishing inflation—i.e. maximization of the number of articles produced through repetition, the lowering of quality standards, or the breakdown of research into publishable units of minimal size. This phenomenon has echoes of the substantial literature on problems with physical success indicators in centrally planned economies and their manipulation.

The aim of performance measurement is to capture a variety of attributes of the higher education process in circumstances when a monetary valuation of the output is not readily available. If this approach is going to succeed, it is essential that all relevant aspects of the activity in question should be measured, to avoid the well-known problem of the measurable driving out the unmeasurable. Thus in the case of higher education, it will be necessary to collect measures on students preferences for entry into particular institutions, their experience while undergoing the educational process reflected in cost data and the quality of the teaching process, and outcomes, in terms of such variables as employability. It will, in addition, be necessary to measure research outputs when the institution in question is engaged in research.

In terms of teaching-performance measures, arguably the best measure of the educational process is value added, defined as the difference between a student's knowledge and ability on entering the institution and capacities on leaving it. Several attempts have been made to devise indices of value added using a weighted measure of students qualifications on entry (based, for example, on A-level scores) and a weighted measure of qualifications on exit (based on degree classifications, completion rates of intermediate years, etc.). Simple approaches of this kind are vulnerable to the objection that they depend crucially upon the weighting ascribed to entry and exit qualifications. This is, of course, in addition to the objection that the institutions themselves in many cases award degree classes, so that exit qualifications may be subject to manipulation.

One way of avoiding the former problem is to adopt an approach based upon the so-called comparative method proposed in the final report of a joint PCFC/CNAA (1990) project to test different approaches to the calculation of value added. The method involves comparing the performance of a particular unit in generating exit qualifications for entrants of a particular type with the national average of exit qualifications for equivalently qualified entrants:

The expected degree class is derived from the national relationship between degree results and entry qualifications . . . The value added score of a course is thus a function of the difference between the degree result achieved and the result predicted from entry qualifications. (ibid., para 3.7)

The method thus takes national average performance as the yardstick against which the value added for a particular unit will be judged. In effect, the comparative method eliminates the need to weight entry qualifications, but still requires the weighting of exit qualifications. It thus solves half the problem of arbitrariness in scaling, but not all of it. Indeed, the presence of some arbitrariness of this kind is inevitable when units differ from the national average in the composition of both their inputs and their outputs. None the less, it is an approach which deserves attention, although current prospects for value added measures are not good (Cave, Hanney, and Henkel, 1995).

2. Economies of scale and scope

Performance measures for higher education are designed to monitor, normally on a comparative basis, the performance of HEIs in various aspects of their work. But what do we know, in terms of rather more fundamental analysis, about the processes by which inputs are turned into outputs in higher education? To what extent do they exhibit economies of scale, or decreasing unit cost as output expands? How significant are economies of scope between teaching and research, so that the two activities are more cheaply performed together? These issues have an obvious bearing not merely upon the efficient organization of higher education but also upon the costs associated with the government's current expansion.

Evidence of economies of scale in UK higher education institutions is extremely sparse. Perhaps this is hardly surprising, given the basis upon which higher education has been controlled in the post-war period. For the US Bowen (1980) formulated the interesting hypothesis that spending in any higher education institution is basically determined by its revenue: because HEIs do not maximize profits or surplus, their managements spend what they get, rather than cut costs. On this basis, we would expect that a well-provided large institution would increase its unit costs with as much vigour as an equally well-endowed small institution. Observations of the underlying technology would thus be muddied by the peculiar nature of the incentives. It is reasonable to suppose that this problem afflicts estimates of the cost functions of UK institutions.

One of the most original studies of economies of scale in HEIs was carried out by Verry and Davies (1976) using UK data. This study was path-breaking in its use of quality and other adjustments. The authors found that marginal costs for both graduate and undergraduate students in the UK were generally constant over enrolment levels. These views were consistent with many of the earlier US studies (for example, Radner and Miller, 1975) which found that economies of scale in undergraduate-only institutions were fully exploited at enrolment levels of about 3,000 students.

Other studies (Cohn, Rhine, and Santos, 1989; de Groot, McMahon, and Volkwein, 1991) have used a more sophisticated theoretical apparatus to examine the data. In particular, they have adopted multi-input, multi-output cost-modelling to estimate not only economies of scale in undergraduate and graduate tuition but also economies of scope between teaching and research. Both studies find cost reduction in average universities continuing at output levels substantially in excess of 3,000 students. They also find economies of scope between teaching and research.

However, another study by Getz and Siegfried (1991) draws attention to the difference in estimates of economies of scale between institutions which are expanding their enrolments and those which are not. Institutions with declining enrolments tend to exhibit higher operating costs, while those with increasing enrolments tend to have lower costs per student. This implies that US HEIs appear to be slow in adjusting their operations to changing enrolment levels. One possible implication is that the quality of instruction declines during periods of expansion.

3. The costs of expansion

The extent of economies of scale is important for the pattern of costs arising from the government's intended expansion of higher education in recent years. The number of students enrolled, in terms of full-time equivalents (FTEs) doubled between 1979 and 1994, and by 1994 the age participation index reached about 30 per cent, the target set for 2000.

Not surprisingly, the expansion had major consequences for total unit costs. Unit public funding in universities remained constant throughout the 1980s, while unit costs in polytechnics fell by about 20 per cent from 1980/81 to 1988/89. In the three years following 1988/89, unit public funding in universities is estimated to have fallen by 16 per cent, while polytechnics and colleges have experienced a decline of 20 per cent. Data for the two sectors were not fully comparable for a number of reasons. However, the data suggest that the PCFC and the UFC at that time provided their institutions with broadly the same level of funding per student for teaching purposes, after allowance has been made for differences in subject mix.

Following the amalgamation of the funding of all higher education institutions by the Higher Education Funding Council for England (HEFCE), unit public funding data and projections are now available for all English institutions. These are shown in Table 15.1, which demonstrates that a reduction in unit costs of approximately one third is projected over the eight year period to 1997/98. The projection of unit costs can be broken down into a projection of productivity gains and of changes in input prices. (In addition, unit costs are affected by changes in subject mix, and data show that in the 1980s this factor reduced costs by about 3 per cent over the decade as a whole, as a result of shifts to cheaper subjects.) Productivity changes depend themselves upon static improvements and on the effects of economies of scale. Changes in input prices depend critically upon academic salaries. As Keep and Sissons (1992) show, academic salaries have lagged behind average earnings of non-manual workers by about 2 per cent per year in recent years. Largely as a consequence of this, input prices in universities grew

Table 15.1. Unit public funding index for higher education in real terms 1988/89 to 1997/98

Financial Year	Funding
1989/90	100
1990/91	92
1991/92	86
1992/93	79
1993/94*	77
1994/95**	75
1995/96**	73
1996/97**	71
1997/98**	69

* Provisional
** Projected
Source: Department for Education and Employment.

more slowly than the GDP deflator. However, it is unlikely that such a trend can be maintained permanently. As a consequence input prices are likely to rise in real terms.

The projections in Table 15.1 embody an annual reduction in unit public funding of about 3 per cent per year. With input costs at best constant, and few further opportunities for altering subject mix, the implied annual productivity increase is also of the order of 3 per cent, to come either through static improvements or economies of scale. Yet, as the following section shows, the period of expansion has now come to an end, eliminating economies of scale. It is unlikely that static efficiency gains will be forthcoming on the scale required, unless accompanied by degradation of quality. The focus has thus turned to alternative sources of funding.

The cost data shown above relate only to recurrent costs. It has also been calculated that the capital costs of the proposed expansion of higher education (including the backlog of repairs) will, in the absence of measures to improve capacity utilization, require additional further capital expenditure of £2 billion over the decade. It is likely that many institutions, especially in the former UFC sector, have space which can be remodelled at relatively low cost to accommodate additional students. However, the projected expansion will require further construction, unless measures are taken to make better use of existing facilities. Some measures of this kind, such as extending the working day, have few implications for the structure of academic life. Others, such as switching to three semesters or four terms, have major consequences. The considerable differences in space requirements across subjects make the extra investment demands dependent on the subject composition of the expanded numbers. Such differences are often neglected in the costing of various degrees, especially as many institutions assign space directly to departments, without even notional costing procedures. These projections of the costs of expansion naturally raise the issue of what options there are for shifting some of the burden of teaching costs from the Exchequer to students or their prospective employers.

III. Funding

1. Funding tuition

The previous section has highlighted the costs associated with the development of higher education. This section considers some of the funding implications. As Williams (1992) reported, UK higher education was characterized until the mid 1980s by a relatively low level of participation in degree-level studies, comparatively short durations of first degrees, and generous public funding. In addition to the payment of tuition fees for qualified home and EC students, the government also makes available parental means-tested maintenance grants. Indeed, a higher proportion of GNP is devoted to student maintenance in the UK than in all but one of the 10 countries for which data were provided in an OECD report (OECD, 1990). These circumstances combined to generate the relatively high private rates of return to higher education reported below.

Arrangements for the funding of both tuition and maintenance are now in a state of flux. As far as tuition is concerned, the government and the funding councils made attempts during the period of expansion up to 1994 to introduce a degree of competition among institutions for student places. This replaced the previous system whereby student places were funded in quantities determined by the funding council at a standard rate, with some adjustment for special factors.

In 1989, the bulk of public funds for teaching and research in higher education institutions was allocated through two parallel bodies

- the Universities Funding Council or UFC (which replaced the earlier University Grants Committee (or UGC).
- The Polytechnics and Colleges Funding Council or PCFC (for further details, see Cave et al., 1992).

The latter body in particular experimented with competitive methods for funding teaching places at the

margin, and the UFC later came under pressure to introduce a more ambitious tendering system for the allocation of places. The arrangements thus had the characteristics of a quasi-market: institutions competed with one another not to sell their services directly to students, but for funding from an agency acting on behalf of final consumers. Places were then allocated to individual students in accordance with criteria established by individual institutions.

In relation to the allocation of funding for student places, the PCFC explicitly introduced a form of quality evaluation: institutions seeking to provide additional places in programmes deemed to be of above average quality were specially favoured in the tendering arrangements. The UFC also proposed to adopt a quality threshold, rather than a handicapping system in its proposed system for the competitive allocation of funding. In the event, however, the UFC's plans were aborted as a result of competition among the universities.

When the funding of HEIs in Great Britain was unified between universities and polytechnics, and conducted through separate Higher Education Funding Councils for England, Scotland and Wales, institutions still enjoyed substantial incentives to expand, on the basis of marginal student fee levels which were less than the average unit of funding, but still quite substantial. The result of all these changes was a massive expansion in enrolments in higher education, accompanied by a substantial decline in public funding of each student as Table 15.1 indicates. From 1994, however, the Department for Education, concerned at the increasing cost to the Exchequer of higher education places and also—possibly—about the deterioration of quality, introduced a new system designed to stabilize student numbers. This system establishes for each institution a MASN (Maximum Aggregate Student Number), deviations from which (beyond a permitted threshold of 1 per cent) in either direction are punished by withdrawal of funds. This has meant that competition among institutions for additional student numbers has been replaced by competition for the best students to fill given student places. It might be expected that this major funding change would alter the incentives to improve quality, provided that the student targets can be met, thus strengthening the potential importance of performance indicators. In practice, however, the effect has been less marked. As a generalization, institutions enjoying high student demand for places have been unwilling to expand student numbers, perhaps from a fear that the resulting decline in unit public funding would dent their perceived quality. Institutions which have expanded numbers substantially in the past few years may still have difficulty in meeting their MASN, and thus have strong incentives to gain a reputation for higher quality.

Although arrangements in Scotland and Wales are slightly different, the Higher Education Funding Council for England (HEFCE) is now pursuing a policy of progressively equalizing the average unit of Council funding (AUCF) across its institutions. However, a recent history of divergent levels of funding has created substantial differences in current levels. HEFCE proposes progressively to eliminate these, although at current rates the process will take several decades.

2. Quality regulation in a competitive system

Price competition among institutions and declining public funding immediately raise the issue of quality regulation. Traditionally, the universities have relied upon the professional independence of their staff to maintain quality standards, and the system has been supported by external examiners from other institutions whose task is to maintain comparability. The polytechnics and colleges sector, by contrast, had more formal validation procedures provided by the Council for National Academic Awards.

Anxieties about the effects of competitive tendering and observed declines in unit costs have refocused attention on quality. Higher education has a number of stake-holders: the staff of the institution, the students themselves, their employers, and the government which funds much of the system. Each is likely to have its own understanding of quality. The academics may emphasize the acquisition of specialist knowledge in their disciplines; students, the quality of their learning experience and its subsequent value in the labour market; and employers, the acquisition of usable skills. For these reasons, defining and regulating quality standards is peculiarly difficult. Cave, Dodsworth, and Thompson (1992) describe the two approaches now in use.

There have been two strands to the quality assurance procedures in HE since 1992. The first, the Higher Education Quality Council (HEQC) is owned by the institutions and addresses the procedures institutions have in place to assure quality. Trained groups of auditors, drawn from HEIs in the main, visit each institution for three to four days, meeting staff and students to evaluate the rigour of the procedures (as described in material provided by the institution). The approach is based on seven questions ranging from 'What are you trying to do?' through 'Why do you think that is the best way

to do it?' and 'How do you improve it?' The full cycle of audits will be complete in 1996/97.

The second strand has been teaching quality assurance. Assessments are conducted on a subject-by-subject basis by HEFCE, which assigns one contract assessor (a HEFCE employee) and some three subject assessors (drawn from the HEIs) to undertake visits of three days or so in length. The visits involve attendance in teaching sessions, and interviews with staff, students and graduates. Quality is determined by reference to a self-assessment document which includes a statement of the aims and objectives of the teaching provision. The methodology has evolved from one in which three grades were assigned 'excellent', 'satisfactory' and 'unsatisfactory' to a four-point scale which is applied to 6 separate 'aspects of provision'. The cycle is planned to run until 2001 and reports of each institutional visit, and overall reports on each subject, are published.

The universities have complained bitterly about HEFCE's methodology and alleged overlap between its activities, those of the HEQC and the professional accrediting bodies. The Secretary of State obliged HEFCE and institutions to submit proposals for a single quality assurance body which would meet both the requirements of the 1992 Education Act and the criticisms of the HEIs. The basic principles of such a system have now been agreed (regular and systematic internal reviews with external peer involvement, periodic external evaluations—of the institution, all to agreed national guidelines) and its introduction from 1997 is currently planned.

Although the British system is likely to become increasingly competitive and, as we argue in the next section, private funding will account for an increasing amount of total expenditure on higher education, the proposed reforms will keep British higher education significantly different from the system in the US, in terms of use of market forces. The US system contains significant elements of private production (although by not-for-profit organizations) and explicit price differentiation. In the UK, by contrast, private universities are still insignificant, and proposals for price differentiation, through top-up fees paid by students, or through quality-related differences in funding council payments for student places, are in the former case non-existent, and in the latter case still limited to a relatively small part of expenditure by the PCFC.

The development of an efficient market in higher education, in which consumers (or purchasers) make informed decisions among alternative price and quality combinations, faces many difficulties. Information is asymmetric, as students often have little knowledge of courses available. Moreover, higher education is a long-term experience good: its effects only become apparent over a long period after graduation, and only limited information about it can be acquired through *ex ante* searching.

The current and proposed system of finance seeks to overcome these problems essentially by paying a uniform price for what is intended at least to be a uniform quality. But the pressures of competition and increased private funding may make this unsustainable. As variation across institutions increases, better information will be required. This may take the direct form of consumers guides or the indirect form of the development of brand names, or other commitments to high quality through investment in reputation. The process of overcoming informational market failures is likely to be a long and painful one.

3. Additional funding sources

The expansion of student numbers has created extra demands on maintenance as well as on tuition expenditure. Government expenditure on student maintenance in the United Kingdom amounted in 1994/95 to about £1.1 bn—a higher proportion of its GDP than most OECD countries. The UK government has already taken steps to limit expenditures on student maintenance by the introduction of a student loan scheme. Maintenance grants are now capped in nominal terms, but students have access to loans at a zero real rate of interest. Net of repayments, loans amounted in 1994/95 to over £50.0m per annum, projected to rise to £90.0m by 1997/98. The introduction of arrangements whereby students fund their maintenance has led to suggestions that the system should be extended to tuition fees.

Loans are not the only form of deferred payment for maintenance and tuition. Many countries have experimented with alternative methods of deferred payment of student tuition and maintenance expenditures. The options fall broadly into the following categories: a loan repayable over a fixed period, an income-contingent loan (whereby the rate of repayment depends upon the graduates attained level of income in any year), or a graduate tax (whereby graduates pay over their lifetime an additional and possibly progressive income tax). The main features of the alternatives are laid out in Table15. 2, taken from Albrecht and Ziderman (1992).

The current UK scheme lies somewhere between the first and second types of loan, with the full debt being repayable, but with repayments ceasing if income drops below a specified level, and with the debt lapsing if income remains low for a long period. The merits of these

Table 15.2. Student loans versus graduate taxes: contrasts and similarities

Mortgage loan	Income-contingent loan	Graduate tax
Government provides student loans to pay fees or living costs	Government provides student loans to pay fees or living costs	Government acquires share in human capital equity
Government recovery of costs	Government recovery of costs	Government shares in benefits
Loan pays fees (tuition or living)	Loan pays fees (tuition or living)	Tax applies to subsidized education
Payments accrue to loan fund	Payments accrue to loan fund	Taxes accrue to the Treasury
Level of annual payments fixed	Level of payment contingent on annual income	Level of tax payments contingent on annual income
Annual payments: a declining proportion of income	Annual payments: a fixed proportion of income	Tax payments: a fixed proportion of income
Fixed term payment obligation	Payment obligation until loan repaid	Tax obligation within employment
Loan disbursement institutions	Loan disbursement institutions	No disbursement
Need to maintain individual accounts	Need to maintain individual accounts	No individual accounts

alternative schemes naturally depend upon the government's objectives as well as upon estimates of their costs in terms of administration costs, default rates, etc. Many countries introducing deferred payment schemes have seen advantages in terms of equity in linking repayments to graduates subsequent income. To the extent that the interest rate in an income-contingent repayment scheme is subsidized, deferment of repayment by lower earners reduces their overall costs. One of the most interesting recent experiments with an income-contingent scheme has recently been conducted in Australia. The Australian experience suggests that one of the main objections to such schemes— a fear that they will reduce access to higher education for disadvantaged groups in the community—has not materialized (Chapman, 1992). If, as seems likely, pressures mount in the UK to shift maintenance and tuition costs increasingly to students, it is desirable that each of the three basic variants discussed above be re-evaluated.

The mortgage loan and the income-contingent loan have the advantage that, in one form or another students can be charged for what their higher education actually costs; the mortgage loan is a simple charge while the income-contingent loan has the advantage over the mortgage loan that it reduces the post-repayment income uncertainty of the borrower in the same way that equity finance offers lower risk than loan finance for an entrepreneur. The graduate tax gains over both of these in terms of simplicity. The imposition of a higher rate of tax on graduates (and not just on new graduates) is quite straightforward.

But it is doubtful that one could operate a pure tax system which charged different people at different rates for differing types of higher education. As a consequence individuals' choices would not be influenced by price differentials and this would entail a loss of efficiency purchased by greater simplicity.

While we have doubts that the simple mortgage loan is a sensible way to charge people for higher education which brings uncertain benefits, we can be quite clear that both the income-contingent loan and the graduate tax offer a much fairer means of finance than does the present approach to public provision. The case for a shift to one of these two is very strong indeed.

4. Funding of research

Funding of research in UK universities has become increasingly selective over the past ten years. The UFC carried out three evaluations of research in university departments, and HEFCE is now carrying out a fourth. The principal basis for the evaluation is peer review, now supplemented by a limited amount of bibliographic information. No systematic attempt has been made to apply some of the more elaborate bibliometric performance indicators, such as output or citation measures, discussed by Johnes (1992). *Ex post* analysis of assessments has, however, suggested that a high proportion of the variation in assessment is accounted for by a handful of explanatory variables, which differ among broad groups of subjects (Taylor, 1995).

Hare and Wyatt (1992) investigated some of the implications of higher education institutions participation in both teaching and research. Their model suggests that institutions may have different capacities and different propensities to engage in the two activities. If true, this would lead to polarization of institutions into those which are teaching-based and those which are research-based. The funding councils are apparently encouraging this specialization on a subject-by-subject basis through its current peer review arrangements. Over the past decade, funding has been increasingly directed to those departments which are seen to be best in research. As a consequence, research funding per staff member in such departments is many times higher than funding allocated to departments which are seen to be the worst. In the current round of evaluations, the apparent yardstick employed is research output per staff member rather than per unit of research funding. This approach naturally extends the polarization of funding.

The trend in research funding in UK higher education is to reduce automatic allocations and introduce more competition. It has been proposed (although not yet accepted) that research resources should increasingly be channelled to the research councils rather than the Higher Education Funding Councils. In the end, teaching and research may be funded by entirely separate bodies, and institutions may be required to demonstrate that their funds have been allocated as intended by the funding bodies.

IV. Outturns

It should not be presumed that higher education necessarily has a positive social economic return. Some commentators argue that a negative social return appears to be a feature of some types of undergraduate education, and of many more types of post-graduate education.

The most obvious way of measuring the consequence of higher education is by looking at the effect on the incomes of those who have experienced higher education. One has to consider both the return to the individual and the return to society. The private rate of return exceeds the social rate of return in the UK because students typically both do not pay tuition fees and receive a grant to cover part of their living expenses. Against that must be offset the fact that society benefits from increases in income gross of income tax, while individuals only benefit from post-tax enhancement of their incomes. The calculations do not take into account the possibility that the social benefit of some types of work may not be fully reflected in rates of pay, and it is difficult to see how they could.

Estimates of private rates of return produced by the Department for Education and Employment (HMSO, 1988) suggest that the social return to education is of the order of 5 per cent p.a. with the private return being over 20 per cent p.a. Nevertheless, there is considerable variation by subject. Social science degrees show the highest return at 26 per cent private return and 8 per cent p.a. social return. Arts degrees are found to have a private return of under 10 per cent and a negative social return. Bennett, Glennerster, and Nevison

(1992) argue that the DES figures overstate true returns once one corrects for the benefits of family background; people from professional/managerial backgrounds form a disproportionate number of university students but would have enhanced earning power even if they did not go to university. The private rate of return which they identify, in the region of 6–7 per cent p.a. post tax, should be compared with the long-term return on equity capital which is probably around 6 per cent pre-tax. Weale (1992) suggests there may be important differences between different types of higher education. The old universities have typically offered higher rewards to those with good A-level results, while education in the new universities has done more for those with poor A-level results. These figures do not translate happily into rates of return, but they do offer some clues as to the appropriate expansion of the higher education system. Nearly all men with good A-levels already go to university; increases in participation are taking place by expanding the number of female students, mature students, and those with poor A-level results. The latter seem to be more suited to the type of education offered by the new universities and it is probably appropriate that this is where the main expansion has taken place.

These figures do not take account of the fact that research is, at least to some extent, a joint product of higher education, or that education may have external benefits. We discuss these later in this section. They do not affect the private return but obviously raise estimates of the social return to education.

While there is, then, an element of uncertainty over the rate of return to undergraduate degrees, the evidence against there being a positive private return to postgraduate study is rather firmer. Rudd (1990) describes in detail the results of a survey looking at the benefit of a social science Ph.D. He found that, for a male social scientist with a first-class degree, graduating between 1972 and 1977, the median salary in 1987 was £13,100. For a social scientist who failed to complete a Ph.D. or took a research-based Masters degree, the median salary was £18,100, while for those with a taught Masters degree the median salary was £18,000. For those with no post-graduate qualification the median salary was £20,900. Similar patterns are found for men with 2.1 degrees and for women with both firsts and 2.1s.

Rudd offers two explanations of this. First of all, while post-graduate university training may be useful, employers seem to regard on the job training as more useful (see Booth, 1992). Secondly the poor return to Ph.D.s arises substantially because many Ph.D.s become teachers in higher education, where they face a monopsonist employer who pays them badly. This raises a second important issue. Is the route of Master's degree followed by Ph.D. the best method of producing higher education teachers? We do not discuss the point here, although it certainly merits wide debate in view of these figures. One should add that Rudd's figures are calculated from simple cross-tabulations. Dolton et al. (1990) use regression analysis to show post-graduate education in a more positive light, but there is no suggestion that the returns approach those associated with undergraduate education.

Financial benefit is an important aspect of an assessment of higher education. But there are a number of others. An international comparison (OECD, 1989) of the chance of unemployment for graduates as compared to other types of workers suggests that it is generally lower. In the UK in 1987 a man who had left school at the earliest opportunity was four times as likely to be unemployed as a graduate. Only Greece had higher unemployment among graduates than among early school-leavers. But the issue is not as clear-cut as it might seem. Among men over 50 the unemployment rate of graduates was higher than that of men who had stayed at school to the age of 18.

A third point which has to be borne in mind in assessing different courses is the extent to which degree courses match jobs. In 1981 8 per cent of science and engineering graduates became accountants. This fraction had risen to 12.8 per cent in 1988. There is no point in gearing higher education to meet supposed manpower needs if graduates tend to take jobs for which their degrees are unsuited or unnecessary. Dolton (1992) presents entropy scores for the 1980 cohort of graduates. These show that students of more vocational subjects like education and law are more likely to choose relevant jobs, but physical scientists are well dispersed. Of course, this may reflect the importance of a physical science degree as offering teaching to think.

The effects of higher education should ideally be considered jointly with those of employer-provided training. Booth (1992) finds that men are more likely than women to be offered further training. In the case of men it is reasonably clear that the benefits of this training are portable from one job to the next, although long periods of training appear worse than short periods in this respect. As far as training offered by current employment is concerned, only courses taken outside the firm appear to have a significant effect on graduate earnings. A week of training seems to raise income by 1 per cent, suggesting that the effects are of the order of three times as great as those of higher education. Since training is likely to be tightly focused, this should come as no great surprise.

The other side of this coin to be explored is the role of the higher education sector in offering short training courses or retraining to people with considerable work experience. This is a departure from their traditional market, but it is likely to become important in the future.

In addition to these effects of higher education and training, there are of course other intangible benefits of higher education which may be important despite the fact that they are difficult to measure. Graduates may be able to make more of their leisure as well as their work. There may be spill-over influences on other people. One particular aspect of this is the possibility of an external benefit of education on economic activity: we look at this next.

1. Externalities

The idea that there may be external benefits from education has returned to the fore with the work of Lucas (1988). His argument is that a high level of education is likely to accelerate the rate of technical progress, perhaps because the extent to which a country can catch up with others through the import of technical knowledge is likely to depend on the level of education and training.

Since the benefits of technical progress are typically going to be passed on from one generation to the next, education benefits future generations as well as the current generation, creating an external benefit (and, incidentally, a good reason for financing education partly from public borrowing) quite separate from the possibility that education may raise the productivity of the uneducated as well as the educated.

While these externalities may be present, they are very difficult to quantify, particularly with respect to higher education. Barro (1991), looking at a large sample of developed and under-developed countries, finds school enrolments in 1960 are a significant factor explaining growth between 1960 and 1985. One should not attribute all of this to externalities. If one assumes that access to education rose sharply between 1945 and 1960, then the countries with high enrolments in 1960 will also have a sharply increasing level of educational attainment of their working population. This will lead to an increase in human capital and economic growth even in the absence of an externality. Indeed Matthews *et al.* (1982) suggest that, out of a total increase in labour productivity of 1.2 per cent p.a. between 1856 and 1973, half can be directly attributed to increased attainment, without any externality being present.

Nevertheless, some evidence for external benefits of education can be found. Weale (1992) suggested that a part of the growth residual of OECD countries for the years 1973–85, calculated after adjustment for changes in effective labour and capital input as well as catch-up, could be explained by educational attainment of the workforce in 1974. The results are open to the objection that they rely on the inclusion of Mediterranean countries in the sample, but they suggest an increase in the rate of growth of 0.14 per cent p.a. for one extra year of education of the workforce as a whole, and the magnitude of this at least seems plausible.

It should be noted that, if the external benefits of higher education are of this magnitude, it is most unreasonable to expect a sharp increase in the take-up of higher education to have much effect on economic growth. An increase in the take-up from 30 per cent to 50 per cent of the workforce would raise the attainment level of the workforce by 0.6 years per worker, and would raise the growth rate by 0.08 per cent p.a. But it would take the full working life of a graduate, nearly 45 years, for the growth rate to rise to its full extent.

The implication of these calculations is that, while there may be external benefits from higher education, and while they are almost certainly extremely important in assessing the case for public finance of higher education, their macroeconomic effects take a very long time to appear. We should not expect an increase in the resources devoted to higher education to have a visible effect on the UK's economic performance in the short term. The converse is also true. It will be a long time before any neglect of higher education, or of any other part of the education system starts to show in the country's macroeconomic performance.

2. Benefits of research

The benefits of research expenditures are much harder to assess. There is one argument that any prosperous, self-respecting country ought to have a viable research community, for much the same reason as it ought to have a national opera; but, even for those areas of research which are *prima facie* quite unrelated to scientific progress, it is possible to be more specific than this. First of all, it is hard to imagine the provision of higher education taking place in an atmosphere completely divorced from research. Research-training is seen as an important ingredient of preparation for teaching in higher education and, even if teachers do not do much subsequent research, the skills they have learnt are likely to be helpful in deciding what to teach and how it should be taught. Second, the UK attracts a large number of students from overseas who study a wide range of subjects. It is probable that what attracts them to the UK is, among other things, the academic reputation of the higher education sector. This reputation is maintained by research. Third, there is a general argument, which cannot be dismissed simply because it is rather vague, that the utility of the public at large may be enhanced by discoveries, broadly defined, even though these discoveries have no specific economic application.

In the case of scientific research one can be much more precise, because many, but not all, types of scientific research lead either to new goods and services which can be marketed or to results which impinge directly on people's welfare even if they are not directly marketed. Patents are often used as a way of measuring discoveries, and Griliches *et al.* (1987) argue that they are a good measure of inventive activity. Narin and Frame (1989) argue that the number of publications cited by US patents has risen from 0.2 in 1975 to somewhere between 0.4 and 0.9 in 1986, depending on the origin of the patent. Since around 80 per cent of academic papers describe the results of publicly-supported research the implication is clearly that scientific research is useful, and perhaps increasingly useful in the development of new technologies. Jaffe (1989) found corporate patent activity associated with spillovers from academic research and Acs *et al.* (1992) reported that his conclusions were strengthened if one looked at innovations rather than patent activity.

But, whatever the difficulties of measurement of the effects of basic research on patenting, it is important to note the links between patenting and economic performance. Archibugi and Pianta (1992) observe that, among the major industrial countries, patenting performance is related to specialization in research, suggesting that economies of scale are present (see Dasgupta, 1987). In the 1980s there was a correlation between economic growth and the growth in the number of patents granted in the US. This provides some evidence that scientific research has economic benefits.

There is also the suggestion that working on academic research projects provides useful skills for non-academic work (Irvine and Martin, 1980) and there may be other spill-over effects present. But can one actually calculate a social rate of return to basic scientific research? Although such calculations are possible, Pavitt (1990) is sceptical. His worry is that it is not possible to take account of the way in which the results of basic research feed through into subsequent applied research, and it is therefore not possible to measure the full benefits of such research.

V. Conclusions

There is good evidence that investment in higher education offers a social return at least as good as that on physical capital, and this provides a strong justification for expansion of the system. Since students with good A levels are already well represented at university, the expansion has taken place by increasing the participation of students with poor A levels or of part-time and mature students. There is some evidence to suggest that some of these students tend to do better out of polytechnic-type education, with obvious implications for the way in which the system should be expanded. Obviously, these conclusions must be qualified by the possibility that increased participation at 16 may enlarge the pool of 18-year-olds with good A levels and thus expand the number of students who seem to do well out of the sort of higher education which has traditionally been offered by the old universities.

There are good arguments, based on principles of equity, to say that those who receive the education should meet its costs. Nevertheless, a simple charge or loan scheme seems inappropriate because the benefits of higher education are highly uncertain. Both an income-contingent loan and a graduate tax offer satisfactory alternatives. The graduate tax gains in terms of simplicity but cannot be fine-tuned to reflect the cost of education exactly.

In performing these calculations one should not ignore two points. First of all, externalities may mean that social returns to education exceed those thrown up by these calculations. Second, the research activity of the higher education sector has benefits which are more tangible in the case of science subjects than arts subjects. These benefits should not be ignored simply because they are difficult to measure.

Could the universities offer better value for money? The shift towards a system whereby the income of institutions depends on numbers of students recruited and research performance, and the efforts to end cross-subsidies between research and teaching funds, are moves in this direction. But these policies, combined with the government's reluctance to match expansion of provision with more public funding, are likely to lead ineluctably towards a more explicit market-based system in which education is paid for by students rather than the tax-payer. The issues in the next decade will be increasingly those of combating not government, but market failure, and of finding ways by which institutions can appropriately combine the professional commitment of their staffs with their customers' growing market power.

References

Acs, Z. J., Andretsch, D. B., and Feldman, M. P. (1992), 'Real Effects of Academic Research: Comment', *American Economic Review*, **82**, 363–7.

Albrecht, D., and Ziderman, A. (1992), 'Student Loans and Their Alternatives: Improving the Performance of Deferred Payment Programmes', *Higher Education*, **23**(4), June.

Archibugi, D., and Pianta, M. (1992), *European Technological Specialization*, Report for Commission of the European Communities, DG. XII.

Barro, R. J. (1991), 'Economic Growth in a Cross Section of Countries', *Quarterly Journal of Economics*, **104**(2), 407–44.

Benhabib, J., and Jovanovic, B. (1991), 'Externalities and Growth Accounting', *American Economic Review*, **81**, 82–113.

Bennett, R., Glennerster, H., and Nevison, D. (1992), 'Investing in Skill: To Stay on or Not to Stay On', *Oxford Review of Economic Policy*, **8**(2), pp 130–45.

Booth, A. (1992), 'Private Sector Training and Graduate Earnings', *Review of Economics and Statistics*.

Bowen, H. R. (1980) *The Cost of Higher Education: How Much do Colleges and Universities Spend Per Student and How Much Should They Spend?*, San Francisco, Jossey Bass.

Cave, M., Kogan, M., and Hanney, S. (1991), *The Use of Performance Indicators in Higher Education*, Jessica Kingsley Publishers, 2nd edition.

—— Hanney, S., and Henkel, M. (1995), 'Performance Measurement in Higher Education Revisited', *Public Money and Management*, October–December, pp. 17–25.

—— Dodsworth, R., and Thompson, D. (1992), 'Regulatory Reform in Higher Education: Incentives for Efficiency and Product Quality', *Oxford Review of Economic Policy*, **8**(2), pp. 79–102.

Chapman, B. (1992), *AUSTUDY: Towards a More Flexible Approach*, Canberra, AGPS.

Cohn, E., Rhine, S., and Santos, M. (1989), 'Institutions of Higher Education as Market Products: Economies of Scale and Scope', *Review of Economics and Statistics*, **71**, (May), 284–390.

Dasgupta, P. (1987), 'The Economic Theory of Technology Policy', in P. Dasgupta and P. Stoneman (eds.), *Economic Policy and Technological Performance*, Cambridge, Cambridge University Press, 7–23.

de Groot, H., McMahon, W. W., and Volkwein, J. F. (1991), 'The Cost Structure of American Research Universities', *Review of Economics and Statistics*, **73**, 424–31.

Dolton, P., Makepeace, G. H., and Inchley, G. D. (1990), *The Early Careers of 1980 Graduates*, Department of Employment Research Paper No. 78.

Getz, M., and Siegfried, J. J. (1991), 'Costs and Productivity in American Colleges and Universities', in C. T. Clotfelter *et al.* (eds.), *Economic Challenges in Higher Education*, University of Chicago Press.

Griliches, Z., Pakes, A., and Hall, B. H. (1987), 'Patents as Indicators of Inventive Activity', in P. Dasgupta and P. Stoneman (eds.), *Economic Policy and Technological Performance*, Cambridge, Cambridge University Press, 97–124.

Hare, P., and Wyatt (1992), 'Economies of Academic Research and its Implication for Higher Education', *Oxford Review of Economic Policy*, **8**(2), pp. 48–66.

HMSO (1960), *Grants to Students*, Cmnd 1051, HMSO.

—— (1963a), *Higher Education: Report of the Committee Appointed by the Prime Minister under the Chairmanship of Lord Robbins*, Cmnd 2154, HMSO.

—— (1963b), *Higher Education: Government Statement on the Report of the Committee under the Chairmanship of Lord Robbins*, Cmnd 2165, HMSO.

—— (1966), *A Plan for Polytechnics and Other Colleges. Higher Education in the Further Education Sector*, Cmnd 3006, HMSO.

—— (1984), *Qualified Manpower: Great Britain, Census 1981*, HMSO.

—— (1987), *Higher Education: Meeting the Challenge*, Cm 114, HMSO.

—— (1988), *Top-up Loans for Students*, Cm 520, HMSO.

—— (1990), *Higher Education: a New Framework*. Cm 1514, HMSO.

Irvine, J., and Martin, B. (1980), *The Economic Effects of Big Science: the Case of Radio-Astronomy*, Proceedings of the International Colloquium on Economic Effects of Space and Other Advanced Technologies, European Space Agency.

Jaffe, A. B. (1989), 'Real Effects of Academic Research', *American Economic Review*, **79**, 957–70.

Johnes, G. (1992), 'Bidding for Students in Britain: Why the UFC Auction Failed', *Higher Education*, **23**, 173–92.

—— (1992), 'Performance Indicators in Higher Education: A Survey of Recent Work', *Oxford Review of Economic Policy*, **8**(2), pp. 19–34.

Keep, E., and Sissons, K. (1992), 'Owning the Problem: Personel Issues in Higher Education Policy Making in the 1990s', *Oxford Review of Economic Policy*, **8**(2), pp. 67–78.

London Economics (1991), *The PCFC Funding System: A Summary Report*.

Lucas, R. E. (1988), 'On the Mechanics of Economic Development', *Journal of Monetary Economics*, **22**, 3–42.

Matthews, R. C. O., Feinstein, C. H., and Odling-Smee, J. (1982), *British Economic Growth 1856–1973*, Oxford, Clarendon Press.

Narin, F., and Frame, J. (1989), 'The Growth of Japanese Science and Technology', *Science*, No. 245, 600–4.

OECD (1989), *Employment Outlook*, Chapter 2, Paris, OECD.

—— (1990), *Financing Higher Education: Current Patterns*, Paris, OECD.

Pavitt, K. (1990), 'What Makes Basic Research Economically Useful?', *Research Policy*, **19**, 110–21.

PCFC/CNAA (1990), *The Measurement of Value-Added in Higher Education*.

PCFC/UFC (1992), *A Funding Methodology for Teaching in Higher Education: Report from the Joint Working Group*.

Radner, R., and Miller, J. (1975), *Demand and Supply in US Higher Education*, New York, McGraw-Hill.

Romer, P. M. (1986), 'Increasing Returns and Long-run Growth', *Journal of Political Economy*, **94**, 1002–37.

Rudd, E. (1990), 'The Early Careers of Social Science Graduates and the Value of a PhD', *Journal of the Royal Statistical Society*, Series A, **153**, 203–32.

Taylor, J. (1995), 'A Statistical Analysis of the 1992 Research Assessment Exercise', *Journal of the Royal Statistical Society*, 158, 2, pp. 241–61.

Verry, D., and Davies, B. (1976), *University Costs and Outputs*, Amsterdam, Elsevier.

Weale, M. R. (1992), 'Externalities from Education', in F. Hahn (ed.), *The Market: Practice and Policy*, Macmillan.

Index